AUTOTOOLS

AUTOTOOLS

A Practitioner's Guide to GNU Autoconf, Automake, and Libtool

by John Calcote

no starch
press

San Francisco

14 13 12 11 10   1 2 3 4 5 6 7 8 9

ISBN-10: 1-59327-206-5
ISBN-13: 978-1-59327-206-7

Publisher: William Pollock
Production Editor: Ansel Staton
Cover and Interior Design: Octopod Studios
Developmental Editor: William Pollock
Technical Reviewer: Ralf Wildenhues
Copyeditor: Megan Dunchak
Compositor: Susan Glinert Stevens
Proofreader: Linda Seifert
Indexer: Nancy Guenther

For information on book distributors or translations, please contact No Starch Press, Inc. directly:

No Starch Press, Inc.
38 Ringold Street, San Francisco, CA 94103
phone: 415.863.9900; fax: 415.863.9950; info@nostarch.com; www.nostarch.com

Library of Congress Cataloging-in-Publication Data

```
Calcote, John, 1964-
  Autotools : a practitioner's guide to GNU Autoconf, Automake, and Libtool / by John Calcote.
      p. cm.
  ISBN-13: 978-1-59327-206-7 (pbk.)
  ISBN-10: 1-59327-206-5 (pbk.)
 1.  Autotools (Electronic resource) 2.  Cross-platform software development. 3.  Open source software.
4.  UNIX (Computer file)  I. Title.
  QA76.76.D47C335 2010
  005.3--dc22
                                          2009040784
```

For Michelle

But to see her was to love her;
Love but her, and love forever.
—Robert Burns

BRIEF CONTENTS

Foreword by Ralf Wildenhues..xv

Preface xvii

Introduction xxi

Chapter 1: A Brief Introduction to the GNU Autotools 1

Chapter 2: Understanding the GNU Coding Standards 19

Chapter 3: Configuring Your Project with Autoconf 57

Chapter 4: More Fun with Autoconf: Configuring User Options 89

Chapter 5: Automatic Makefiles with Automake...............................119

Chapter 6: Building Libraries with Libtool 145

Chapter 7: Library Interface Versioning and Runtime Dynamic Linking 171

Chapter 8: FLAIM: An Autotools Example.......................................195

Chapter 9: FLAIM Part II: Pushing the Envelope 229

Chapter 10: Using the M4 Macro Processor with Autoconf 251

Chapter 11: A Catalog of Tips and Reusable Solutions for Creating Great Projects 271

Index 313

CONTENTS IN DETAIL

FOREWORD by Ralf Wildenhues   **xv**

PREFACE   **xvii**

Why Use the Autotools? xviii
Acknowledgments xx
I Wish You the Very Best xx

INTRODUCTION   **xxi**

Who Should Read This Book xxii
How This Book Is Organized xxii
Conventions Used in This Book xxiii
Autotools Versions Used in This Book xxiii

1
A BRIEF INTRODUCTION TO THE GNU AUTOTOOLS   1

Who Should Use the Autotools? 2
When Should You Not Use the Autotools? 2
Apple Platforms and Mac OS X 3
The Choice of Language 4
Generating Your Package Build System 5
Autoconf 6
    autoconf 7
    autoreconf 7
    autoheader 7
    autoscan 7
    autoupdate 7
    ifnames 8
    autom4te 8
    Working Together 8
Automake 9
    automake 10
    aclocal 10
Libtool 11
    libtool 12
    libtoolize 12
    ltdl, the Libtool C API 12
Building Your Package 13
    Running configure 13
    Running make 15
Installing the Most Up-to-Date Autotools 16
Summary 18

2
UNDERSTANDING THE GNU CODING STANDARDS   19

Creating a New Project Directory Structure 20
Project Structure 21
Makefile Basics 22
    Commands and Rules 23
    Variables 24
    A Separate Shell for Each Command 25
    Variable Binding 26
    Rules in Detail 27
    Resources for Makefile Authors 32
Creating a Source Distribution Archive 32
    Forcing a Rule to Run 34
    Leading Control Characters 35
Automatically Testing a Distribution 36
Unit Testing, Anyone? 37
Installing Products 38
    Installation Choices 40
    Uninstalling a Package 41
    Testing Install and Uninstall 42
The Filesystem Hierarchy Standard 44
Supporting Standard Targets and Variables 45
    Standard Targets 46
    Standard Variables 46
    Adding Location Variables to Jupiter 47
Getting Your Project into a Linux Distro 48
Build vs. Installation Prefix Overrides 50
User Variables 52
Configuring Your Package 54
Summary 55

3
CONFIGURING YOUR PROJECT WITH AUTOCONF   57

Autoconf Configuration Scripts 58
The Shortest configure.ac File 59
Comparing M4 to the C Preprocessor 60
The Nature of M4 Macros 60
Executing autoconf 61
Executing configure 62
Executing config.status 63
Adding Some Real Functionality 64
Generating Files from Templates 67
Adding VPATH Build Functionality 68
Let's Take a Breather 70
An Even Quicker Start with autoscan 71
    The Proverbial autogen.sh Script 73
    Updating Makefile.in 75
Initialization and Package Information 76
    AC_PREREQ 76
    AC_INIT 76
    AC_CONFIG_SRCDIR 77

The Instantiating Macros 78
    AC_CONFIG_HEADERS 83
       Using autoheader to Generate an Include File Template 84
Back to Remote Builds for a Moment 87
Summary 88

4
MORE FUN WITH AUTOCONF:
CONFIGURING USER OPTIONS

89

Substitutions and Definitions 90
    AC_SUBST 90
    AC_DEFINE 91
Checking for Compilers 91
Checking for Other Programs 93
A Common Problem with Autoconf 95
Checks for Libraries and Header Files 98
    Is It Right or Just Good Enough? 101
    Printing Messages 106
Supporting Optional Features and Packages 107
    Coding Up the Feature Option 109
    Formatting Help Strings 112
Checks for Type and Structure Definitions 112
The AC_OUTPUT Macro 116
Summary 117

5
AUTOMATIC MAKEFILES
WITH AUTOMAKE

119

Getting Down to Business 120
    Enabling Automake in configure.ac 121
    A Hidden Benefit: Automatic Dependency Tracking 124
What's in a Makefile.am File? 125
Analyzing Our New Build System 126
    Product List Variables 127
    Product Source Variables 132
    PLV and PSV Modifiers 132
Unit Tests: Supporting make check 133
Reducing Complexity with Convenience Libraries 134
    Product Option Variables 136
    Per-Makefile Option Variables 138
Building the New Library 138
What Goes into a Distribution? 140
Maintainer Mode 141
Cutting Through the Noise 142
Summary 144

6
BUILDING LIBRARIES WITH LIBTOOL   145

The Benefits of Shared Libraries 146
How Shared Libraries Work 146
    Dynamic Linking at Load Time 147
    Automatic Dynamic Linking at Runtime 148
    Manual Dynamic Linking at Runtime 149
Using Libtool 150
    Abstracting the Build Process 150
    Abstraction at Runtime 151
Installing Libtool 152
Adding Shared Libraries to Jupiter 152
    Using the LTLIBRARIES Primary 153
    Public Include Directories 153
    Customizing Libtool with LT_INIT Options 157
    Reconfigure and Build 161
    So What Is PIC, Anyway? 164
    Fixing the Jupiter PIC Problem 167
Summary 170

7
LIBRARY INTERFACE VERSIONING AND
RUNTIME DYNAMIC LINKING   171

System-Specific Versioning 172
    Linux and Solaris Library Versioning 172
    IBM AIX Library Versioning 173
    HP-UX/AT&T SVR4 Library Versioning 176
The Libtool Library Versioning Scheme 176
    Library Versioning Is Interface Versioning 177
    When Library Versioning Just Isn't Enough 180
Using libltdl 181
    Necessary Infrastructure 181
    Adding a Plug-In Interface 183
    Doing It the Old-Fashioned Way 184
    Converting to Libtool's ltdl Library 188
    Preloading Multiple Modules 192
    Checking It All Out 193
Summary 194

8
FLAIM: AN AUTOTOOLS EXAMPLE   195

What Is FLAIM? 196
Why FLAIM? 196
An Initial Look 197
Getting Started 199
    Adding the configure.ac Files 199
    The Top-Level Makefile.am File 202
The FLAIM Subprojects 204
    The FLAIM Toolkit configure.ac File 205
    The FLAIM Toolkit Makefile.am File 212

Designing the ftk/src/Makefile.am File 215
Moving On to the ftk/util Directory 217
Designing the XFLAIM Build System 218
The XFLAIM configure.ac File 219
Creating the xflaim/src/Makefile.am File 222
Turning to the xflaim/util Directory 223
Summary 227

9
FLAIM PART II: PUSHING THE ENVELOPE   229

Building Java Sources Using the Autotools 230
Autotools Java Support 230
Using ac-archive Macros 233
Canonical System Information 234
The xflaim/java Directory Structure 234
The xflaim/src/Makefile.am File 235
Building the JNI C++ Sources 236
The Java Wrapper Classes and JNI Headers 237
A Caveat About Using the JAVA Primary 239
Building the C# Sources 239
Manual Installation 242
Cleaning Up Again 243
Configuring Compiler Options 243
Hooking Doxygen into the Build Process 245
Adding Nonstandard Targets 247
Summary 250

10
USING THE M4 MACRO PROCESSOR WITH AUTOCONF   251

M4 Text Processing 252
Defining Macros 253
Macros with Arguments 255
The Recursive Nature of M4 256
Quoting Rules 258
Autoconf and M4 259
The Autoconf M4 Environment 260
Writing Autoconf Macros 260
Simple Text Replacement 260
Documenting Your Macros 263
M4 Conditionals 264
Diagnosing Problems 268
Summary 269

11
A CATALOG OF TIPS AND REUSABLE SOLUTIONS
FOR CREATING GREAT PROJECTS   271

Item 1: Keeping Private Details out of Public Interfaces 272
Solutions in C 273
Solutions in C++ 273

Item 2: Implementing Recursive Extension Targets 276
Item 3: Using a Repository Revision Number in a Package Version 279
Item 4: Ensuring Your Distribution Packages Are Clean 281
Item 5: Hacking Autoconf Macros 282
    Providing Library-Specific Autoconf Macros 287
Item 6: Cross-Compiling 287
Item 7: Emulating Autoconf Text Replacement Techniques 293
Item 8: Using the ac-archive Project 298
Item 9: Using pkg-config with Autotools 299
    Providing pkg-config Files for Your Library Projects 300
    Using pkg-config Files in configure.ac 301
Item 10: Using Incremental Installation Techniques 302
Item 11: Using Generated Source Code 302
    Using the BUILT_SOURCES Variable 302
    Dependency Management 303
    Built Sources Done Right 306
Item 12: Disabling Undesirable Targets 309
Item 13: Watch Those Tab Characters! 310
Item 14: Packaging Choices 311
Wrapping Up 312

INDEX   313

FOREWORD

When I was asked to do a technical review on a book about the Autotools, I was rather skeptical. Several online tutorials and a few books already introduce readers to the use of GNU Autoconf, Automake, and Libtool. However, many of these texts are less than ideal in at least some ways: They were either written several years ago and are starting to show their age, contain at least some inaccuracies, or tend to be incomplete for typical beginner's tasks. On the other hand, the GNU manuals for these programs are fairly large and rather technical, and as such, they may present a significant entry barrier to learning your ways around the Autotools.

John Calcote began this book with an online tutorial that shared at least some of the problems facing other tutorials. Around that time, he became a regular contributor to discussions on the Autotools mailing lists, too. John kept asking more and more questions, and discussions with him uncovered some bugs in the Autotools sources and documentation, as well as some issues in his tutorial.

Since that time, John has reworked the text a lot. The review uncovered several more issues in both software and book text, a nice mutual benefit. As a result, this book has become a great introductory text that still aims to be accurate, up to date with current Autotools, and quite comprehensive in a way that is easily understood.

Always going by example, John explores the various software layers, portability issues and standards involved, and features needed for package build development. If you're new to the topic, the entry path may just have become a bit less steep for you.

Ralf Wildenhues
Bonn, Germany
June 2010

PREFACE

I've often wondered during the last ten years how it could be that the *only* third-party book on the GNU Autotools that I've been able to discover is *GNU AUTOCONF, AUTOMAKE, and LIBTOOL* by Gary Vaughan, Ben Elliston, Tom Tromey, and Ian Lance Taylor, affectionately known by the community as *The Goat Book* (so dubbed for the front cover—an old-fashioned photo of goats doing acrobatic stunts).[1]

I've been told by publishers that there is simply no market for such a book. In fact, one editor told me that he himself had tried unsuccessfully to entice authors to write this book a few years ago. His authors wouldn't finish the project, and the publisher's market analysis indicated that there was very little interest in the book. Publishers believe that open source software developers tend to disdain written documentation. Perhaps they're right. Interestingly, books on IT utilities like Perl sell like Perl's going out of style—which is actually somewhat true these days—and yet people are still buying enough

---

1. Vaughan, Elliston, Tromey, and Taylor, *GNU Autoconf, Automake, and Libtool* (Indianapolis: Sams Publishing, 2000).

Perl books to keep their publishers happy. All of this explains why there are ten books on the shelf with animal pictures on the cover for Perl, but literally nothing for open source software developers.

I've worked in software development for 25 years, and I've used open source software for quite some time now. I've learned a lot about open source software maintenance and development, and most of what I've learned, unfortunately, has been by trial and error. Existing GNU documentation is more often reference material than solution-oriented instruction. Had there *been* other books on the topic, I would have snatched them all up immediately.

What we need is a cookbook-style approach with the recipes covering real problems found in real projects. First the basics are covered, sauces and reductions, followed by various cooking techniques. Finally, master recipes are presented for culinary wonders. As each recipe is mastered, the reader makes small intuitive leaps—I call them *minor epiphanies*. Put enough of these under your belt and overall mastery of the Autotools is ultimately inevitable.

Let me give you an analogy. I'd been away from math classes for about three years when I took my first college calculus course. I struggled the entire semester with little progress. I understood the theory, but I had trouble with the homework. I just didn't have the background I needed. So the next semester, I took college algebra and trigonometry back to back as half-semester classes. At the end of that semester, I tried calculus again. This time I did very well—finishing the class with a solid *A* grade. What was missing the first time? Just basic math skills. You'd think it wouldn't have made *that* much difference, but it really does.

The same concept applies to learning to properly use the Autotools. You need a solid understanding of the tools upon which the Autotools are built in order to become proficient with the Autotools themselves.

Why Use the Autotools?

In the early 1990s, I was working on the final stages of my bachelor's degree in computer science at Brigham Young University. I took an advanced computer graphics class where I was introduced to C++ and the object-oriented programming paradigm. For the next couple of years, I had a love-hate relationship with C++. I was a pretty good C coder by that time, and I thought I could easily pick up C++, as close in syntax as it was to C. How wrong I was! I fought with the C++ compiler more often than I'd care to recall.

The problem was that the most fundamental differences between C and C++ are not obvious to the casual observer, because they're buried deep within the C++ language specification rather than on the surface in the language syntax. The C++ compiler generates an amazing amount of code beneath the covers, providing functionality in a few lines of C++ code that require dozens of lines of C code.

Just as programmers then complained of their troubles with C++, so likewise programmers today complain about similar difficulties with the GNU Autotools. The differences between make and Automake are very similar to the differences between C and C++. The most basic single-line *Makefile.am* generates a *Makefile.in* (an Autoconf template) containing 300–400 lines of parameterized make script, and it tends to increase with each revision of the tool as more features are added.

Thus, when you use the Autotools, you have to understand the underlying infrastructure managed by these tools. You need to take the time to understand the open source software distribution, build, test, and installation philosophies embodied by—in many cases even enforced by—these tools, or you'll find yourself fighting against the system. Finally, you need to learn to agree with these basic philosophies because you'll only become frustrated if you try to make the Autotools operate outside of the boundaries set by their designers.

Source-level distribution relegates to the end user a particular portion of the responsibility of software development that has traditionally been assumed by the software developer—namely, building products from source code. But end users are often not developers, so most of them won't know how to properly build the package. The solution to this problem, from the earliest days of the open source movement, has been to make the package build and installation processes as simple as possible for the end user so that he could perform a few well-understood steps to have the package built and installed cleanly on his system.

Most packages are built using the make utility. It's very easy to type make, but that's not the problem. The problem crops up when the package doesn't build successfully because of some unanticipated difference between the user's system and the developer's system. Thus was born the ubiquitous configure script—initially a simple shell script that configured the end user's environment so that make could successfully find the required external resources on the user's system. Hand-coded configuration scripts helped, but they weren't the final answer. They fixed about 65 percent of the problems resulting from system configuration differences—and they were a pain in the neck to write properly and to maintain. Dozens of changes were made incrementally over a period of years, until the script worked properly on most of the systems anyone cared about. But the entire process was clearly in need of an upgrade.

Do you have any idea of the number of build-breaking differences there are between existing systems today? Neither do I, but there are a handful of developers in the world who know a large percentage of these differences. Between them and the open source software community, the GNU Autotools were born. The Autotools were designed to create configuration scripts and makefiles that work correctly and provide significant chunks of valuable end-user functionality under most circumstances, and on most systems— even on systems not initially considered (or even conceived of) by the package maintainer.

With this in mind, the primary purpose of the Autotools is not to make life simpler for the package maintainer (although it really does in the long run). *The primary purpose of the Autotools is to make life simpler for the end user.*

Acknowledgments

I could not have written a technical book like this without t̶h̶e̶ people. I would like to thank Bill Pollock and the editors and st̶ Press for their patience with a first-time author. They made it̶ esting and fun (and a little painful at times).

Additionally, I'd like to thank the authors and maintainers of Autotools for giving the world a standard to live up to and a set of make it simpler to do so. Specifically, I'd like to thank Ralf Wilde believed in this project enough to spend hundreds of hours of his time in technical review. His comments and insight were invaluable i̶ this book from mere wishful thinking to an accurate and useful text.

I would also like to thank my friend Cary Petterborg for encourag̶ to "just go ahead and do it" when I told him it would probably never h̶a̶ ̶

Finally, I'd like to thank my wife Michelle and my children Ethan, Mason, Robby, Haley, Joey, Nick, and Alex for allowing me to spend all of that time away from them while I worked on the book. A novel would have been easier (and more lucrative), but the world has plenty of novels and n̶ enough books about the Autotools.

I Wish You the Very Best

I spent a long time and a lot of effort learning what I now know about the Autotools. Most of this learning process was more painful than it really had to be. I've written this book so that you won't have to struggle to learn what should be a core set of tools for the open source programmer. Please feel free to contact me, and let me know your experiences with learning the Autotools. I can be reached at my personal email address at *john.calcote @gmail.com*. Good luck in your quest for a better software development experience!

John Calcote
Elk Ridge, Utah
June 2010

INTRODUCTION

Few software developers would deny that GNU Autoconf, Automake, and Libtool (the *Autotools*) have revolutionized the open source software world. But while there are many thousands of Autotools advocates, there are also many developers who *hate* the Autotools—with a passion. The reason for this dread of the Autotools, I think, is that when you use the Autotools, you have to understand the underlying infrastructure that they manage. Otherwise, you'll find yourself fighting against the system.

This book solves this problem by first providing a framework for understanding the underlying infrastructure of the Autotools and then building on that framework with a tutorial-based approach to teaching Autotools concepts in a logically ordered fashion.

Who Should Read This Book

This book is for the open source software package maintainer who wants to become an Autotools expert. Existing material on the subject is limited to the GNU Autotools manuals and a few Internet-based tutorials. For years most real-world questions have been answered on the Autotools mailing lists, but mailing lists are an inefficient form of teaching because the same answers to the same questions are given time and again. This book provides a cookbook style approach, covering real problems found in real projects.

How This Book Is Organized

This book moves from high-level concepts to mid-level use cases and examples and then finishes with more advanced details and examples. As though we were learning arithmetic, we'll begin with some basic math—algebra and trigonometry—and then move on to analytical geometry and calculus.

Chapter 1 presents a general overview of the packages that are considered part of the GNU Autotools. This chapter describes the interaction between these packages and the files consumed by and generated by each one. In each case, figures depict the flow of data from hand-coded input to final output files.

Chapter 2 covers open source software project structure and organization. This chapter also goes into some detail about the *GNU Coding Standards (GCS)* and the *Filesystem Hierarchy Standard (FHS)*, both of which have played vital roles in the design of the GNU Autotools. It presents some fundamental tenets upon which the design of each of the Autotools is based. With these concepts, you'll better understand the theory behind the architectural decisions made by the Autotools designers.

In this chapter, we'll also design a simple project, Jupiter, from start to finish using hand-coded makefiles. We'll add to Jupiter in a stepwise fashion as we discover functionality that we can use to simplify tasks.

Chapters 3 and 4 present the framework designed by the GNU Autoconf engineers to ease the burden of creating and maintaining portable, functional project configuration scripts. The GNU Autoconf package provides the basis for creating complex configuration scripts with just a few lines of information provided by the project maintainer.

In these chapters, we'll quickly convert our hand-coded makefiles into Autoconf *Makefile.in* templates and then begin adding to them in order to gain some of the most significant Autoconf benefits. Chapter 3 discusses the basics of generating configuration scripts, while Chapter 4 moves on to more advanced Autoconf topics, features, and uses.

Chapter 5 discusses converting the Jupiter project *Makefile.in* templates into Automake *Makefile.am* files. Here you'll discover that Automake is to makefiles what Autoconf is to configuration scripts. This chapter presents the major features of Automake in a manner that will not become outdated as new versions of Automake are released.

Chapters 6 and 7 explain basic shared-library concepts and show how to build shared libraries with Libtool—a stand-alone abstraction for shared library functionality that can be used with the other Autotools. Chapter 6 begins with a shared-library primer and then covers some basic Libtool extensions that allow Libtool to be a drop-in replacement for the more basic library generation functionality provided by Automake. Chapter 7 covers library versioning and runtime dynamic module management features provided by Libtool.

Chapters 8 and 9 show the transformation of an existing, fairly complex, open source project (FLAIM) from using a hand-built build system to using an Autotools build system. This example will help you to understand how you might *autoconfiscate* one of your own existing projects.

Chapter 10 provides an overview of the features of the M4 macro processor that are relevant to obtaining a solid understanding of Autoconf. This chapter also considers the process of writing your own Autoconf macros.

Chapter 11 is a compilation of tips, tricks, and reusable solutions to Autoconf problems. The solutions in this chapter are presented as a set of individual topics or items. Each item can be understood without context from the surrounding items.

Most of the examples shown in listings in this book are available for download from *http://www.nostarch.com/autotools.htm*.

Conventions Used in This Book

This book contains hundreds of program listings in roughly two categories: console examples and file listings. Console examples have no captions, and their commands are bolded. File listings contain full or partial listings of the files discussed in the text. All named listings are provided in the downloadable archive. Listings without filenames are entirely contained in the printed listing itself. In general, bolded text in listings indicates changes made to a previous version of that listing.

For listings related to the Jupiter and FLAIM projects, the caption specifies the path of the file relative to the project root directory.

Throughout this book, I refer to the GNU/Linux operating system simply as *Linux*. It should be understood that by the use of the term *Linux*, I'm referring to GNU/Linux, its actual official name. I use *Linux* simply as shorthand for the official name.

Autotools Versions Used in This Book

The Autotools are always being updated—on average, a significant update of each of the three tools, Autoconf, Automake, and Libtool, is released every year and a half, and minor updates are released every three to six months. The Autotools designers attempt to maintain a reasonable level of backward compatibility with each new release, but occasionally something significant is broken, and older documentation simply becomes out of date.

While I describe new significant features of recent releases of the Autotools, in my efforts to make this a more timeless work, I've tried to stick to descriptions of Autoconf features (macros for instance) that have been in widespread use for several years. Minor details change occasionally, but the general use has stayed the same through many releases.

At appropriate places in the text, I mention the versions of the Autotools that I've used for this book, but I'll summarize here. I've used version 2.64 of Autoconf, version 1.11 of Automake, and version 2.2.6 of Libtool. These were the latest versions as of this writing, and even through the publication process, I was able to make minor corrections and update to new releases as they became available.

1

A BRIEF INTRODUCTION
TO THE GNU AUTOTOOLS

We shall not cease from exploration
And the end of all our exploring
Will be to arrive where we started
And know the place for the first time.
—T.S. Eliot, "Quartet No. 4: Little Gidding"

As stated in the preface to this book, the purpose of the GNU Autotools is to make life simpler for the end user, not the maintainer. Nevertheless, using the Autotools will make your job as a project maintainer easier in the long run, although maybe not for the reasons you suspect. The Autotools framework is as simple as it can be, given the functionality it provides. The real purpose of the Autotools is twofold: it serves the needs of your users, and it makes your project incredibly portable—even to systems on which you've never tested, installed, or built your code.

Throughout this book, I will often use the term *Autotools*, although you won't find a package in the GNU archives with this label. I use this term to signify the following three GNU packages, which are considered by the community to be part of the GNU build system:

- Autoconf, which is used to generate a configuration script for a project
- Automake, which is used to simplify the process of creating consistent and functional makefiles
- Libtool, which provides an abstraction for the portable creation of shared libraries

Other build tools, such as the open source packages *CMake* and *SCons*, attempt to provide the same functionality as the Autotools but in a more user-friendly manner. However, the functionality these tools attempt to hide behind GUI interfaces and script builders actually ends up making them less functional.

Who Should Use the Autotools?

If you're writing open source software that targets Unix or Linux systems, you should absolutely be using the GNU Autotools, and even if you're writing proprietary software for Unix or Linux systems, you'll still benefit significantly from using them. The Autotools provide you with a build environment that will allow your project to build successfully on future versions or distributions with virtually no changes to the build scripts. This is useful even if you only intend to target a single Linux distribution, because—let's be honest—you really *can't* know in advance whether or not your company will want your software to run on other platforms in the future.

When Should You Not Use the Autotools?

About the only time it makes sense not to use the Autotools is when you're writing software that will only run on non-Unix platforms, such as Microsoft Windows. Although the Autotools have limited support for building Windows software, it's my opinion that the POSIX/FHS runtime environment embraced by these tools is just too different from the Windows runtime environment to warrant trying to shoehorn a Windows project into the Autotools paradigm.

Autotools support for Windows requires a Cygwin[1] or MSYS[2] environment in order to work correctly, because Autoconf-generated configuration scripts are Bourne-shell scripts, and Windows doesn't provide a native Bourne shell. Unix and Microsoft tools are just different enough in command-line options and runtime characteristics that it's often simpler to use Windows ports of GNU tools, such as GCC or MinGW, to build Windows programs with an Autotools build system.

I've seen truly portable build systems that use these environments and tool sets to build Windows software using Autotools scripts that are common between Windows and Unix. The shim libraries provided by portability environments like Cygwin make the Windows operating system look POSIX enough to pass for Unix in a pinch, but they sacrifice performance and functionality for the sake of portability. The MinGW approach is a little better in that it targets the native Windows API. In any case, these sorts of least-common-denominator approaches merely serve to limit the possibilities of your code on Windows.

I've also seen developers customize the Autotools to generate build scripts that use native (Microsoft) Windows tools. These people spend much of their time tweaking their build systems to do things they were never intended to do, in a hostile and foreign environment. Their makefiles contain entirely

---

1. Cygwin Information and Installation, *http://www.cygwin.com/*.
2. MinGW and MSYS, Minimalist GNU for Windows, *http://www.mingw.org/*.

different sets of functionality based on the target and host operating systems: one set of code to build a project on Windows and another to build on POSIX systems. This does not constitute a portable build system; it only portrays the vague illusion of one.

For these reasons, I focus exclusively in this book on using the Autotools on POSIX-compliant platforms.

NOTE   *I'm not a typical Unix bigot. While I love Unix (and especially Linux), I also appreciate Windows for the areas in which it excels.[3] For Windows development, I highly recommend using Microsoft tools. The original reasons for using GNU tools to develop Windows programs are more or less academic nowadays, because Microsoft has made the better part of its tools available for download at no cost. (For download information, see Microsoft Express at* http://www.microsoft.com/Express.*)*

Apple Platforms and Mac OS X

The Macintosh operating system has been POSIX compliant since 2002 when Mac OS version 10 (OS X) was released. OS X is derived from NeXTSTEP/ OpenStep, which is based on the Mach kernel, with parts taken from FreeBSD and NetBSD. As a POSIX-compliant operating system, OS X provides all the infrastructure required by the Autotools. The problems you'll encounter with OS X will mostly likely involve Apple's user interface and package-management systems, both of which are specific to the Mac.

The user interface presents the same issues you encounter when dealing with X Windows on other Unix platforms, and then some. The primary difference is that X Windows is used exclusively on most Unix systems, but Mac OS has its own graphical user interface called Cocoa. While X Windows can be used on the Mac (Apple provides a window manager that makes X applications look a lot like native Cocoa apps), Mac programmers will sometimes wish to take full advantage of the native user interface features provided by the operating system.

The Autotools skirt the issue of package management differences between Unix platforms by simply ignoring it. They create packages that are little more than compressed archives using the tar and gzip utilities, and they install and uninstall products from the make command line. The Mac OS package management system is an integral part of installing an application on an Apple system and projects like Fink (*http://www.finkproject.org/*) and MacPorts (*http:// www.macports.org/*) help make existing open source packages available on the Mac by providing simplified mechanisms for converting Autotools packages into installable Mac packages.

The bottom line is that the Autotools can be used quite effectively on Apple Macintosh systems running OS X or later, as long as you keep these caveats in mind.

---

3. Hard core gamers will agree with me, I'm sure. I'm writing this book on a laptop running Windows 7, but I'm using OpenOffice.org as my text editor, and I'm writing the book's sample code on my 3GHz 64-bit dual processor Opensuse 11.2 Linux workstation.

The Choice of Language

Your choice of programming language is another important factor to consider when deciding whether to use the Autotools. Remember that the Autotools were designed by GNU people to manage GNU projects. In the GNU community, there are two factors that determine the importance of a computer programming language:

- Are there any GNU packages written in the language?
- Does the GNU compiler toolset support the language?

Autoconf provides native support for the following languages based on these two criteria (by *native support*, I mean that Autoconf will compile, link, and run source-level feature checks in these languages):

- C
- C++
- Objective C
- Fortran
- Fortran 77
- Erlang

Therefore, if you want to build a Java package, you can configure Automake to do so (as we'll see in Chapters 8 and 9), but you can't ask Autoconf to compile, link, or run Java-based checks,[4] because Autoconf simply doesn't natively support Java. However, you can find Autoconf macros (which I will cover in more detail in later chapters) that enhance Autoconf's ability to manage the configuration process for projects written in Java.

Open source software developers are actively at work on the gcj compiler and toolset, so some native Java support may ultimately be added to Autoconf. But as of this writing, gcj is still a bit immature, and very few GNU packages are currently written in Java, so the issue is not yet critical to the GNU community.

Rudimentary support does exist in Automake for both GNU (gcj) and non-GNU Java compilers and JVMs. I've used these features myself on projects and they work well, as long as you don't try to push them too far.

If you're into Smalltalk, ADA, Modula, Lisp, Forth, or some other non-mainstream language, you're probably not too interested in porting your code to dozens of platforms and CPUs. However, if you *are* using a non-mainstream language, and you're concerned about the portability of your build systems, consider adding support for your language to the Autotools yourself. This is not as daunting a task as you may think, and I guarantee that you'll be an Autotools expert when you're finished.[5]

---

4. This statement is not strictly true: I've seen third-party macros that use the JVM to execute Java code within checks, but these are usually very special cases. None of the built-in Autoconf checks rely on a JVM in any way. Chapters 8 and 9 outline how you might use a JVM in an Autoconf check. Additionally, the portable nature of Java and the Java virtual machine specification make it fairly unlikely that you'll need to perform a Java-based Autoconf check in the first place.

5. For example, native Erlang support made it into the Autotools because members of the Erlang community thought it was important enough to add it themselves.

Generating Your Package Build System

The GNU Autotools framework includes three main packages: Autoconf, Automake, and Libtool. The tools in these packages can generate code that depends on utilities and functionality from the *gettext, m4, sed, make,* and *perl* packages, among others.

With respect to the Autotools, it's important to distinguish between a *maintainer's* system and an *end user's* system. The design goals of the Autotools specify that an Autotools-generated build system should rely only on tools that are readily available and preinstalled on the end user's machine. For example, the machine a maintainer uses to create distributions requires a Perl interpreter, but a machine on which an end-user builds products from release distribution packages should not require Perl.

A corollary is that an end user's machine doesn't need to have the Autotools installed—an end user's system only requires a reasonably POSIX-compliant version of make and some variant of the Bourne shell that can execute the generated configuration script. And, of course, any package will also require compilers, linkers, and other tools deemed necessary by the project maintainer to convert source files into executable binary programs, help files, and other runtime resources.

If you've ever downloaded, built, and installed software from a *tarball*—a compressed archive with a *.tar.gz, .tgz, .tar.bz2,* or other such extension—you're undoubtedly aware of the general process. It usually looks something like this:

```
$ gzip -cd hackers-delight-1.0.tar.gz | tar xvf -
...
$ cd hackers-delight-1.0
$ ./configure && make
...
$ sudo make install
...
```

NOTE *If you've performed this sequence of commands, you probably know what they mean, and you have a basic understanding of the software development process. If this is the case, you'll have no trouble following the content of this book.*

Most developers understand the purpose of the make utility, but what's the point of configure? While Unix systems have followed the de facto standard Unix kernel interface for decades, most software has to stretch beyond these boundaries.

Originally, configuration scripts were hand-coded shell scripts designed to set variables based on platform-specific characteristics. They also allowed users to configure package options before running make. This approach worked well for decades, but as the number of Linux distributions and custom Unix systems grew, the variety of features and installation and configuration options exploded, so it became very difficult to write a decent portable configuration script. In fact, it was much more difficult to write a portable configuration script than it was to write makefiles for a new project. Therefore, most people just created configuration scripts for their projects by copying and modifying the script for a similar project.

In the early 1990s, it was apparent to many open source software developers that project configuration would become painful if something wasn't done to ease the burden of writing massive shell scripts to manage configuration options. The number of GNU project packages had grown to hundreds, and maintaining consistency between their separate build systems had become more time consuming than simply maintaining the code for these projects. These problems had to be solved.

Autoconf

Autoconf[6] changed this paradigm almost overnight. David MacKenzie started the Autoconf project in 1991, but a look at the *AUTHORS* file in the Savannah Autoconf project[7] repository will give you an idea of the number of people that had a hand in making the tool. Although configuration scripts were long and complex, users only needed to specify a few variables when executing them. Most of these variables were simply choices about components, features, and options, such as: *Where can the build system find libraries and header files? Where do I want to install my finished products? Which optional components do I want to build into my products?*

Instead of modifying and debugging hundreds of lines of supposedly portable shell script, developers can now write a short meta-script file using a concise, macro-based language, and Autoconf will generate a perfect configuration script that is more portable, more accurate, and more maintainable than a hand-coded one. In addition, Autoconf often catches semantic or logic errors that could otherwise take days to debug. Another benefit of Autoconf is that the shell code it generates is portable between most variations of the Bourne shell. Mistakes made in portability between shells are very common, and, unfortunately, are the most difficult kinds of mistakes to find, because no one developer has access to all Bourne-like shells.

NOTE   *While scripting languages like Perl and Python are now more pervasive than the Bourne shell, this was not the case when the idea for Autoconf was first conceived.*

Autoconf-generated configuration scripts provide a common set of options that are important to all portable software projects running on POSIX systems. These include options to modify standard locations (a concept I'll cover in more detail in Chapter 2), as well as project-specific options defined in the *configure.ac* file (which I'll discuss in Chapter 3).

The *autoconf* package provides several programs, including the following:

- autoconf
- autoheader
- autom4te

---

6. For more on Autoconf origins, see the GNU webpage on the topic at *http://www.gnu.org/software/autoconf*.

7. See *http://savannah.gnu.org/projects/autoconf*.

- autoreconf
- autoscan
- autoupdate
- ifnames

autoconf

autoconf is a simple Bourne shell script. Its main task is to ensure that the current shell contains the functionality necessary to execute the M4 macro processor. (I'll discuss Autoconf's use of M4 in detail in Chapter 3.) The remainder of the script parses command-line parameters and executes autom4te.

autoreconf

The autoreconf utility executes the configuration tools in the *autoconf, automake,* and *libtool* packages as required by each project. autoreconf minimizes the amount of regeneration required to address changes in timestamps, features, and project state. It was written as an attempt to consolidate existing maintainer-written, script-based utilities that ran all the required Autotools in the right order. You can think of autoreconf as a sort of smart Autotools bootstrap utility. If all you have is a *configure.ac* file, you can run autoreconf to execute all the tools you need, in the correct order, so that configure will be properly generated.

autoheader

The autoheader utility generates a C/C++–compatible header file template from various constructs in *configure.ac.* This file is usually called *config.h.in.* When the end user executes configure, the configuration script generates *config.h* from *config.h.in.* As maintainer, you'll use autoheader to generate the template file that you will include in your distribution package. (We'll examine autoheader in greater detail in Chapter 3.)

autoscan

The autoscan program generates a default *configure.ac* file for a new project; it can also examine an existing Autotools project for flaws and opportunities for enhancement. (We'll discuss autoscan in more detail in Chapters 3 and 8.) autoscan is very useful as a starting point for a project that uses a non-Autotools-based build system, but it may also be useful for suggesting features that might enhance an existing Autotools-based project.

autoupdate

The autoupdate utility is used to update *configure.ac* or the template (*.in*) files to match the syntax supported by the current version of the Autotools.

ifnames

The ifnames program is a small and generally underused utility that accepts a list of source file names on the command line and displays a list of C-preprocessor definitions on the stdout device. This utility was designed to help maintainers determine what to put into the *configure.ac* and *Makefile.am* files to make them portable. If your project was written with some level of portability in mind, ifnames can help you determine where those attempts at portability are located in your source tree and give you the names of potential portability definitions.

autom4te

The autom4te utility is an intelligent caching wrapper for M4 that is used by most of the other Autotools. The autom4te cache decreases the time successive tools spend accessing *configure.ac* constructs by as much as 30 percent.

I won't spend a lot of time on autom4te (pronounced *automate*) because it's primarily used internally by the Autotools. The only sign that it's working is the *autom4te.cache* directory that will appear in your top-level project directory after you run autoconf or autoreconf.

Working Together

Of the tools listed above, autoconf and autoheader are the only ones project maintainers will use directly when generating a configure script, and autoreconf is the only one that the developer needs to directly execute. Figure 1-1 shows the interaction between input files and autoconf and autoheader that generates the corresponding product files.

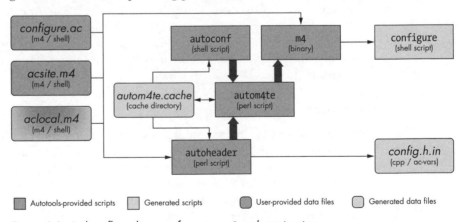

Figure 1-1: A data flow diagram for autoconf and autoheader

NOTE   *I will use the data flow diagram format shown in Figure 1-1 throughout this book. Dark boxes represent objects provided either by the user or by an Autotools package. Light boxes represent generated objects. Boxes with square corners are scripts, and boxes with rounded corners are data files. The meaning of most of the labels here should be obvious, but at least one deserves an explanation: The term* ac-vars *refers to Autoconf-specific replacement text. I'll explain the gradient shading of the aclocal.m4 box shortly.*

The primary task of this suite of tools is to generate a configuration script that can be used to configure a project build directory. This script will not rely on the Autotools themselves; in fact, autoconf is designed to generate configuration scripts that will run on all Unix-like platforms and in most variations of the Bourne shell. This means that you can generate a configuration script using autoconf and then successfully execute that script on a machine that does not have the Autotools installed.

The autoconf and autoheader programs are executed either directly by the user or indirectly by autoreconf. They take their input from your project's *configure.ac* file and various Autoconf-flavored M4 macro definition files, using autom4te to maintain cache information. autoconf generates a configuration script called configure, a very portable Bourne shell script that enables your project to offer many useful configuration capabilities. autoheader generates the *config.h.in* template based on certain macro definitions in *configure.ac*.

Automake

Once you've done it a few times, writing a basic makefile for a new project is fairly simple. But problems may occur when you try to do more than just the basics. And let's face it—what project maintainer has ever been satisfied with just a basic makefile?

Attention to detail is what makes an open source project successful. Users lose interest in a project fairly easily—especially when functionality they expect is missing or improperly written. For example, users have come to expect makefiles to support certain standard targets or goals, specified on the make command line, like this:

```
$ make install
```

Common make targets include all, clean, and install. In this example, install is the target. But you should realize that none of these are *real* targets: A *real target* is a filesystem object that is produced by the build system—usually a file. When building an executable called *doofabble*, for instance, you'd expect to be able to enter:

```
$ make doofabble
```

For this project, *doofabble* is a real target, and this command works for the doofabble project. However, requiring the user to enter real targets on the make command line is asking a lot of them, because each project must be built differently—make doofabble, make foodabble, make abfooble, and so on. Standardized targets for make allow all projects to be built in the same way using commonly known commands like make all or make clean. But *commonly known* doesn't mean *automatic*, and writing and maintaining makefiles that support these targets is tedious and error prone.

Automake's job is to convert a simplified specification of your project's build process into boilerplate makefile syntax that always works correctly the first time *and provides all the standard functionality expected.* Automake creates projects that support the guidelines defined in the *GNU Coding Standards* (discussed in Chapter 2).

The *automake* package provides the following tools in the form of Perl scripts:

- automake
- aclocal

automake

The automake program generates standard makefile templates (named *Makefile.in*) from high-level build specification files (named *Makefile.am*). These *Makefile.am* input files are essentially just regular makefiles. If you were to put only the few required Automake definitions in a *Makefile.am* file, you'd get a *Makefile.in* file containing several hundred lines of parameterized make script.

If you add additional make syntax to a *Makefile.am* file, Automake will move this code to the most functionally correct location in the resulting *Makefile.in* file. In fact, you can write your *Makefile.am* files so all they contain is ordinary make script, and the resulting makefiles will work just fine. This pass-through feature gives you the ability to extend Automake's functionality to suit your project's specific requirements.

aclocal

In the *GNU Automake Manual,* the aclocal utility is documented as a temporary work-around for a certain lack of flexibility in Autoconf. Automake extends Autoconf by adding an extensive set of macros, but Autoconf was not really designed with this level of extensibility in mind.

The original documented method for adding user-defined macros to an Autoconf project was to create a file called *aclocal.m4*, place the user-defined macros in this file, and place the file in the same directory as *configure.ac*. Autoconf then automatically included this file of macros while processing *configure.ac*. The designers of Automake found this extension mechanism too useful to pass up; however, users would have been required to add an m4_include statement to a possibly unnecessary *aclocal.m4* file in order to include the Automake macros. Since both user-defined macros and M4 itself are considered advanced concepts, this was deemed too harsh a requirement.

aclocal was designed to solve this problem—this utility generates an *aclocal.m4* file for a project that contains both user-defined macros and all required Automake macros.[8] Instead of adding user-defined macros directly to *aclocal.m4*, project maintainers should now add them to a new file called *acinclude.m4*.

---

8. Automake macros are copied into this file, but the user-written *acinclude.m4* file is merely referenced with an m4_include statement at the end of the file.

To make it clear to readers that Autoconf doesn't depend on Automake (and perhaps due to a bit of stubbornness), the *GNU Autoconf Manual* doesn't make much mention of the aclocal utility. The *GNU Automake Manual* originally suggested that you rename *aclocal.m4* to *acinclude.m4* when adding Automake to an existing Autoconf project, and this approach is still commonly used. The flow of data for aclocal is depicted in Figure 1-2.

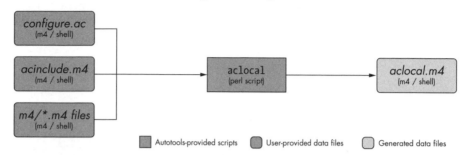

Figure 1-2: A data flow diagram for aclocal

However, the latest documentation for both Autoconf and Automake suggests that the entire paradigm is now obsolete. Developers should now specify a directory that contains a set of M4 macro files. The current recommendation is to create a directory in the project root directory called *m4* and add macros as individual *.m4* files to it. All files in this directory will be gathered into *aclocal.m4* before Autoconf processes *configure.ac*.[9]

It should now be more apparent why the *aclocal.m4* box in Figure 1-1 couldn't decide which color it should be. When you're using it without Automake and Libtool, you write the *aclocal.m4* file by hand. However, when you're using it with Automake, the file is generated by the aclocal utility, and you provide project-specific macros either in *acinclude.m4* or in an *m4* directory.

Libtool

How do you build shared libraries on different Unix platforms without adding a lot of very platform-specific conditional code to your build system and source code? This is the question that the *libtool* package tries to address.

There's a significant amount of common functionality among Unix-like platforms. However, one very significant difference has to do with how shared libraries are built, named, and managed. Some platforms name their libraries *lib*name.*so*, others use *lib*name.*a* or even *lib*name.*sl*, and still others don't even provide native shared libraries. Some platforms provide *libdl.so* to allow software to dynamically load and access library functionality at runtime, while others provide different mechanisms, and some platforms don't provide this functionality at all.

---

9. As with *acinclude.m4*, this gathering is virtual; *aclocal.m4* merely contains m4_include statements that reference these other files in place.

The developers of Libtool have carefully considered all of these differences. Libtool supports dozens of platforms, providing not only a set of Autoconf macros that hide library naming differences in makefiles, but also offering an optional library of dynamic loader functionality that can be added to programs. This functionality allows maintainers to make their runtime, dynamic shared-object management code more portable.

The *libtool* package provides the following programs, libraries, and header file:

- libtool (program)
- libtoolize (program)
- *ltdl* (static and shared libraries)
- *ltdl.h* (header file)

libtool

The libtool shell script that ships with the *libtool* package is a generic version of the custom script that libtoolize generates for a project.

libtoolize

The libtoolize shell script prepares your project to use Libtool. It generates a custom version of the generic libtool script and adds it to your project directory. This custom script is shipped with the project along with the Automake-generated makefiles, which execute the script on the user's system at the appropriate time.

ltdl, the Libtool C API

The *libtool* package also provides the *ltdl* library and associated header files, which provide a consistent runtime shared-object manager across platforms. The *ltdl* library may be linked statically or dynamically into your programs, giving them a consistent runtime shared-library access interface between platforms.

Figure 1-3 illustrates the interaction between the automake and libtool scripts, and the input files used to create products that configure and build your projects.

Automake and Libtool are both standard pluggable options that can be added to *configure.ac* with just a few simple macro calls.

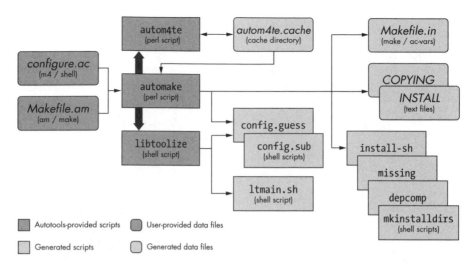

Figure 1-3: A data flow diagram for automake and libtool

Building Your Package

As maintainer, you probably build your software packages fairly often, and you're also probably intimately familiar with your project's components, architecture, and build system. However, you should make sure that your users' build experiences are much simpler than your own. One way to do this is to give users a simple, easy-to-understand pattern to follow when building your software packages. In the following sections, I'll show you the build pattern provided by the Autotools.

Running configure

After running the Autotools, you're left with a shell script called configure and one or more *Makefile.in* files. These files are intended to be shipped with your project release distribution packages. Your users will download these packages, unpack them, and enter ./configure && make from the top-level project directory. Then the configure script will generate makefiles (called *Makefile*) from the *Makefile.in* templates created by automake and a *config.h* header file from the *config.h.in* template generated by autoheader.

Automake generates *Makefile.in* templates rather than makefiles because without makefiles, your users can't run make; you don't want them to run make until after they've run configure, and this functionality guards against them doing so. *Makefile.in* templates are nearly identical to makefiles you might write by hand, except that you didn't have to. They also do a lot more than most people are willing to hand code. Another reason for not shipping ready-to-run makefiles is that it gives configure the chance to insert platform characteristics and user-specified optional features directly into the makefiles. This makes them a better fit for their target platforms and the end user's build preferences.

Figure 1-4 illustrates the interaction between configure and the scripts it executes during the configuration process in order to create the makefiles and the *config.h* header file.

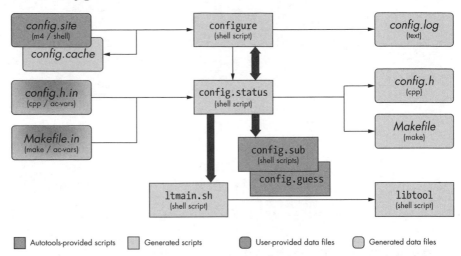

Figure 1-4: A data flow diagram for configure

The configure script has a bidirectional relationship with another script called config.status. You may have thought that your configure script generated your makefiles. But actually, the only file (besides a log file) that configure generates is config.status.

configure is designed to determine platform characteristics and features available on the user's system, as specified in *configure.ac*. Once it has this information, it generates config.status, which contains all of the check results, and then it executes this script. The config.status script, in turn, uses the check information embedded within it to generate platform-specific *config.h* and makefiles, as well as any other files specified for instantiation in *configure.ac*.

NOTE   *As the double-ended fat arrow in Figure 1-4 shows, config.status can also call configure. When used with the --recheck option, config.status will call configure using the same command-line options used to originally generate config.status.*

The configure script also generates a log file called *config.log*, which will contain very useful information in the event that an execution of configure fails on the user's system. As the maintainer, you can use this information for debugging. The *config.log* file also logs how configure was executed. (You can run config.status --version to discover the command-line options used to generate config.status.) This feature can be particularly handy when, for example, a user returns from a long vacation and can't remember which options he used to originally generate the project build directory.

NOTE   *To regenerate makefiles and the* config.h *header files, just enter ./config.status from within the project build directory. The output files will be generated using the same options originally used to generate the* config.status *file.*

Building Outside the Source Directory

A little-known feature of Autotools build environments is that they don't need to be generated within a project source tree. That is, if a user executes configure from a directory other than the project source directory, he can generate a full build environment within an isolated build directory.

In the following example, Joe User downloads *doofabble-3.0.tar.gz*, unpacks it, and creates two sibling directories called *doofabble-3.0.debug* and *doofabble-3.0.release*. He changes into the *doofabble-3.0.debug* directory, executes doofabble-3.0's configure script, using a relative path, with a doofabble-specific debug option, and then runs make from within this same directory. Finally, he switches over to the *doofabble-3.0.release* directory and does the same thing, this time running configure without the debug option enabled:

```
$ gzip -dc doofabble-3.0.tar.gz | tar zxf -
$ mkdir doofabble-3.0.debug
$ mkdir doofable-3.0.release
$ cd doofabble-3.0.debug
$ ../doofabble-3.0/configure --enable-debug
...
$ make
...
$ cd ../dofable-3.0.release
$ ../doofabble-3.0/configure
...
$ make
...
```

Users generally don't care about remote build functionality, because all they usually want to do is configure, build, and install your code on their platforms. Maintainers, on the other hand, find remote build functionality very useful, as it allows them to not only maintain a reasonably pristine source tree, but it also allows them to maintain multiple build environments for their project, each with complex configuration options. Rather than reconfigure a single build environment, a maintainer can simply switch to another build directory that has been configured with different options.

Running make

Finally, you run plain old make. The designers of the Autotools went to a *lot* of trouble to ensure that you didn't need any special version or brand of make. Figure 1-5 depicts the interaction between make and the makefiles that are generated during the build process.

As you can see, make runs several generated scripts, but these are all really ancillary to the make process. The generated makefiles contain commands that execute these scripts under the appropriate conditions. These scripts are part of the Autotools, and they are either shipped with your package or generated by your configuration script.

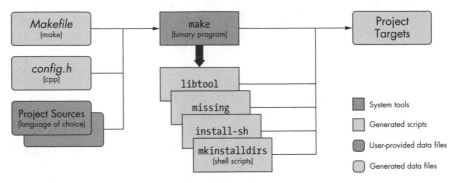

Figure 1-5: A data flow diagram for make

Installing the Most Up-to-Date Autotools

If you're running a variant of Linux and you've chosen to install the compilers and tools used for developing C-language software, you probably already have some version of the Autotools installed on your system. To determine which versions of autoconf, automake, and libtool you're using, simply open a terminal window and type the following commands:

```
$ which autoconf
/usr/local/bin/autoconf
$ autoconf --version
autoconf (GNU Autoconf) 2.65
Copyright (C) 2009 Free Software Foundation, Inc.
License GPLv3+/Autoconf: GNU GPL version 3 or later
<http://gnu.org/licenses/gpl.html>, <http://gnu.org/licenses/exceptions.html>
This is free software: you are free to change and redistribute it.
There is NO WARRANTY, to the extent permitted by law.

Written by David J. MacKenzie and Akim Demaille.
$
$ which automake
/usr/local/bin/automake
$ automake --version
automake (GNU automake) 1.11
Copyright (C) 2009 Free Software Foundation, Inc.
License GPLv2+: GNU GPL version 2 or later <http://gnu.org/licenses/gpl-
2.0.html>
This is free software: you are free to change and redistribute it.
There is NO WARRANTY, to the extent permitted by law.

Written by Tom Tromey <tromey@redhat.com>
        and Alexandre Duret-Lutz <adl@gnu.org>.
$
$ which libtool
/usr/local/bin/libtool
```

```
$ libtool --version
ltmain.sh (GNU libtool) 2.2.6b
Written by Gordon Matzigkeit <gord@gnu.ai.mit.edu>, 1996

Copyright (C) 2008 Free Software Foundation, Inc.
This is free software; see the source for copying conditions. There is NO
warranty; not even for MERCHANTABILITY or FITNESS FOR A PARTICULAR PURPOSE.
$
```

NOTE   *If you have the Linux-distribution varieties of these Autotools packages installed on your system, the executables will probably be found in* /usr/bin, *rather than* /usr/local/bin, *as you can see from the output of the* which *command here.*

If you choose to download, build, and install the latest version of any one of these packages from the GNU website, you must do the same for all of them, because the *automake* and *libtool* packages install macros into the Autoconf macro directory. If you don't already have the Autotools installed, you can install them from their GNU distribution source archives with the following commands (be sure to change the version numbers as necessary):

```
$ mkdir autotools && cd autotools
$ wget -q ftp://ftp.gnu.org/gnu/autoconf/autoconf-2.65.tar.gz
$ gzip -cd autoconf* | tar xf -
$ cd autoconf*
$ ./configure && make all check
...
$ su
Password: ******
# make install
...
# exit
$ cd ..
$
$ wget -q ftp://ftp.gnu.org/gnu/automake/automake-1.11.tar.gz
$ gzip -cd automake* | tar xf -
$ cd automake*
$ ./configure && make all check
...
$ su
Password: ******
# make install
# exit
$ cd ..
$
$ wget -q ftp://ftp.gnu.org/gnu/libtool/libtool-2.2.6b.tar.gz
$ gzip -cd libtool* | tar xf -
$ cd libtool*
$ ./configure && make all check
...
```

```
$ su
Password: ******
# make install
...
# exit
$ cd ..
$
```

You should now be able to successfully execute the version check commands from the previous example.

Summary

In this chapter, I've presented a high-level overview of the Autotools to give you a feel for how everything ties together. I've also shown you the pattern to follow when building software from distribution tarballs created by Autotools build systems. Finally, I've shown you how to install the Autotools and how to tell which versions you have installed.

In Chapter 2, we'll step away from the Autotools briefly and begin creating a hand-coded build system for a toy project called *Jupiter*. You'll learn the requirements of a reasonable build system, and you'll become familiar with the rationale behind the original design of the Autotools. With this background knowledge, you'll begin to understand why the Autotools do things the way they do. I can't really emphasize this enough: *Chapter 2 is one of the most important chapters in this book.*

2

UNDERSTANDING THE GNU
CODING STANDARDS

*I don't know what's the matter with people: they don't
learn by understanding, they learn by some other way—
by rote or something. Their knowledge is so fragile!*
—*Richard Feynman,*
Surely You're Joking, Mr. Feynman!

In Chapter 1, I gave an overview of the GNU
Autotools and some resources that can help
reduce the learning curve required to master
them. In this chapter, we're going to step back a
little and examine project organization techniques
that you can apply to any project, not just one that uses
the Autotools.

When you're done reading this chapter, you should be familiar with the
common make targets and why they exist. You should also have a solid understanding of why projects are organized the way they are. By the time you finish this chapter, you'll be well on your way to becoming an Autotools expert.

The information provided in this chapter comes primarily from two sources:

- The *GNU Coding Standards (GCS)*[1]
- The *Filesystem Hierarchy Standard (FHS)*[2]

---

1. See the Free Software Foundation's *GNU Coding Standards* at *http://www.gnu.org/prep/standards/*.
2. See Daniel Quinlan's overview at *http://www.pathname.com/fhs/*.

If you'd like to brush up on your make syntax, you may also find the *GNU Make Manual*[3] very useful. If you're particularly interested in portable make syntax (and you probably should be), then check out the POSIX man page for make.[4]

Creating a New Project Directory Structure

There are two questions you need to ask yourself when you're setting up the build system for an open source software project:

- Which platforms will I target?
- What do my users expect?

The first is an easy question—you get to decide which platforms to target, but you shouldn't be too restrictive. Open source software projects attain greatness by virtue of the number of people who've adopted them, and arbitrarily limiting the number of platforms reduces the potential size of your community.

The second question is more difficult to answer. First, let's narrow the scope to something manageable. What you really need to ask is: *What do my users expect of my build system?* Experienced open source software developers become familiar with these expectations by downloading, unpacking, building, and installing thousands of packages. Eventually, they come to know intuitively what users expect of a build system. But, even so, the processes of package configuration, build, and installation vary widely, so it's difficult to define any solid norm.

Rather than taking a survey of every build system out there yourself, you can consult the Free Software Foundation (FSF), sponsor of the GNU project, which has done a lot of the leg work for you. The FSF is one of the best definitive sources for information on free, open source software, including the *GCS*, which covers a wide variety of topics related to writing, publishing, and distributing free, open source software. Even many non-GNU open source software projects align themselves with the *GCS*. Why? Well, they invented the concept of free software, and their ideas make sense, for the most part.[5] There are dozens of issues to consider when designing a system that manages packaging, building, and installing software, and the *GCS* takes most of them into account.

3. See the Free Software Foundation's *GNU Make Manual* at *http://www.gnu.org/software/make/manual/*.

4. See the Open Group Base Specifications, Issue 6, at *http://www.opengroup.org/onlinepubs/009695399/utilities/make.html*.

5. In truth, it's likely that the standards that came about from the BSD project were written much earlier than the standards of the FSF, but the FSF had a big hand in spreading the information to many different platforms and non–system specific software projects. Thus, it had a large part in making these standards publicly visible and widely used.

Project Structure

We'll start with a basic sample project and build on it as we continue our exploration of source-level software distribution. I'll call our project *Jupiter* and I'll create a project directory structure using the following commands:

```
$ cd projects
$ mkdir -p jupiter/src
$ touch jupiter/Makefile
$ touch jupiter/src/Makefile
$ touch jupiter/src/main.c
$ cd jupiter
$
```

We now have one source code directory called *src*, one C source file called *main.c*, and a makefile for each of the two directories in our project. Minimal, yes; but this is a new endeavor, and everyone knows that the key to a successful open source software project is evolution. Start small and grow as needed—and as you have the time and inclination.

Let's start by adding support for building and cleaning our project. (We'll need to add other important capabilities to our build system later on, but these two will get us going.) The top-level makefile does very little at this point; it merely passes requests down to *src/Makefile*, recursively. This constitutes a fairly common type of build system, known as a *recursive build system*, so named because makefiles recursively invoke make on subdirectory makefiles.[6]

---

6. Peter Miller's seminal paper, "Recursive Make Considered Harmful" (*http://miller.emu.id.au/pmiller/books/rmch/*), published over 10 years ago, discusses some of the problems recursive build systems can cause. I encourage you to read this paper and understand the issues Miller presents. While the issues are valid, the sheer simplicity of implementing and maintaining a recursive build system makes it, by far, the most widely used form of build system.

Listings 2-1 through 2-3 show the contents of each of these three files, thus far.

```
all clean jupiter:
        cd src && $(MAKE) $@

.PHONY: all clean
```

Listing 2-1: Makefile: An initial draft of a top-level makefile for Jupiter

```
all: jupiter

jupiter: main.c
        gcc -g -O0 -o $@ main.c

clean:
        -rm jupiter

.PHONY: all clean
```

Listing 2-2: src/Makefile: The first draft of Jupiter's src directory makefile

```
#include <stdio.h>
#include <stdlib.h>

int main(int argc, char * argv[])
{
    printf("Hello from %s!\n", argv[0]);
    return 0;
}
```

Listing 2-3: src/main.c: The first version of the one source file in the Jupiter project

NOTE *As you read this code, you will probably notice places where a makefile or a source code file contains a construct that is not written in the simplest manner or is perhaps not written the way you would have chosen to write it. There is a method to my madness: I've tried to use constructs that are portable to many flavors of the make utility.*

Now let's discuss the basics of make. If you're already pretty well versed in it, then you can skip the next section. Otherwise, give it a quick read, and we'll return our attention to the Jupiter project later in the chapter.

Makefile Basics

If you don't use make on a regular basis, it's often difficult to remember exactly what goes where in a makefile, so here are a few things to keep in mind. Besides comments, which begin with a hash mark (#), there are only three basic types of entities in a makefile:

- Variable assignments
- Rules
- Commands

While there are several other types of constructs in a makefile (including conditional statements, directives, extension rules, pattern rules, function variables, and include statements, among others), for our purposes, we'll just touch lightly on them as needed instead of covering them all in detail. This doesn't mean they're unimportant, however—on the contrary, they're very useful if you're going to write your own complex build system by hand. However, our purpose is to gain the background necessary for understanding the GNU Autotools, so I'll only cover the aspects of make you need to know to accomplish that goal.

If you want a broader education on make syntax, refer to the *GNU Make Manual.* For strictly portable syntax, the POSIX man page for make is an excellent reference. If you want to become a make expert, be prepared to spend a good deal of time studying these resources—there's much more to the make utility than is initially apparent.

Commands and Rules

When a line in a makefile begins with a TAB character, make will always consider it to be a command. Indeed, one of the most frustrating aspects of makefile syntax to neophytes and experts alike is that commands must be prefixed with an essentially invisible character. The error messages generated by the legacy UNIX make utility when a required TAB is missing (or has been converted to spaces by your editor) or an unintentional TAB is inserted are obscure at best. GNU make does a better job with such error messages. Nonetheless, be careful to use leading TAB characters properly in your makefiles—always and only before commands.

A list of one or more commands is always associated with a preceding rule. A *rule* takes the form of a target followed by a list of dependencies. In general, *targets* are objects that need to be built, and *dependencies* are objects that provide source material for targets. Thus, targets are said to depend upon the dependencies. Dependencies are essentially *prerequisites* of the targets, and thus they should be updated first.[7]

Listing 2-4 shows the general layout of a makefile.

```
var1=val1
var2=val2
...
target1 : t1_dep1 t1_dep2 ... t1_depN
<TAB>    shell-command1a
<TAB>    shell-command1b
         ...
target2 : t2_dep1 t2_dep2 ... t2_depN
<TAB>    shell-command2a
<TAB>    shell-command2b
         ...
```

Listing 2-4: The general layout of a makefile

---

7. You'll often hear dependencies referred to as *prerequisites* for this reason.

The make utility is a rule-based command engine, and the rules at work indicate which commands should be executed and when. When you prefix a line with a TAB character, you're telling make that you want it to execute the following statements from a shell according to the preceding rule. The existence and timestamps of the files mentioned in the rules indicate whether the commands should be executed, and in what order.

As make processes the text in a makefile, it builds a web of dependency chains (technically called a *directed graph*). When building a particular target, make must walk backward through the entire graph to the beginning of each "chain." make then executes the commands for each rule in these chains, beginning with the rule farthest from the target and working forward to the rule for the desired target. As make discovers targets that are older than their dependencies, it must execute the associated set of commands to update those targets before it can process the next rule in the chain. As long as the rules are written correctly, this algorithm ensures that make will build a completely up-to-date product using the least number of operations possible.

Variables

Lines in a makefile containing an equal sign (=) are variable definitions. Variables in makefiles are somewhat similar to shell or environment variables, but there are some key differences.

In Bourne-shell syntax, you'd reference a variable in this manner: ${my_var}. The syntax for referencing variables in a makefile is identical, except that you have the choice of using parentheses or curly brackets: $(my_var). To minimize confusion, it has become somewhat of a convention to use parentheses rather than curly brackets when dereferencing make variables. For single-character make variables, using these delimiters is optional, but you should use them in order to avoid ambiguities. For example, $X is functionally equivalent to $(X) or ${X}, but $(my_var) would require parentheses so make does not interpret the reference as $(m)y_var.

NOTE   *To dereference a shell variable inside a make command, escape the dollar sign by doubling it—for example, $${shell_var}. Escaping the dollar sign tells make not to interpret the variable reference, but rather to treat it as literal text in the command.*

By default, make reads the process environment into its variable table before processing the makefile; this allows you to access most environment variables without explicitly defining them in the makefile. Note, however, that variables set inside the makefile will override those obtained from the environment.[8] It's generally not a good idea to depend on the existence of environment variables in your build process, although it's okay to use them conditionally. In addition, make defines several useful variables of its own, such as the MAKE variable, the value of which is the complete command line (with options) used to invoke the current make process.

---

8. You can use the -e option on the make command line to reverse this default behavior so that variables defined within the environment override those defined within the makefile. However, relying on this option can lead to problems caused by subtle environmental differences between systems.

You can assign variables at any point in the makefile. However, you should be aware that make processes a makefile in two passes. In the first pass, it gathers variables and rules into tables and internal structures. In the second pass, it resolves dependencies defined by the rules, invoking those rules as necessary to rebuild the dependencies based on filesystem timestamps. If a dependency in a rule is newer than the target or if the target is missing, then make executes the commands of the rule to update the target. Some variable references are resolved immediately during the first pass while processing rules, and others are resolved later during the second pass while executing commands.

A Separate Shell for Each Command

As it processes rules, make executes each command independently of those around it. That is, each individual command under a rule is executed in its own shell. This means that you cannot export a shell variable in one command and then try to access its value in the next.

To do something like this, you would have to string commands together on the same command line with command separator characters (e.g., semicolons, in Bourne shell syntax). When you write commands like this, make passes the set of concatenated commands as one command line to the same shell. To avoid long command lines and increase readability, you can wrap them using a backslash at the end of each line—usually after the semicolon. The wrapped portion of such commands may also be preceded by a TAB character. POSIX specifies that make should remove all leading TAB characters (even those following escaped newlines) before processing commands, but be aware that some make implementations do output—usually harmlessly—the TAB characters embedded within wrapped commands.[9]

Listing 2-5 shows a few simple examples of multiple commands that will be executed by the same shell.

```
❶ foo: bar.c
        sources=bar.c; \
        gcc -o foo $${sources}

❷ fud: baz.c
        sources=baz.c; gcc -o fud $${sources}

❸ doo: doo.c
        TMPDIR=/var/tmp gcc -o doo doo.c
```

Listing 2-5: Some examples of multiple commands executed by the same shell

In the first example at ❶, both lines are executed by the same shell because the backslash escapes the newline character between the lines. The make utility will remove any escaped newline characters before passing a single, multi-command statement to the shell. The second example at ❷ is identical to the first, from make's perspective.

9. Experiments have shown that many make implementations generate cleaner output if you don't use TAB characters after escaped newlines. Nevertheless, the community seems to have settled on the consistent use of TAB characters in all command lines, whether wrapped or not.

The third example at ❸ is a bit different. In this case, I've defined the TMPDIR variable only for the child process that will run gcc.[10] Note the missing semicolon; as far as the shell is concerned, this is a single command.[11]

NOTE   *If you choose to wrap commands with a trailing backslash, be sure that there are no spaces or other invisible characters after it. The backslash escapes the newline character, so it must immediately precede that character.*

Variable Binding

Variables referenced in commands may be defined after the command in the makefile because such references are not bound to their values until just before make passes the command to the shell for execution—long after the entire makefile has been read. In general, make binds variables to values as late as it possibly can.

Since commands are processed at a later stage than rules, variable references in commands are bound later than those in rules. Variable references found in rules are expanded when make builds the directed graph from the rules in the makefile. Thus, a variable referenced in a rule must be fully defined in a makefile before the referencing rule. Listing 2-6 shows a portion of a makefile that illustrates both of these concepts.

```
...
mytarget=foo
❶ $(mytarget): $(mytarget).c
❷         gcc -o $(mytarget) $(mytarget).c

mytarget=bar
...
```

Listing 2-6: Variable expansion in a makefile

In the rule at ❶, both references to $(mytarget) are expanded to foo because they're processed during the first pass, when make is building the variable list and directed graph. However, the outcome is probably not what you'd expect, because both references to $(mytarget) in the command at ❷ are not expanded until much later, long after make has already assigned bar to mytarget, overwriting the original assignment of foo.

Listing 2-7 shows the same rule and command the way make sees them after the variables are fully expanded.

```
...
foo: foo.c
        gcc -o bar bar.c
...
```

Listing 2-7: The results after variable expansion of the code in Listing 2-6

---

10. gcc uses the value of the TMPDIR variable to determine where to write temporary intermediate files between tools such as the C-preprocessor and the compiler.

11. You cannot dereference TMPDIR on the command line when it's defined in this manner. Only the child process has access to this variable; the current shell does not.

The moral of this story is that you should understand where variables will be expanded in makefile constructs so you're not surprised when make refuses to act in a sane manner when it processes your makefile. It is good practice (and a good way to avoid headaches) to always assign variables before you intend to use them. For more information on immediate and deferred expansion of variables in makefiles, refer to "How make Reads a Makefile" in the *GNU Make Manual.*

Rules in Detail

Lines in my sample makefiles that are not variable assignments (i.e., don't contain an equal sign), and are not commands (i.e., are not prefixed with a TAB character) are all rules of one type or another. The rules used in my examples are known as *common* make rules, containing a single colon character (:). The colon separates targets on the left from dependencies on the right.

Remember that targets are products—that is, filesystem entities that can be produced by running one or more commands, such as a C or C++ compiler, a linker, or a documentation generator like Doxygen or LaTeX. Dependencies, on the other hand, are source objects, or objects from which targets are created. These may be computer language source files, intermediate products built by a previous rule, or anything else that can be used by a command as a resource.

You can specify any target defined within a makefile rule directly on the make command line, and make will execute all the commands necessary to generate that target.

NOTE *If you don't specify any targets on the make command line, make will use the default target—the first one it finds in the makefile.*

For example, a C compiler takes dependency *main.c* as input and generates target *main.o.* A linker then takes dependency *main.o* as input and generates a named executable target—program, in this case.

Figure 2-1 shows the flow of data as it might be specified by the rules defined in a makefile.

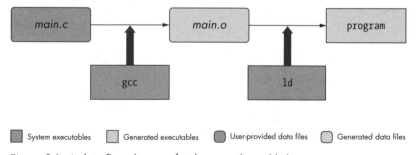

Figure 2-1: A data flow diagram for the compile and link processes

The make utility implements some fairly complex logic to determine when a rule should be run, based on whether a target exists and whether it is older than its dependencies. Listing 2-8 shows a makefile containing rules that execute the actions in Figure 2-1.

```
program: main.o print.o display.o
❶        ld main.o print.o display.o ... -o program

main.o: main.c
        gcc -c -g -O2 -o main.o main.c

print.o: print.c
        gcc -c -g -O2 -o print.o print.c

main.o: main.c
        gcc -c -g -O2 -o display.o display.c
```

Listing 2-8: Using multiple make rules to compile and link a program

The first rule in this makefile says that program depends on *main.o, print.o,* and *display.o.* The remaining rules say that each *.o* file depends on the corresponding *.c* file. Ultimately, program depends on the three source files, but the object files are necessary as intermediate dependencies because there are two steps to the process—compile and link—with a result in between. For each rule, make uses an associated list of commands to build the rule's target from its list of dependencies.

Unix compilers are designed as higher-level tools than linkers. They have built-in, low-level knowledge about system-specific linker requirements. In the makefile in Listing 2-8, the ellipsis in the line at ❶ is a placeholder for a list of system-specific, low-level objects and libraries required to build all programs on this system. The compiler can be used to call the linker, silently passing these system-specific objects and libraries. (It's so effective and widely used that it's often difficult to discover how to manually execute the linker on a given system.) Listing 2-9 shows how you might rewrite the makefile from Listing 2-8 to use the compiler to compile the sources and call the linker in a single rule.[12]

```
sources = main.c print.c display.c

program: $(sources)
        gcc -g -O0 -o program $(sources)
```

Listing 2-9: Using a single make rule to compile sources into an executable

In this example, I've added a make variable (sources) that allows us to consolidate all product dependencies into one location. We now have a list of source files captured in a variable definition that is referenced in two places: in the dependency list and on the command line.

---

12. Using a single rule and command to process both steps is possible in this case because the example is very basic. For larger projects, skipping from source to executable in a single step is usually not the wisest way to manage the build process. However, in either case, using the compiler to call the linker can ease the burden of determining the many system objects that need to be linked into an application, and, in fact, this very technique is used quite often. More complex examples, wherein each file is compiled separately, use the compiler to compile each source file into an object file and then use the compiler to call the linker to link them all together into an executable.

Automatic Variables

There may be other kinds of objects in a dependency list that are not in the sources variable, including precompiled objects and libraries. These other objects would have to be listed separately, both in the rule and on the command line. Wouldn't it be nice if we had shorthand notation for referencing the rule's entire dependency list in the commands?

As it happens, there are various *automatic* variables that can be used to reference portions of the controlling rule during the execution of a command. Unfortunately, most of these are all but useless if you care about portability between implementations of make. The $@ variable (which references the current target) happens to be portable and useful, but most of the other automatic variables are too limited to be very useful.[13] The following is a complete list of portable automatic variables defined by POSIX for make:

- $@ refers to the full target name of the current target or the archive filename part of a library archive target. This variable is valid in both explicit and implicit rules.

- $% refers to a member of an archive and is valid only when the current target is an archive member—that is, an object file that is a member of a static library. This variable is valid in both explicit and implicit rules.

- $? refers to the list of dependencies that are newer than the current target. This variable is valid in both explicit and implicit rules.

- $< refers to the member of the dependency list whose existence allowed the rule to be chosen for the target. This variable is only valid in implicit rules.

- $* refers to the current target name with its suffix deleted. This variable is guaranteed by POSIX to be valid only in implicit rules.

GNU make dramatically extends the POSIX-defined list, but since GNU extensions are not portable, it's unwise to use any of these except $@.

Dependency Rules

In Listing 2-10, I've replaced the sources variable with an objects variable and replaced the list of source files with a list of object files. This listing also eliminates redundancy by making use of both standard and automatic variables.

```
objects = main.o print.o display.o

main.o: main.c print.h display.h
print.o: print.c print.h
display.o: display.c display.h

program: $(objects)
        gcc -g -O0 -o $@ $(objects)
```

Listing 2-10: Using automatic variables in a command

---

13. This is because POSIX is not so much a specification for the way things *should be* done as it is a specification for the way things *are* done. Essentially, the purpose of the POSIX standard is to keep Unix implementations from deviating any further from the norm than necessary. Unfortunately, most make implementations had wide acceptance within their own communities long before the idea for a POSIX standard was conceived.

I've also added three *dependency rules*, which are rules without commands that clarify the relationships between compiler output files and dependent source and header files. Because *print.h* and *display.h* are (presumably) included by *main.c*, *main.c* must be recompiled if either of those files changes; however, make has no way of knowing that these two header files are included by *main.c*. Dependency rules allow the developer to tell make about such back-end relationships.

Implicit Rules

If you attempt to mentally follow the dependency graph that make would build from the rules within the makefile in Listing 2-10, you'll find what appears to be a hole in the web. According to the last rule in the file, the program executable depends on *main.o*, *print.o*, and *display.o*. This rule also provides the command to link these objects into an executable (using the compiler only to call the linker this time). The object files are tied to their corresponding C source and header files by the three dependency rules. But where are the commands that compile the *.c* files into *.o* files?

We could add these commands to the dependency rules, but there's really no need, because make has a built-in rule that knows how to build *.o* files from *.c* files. There's nothing magic about make—it only knows about the relationships you describe to it through the rules you write. But make does have certain built-in rules that describe the relationships between, for example, *.c* files and *.o* files. This particular built-in rule provides commands for building anything with a *.o* extension from a file of the same base name with a *.c* extension. These built-in rules are called *suffix rules*, or more generally, *implicit rules*, because the name of the dependency (source file) is implied by the name of the target (object file).

You can write implicit rules yourself, if you wish. You can even override the default implicit rules with your own versions. Implicit rules are a powerful tool, and they shouldn't be overlooked, but for the purposes of this book, we won't go into any more detail. You can learn more about writing and using implicit rules within makefiles in "Using Implicit Rules" in the *GNU Make Manual*.

To illustrate this implicit functionality, I created simple C source and header files to accompany the sample makefile from Listing 2-10. Here's what happened when I executed make on this makefile:

```
❶ $ make
   cc     -c -o main.o main.c
   $
❷ $ make program
   cc     -c -o print.o print.c
   cc     -c -o display.o display.c
   gcc -g -O0 -o program main.o print.o display.o
   $
```

As you can see, cc was magically executed with -c and -o options to generate *main.o* from *main.c*. This is common command-line syntax used to make a C-language compiler build objects from sources—it's so common, in fact, that the functionality is built into make. If you look for cc on a modern GNU/Linux system, you'll find that it's a soft link in */usr/bin* that refers to the system's GNU C compiler. On other systems, it refers to the system's native C compiler. Calling the system C compiler *cc* has been a de facto standard for decades.[14]

But why did the make utility build only *main.o* when we typed make at ❶? Simply because the dependency rule for *main.o* provided the first (and thus, the default) target for the makefile. In this case, to build program, we needed to execute make program, like we did in ❷. Remember that when you enter make on the command line, the make utility attempts to build the first explicitly defined target within the file called *Makefile* in the current directory. If we wanted to make program the default target, we could rearrange the rules so the program rule would be the first one listed in the makefile.

To see the dependency rules in action, touch one of the header files and then rebuild the program target:

```
$ touch display.h
$ make program
cc     -c -o main.o main.c
cc     -c -o display.o display.c
gcc -g -O0 -o program main.o print.o display.o
$
```

After updating *display.h*, only *display.o*, *main.o*, and program were rebuilt. The *print.o* object didn't need to be rebuilt because *print.c* doesn't depend on *display.h*, according to the rules specified in the makefile.

Phony Targets

Targets are not always files. They can also be so-called *phony targets*, as in the case of all and clean. These targets don't refer to true products in the filesystem, but rather to particular outcomes or actions—when you make these targets, the project is *cleaned*, *all* products are built, and so on.

Multiple Targets

In the same way that you can list multiple dependencies on the right side of a colon, you can combine rules for multiple targets with the same dependencies and commands by listing the targets on the left side of a colon, as shown in Listing 2-11.

```
all clean:
        cd src && $(MAKE) $@
```

Listing 2-11: Using multiple targets in a rule

---

14. POSIX has standardized the program (or link) names *c89* and *c99* to refer to 1989 and 1999 C-language standard compatible compilers. Since these commands can refer to the same compiler with different command-line options, they're often implemented as binary programs or shell scripts, rather than merely as soft links.

While it may not be immediately apparent, this example contains two separate rules: one for each of the two targets, all and clean. Because these two rules have the same set of dependencies (none, in this case), and the same set of commands, we're able to take advantage of a shorthand notation supported by make that allows us to combine their rules into one specification.

To help you understand this concept, consider the $@ variable in Listing 2-11. Which target does it refer to? That depends on which rule is currently executing—the one for all or the one for clean. Since a rule can only be executed on a single target at any given time, $@ can only ever refer to one target, even when the controlling rule specification contains several.

Resources for Makefile Authors

GNU make is significantly more powerful than the original AT&T UNIX make utility, although GNU make is completely backward compatible, as long as you avoid GNU extensions. The *GNU Make Manual*[15] is available online, and O'Reilly has published an excellent book on the original AT&T UNIX make utility[16] and all of its many nuances. While you can still find this title, the publisher has recently merged its content into a new edition that also covers GNU make extensions.[17]

This concludes the general discussion of makefile syntax and the make utility, although we will look at additional makefile constructs as we encounter them throughout the rest of this chapter. With this general information behind us, let's return to the Jupiter project and begin adding some more interesting functionality.

Creating a Source Distribution Archive

In order to actually get source code for Jupiter to our users, we're going to have to create and distribute a *source archive*—a tarball. We could write a separate script to create the tarball, but since we can use phony targets to create arbitrary sets of functionality in makefiles, let's design a make target to perform this task instead. Building a source archive for distribution is usually relegated to the dist target.

When designing a new make target, we need to consider whether its functionality should be distributed among the makefiles of the project or handled in a single location. Normally, the rule of thumb is to take advantage of a recursive build system's nature by allowing each directory to manage its own portions of a process. We did just this when we passed control of building the jupiter program down to the *src* directory, where the source code is located.

---

15. See the Free Software Foundation's *GNU Make Manual* at *http://www.gnu.org/software/make/manual/*.

16. Andy Oram and Steve Talbott, *Managing Projects with make, Second Edition: The Power of GNU make for Building Anything* (Sebastopol, CA: O'Reilly Media, 1991), *http://oreilly.com/catalog/9780937175903/*.

17. Robert Mecklenburg, *Managing Projects with GNU Make, Third Edition: The Power of GNU make for Building Anything* (Sebastopol, CA: O'Reilly Media, 2004), *http://www.oreilly.com/catalog/9780596006105/*.

However, building a compressed archive from a directory structure isn't really a recursive process.[18] This being the case, we'll have to perform the entire task in one of the two makefiles.

Global processes are often handled by the makefile at the highest relevant level in the project directory structure. We'll add the dist target to our top-level makefile, as shown in Listing 2-12.

```
❶ package = jupiter
  version = 1.0
  tarname = $(package)
  distdir = $(tarname)-$(version)

  all clean jupiter:
          cd src && $(MAKE) $@

❷ dist: $(distdir).tar.gz

❸ $(distdir).tar.gz: $(distdir)
          tar chof - $(distdir) | gzip -9 -c > $@
          rm -rf $(distdir)

❹ $(distdir):
          mkdir -p $(distdir)/src
          cp Makefile $(distdir)
          cp src/Makefile $(distdir)/src
          cp src/main.c $(distdir)/src

❺ .PHONY: all clean dist
```

Listing 2-12: Makefile: *Adding the* dist *target to the top-level makefile*

Besides the addition of the dist target at ❷, I've also made several other modifications. Let's look at them one at a time. I've added the dist target to the .PHONY rule at ❺. .PHONY is a special kind of built-in rule called a *dot-rule* or a *directive.* The make utility understands several different dot-rules. The purpose of .PHONY is simply to tell make that certain targets don't generate filesystem objects. Normally, make determines which commands to run by comparing the timestamps of the targets to those of their dependencies in the filesystem— but phony targets don't have associated filesystem objects. Using .PHONY ensures that make won't go looking for nonexistent product files named after these targets.

Adding a target to the .PHONY rule has another effect. Since make won't be able to use timestamps to determine whether the target is up to date (that is, newer than its dependencies), make has no recourse but to *always* execute the commands associated with phony targets whenever these targets either are requested on the command line or appear in a dependency chain.

---

18. Well, okay, it is a recursive process, but the recursive portions of the process are tucked away inside the tar utility.

I've separated the functionality of the dist target into three separate rules (❷, ❸, and ❹) for the sake of readability, modularity, and maintenance. This is a great rule of thumb to follow in any software engineering process: *Build large processes from smaller ones, and reuse the smaller processes where it makes sense.*

The dist target at ❷ depends on the existence of the ultimate goal—in this case a source-level compressed archive package, *jupiter-1.0.tar.gz.* I've used one variable to hold the version number (which makes it easier to update the project version later) and another variable for the package name at ❶, which will make it easier to change the name if I ever decide to reuse this makefile for another project. I've also logically split the functions of package name and tarball name; the default tarball name is the package name, but we do have the option of making them different.

The rule that builds the tarball at ❸ indicates how this should be done with a command that uses the gzip and tar utilities to create the file. But, notice that the rule has a dependency—the directory to be archived. The directory name is derived from the tarball name and the package version number; it's stored in yet another variable called distdir.

We don't want object files and executables from our last build attempt to end up in the archive, so we need to build an image directory containing exactly what we want to ship—including any files required in the build and install processes and any additional documentation or license files. Unfortunately, this pretty much mandates the use of individual copy (cp) commands.

Since there's a rule in the makefile (at ❹) that tells how this directory should be created, and since that rule's target is a dependency of the tarball, make runs the commands for that rule *before* running the commands for the tarball rule. Recall that make processes rules to build dependencies recursively, from the bottom up, until it can run the commands for the requested target.[19]

Forcing a Rule to Run

There's a subtle flaw in the $(distdir) target that may not be obvious right now, but it will rear its ugly head at the worst of times. If the archive image directory (*jupiter-1.0*) already exists when you execute make dist, then make won't try to create it. Try this:

```
$ mkdir jupiter-1.0
$ make dist
tar chof - jupiter-1.0 | gzip -9 -c > jupiter-1.0.tar.gz
rm -rf jupiter-1.0
$
```

Notice that the dist target didn't copy any files—it just built an archive out of the existing *jupiter-1.0* directory, which was empty. Our users would get a real surprise when they unpack this tarball! Worse still, if the image directory from the previous attempt to archive happened to still be there, the new tarball would contain the now outdated sources from our last attempt to create a distribution tarball.

---

19. This process is formally called *post-order recursion.*

The problem is that the $(distdir) target is a real target with no dependencies, which means that make will consider it up to date as long as it exists in the filesystem. We could add the $(distdir) target to the .PHONY rule to force make to rebuild it every time we make the dist target, but it's not a phony target—it's a real filesystem object. The proper way to ensure that $(distdir) is always rebuilt is to ensure that it doesn't exist before make attempts to build it. One way to accomplish this is to create a true phony target that will always execute, and then add that target to the dependency chain for the $(distdir) target. A common name for this kind of target is FORCE, and I've implemented this concept in Listing 2-13.

```
    ...
❶ $(distdir).tar.gz: $(distdir)
        tar chof - $(distdir) | gzip -9 -c > $@
        rm -rf $(distdir)

❷ $(distdir): FORCE
        mkdir -p $(distdir)/src
        cp Makefile $(distdir)
        cp src/Makefile $(distdir)/src
        cp src/main.c $(distdir)/src

❸ FORCE:
        -rm $(distdir).tar.gz >/dev/null 2>&1
        -rm -rf $(distdir) >/dev/null 2>&1

.PHONY: FORCE all clean dist
```

Listing 2-13: Makefile: *Using the FORCE target*

The FORCE rule's commands (at ❸) are executed every time because FORCE is a phony target. Since we made FORCE a dependency of the $(distdir) target (at ❷), we have the opportunity to delete any previously created files and directories *before* make begins to evaluate whether it should execute the commands for $(distdir).

Leading Control Characters

A leading dash character (-) on a command tells make not to care about the status code of the command it precedes. Normally, when make encounters a command that returns a nonzero status code to the shell, it will stop execution and display an error message—but if you use a leading dash, it will just ignore the error and continue. I use a leading dash on the rm commands in the FORCE rule because I want to delete previously created product files that may *or may not* exist, and rm will return an error if I attempt to delete a nonexistent file.[20]

---

20. Another option would have been to use a -f command-line option with the rm command, which would narrow the failure conditions to those not related to removing nonexistent files.

Note that I did not use a leading dash on the rm command in the tarball rule at ❶. This is because I want to know if something goes wrong with this command—if it doesn't succeed, something is very wrong, since the preceding command should have created a tarball from this directory.

Another leading character that you may encounter is the at sign (@). A command prefixed with an at sign tells make not to perform its normal behavior of printing the command to the stdout device as it executes it. It is common to use a leading at sign on echo statements. You don't want make to print echo statements, because then your message will be printed twice: once by make, and then again by the echo statement itself.

It's best to use the at sign judiciously. I usually reserve it for commands I *never* want to see, such as echo statements. If you like quiet build systems, consider using the global .SILENT directive in your makefiles. Or better still, simply allow the user the option of adding the -s option to her make command lines. This enables her to choose how much noise she wants to see.

Automatically Testing a Distribution

The rule for building the archive directory is probably the most frustrating rule in this makefile, because it contains commands to copy individual files into the distribution directory. Every time we change the file structure in our project, we have to update this rule in our top-level makefile, or we'll break the dist target. But there's nothing more we can do—we've made the rule as simple as possible. Now we just have to remember to manage this process properly.

Unfortunately though, breaking the dist target is not the worst thing that could happen if you forget to update the distdir rule's commands. It may *appear* that the dist target is working, but it may not actually be copying all of the required files into the tarball. In fact, it is far more likely that this, rather than an error, will occur, because adding files to a project is a more common activity than moving them around or deleting them. New files will not be copied, but the dist rule won't notice the difference.

There is a way to perform a sort of self-check on the dist target. We can create another phony target called distcheck that does exactly what our users will do: unpack the tarball and build the project. We can have this rule's commands perform this task in a temporary directory. If the build process fails, then the distcheck target will break, telling us that we forgot something crucial in our distribution.

Listing 2-14 shows the modifications to our top-level makefile that are required to implement the distcheck target.

```
...
distcheck: $(distdir).tar.gz
        gzip -cd $(distdir).tar.gz | tar xvf -
        cd $(distdir) && $(MAKE) all
        cd $(distdir) && $(MAKE) clean
        rm -rf $(distdir)
```

```
        @echo "*** Package $(distdir).tar.gz is ready for distribution."
...
.PHONY: FORCE all clean dist distcheck
```

Listing 2-14: Makefile: Adding a distcheck target to the top-level makefile

The distcheck target depends on the tarball itself, so the rule that builds the tarball is executed first. make then executes the distcheck commands, which unpack the tarball just built and then recursively run make on the all and clean targets within the resulting directory. If that process succeeds, it prints out a message indicating that your users will likely not have a problem with this tarball.

Now all you have to do is remember to execute make distcheck *before* you post your tarballs for public distribution!

Unit Testing, Anyone?

Some people insist that unit testing is evil, but the only honest rationale they can come up with for not doing it is laziness. Proper unit testing is hard work, but it pays off in the end. Those who do it have learned a lesson (usually in childhood) about the value of delayed gratification.

A good build system should incorporate proper unit testing. The most commonly used target for testing a build is the check target, so we'll go ahead and add it in the usual manner. The actual unit test should probably go in *src/Makefile* because that's where the jupiter executable is built, so we'll pass the check target down from the top-level makefile.

But what commands do we put in the check rule? Well, jupiter is a pretty simple program—it prints a message, *Hello from* some/path/*jupiter!* where *some/path* depends on the location from which jupiter was executed. I'll use the grep utility to test that jupiter actually outputs such a string.

Listings 2-15 and 2-16 illustrate the modifications to our top-level and *src* directory makefiles, respectively.

```
...
all clean check jupiter:
        cd src && $(MAKE) $@
...
.PHONY: FORCE all clean check dist distcheck
```

Listing 2-15: Makefile: Passing the check target to src/Makefile

```
...
check: all
        ./jupiter | grep "Hello from .*jupiter!"
        @echo "*** ALL TESTS PASSED ***"
...
.PHONY: all clean check
```

Listing 2-16: src/Makefile: Implementing the unit test in the check target

Note that check depends on all. We can't really test our products unless they are up to date, reflecting any recent source code or build system changes that may have been made. It makes sense that if the user wants to test the products, he also wants the products to exist and be up to date. We can ensure they exist and are up to date by adding all to check's dependency list.

There's one more enhancement we could make to our build system: We can add check to the list of targets executed by make in our distcheck rule, between the commands to make all and clean. Listing 2-17 shows where this is done in the top-level makefile.

```
...
distcheck: $(distdir).tar.gz
        gzip -cd $(distdir).tar.gz | tar xvf -
        cd $(distdir) && $(MAKE) all
        cd $(distdir) && $(MAKE) check
        cd $(distdir) && $(MAKE) clean
        rm -rf $(distdir)
        @echo "*** Package $(distdir).tar.gz is ready for distribution."
...
```

Listing 2-17: Makefile: *Adding the check target to the $(MAKE) command*

Now when we run make distcheck, it will test the entire build system shipped with the package.

Installing Products

We've reached the point where our users' experiences with Jupiter should be fairly painless—even pleasant—as far as building the project is concerned. Users will simply unpack the distribution tarball, change into the distribution directory, and type make. It really can't get any simpler than that.

But we still lack one important feature—installation. In the case of the Jupiter project, this is fairly trivial. There's only one program, and most users would guess correctly that to install it, they should copy jupiter into either their */usr/bin* or */usr/local/bin* directory. More complex projects, however, could cause users some real consternation when it comes to where to put user and system binaries, libraries, header files, and documentation including man pages, info pages, PDF files, and the more-or-less obligatory *README, AUTHORS, NEWS, INSTALL,* and *COPYING* files generally associated with GNU projects.

We don't really want our users to have to figure all that out, so we'll create an install target to manage putting things where they go once they're built properly. In fact, why not just make installation part of the all target? Well, let's not get carried away. There are actually a few good reasons for not doing this.

First, build and installation are separate logical concepts. The second reason is a matter of filesystem rights. Users have rights to build projects in their own home directories, but installation often requires *root*-level rights to copy files into system directories. Finally, there are several reasons why a user may wish to build but not install a project, so it would be unwise to tie these actions together.

While creating a distribution package may not be an inherently recursive process, installation certainly is, so we'll allow each subdirectory in our project to manage installation of its own components. To do this, we need to modify both the top-level and the *src*-level makefiles. Changing the top-level makefile is easy: Since there are no products to be installed in the top-level directory, we'll just pass the responsibility on to *src/Makefile* in the usual way.

The modifications for adding an install target are shown in Listings 2-18 and 2-19.

```
...
all clean check install jupiter:
        cd src && $(MAKE) $@
...
.PHONY: FORCE all clean check dist distcheck install
```

Listing 2-18: Makefile: Passing the install target to src/Makefile

```
...
install:
        cp jupiter /usr/bin
        chown root:root /usr/bin/jupiter
        chmod +x /usr/bin/jupiter

.PHONY: all clean check install
```

Listing 2-19: src/Makefile: Implementing the install target

In the top-level makefile shown in Listing 2-18, I've added install to the list of targets passed down to *src/Makefile*. The installation of files is actually handled by the *src*-level makefile shown in Listing 2-19.

Installation is a bit more complex than simply copying files. If a file is placed in the */usr/bin* directory, then *root* should own it, so that only *root* can delete or modify it. Additionally, the jupiter binary should be flagged executable, so I've used the chmod command to set the mode of the file as such. This is probably redundant, as the linker ensures that jupiter is created as an executable file, but some types of executable products are not generated by a linker—shell scripts, for example.

Now our users can just type the following sequence of commands and the Jupiter project will be built, tested, and installed with the correct system attributes and ownership on their platforms:

```
$ gzip -cd jupiter-1.0.tar.gz | tar xf -
$ cd jupiter-1.0
$ make all check
...
```

```
$ sudo make install
Password: ******
...
```

Installation Choices

All of this is well and good, but it could be a bit more flexible with regard to where things are installed. Some users may be okay with having jupiter installed into the */usr/bin* directory. Others are going to ask why it isn't installed into the */usr/local/bin* directory—after all, this is a common convention. We could change the target directory to */usr/local/bin*, but then users may ask why they don't have the option of installing into their home directories. This is the perfect situation for a little command-line supported flexibility.

Another problem with our current build system is that we have to do a lot of stuff just to install files. Most Unix systems provide a system-level program—usually a shell script—called install that allows a user to specify various attributes of the files being installed. The proper use of this utility could simplify things a bit for Jupiter's installation, so while we're adding location flexibility, we might as well use the install utility, too. These modifications are shown in Listings 2-20 and 2-21.

```
...
prefix=/usr/local
❶ export prefix

all clean check install jupiter:
        cd src && $(MAKE) $@
...
```

Listing 2-20: Makefile: *Adding a* prefix *variable*

```
...
install:
❷       install -d $(prefix)/bin
        install -m 0755 jupiter $(prefix)/bin
...
```

Listing 2-21: src/Makefile: *Using the* prefix *variable in the* install *target*

Notice that I only declared and assigned the prefix variable in the top-level makefile, but I referenced it in *src/Makefile*. I can do this because I used the export modifier at ❶ in the top-level makefile—this modifier exports the make variable to the shell that make spawns when it executes itself in the *src* directory. This feature of make allows us to define all of our user variables in one obvious location—at the beginning of the top-level makefile.

NOTE *GNU make allows you to use the export keyword on the assignment line, but this syntax is not portable between GNU make and other versions of make.*

I've now declared the prefix variable to be */usr/local*, which is very nice for those who want to install jupiter in */usr/local/bin*, but not so nice for those who want it in */usr/bin*. Fortunately, make allows you to define make variables on the command line, in this manner:

```
$ sudo make prefix=/usr install
...
```

Remember that variables defined on the command line override those defined within the makefile.[21] Thus, users who want to install jupiter into the */usr/bin* directory now have the option of specifying this on the make command line.

With this system in place, our users may install jupiter into a *bin* directory beneath any directory they choose, including a location in their home directory (for which they do not need additional rights). This is, in fact, the reason we added the install -d $(prefix)/bin command at ❷ in Listing 2-21—this command creates the installation directory if it doesn't already exist. Since we allow the user to define prefix on the make command line, we don't actually know where the user is going to install jupiter; therefore, we have to be prepared for the possibility that the location may not yet exist. Give this a try:

```
$ make all
$ make prefix=$PWD/_inst install
$
$ ls -1p
_inst/
Makefile
src/
$
$ ls -1p _inst
bin/
$
$ ls -1p _inst/bin
jupiter
$
```

Uninstalling a Package

What if a user doesn't like our package after he's installed it, and he just wants to get it off his system? This is a fairly likely scenario for the Jupiter project, as it's rather useless and takes up valuable space in his *bin* directory. In the case of *your* projects, however, it's more likely that a user would want to do a clean install of a newer version of the project or replace the test build he downloaded from the project website with a professionally packaged version that

---

21. Unfortunately, some make implementations do not propagate such command-line variables to recursive $(MAKE) processes. To alleviate this potential problem, variables that might be set on the command line can be passed as var="$(var)" on sub-make command lines. My simple examples ignore this issue because it's a corner case, but you should at least be aware of this problem.

comes with his Linux distribution. Support for an uninstall target would be very helpful in situations like these.

Listings 2-22 and 2-23 show the addition of an uninstall target to our two makefiles.

```
...
all clean install uninstall jupiter:
        cd src && $(MAKE) $@
...
.PHONY: FORCE all clean dist distcheck install uninstall
```

Listing 2-22: Makefile: *Adding the* uninstall *target to the top-level makefile*

```
...
uninstall:
        -rm $(prefix)/bin/jupiter

.PHONY: all clean check install uninstall
```

Listing 2-23: src/Makefile: *Adding the* uninstall *target to the src-level makefile*

As with the install target, this target requires *root*-level rights if the user is using a system prefix, such as */usr* or */usr/local.* You should be very careful about how you write your uninstall targets; unless a directory belongs specifically to your package, you shouldn't assume you created it. If you do, you may end up deleting a system directory like */usr/bin*!

The list of things to maintain in our build system is getting out of hand. There are now two places we need to update when we change our installation processes: the install and uninstall targets. Unfortunately, this is really about the best we can hope for when writing our own makefiles, unless we resort to fairly complex shell script commands. But hang in there—in Chapter 5 I'll show you how to rewrite this makefile in a much simpler way using GNU Automake.

Testing Install and Uninstall

Now let's add some code to our distcheck target to test the functionality of the install and uninstall targets. After all, it's fairly important that both of these targets work correctly from our distribution tarballs, so we should test them in distcheck before declaring the tarball release-worthy. Listing 2-24 illustrates the necessary changes to the top-level makefile.

```
...
distcheck: $(distdir).tar.gz
        gzip -cd $(distdir).tar.gz | tar xvf -
        cd $(distdir) && $(MAKE) all
        cd $(distdir) && $(MAKE) check
        cd $(distdir) && $(MAKE) prefix=$${PWD}/_inst install
        cd $(distdir) && $(MAKE) prefix=$${PWD}/_inst uninstall
        cd $(distdir) && $(MAKE) clean
```

```
        rm -rf $(distdir)
        @echo "*** Package $(distdir).tar.gz is ready for distribution."
...
```

Listing 2-24: Makefile: Adding distcheck tests for the install and uninstall targets

Note that I used a double dollar sign on the $${PWD} variable references, ensuring that make passes the variable reference to the shell with the rest of the command line, rather than expanding it inline before executing the command. I wanted this variable to be dereferenced by the shell, rather than the make utility.[22]

What we're doing here is testing to ensure the install and uninstall targets don't generate errors—but this isn't very likely because all they do is install files into a temporary directory within the build directory. We could add some code immediately after the make install command that looks for the products that are supposed to be installed, but that's more than I'm willing to do. One reaches a point of diminishing returns, where the code that does the checking is just as complex as the installation code—in which case the check becomes pointless.

But there is something else we can do: We can write a more or less generic test that checks to see if everything we installed was properly removed. Since the stage directory was empty before our installation, it had better be in a similar state after we uninstall. Listing 2-25 shows the addition of this test.

```
...
distcheck: $(distdir).tar.gz
        gzip -cd $(distdir).tar.gz | tar xvf -
        cd $(distdir) && $(MAKE) all
        cd $(distdir) && $(MAKE) check
        cd $(distdir) && $(MAKE) prefix=$${PWD}/_inst install
        cd $(distdir) && $(MAKE) prefix=$${PWD}/_inst uninstall
❶      @remaining="`find $${PWD}/$(distdir)/_inst -type f | wc -l`"; \
        if test "$${remaining}" -ne 0; then \
          echo "*** $${remaining} file(s) remaining in stage directory!"; \
          exit 1; \
        fi
        cd $(distdir) && $(MAKE) clean
        rm -rf $(distdir)
❷      @echo "*** Package $(distdir).tar.gz is ready for distribution."
...
```

Listing 2-25: Makefile: Adding a test for leftover files after uninstall finishes

The test first generates a numeric value at ❶ in a shell variable called remaining, which represents the number of regular files found in the stage directory we used. If this number is not zero, it prints a message to the console

---

22. Technically, I didn't have to do this because the PWD make variable was initialized from the environment, but it serves as a good example of this process. Additionally, there are corner cases where the PWD make variable is not quite as accurate as the PWD shell variable. It may be left pointing to the parent directory on a subdirectory make invocation.

at ❷ indicating how many files were left behind by the uninstall commands and then it exits with an error. Exiting early leaves the stage directory intact so we can examine it to find out which files we forgot to uninstall.

NOTE *This test code represents a good use of multiple shell commands passed to a single shell. I had to do this here so that the value of remaining would be available for use by the if statement. Conditionals don't work very well when the closing fi is not executed by the same shell as the opening if!*

I don't want to alarm people by printing the embedded echo statement unless it really should be executed, so I prefixed the entire test with an at sign (@) so that make wouldn't print the code to stdout. Since make considers these five lines of code to be a single command, the only way to suppress printing the echo statement is to suppress printing the entire command.

Now, this test isn't perfect—not by a long shot. This code only checks for regular files. If your installation procedure creates any soft links, this test won't notice if they're left behind. The directory structure that's built during installation is purposely left in place because the check code doesn't know whether a subdirectory within the stage directory belongs to the system or to the project. The uninstall rule's commands can be aware of which directories are project specific and properly remove them, but I don't want to add project-specific knowledge into the distcheck tests—it's that problem of diminishing returns again.

The Filesystem Hierarchy Standard

You may be wondering by now where I'm getting these directory names. What if some Unix system out there doesn't use */usr* or */usr/local*? For one thing, this is another reason for providing the prefix variable—to allow the user some choice in these matters. However, most Unix-like systems nowadays follow the *Filesystem Hierarchy Standard* as closely as possible. The *FHS* defines a number of standard places including the following root-level directories:

/bin	*/etc*	*/home*
/opt	*/sbin*	*/srv*
/tmp	*/usr*	*/var*

This list is by no means exhaustive. I've only mentioned the directories that are most relevant to our study of open source project build systems. In addition, the *FHS* defines several standard locations beneath these root-level directories. For instance, the */usr* directory should contain the following subdirectories:

/usr/bin	*/usr/include*	*/usr/lib*
/usr/local	*/usr/sbin*	*/usr/share*
/usr/src		

The */usr/local* directory should contain a structure very similar to that of the */usr* directory. The */usr/local* directory provides a location for software installation that overrides versions of the same packages installed in the */usr* directory structure, because system software updates often overwrite software in */usr* without prejudice. The */usr/local* directory structure allows a system administrator to decide which version of a package to use on her system, because */usr/local/bin* may be (and usually is) added to the PATH before */usr/bin*. A fair amount of thought has gone into designing the *FHS*, and the GNU Autotools take full advantage of this consensus of understanding.

Not only does the *FHS* define these standard locations, but it also explains in detail what they're for and what types of files should be kept there. All in all, the *FHS* leaves you, as project maintainer, just enough flexibility and choice to keep your life interesting but not enough to make you wonder if you're installing your files in the right places.[23]

Supporting Standard Targets and Variables

In addition to those I've already mentioned, the *GNU Coding Standards* lists some important targets and variables that you should support in your projects—mainly because your users will expect support for them.

Some of the chapters in the *GCS* document should be taken with a grain of salt (unless you're actually working on a GNU-sponsored project). For example, you probably won't care much about the C source code formatting suggestions in Chapter 5. Your users certainly won't care, so you can use whatever source code formatting style you wish.

That's not to say that all of Chapter 5 is worthless to non-GNU open source projects. The "Portability between System Types" and "Portability between CPUs" subsections, for instance, provide excellent information on C source code portability. The "Internationalization" subsection gives some useful tips on using GNU software to internationalize your projects.

While Chapter 6 discusses documentation the GNU way, some sections of Chapter 6 describe various top-level text files commonly found in projects, such as the *AUTHORS, NEWS, INSTALL, README*, and *ChangeLog* files. These are all bits of information that the well-indoctrinated open source software user expects to see in any reputable project.

The *really* useful information in the *GCS* document begins in Chapter 7: "The Release Process." This chapter is critical to you as a project maintainer because it defines what your users will expect of your projects' build systems. Chapter 7 contains the de facto standards for the user options that packages provide in source-level distributions.

---

23. Before I discovered the FHS, I relied on my personal experience to decide where files should be installed in my projects. Mostly I was right, because I'm a careful guy, but after I read the FHS documentation, I went back to some of my past projects with a bit of chagrin and changed things around. I heartily recommend you become thoroughly familiar with the FHS if you seriously intend to develop Unix software.

Standard Targets

The "How Configuration Should Work" subsection of Chapter 7 of the *GCS* defines the configuration process, which I cover briefly in "Configuring Your Package" on page 54. The "Makefile Conventions" subsection covers all of the standard targets and many of the standard variables that users have come to expect in open source software packages. Standard targets defined by the *GCS* include the following:

all	install	install-html
install-dvi	install-pdf	install-ps
install-strip	uninstall	clean
distclean	mostlyclean	maintainer-clean
TAGS	info	dvi
html	pdf	ps
dist	check	installcheck
installdirs		

You don't need to support all of these targets, but you should consider supporting the ones that make sense for your project. For example, if you build and install HTML pages, you should probably consider supporting the html and install-html targets. Autotools projects support these and more. Some targets are useful to end users, while others are only useful to project maintainers.

Standard Variables

Variables you should support as you see fit include those listed in the following table. In order to provide flexibility for the end user, most of these variables are defined in terms of a few of them, and ultimately only one of them: prefix. For lack of a more standard name, I call these *prefix variables*. Most of these could be classified as *installation directory variables* that refer to standard locations, but there are a few exceptions, such as srcdir. Table 2-1 lists these prefix variables and their default values.

Table 2-1: Prefix Variables and Their Default Values

Variable	Default Value
prefix	*/usr/local*
exec_prefix	$(prefix)
bindir	$(exec_prefix)/*bin*
sbindir	$(exec_prefix)/*sbin*
libexecdir	$(exec_prefix)/*libexec*
datarootdir	$(prefix)/*share*
datadir	$(datarootdir)
sysconfdir	$(prefix)/*etc*
sharedstatedir	$(prefix)/*com*

Table 2-1: Prefix Variables and Their Default Values (continued)

Variable	Default Value
localstatedir	$(prefix)/var
includedir	$(prefix)/include
oldincludedir	/usr/include
docdir	$(datarootdir)/doc/$(package)
infodir	$(datarootdir)/info
htmldir	$(docdir)
dvidir	$(docdir)
pdfdir	$(docdir)
psdir	$(docdir)
libdir	$(exec_prefix)/lib
lispdir	$(datarootdir)/emacs/site-lisp
localedir	$(datarootdir)/locale
mandir	$(datarootdir)/man
manNdir	$(mandir)/manN (N = 1..9)
manext	.1
manNext	.N (N = 1..9)
srcdir	The source-tree directory corresponding to the current directory in the build tree

Autotools-based projects support these and other useful variables automatically, as needed; Automake provides full support for them, while Autoconf's support is more limited. If you write your own makefiles and build systems, you should support as many of these as you use in your build and installation processes.

Adding Location Variables to Jupiter

To support the variables that we've used so far in the Jupiter project, we need to add the bindir variable, as well as any variables that it relies on—in this case, the exec_prefix variable. Listings 2-26 and 2-27 show how to do this in the top-level and *src* directory makefiles.

```
...
prefix        = /usr/local
exec_prefix   = $(prefix)
bindir        = $(exec_prefix)/bin

export prefix
export exec_prefix
export bindir
...
```

Listing 2-26: Makefile: Adding the bindir variable

```
...
install:
        install -d $(bindir)
        install -m 0755 jupiter $(bindir)

uninstall:
        -rm $(bindir)/jupiter
...
```

Listing 2-27: src/Makefile: *Adding the* bindir *variable*

Even though we only use `bindir` in *src/Makefile*, we have to export `prefix`, `exec_prefix`, and `bindir` because `bindir` is defined in terms of `exec_prefix`, which is itself defined in terms of `prefix`. When `make` runs the `install` commands, it will first resolve `bindir` to $(exec_prefix)/*bin*, then to $(prefix)/*bin*, and finally to */usr/local/bin*. Thus, *src/Makefile* needs to have access to all three variables during this process.

How do such recursive variable definitions make life better for the end user? After all, the user can change the root install location from */usr/local* to */usr* by simply typing the following:

```
$ make prefix=/usr install
...
```

The ability to change prefix variables at multiple levels is particularly useful to a Linux distribution packager (an employee or volunteer at a Linux company whose job it is to professionally package your project as an RPM or APT package), who needs to install packages into very specific system locations. For example, a distro packager could use the following command to change the installation prefix to */usr* and the system configuration directory to */etc*:

```
$ make prefix=/usr sysconfdir=/etc install
...
```

Without the ability to change prefix variables at multiple levels, configuration files would end up in */usr/etc* because the default value of $(`sysconfdir`) is $(`prefix`)/*etc*.

Getting Your Project into a Linux Distro

Open source software maintainers often hope that their projects will be picked up by a Linux distribution. When a Linux distro picks up your package for distribution on its CDs and DVDs, your project magically moves from the realm of tens of users to that of tens of thousands of users—almost overnight. Some people will be using your software without even knowing it.

By following the *GCS* within your build system, you remove many of the barriers to including your project in a Linux distro. If your tarball follows all the usual conventions, distro packagers will immediately know what to do with it. These packagers generally get to decide, based on needed functionality and their feelings about your package, whether it should be included in their flavor of Linux. Since they have a fair amount of power in this process, it behooves you to please them.

Section 7 of the *GCS* contains a small subsection that talks about supporting *staged installations*. It is easy to support this concept in your build system, but if you neglect to support it, it will almost always cause problems for packagers.

Packaging systems such as the Red Hat Package Manager (RPM) accept one or more tarballs, a set of patch files, and a specification file. The so-called *spec file* describes the process of building and packaging your project for a particular system. In addition, it defines all of the products installed into the target installation directory structure. The package manager software uses this information to install your package into a temporary directory, from which it then pulls the specified binaries, storing them in a special binary archive that the package installation software (e.g., RPM) understands.

To support staged installation, all you need is a variable named DESTDIR that acts as a sort of super-prefix to all of your installed products. To show you how this is done, I'll add staged installation support to the Jupiter project. This is so trivial that it only requires three changes to *src/Makefile*. The required changes are bolded in Listing 2-28.

```
...
install:
        install -d $(DESTDIR)$(bindir)
        install -m 0755 jupiter $(DESTDIR)$(bindir)

uninstall:
        -rm $(DESTDIR)$(bindir)/jupiter
...
```

Listing 2-28: src/Makefile: Adding staged build functionality

As you can see, I've added the $(DESTDIR) prefix to the $(bindir) references in the install and uninstall targets that refer to installation paths. You don't need to define a default value for DESTDIR, because when it is left undefined, it expands to an empty string, which has no effect on the paths to which it's prepended.

I didn't need to add $(DESTDIR) to the uninstall rule's rm command for the sake of the package manager, because package managers don't care how your package is uninstalled. They only install your package so they can copy the products from a stage directory. To uninstall the stage directory, package managers simply delete it. Package managers such as RPM use their own rules for removing products from a system, and these rules are based on a package manager database, rather than your uninstall target.

However, for the sake of symmetry, and to be complete, it doesn't hurt to add $(DESTDIR) to uninstall. Besides, we need it to be complete for the sake of the distcheck target, which we'll now modify to take advantage of our staged installation functionality. This modification is shown in Listing 2-29.

```
...
distcheck: $(distdir).tar.gz
        gzip -cd $(distdir).tar.gz | tar xvf -
        cd $(distdir) && $(MAKE) all
        cd $(distdir) && $(MAKE) check
        cd $(distdir) && $(MAKE) DESTDIR=$${PWD}/_inst install
        cd $(distdir) && $(MAKE) DESTDIR=$${PWD}/_inst uninstall
        @remaining="`find $${PWD}/$(distdir)/_inst -type f | wc -l`"; \
        if test "$${remaining}" -ne 0; then \
          echo "*** $${remaining} file(s) remaining in stage directory!"; \
          exit 1; \
        fi
        cd $(distdir) && $(MAKE) clean
        rm -rf $(distdir)
        @echo "*** Package $(distdir).tar.gz is ready for distribution."
...
```

Listing 2-29: Makefile: *Using DESTDIR in the distcheck target*

Changing prefix to DESTDIR in the install and uninstall commands allows us to properly test a complete installation directory hierarchy, as we'll see shortly.

At this point, an RPM spec file could provide the following text as the installation commands for the Jupiter package:

```
%install
make prefix=/usr DESTDIR=%BUILDROOT install
```

Don't worry about package manager file formats. Instead, just focus on providing staged installation functionality through the DESTDIR variable.

You may be wondering why the prefix variable couldn't provide this functionality. For one thing, not every path in a system-level installation is defined relative to the prefix variable. The system configuration directory (sysconfdir), for instance, is often defined as */etc* by packagers. You can see in Table 2-1 that the default definition of sysconfdir is $(prefix)/*etc*, so the only way sysconfdir would resolve to */etc* would be if you explicitly set it to do so on the configure or make command line. If you configured it that way, only a variable like DESTDIR would affect the base location of sysconfdir during staged installation. Other reasons for this will become clearer as we talk about project configuration later on in this chapter, and then again in the next two chapters.

Build vs. Installation Prefix Overrides

At this point, I'd like to digress slightly to explain an elusive (or at least non-obvious) concept regarding prefix and other path variables defined in the *GCS*. In the preceding examples, I used prefix overrides on the make install command line, like this:

```
$ make prefix=/usr install
...
```

The question I wish to address is: What is the difference between using a prefix override for make all and for make install? In our small sample makefiles, we've managed to avoid using prefixes in any targets not related to installation, so it may not be clear to you at this point that a prefix is *ever* useful during the build stage. However, prefix variables can be very useful during the build stage to substitute paths into source code at compile time, as shown in Listing 2-30.

```
program: main.c
        gcc -DCFGDIR="\"$(sysconfdir)\"" -o $@ main.c
```

Listing 2-30: Substituting paths into source code at compile time

In this example, I'm defining a C-preprocessor variable called CFGDIR on the compiler command line for use by *main.c*. Presumably, there's some code in *main.c* like that shown in Listing 2-31.

```
#ifndef CFGDIR
# define CFGDIR "/etc"
#endif

const char cfgdir[FILENAME_MAX] = CFGDIR;
```

Listing 2-31: Substituting CFGDIR at compile time

Later in the code, you might use the C global variable cfgdir to access the application's configuration file.

Linux distro packagers often use different prefix overrides for build and install command lines in RPM spec files. During the build stage, the actual runtime directories are hardcoded into the executable using commands like the one shown in Listing 2-32.

```
%build
%setup
./configure prefix=/usr sysconfdir=/etc
make
```

Listing 2-32: The portion of an RPM spec file that builds the source tree

Note that we have to explicitly specify sysconfdir along with prefix, because, as I mentioned above, the system configuration directory is usually outside of the system prefix directory structure. The package manager installs these executables into a stage directory so it can then copy them out of their installed locations when it builds the binary installation package. The corresponding installation commands might look like those shown in Listing 2-33.

```
%install
make DESTDIR=%BUILDROOT% install
```

Listing 2-33: The installation portion of an RPM spec file

Using DESTDIR during installation will temporarily override *all* installation prefix variables, so you don't have to remember which variables you've overridden during configuration. Given the configuration command shown in Listing 2-32, using DESTDIR in the manner shown in Listing 2-33 has the same effect as the code shown in Listing 2-34.

```
%install
make prefix=%BUILDROOT%/usr sysconfdir=%BUILDROOT%/etc install
```

Listing 2-34: Overriding the default sysconfdir during installation

The key point here is one that I touched on earlier. *Never write your install target to build all or even part of your products in your makefiles.* Installation functionality should be limited to copying files, if possible. Otherwise, your users won't be able to access your staged installation features if they are using prefix overrides.

Another reason for limiting installation functionality in this way is that it allows the user to install sets of packages as a group into an isolated location and then create links to the actual files in the proper locations. Some people like to do this when they are testing out a package and want to keep track of all its components.[24]

One final point: If you're installing into a system directory hierarchy, you'll need *root* permissions. People often run make install like this:

```
$ sudo make install
...
```

If your install target depends on your build targets, and you've neglected to build them beforehand, make will happily build your program before installing it—but the local copies will all be owned by *root*. This inconvenience is easily avoided by having make install fail for lack of things to install, rather than jumping right into a build while running as *root*.

User Variables

The *GCS* defines a set of variables that are sacred to the user. These variables should be *referenced* by a GNU build system, but never *modified* by a GNU build system. These so-called *user variables* include those listed in Table 2-2 for C and C++ programs.

---

24. Some Linux distributions provide a way of installing multiple versions of common packages. Java is a great example; to support packages using multiple versions or brands of Java (perhaps Sun Java versus IBM Java), some Linux distributions provide a script set called the *alternatives* scripts. These allow a user (running as *root*) to swap all of the links in the various system directories from one grouped installation to another. Thus, both sets of files can be installed in different auxiliary locations, but links in the expected installation locations can be changed to refer to each group at different times with a single *root*-level command.

Table 2-2: Some User Variables and Their Purposes

Variable	Purpose
CC	A reference to the system C compiler
CFLAGS	Desired C compiler flags
CXX	A reference to the system C++ compiler
CXXFLAGS	Desired C++ compiler flags
LDFLAGS	Desired linker flags
CPPFLAGS	Desired C/C++ preprocessor flags
...	

This list is by no means comprehensive, and interestingly, there isn't a comprehensive list to be found in the *GCS*. In fact, most of these variables come from the documentation for the make utility itself. These variables are used in the built-in rules of the make utility—they're somewhat hardcoded into make, and so they are effectively defined by make. You can find a fairly complete list of program name and flag variables in the "Variables Used by Implicit Rules" section of the *GNU Make Manual*.

Note that make assigns default values for many of these variables based on common Unix utility names. For example, the default value of CC is cc, which (at least on Linux systems) is a soft link to the GCC C compiler (gcc). On other systems, cc is a soft link to the system's own compiler. Thus we don't need to set CC to gcc, which is good, because GCC may not be installed on non-Linux platforms.

For our purposes, the variables shown in Table 2-2 are sufficient, but for a more complex makefile, you should become familiar with the larger list outlined in the *GNU Make Manual*.

To use these variables in our makefiles, we'll just replace gcc with $(CC). We'll do the same for CFLAGS and CPPFLAGS, although CPPFLAGS will be empty by default. The CFLAGS variable has no default value either, but this is a good time to add one. I like to use -g to build objects with symbols, and -O0 to disable optimizations for debug builds. The updates to *src/Makefile* are shown in Listing 2-35.

```
...
CFLAGS  = -g -O0
...
jupiter: main.c
        $(CC) $(CPPFLAGS) $(CFLAGS) -o $@ main.c
...
```

Listing 2-35: src/Makefile: *Adding appropriate user variables*

This works because the make utility allows such variables to be overridden by options on the command line. For example, to switch compilers and set some compiler command-line options, a user need only type the following:

```
$ make CC=gcc3 CFLAGS='-g -O2' CPPFLAGS=-dtest
```

In this case, our user has decided to use GCC version 3 instead of 4, generate debug symbols, and optimize her code using level-two optimizations. She's also decided to enable the test option through the use of a C-preprocessor definition. Note that if these variables are set on the make command line, this apparently equivalent Bourne-shell syntax will not work as expected:

```
$ CC=gcc3 CFLAGS='-g -O2' CPPFLAGS=-dtest make
```

The reason is that we're merely setting environment variables in the local environment passed to the make utility by the shell. Remember that environment variables do not automatically override those set in the makefile. To get the functionality we want, we could use a little GNU make–specific syntax in our makefile, as shown in Listing 2-36.

```
...
CFLAGS    ?= -g -O0
...
```

Listing 2-36: Using the GNU make–specific query-assign operator (?=) in a makefile

The ?= operator is a GNU make-specific operator, which will only set the variable in the makefile if it hasn't already been set elsewhere. This means we can now override these particular variable settings by setting them in the environment. But don't forget that this will only work in GNU make. In general, it's better to set make variables on the make command line.

Configuring Your Package

The *GCS* describes the configuration process in the "How Configuration Should Work" subsection of Section 7. Up to this point, we've been able to do about everything we've wanted to with Jupiter using only makefiles, so you might be wondering what configuration is actually for. The opening paragraphs of this subsection in the *GCS* answer our question:

> Each GNU distribution should come with a shell script named
> configure. This script is given arguments which describe the kind
> of machine and system you want to compile the program for. The
> configure script must record the configuration options so that they
> affect compilation.
>
> The description here is the specification of the interface for the
> configure script in GNU packages. Many packages implement it
> using GNU Autoconf (see Section "Introduction" in Autoconf)
> and/or GNU Automake (see Section "Introduction" in Automake),
> but you do not have to use these tools. You can implement it any
> way you like; for instance, by making configure be a wrapper
> around a completely different configuration system.

Another way for the `configure` script to operate is to make a link from a standard name such as `config.h` to the proper configuration file for the chosen system. If you use this technique, the distribution should *not* contain a file named `config.h`. This is so that people won't be able to build the program without configuring it first.

Another thing that configure can do is to edit the Makefile. If you do this, the distribution should *not* contain a file named `Makefile`. Instead, it should include a file `Makefile.in` which contains the input used for editing. Once again, this is so that people won't be able to build the program without configuring it first.[25]

So then, the primary tasks of a typical configuration script are as follows:

- Generate files from templates containing replacement variables.
- Generate a C-language header file (*config.h*) for inclusion by project source code.
- Set user options for a particular `make` environment (debug flags, etc.).
- Set various package options as environment variables.
- Test for the existence of tools, libraries, and header files.

For complex projects, configuration scripts often generate the project makefiles from one or more templates maintained by project developers. These templates contain configuration variables in a format that is easy to recognize (and substitute). The configuration script replaces these variables with values determined during the configuration process—either from command-line options specified by the user or from a thorough analysis of the platform environment. This analysis entails such things as checking for the existence of certain system or package header files and libraries, searching various file-system paths for required utilities and tools, and even running small programs designed to indicate the feature set of the shell, C compiler, or desired libraries.

The tool of choice for variable replacement has, in the past, been the `sed` stream editor. A simple `sed` command can replace all the configuration variables in a makefile template in a single pass through the file. However, Autoconf versions 2.62 and newer prefer `awk` to `sed` for this process. The `awk` utility is almost as pervasive as `sed` these days, and it provides more functionality to allow for efficient replacement of many variables. For our purposes on the Jupiter project, either of these tools would suffice.

Summary

We have now created a complete project build system by hand, with one important exception: We haven't designed a `configure` script according to the design criteria specified in the *GNU Coding Standards*. We could do this, but it would take a dozen more pages of text to build one that even comes close to conforming to these specifications. Still, there are a few key build features

---

25. See Section 7.1, "How Configuration Should Work," in the *GNU Coding Standards* document at *http://www.gnu.org/prep/standards/html_node/Configuration.html#Configuration*. GNU documentation changes quite often. This text came from the March 26, 2010 version of the GCS document.

related specifically to the makefiles that the *GCS* indicate as being desirable. Among these is the concept of *VPATH* building. This is an important feature that can only be properly illustrated by actually writing a configuration script that works as specified by the *GCS*.

Rather than spend the time and effort to do this now, I'd like to simply move on to a discussion of Autoconf in Chapter 3, which will allow us to build one of these configuration scripts in as little as two or three lines of code. With that behind us, it will be trivial to add VPATH building and other common Autotools features to the Jupiter project.

3

CONFIGURING YOUR PROJECT
WITH AUTOCONF

Come my friends,
'Tis not too late to seek a newer world.
—Alfred, Lord Tennyson, "Ulysses"

Because Automake and Libtool are essentially add-on components to the original Autoconf framework, it's useful to spend some time focusing on using Autoconf without Automake and Libtool. This will provide a fair amount of insight into how Autoconf operates by exposing aspects of the tool that are often hidden by Automake.

Before Automake came along, Autoconf was used alone. In fact, many legacy open source projects never made the transition from Autoconf to the full GNU Autotools suite. As a result, it's not unusual to find a file called *configure.in* (the original Autoconf naming convention) as well as handwritten *Makefile.in* templates in older open source projects.

In this chapter, I'll show you how to add an Autoconf build system to an existing project. I'll spend most of this chapter talking about the fundamental features of Autoconf, and in Chapter 4, I'll go into much more detail about how some of the more complex Autoconf macros work and how to properly use them. Throughout this process, we'll continue using the Jupiter project as our example.

Autoconf Configuration Scripts

The input to the autoconf program is shell script sprinkled with macro calls. The input stream must also include the definitions of all referenced macros—both those that Autoconf provides and those that you write yourself.

The macro language used in Autoconf is called *M4*. (The name means *M, plus 4 more letters*, or the word *Macro*.[1]) The m4 utility is a general-purpose macro language processor originally written by Brian Kernighan and Dennis Ritchie in 1977.

While you may not be familiar with it, you can find some form of M4 on every Unix and Linux variant (as well as other systems) in use today. The prolific nature of this tool is the main reason it's used by Autoconf, as the original design goals of Autoconf stated that it should be able to run on all systems without the addition of complex tool chains and utility sets.[2]

Autoconf depends on the existence of relatively few tools: a Bourne shell, M4, and a Perl interpreter. The configuration scripts and makefiles it generates rely on the existence of a different set of tools, including a Bourne shell, grep, ls, and sed or awk.[3]

NOTE   *Do not confuse the requirements of the Autotools with the requirements of the scripts and makefiles they generate. The Autotools are maintainer tools, while the resulting scripts and makefiles are end-user tools. We can reasonably expect a higher level of installed functionality on development systems than we can on end-user systems.*

The configuration script ensures that the end user's build environment is configured to properly build your project. This script checks for installed tools, utilities, libraries, and header files, as well as for specific functionality within these resources. What distinguishes Autoconf from other project configuration frameworks is that Autoconf tests also ensure that these resources can be properly consumed by your project. You see, it's not only important that your users have *libxyz.so* and its public header files properly installed on their systems, but also that they have the correct versions of these files. Autoconf is pathological about such tests. It ensures that the end user's environment is in compliance with the project requirements by compiling and linking a small test program for each feature—a quintessential example, if you will, that does what your project source code does on a larger scale.

Can't I just ensure that libxyz.2.1.0.so *is installed by searching library paths for the filename?* The answer to this question is debatable. There are legitimate situations where libraries and tools get updated quietly. Sometimes, the specific functionality upon which your project relies is added in the form of a security bug fix or enhancement to a library, in which case vendors aren't even required to bump up the version number. But it's often difficult to tell whether you've got version 2.1.0.r1 or version 2.1.0.r2 unless you look at the file size or call a library function to make sure it works as expected.

---

1. As a point of interest, this naming convention is a fairly common practice in some software engineering domains. For example, the term *internationalization* is often abbreviated *i18n*, for the sake of brevity (or perhaps just because programmers love acronyms).

2. In fact, whatever notoriety M4 may have today is likely due to the widespread use of Autoconf.

3. Autoconf versions 2.62 and later generate configuration scripts that require awk in addition to sed on the end user's system.

However, the most significant reason for not relying on library version numbers is that they do not represent specific marketing releases of a library. As we will discuss in Chapter 7, library version numbers indicate binary interface characteristics on a particular platform. This means that library version numbers for the same feature set can be different from platform to platform, which means that you may not be able to tell—short of compiling and linking against the library—whether or not a particular library has the functionality your project needs.

Finally, there are several important cases where the same functionality is provided by entirely different libraries on different systems. For example, you may find cursor manipulation functionality in *libtermcap* on one system, *libncurses* on another, and *libcurses* on yet another system. But it's not critical that you know about all of these side cases, because your users will tell you when your project won't build on their system because of such a discrepancy.

What can you do when such a bug is reported? You can use the Autoconf AC_SEARCH_LIBS macro to test multiple libraries for the same functionality. Simply add a library to the search list, and you're done. Since this fix is so easy, it's likely the user who noticed the problem will simply send a patch to your *configure.ac* file.

Because Autoconf tests are written in shell script, you have a lot of flexibility as to how the tests operate. You can write a test that merely checks for the existence of a library or utility in the usual locations on your user's system, but this bypasses some of the most significant features of Autoconf. Fortunately, Autoconf provides dozens of macros that conform to Autoconf's feature-testing philosophy. You should carefully study and use the list of available macros, rather than write your own, because they're specifically designed to ensure that the desired functionality is available on the widest variety of systems and platforms.

The Shortest configure.ac File

The simplest possible *configure.ac* file has just two lines, as shown in Listing 3-1.

```
AC_INIT([Jupiter], [1.0])
AC_OUTPUT
```

Listing 3-1: The simplest configure.ac *file*

To those new to Autoconf, these two lines appear to be a couple of function calls, perhaps in the syntax of some obscure programming language. Don't let their appearance throw you—these are M4 macro calls. The macros are defined in files distributed with the *autoconf* package. You can find the definition of AC_INIT, for example, in the *autoconf/general.m4* file in Autoconf's installation directory (usually */usr/(local/)share/autoconf*). AC_OUTPUT is defined in *autoconf/status.m4*.

Comparing M4 to the C Preprocessor

M4 macros are similar in many ways to the C-preprocessor (CPP) macros defined in C-language source files. The C preprocessor is also a text replacement tool, which isn't surprising: Both M4 and the C preprocessor were designed and written by Kernighan and Ritchie around the same time.

Autoconf uses square brackets around macro parameters as a quoting mechanism. Quotes are necessary only for cases in which the context of the macro call could cause an ambiguity that the macro processor may resolve incorrectly (usually without telling you). We'll discuss M4 quoting in much more detail in Chapter 10. For now, just use square brackets around every argument to ensure that the expected macro expansions are generated.

Like CPP macros, you can define M4 macros to accept a comma-delimited list of arguments enclosed in parentheses. In both utilities, the opening parenthesis must immediately follow the macro name in its definition, with no intervening whitespace. A significant difference, however, is that in M4, the arguments to parameterized macros are optional, and the caller may simply omit them. If no arguments are passed, you can also omit the parentheses. Extra arguments passed to M4 macros are simply ignored. Finally, M4 does not allow intervening whitespace between a macro name and the opening parenthesis in a macro call.

The Nature of M4 Macros

If you've been programming in C for many years, you've no doubt run across a few C-preprocessor macros from the dark regions of the lower realm. I'm talking about those truly evil macros that expand into one or two pages of C code. They should have been written as C functions, but their authors were either overly worried about performance or just got carried away, and now it's your turn to debug and maintain them. But, as any veteran C programmer will tell you, the slight performance gains you get by using a macro where you should have used a function do not justify the trouble you cause maintainers trying to debug your fancy macros. Debugging such macros can be a nightmare because the source code generated by macros is usually inaccessible from within a symbolic debugger.[4]

Writing such complex macros is viewed by M4 programmers as a sort of macro nirvana—the more complex and functional they are, the "cooler" they are. The two Autoconf macros in Listing 3-1 expand into a file containing over 2,200 lines of Bourne-shell script that total more than 60KB in size! But you wouldn't guess this by looking at their definitions. They're both fairly short—only a few dozen lines each. The reason for this apparent disparity is simple: They're written in a modular fashion, each macro expanding several others, which, in turn, expand several others, and so on.

---

4. A technique I've used in the past for debugging large macros involves manually generating source code using the C preprocessor, and then compiling this generated source. Symbolic debuggers can only work with the source code you provide. By providing source with the macros fully expanded, you enable the debugger to allow you to step through the generated source.

For the same reasons that programmers are taught not to abuse the C preprocessor, the extensive use of M4 causes a fair amount of frustration for those trying to understand Autoconf. That's not to say Autoconf shouldn't use M4 this way; quite the contrary—this is the domain of M4. But there is a school of thought that says M4 was a poor choice for Autoconf because of the problems with macros mentioned above. Fortunately, being able to use Autoconf effectively usually doesn't require a deep understanding of the inner workings of the macros that ship with it.[5]

Executing autoconf

Running autoconf is simple: Just execute it in the same directory as your *configure.ac* file. While I could do this for each example in this chapter, I'm going to use the autoreconf program instead of the autoconf program, because running autoreconf has exactly the same effect as running autoconf, except that autoreconf will also do the right thing when you start adding Automake and Libtool functionality to your build system. That is, it will execute all of the Autotools in the right order based on the contents of your *configure.ac* file.

autoreconf is smart enough to only execute the tools you need, in the order you need them, with the options you want (with one caveat that I'll mention shortly). Therefore, running autoreconf is the recommended method for executing the Autotools tool chain.

Let's start by adding the simple *configure.ac* file from Listing 3-1 to our project directory. The top-level directory currently contains only a *Makefile* and a *src* directory which contains its own *Makefile* and a *main.c* file. Once you've added *configure.ac* to the top-level directory, run autoreconf:

```
$ autoreconf
$
$ ls -1p
autom4te.cache/
configure
configure.ac
Makefile
src/
$
```

First, notice that autoreconf operates silently by default. If you want to see something happening, use the -v or --verbose option. If you want autoreconf to execute the Autotools in verbose mode as well, then add -vv to the command line.[6]

Next, notice that autoconf creates a directory called *autom4te.cache*. This is the autom4te cache directory. This cache speeds up access to *configure.ac* during successive executions of utilities in the Autotools tool chain.

---

5. There are a few exceptions to this rule. Poor documentation can sometimes lead to a misunderstanding about the intended use of some of the published Autoconf macros. This book highlights a few of these situations, but a degree of expertise with M4 is the only way to work your way through most of these problems.
6. You may also pass --verbose --verbose, but this syntax seems a bit . . . verbose to me.

The result of passing *configure.ac* through autoconf is essentially the same file (now called configure), but with all of the macros fully expanded. You're welcome to take a look at configure, but don't be too surprised if you don't immediately understand what you see. The *configure.ac* file has been transformed, through M4 macro expansions, into a text file containing thousands of lines of complex Bourne shell script.

Executing configure

As discussed in "Configuring Your Package" on page 54, the *GNU Coding Standards* indicate that a handwritten configure script should generate another script called config.status, whose job it is to generate files from templates. Unsurprisingly, this is exactly the sort of functionality you'll find in an Autoconf-generated configuration script. This script has two primary tasks:

- Perform requested checks
- Generate and then call config.status

The results of the checks performed by configure are written into config.status in a manner that allows them to be used as replacement text for Autoconf substitution variables in template files (*Makefile.in, config.h.in,* and so on). When you execute configure, it tells you that it's creating config.status. It also creates a log file called *config.log* that has several important attributes. Let's run configure and then see what's new in our project directory.

```
$ ./configure
configure: creating ./config.status
$
$ ls -1p
autom4te.cache/
config.log
config.status
configure
configure.ac
Makefile
src/
$
```

We see that configure has indeed generated both config.status and *config.log.* The *config.log* file contains the following information:

- The command line that was used to invoke configure (very handy!)
- Information about the platform on which configure was executed
- Information about the core tests configure executed
- The line number in configure at which config.status is generated and then called

At this point in the log file, `config.status` takes over generating log information and adds the following information:

- The command line used to invoke `config.status`

After `config.status` generates all the files from their templates, it exits, returning control to `configure`, which then appends the following information to the log:

- The cache variables `config.status` used to perform its tasks
- The list of output variables that may be replaced in templates
- The exit code `configure` returned to the shell

This information is invaluable when debugging a `configure` script and its associated *configure.ac* file.

Why doesn't `configure` just execute the code it writes into `config.status` instead of going to all the trouble of generating a second script, only to immediately call it? There are a few good reasons. First, the operations of performing checks and generating files are conceptually different, and `make` works best when conceptually different operations are associated with separate `make` targets. A second reason is that you can execute `config.status` separately to regenerate output files from their corresponding template files, saving the time required to perform those lengthy checks. Finally, `config.status` is written to remember the parameters originally used on the `configure` command line. Thus, when `make` detects that it needs to update the build system, it can call `config.status` to re-execute `configure`, using the command-line options that were originally specified.

Executing config.status

Now that you know how `configure` works, you might be tempted to execute `config.status` yourself. This was exactly the intent of the Autoconf designers and the authors of the *GCS*, who originally conceived these design goals. However, a more important reason for separating checks from template processing is that `make` rules can use `config.status` to regenerate makefiles from their templates when `make` determines that a template is newer than its corresponding makefile.

Rather than call `configure` to perform needless checks (your environment hasn't changed—just your template files), makefile rules should be written to indicate that output files are dependent on their templates. The commands for these rules run `config.status`, passing the rule's target as a parameter. If, for example, you modify one of your *Makefile.in* templates, `make` calls `config.status` to regenerate the corresponding *Makefile*, after which, `make` re-executes its own original command line—basically restarting itself.[7]

---

7. This is a built-in feature of GNU make. However, for the sake of portability, Automake generates makefiles that carefully reimplement this functionality as much as possible in make script, rather than relying on the built-in mechanism found in GNU make. The Automake solution isn't quite as comprehensive as GNU make's built-in functionality, but it's the best we can do, under the circumstances.

Listing 3-2 shows the relevant portion of such a *Makefile.in* template, containing the rules needed to regenerate the corresponding *Makefile*.

```
...
Makefile: Makefile.in config.status
        ./config.status $@
...
```

Listing 3-2: A rule that causes make to regenerate Makefile if its template has changed

A rule with a target named *Makefile* is the trigger here. This rule allows make to regenerate the source makefile from its template if the template changes. It does this *before* executing either the user's specified targets or the default target, if no specific target was given.

The rule in Listing 3-2 indicates that *Makefile* is dependent on config.status as well as *Makefile.in*, because if configure updates config.status, it may generate the makefile differently. Perhaps different command-line options were provided so that configure can now find libraries and header files it couldn't find previously. In this case, Autoconf substitution variables may have different values. Thus, *Makefile* should be regenerated if either *Makefile.in* or config.status is updated.

Since config.status is itself a generated file, it stands to reason that you could write such a rule to regenerate this file when needed. Expanding on the previous example, Listing 3-3 adds the required code to rebuild config.status if configure changes.

```
...
Makefile: Makefile.in config.status
        ./config.status $@

config.status: configure
        ./config.status --recheck
...
```

Listing 3-3: A rule to rebuild config.status when configure changes

Since config.status is a dependency of *Makefile*, make will look for a rule whose target is config.status and run its commands if configure is newer than config.status.

Adding Some Real Functionality

I've suggested before that you should call config.status in your makefiles to generate those makefiles from templates. Listing 3-4 shows the code in *configure.ac* that actually makes this happen. It's just a single additional macro call between the two original lines of Listing 3-1.

```
AC_INIT([Jupiter],[1.0])
AC_CONFIG_FILES([Makefile src/Makefile])
AC_OUTPUT
```

Listing 3-4: configure.ac: Using the AC_CONFIG_FILES macro

This code assumes that templates exist for *Makefile* and *src/Makefile*, called *Makefile.in* and *src/Makefile.in*, respectively. These template files look exactly like their *Makefile* counterparts, with one exception: Any text that I want Autoconf to replace is marked as an Autoconf substitution variable, using the @VARIABLE@ syntax.

To create these files, simply rename the existing *Makefile*s to *Makefile.in* in both the top-level and *src* directories. This is a common practice when *autoconfiscating* a project:

```
$ mv Makefile Makefile.in
$ mv src/Makefile src/Makefile.in
$
```

Next, let's add a few Autoconf substitution variables to replace the original default values. At the top of these files, I've also added the Autoconf substitution variable, @configure_input@, after a comment hash mark. Listing 3-5 shows the comment text that is generated in *Makefile*.

```
# Makefile.  Generated from Makefile.in by configure.
...
```

Listing 3-5: Makefile: The text generated from the Autoconf @configure_input@ variable

I've also added the makefile regeneration rules from the previous examples to each of these templates, with slight path differences in each file to account for their different positions relative to config.status and configure in the build directory.

Listings 3-6 and 3-7 highlight in bold the required changes to the final versions of *Makefile* and *src/Makefile* from the end of Chapter 2.

```
# @configure_input@

# Package-specific substitution variables
package         = @PACKAGE_NAME@
version         = @PACKAGE_VERSION@
tarname         = @PACKAGE_TARNAME@
distdir         = $(tarname)-$(version)

# Prefix-specific substitution variables
prefix          = @prefix@
exec_prefix     = @exec_prefix@
bindir          = @bindir@

...
```

```
$(distdir): FORCE
        mkdir -p $(distdir)/src
        cp configure.ac $(distdir)
        cp configure $(distdir)
        cp Makefile.in $(distdir)
        cp src/Makefile.in $(distdir)/src
        cp src/main.c $(distdir)/src

distcheck: $(distdir).tar.gz
        gzip -cd $(distdir).tar.gz | tar xvf -
        cd $(distdir) && ./configure
        cd $(distdir) && $(MAKE) all
        cd $(distdir) && $(MAKE) check
        cd $(distdir) && $(MAKE) DESTDIR=$${PWD}/_inst install
        cd $(distdir) && $(MAKE) DESTDIR=$${PWD}/_inst uninstall
        @remaining="`find $${PWD}/$(distdir)/_inst -type f | wc -l`"; \
        if test "$${remaining}" -ne 0; then \
          echo "*** $${remaining} file(s) remaining in stage directory!"; \
          exit 1; \
        fi
        cd $(distdir) && $(MAKE) clean
        rm -rf $(distdir)
        @echo "*** Package $(distdir).tar.gz is ready for distribution."

Makefile: Makefile.in config.status
        ./config.status $@

config.status: configure
        ./config.status --recheck
...
```

Listing 3-6: Makefile.in: Required modifications to Makefile from the end of Chapter 2

```
# @configure_input@

# Package-specific substitution variables
package         = @PACKAGE_NAME@
version         = @PACKAGE_VERSION@
tarname         = @PACKAGE_TARNAME@
distdir         = $(tarname)-$(version)

# Prefix-specific substitution variables
prefix          = @prefix@
exec_prefix     = @exec_prefix@
bindir          = @bindir@

...
Makefile: Makefile.in ../config.status
        cd .. && ./config.status src/$@
```

```
../config.status: ../configure
        cd .. && ./config.status --recheck
...
```

Listing 3-7: src/Makefile.in: *Required modifications to* src/Makefile *from the end of Chapter 2*

I've removed the export statements from the top-level *Makefile.in* and added a copy of all of the make variables (originally only in the top-level *Makefile*) into *src/Makefile.in*. Since config.status generates both of these files, I can reap excellent benefits by substituting values for these variables directly into both files. The primary advantage of doing this is that I can now run make in any subdirectory without worrying about uninitialized variables that would originally have been passed down by a higher-level makefile.

Since Autoconf generates entire values for these make variables, you may be tempted to clean things up a bit by removing the variables and just substituting @prefix@ where we currently use $(prefix) throughout the files. There are a few good reasons for keeping the make variables. First and foremost, we'll retain the original benefits of the make variables; our end users can continue to substitute their own values on the make command line. (Even though Autoconf places default values in these variables, users may wish to override them.) Second, for variables such as $(distdir), whose values are comprised of multiple variable references, it's simply cleaner to build the name in one place and use it everywhere else through a single variable.

I've also changed the commands in the distribution targets a bit. Rather than distribute the makefiles, I now need to distribute the *Makefile.in* templates, as well as the new configure script and the *configure.ac* file.[8]

Finally, I modified the distcheck target's commands to run the configure script before running make.

Generating Files from Templates

Note that you can use AC_CONFIG_FILES to generate *any* text file from a file of the same name with an *.in* extension, found in the same directory. The *.in* extension is the default template naming pattern for AC_CONFIG_FILES, but you can override this default behavior. I'll get into the details shortly.

Autoconf generates sed or awk expressions into the resulting configure script, which then copies them into config.status. The config.status script uses these expressions to perform string replacement in the input template files.

Both sed and awk are text-processing tools that operate on file streams. The advantage of a stream editor (the name *sed* is a contraction of the phrase *stream editor*) is that it replaces text patterns in a byte stream. Thus, both sed and awk can operate on huge files because they don't need to load the entire input file into memory in order to process it. Autoconf builds the expression list that config.status passes to sed or awk from a list of variables defined by

---

8. Distributing *configure.ac* is not merely an act of kindness—it could also be considered a requirement of GNU source licenses, since *configure.ac* is very literally the source code for configure.

various macros, many of which I'll cover in greater detail later in this chapter. It's important to understand that Autoconf substitution variables are the *only* items replaced in a template file while generating output files.

At this point, with very little effort, I've created a basic *configure.ac* file. I can now execute autoreconf, followed by configure and then make, in order to build the Jupiter project. This simple, three-line *configure.ac* file generates a configure script that is fully functional, according to the definition of a proper configuration script defined by the *GCS*.

The resulting configuration script runs various system checks and generates a config.status script that can replace a fair number of substitution variables in a set of specified template files in this build system. That's a lot of functionality in just three lines of code.

Adding VPATH Build Functionality

At the end of Chapter 2, I mentioned that I hadn't yet covered an important concept—that of VPATH builds. A *VPATH build* is a way of using a makefile construct (VPATH) to configure and build a project in a directory other than the source directory. This is important if you need to perform any of the following tasks:

- Maintain a separate debug configuration
- Test different configurations side by side
- Keep a clean source directory for patch diffs after local modifications
- Build from a read-only source directory

The VPATH keyword is short for *virtual search path*. A VPATH statement contains a colon-separated list of places to look for relative-path dependencies when they can't be found relative to the current directory. In other words, when make can't find a prerequisite file relative to the current directory, it searches for that file successively in each of the paths in the VPATH statement.

Adding remote build functionality to an existing makefile using VPATH is very simple. Listing 3-8 shows an example of using a VPATH statement in a makefile.

```
VPATH = some/path:some/other/path:yet/another/path

program: src/main.c
        $(CC) ...
```

Listing 3-8: An example of using VPATH in a makefile

In this (contrived) example, if make can't find *src/main.c* in the current directory while processing the rule, it will look for *some/path/src/main.c*, and then for *some/other/path/src/main.c*, and finally for *yet/another/path/src/main.c* before giving up with an error message about not knowing how to make *src/main.c*.

With just a few simple modifications, we can completely support remote builds in Jupiter. Listings 3-9 and 3-10 illustrate the necessary changes to the project's two makefiles.

```
...
# VPATH-specific substitution variables
srcdir          = @srcdir@
VPATH           = @srcdir@
...
$(distdir): FORCE
        mkdir -p $(distdir)/src
        cp $(srcdir)/configure.ac $(distdir)
        cp $(srcdir)/configure $(distdir)
        cp $(srcdir)/Makefile.in $(distdir)
        cp $(srcdir)/src/Makefile.in $(distdir)/src
        cp $(srcdir)/src/main.c $(distdir)/src
...
```

Listing 3-9: Makefile.in: Adding VPATH build capabilities to the top-level makefile

```
...
# VPATH-related substitution variables
srcdir          = @srcdir@
VPATH           = @srcdir@
...
```

Listing 3-10: src/Makefile.in: Adding VPATH build capabilities to the lower-level makefile

That's it. Really. When config.status generates a file, it replaces an Autoconf substitution variable called @srcdir@ with the relative path to the template's source directory. The value substituted for @srcdir@ in a given *Makefile* within the build directory structure is the relative path to the directory containing the corresponding *Makefile.in* template in the source directory structure. The concept here is that for each *Makefile* in the remote build directory, VPATH provides a relative path to the directory containing the source code for that build directory.

The changes required for supporting remote builds in your build system are summarized as follows:

- Set a make variable, srcdir, to the @srcdir@ substitution variable.
- Set the VPATH variable to @srcdir@.
- Prefix all file dependencies used *in commands* with $(srcdir)/.

NOTE *Don't use $(srcdir) in the VPATH statement itself, because some older versions of make won't substitute variable references within the VPATH statement.*

If the source directory is the same as the build directory, the @srcdir@ substitution variable degenerates to a dot (.). That means all of these $(srcdir)/ prefixes simply degenerate to ./, which is harmless.[9]

---

9. This is not strictly true for non-GNU implementations of make. GNU make is smart enough to know that *file* and *./file* refer to the same filesystem object. However, non-GNU implementations of make aren't always quite so intelligent, so you should be careful to refer to a filesystem object using the same notation for each reference in your *Makefile.in* templates.

A quick example is the easiest way to show you how this works. Now that Jupiter is fully functional with respect to remote builds, let's give it a try. Start in the Jupiter project directory, create a subdirectory called *build*, and then change into that directory. Execute the configure script using a relative path, and then list the current directory contents:

```
$ mkdir build
$ cd build
$ ../configure
configure: creating ./config.status
config.status: creating Makefile
config.status: creating src/Makefile
$
$ ls -1p
config.log
config.status
Makefile
src/
$
$ ls -1p src
Makefile
$
```

The entire build system has been constructed by configure and config.status within the *build* subdirectory. Enter make to build the project from within the *build* directory:

```
$ make
cd src && make all
make[1]: Entering directory '../prj/jupiter/build'
gcc -g -O2 -o jupiter ../../src/main.c
make[1]: Leaving directory '../prj/jupiter/build'
$
$ ls -1p src
jupiter
Makefile
$
```

No matter where you are, if you can access the project directory using either a relative or an absolute path, you can do a remote build from that location. This is just one more thing that Autoconf does for you in Autoconf-generated configuration scripts. Imagine managing proper relative paths to source directories in your own hand-coded configuration scripts!

Let's Take a Breather

So far, I've shown you a nearly complete build system that includes almost all of the features outlined in the *GCS*. The features of Jupiter's build system are all fairly self-contained and reasonably simple to understand. The most difficult feature to implement by hand is the configuration script. In fact, writing a configuration script by hand is so labor intensive, compared to the simplicity of using Autoconf, that I just skipped the hand-coded version entirely in Chapter 2.

Although using Autoconf like I've used it here is quite easy, most people don't create their build systems in the manner I've shown you. Instead, they try to copy the build system of another project, and tweak it to make it work in their own project. Later, when they start a new project, they do the same thing again. This can cause trouble because the code they're copying was never meant to be used the way they're now trying to use it.

I've seen projects in which the *configure.ac* file contained junk that had nothing to do with the project to which it belonged. These leftover bits came from some legacy project, but the maintainer didn't know enough about Autoconf to properly remove all the extraneous text. With the Autotools, it's generally better to start small and add what you need than to start with a copy of *configure.ac* from another full-featured build system, and try to pare it down to size or otherwise modify it to work with a new project.

I'm sure you're feeling like there's a lot more to learn about Autoconf, and you're right. We'll spend the majority of this chapter examining the most important Autoconf macros and how they're used in the context of the Jupiter project. But first, let's go back and see if we might be able to simplify the Autoconf startup process even more by using another utility that comes with the *autoconf* package.

An Even Quicker Start with autoscan

The easiest way to create a (mostly) complete *configure.ac* file is to run the autoscan utility, which is part of the *autoconf* package. This utility examines the contents of a project directory and generates the basis for a *configure.ac* file (which autoscan names *configure.scan*) using existing makefiles and source files.

Let's see how well autoscan does on the Jupiter project. First, I'll clean up the droppings from my earlier experiments, and then run autoscan in the *jupiter* directory. Note that I'm *not* deleting my original *configure.ac* file—I'll just let autoscan tell me how to improve it. In less than a second, I have a few new files in the top-level directory:

```
$ rm -rf autom4te.cache build
$ rm configure config.* Makefile src/Makefile src/jupiter
$ ls -1p
configure.ac
Makefile.in
src/
$
$ autoscan
❶ configure.ac: warning: missing AC_CHECK_HEADERS([stdlib.h]) wanted by: src/main.c:2
configure.ac: warning: missing AC_PREREQ wanted by: autoscan
configure.ac: warning: missing AC_PROG_CC wanted by: src/main.c
configure.ac: warning: missing AC_PROG_INSTALL wanted by: Makefile.in:18
$
```

```
$ ls -1p
autom4te.cache/
autoscan.log
configure.ac
configure.scan
Makefile.in
src/
$
```

The autoscan utility examines the project directory hierarchy and creates
two files called *configure.scan* and *autoscan.log*. The project may or may not
already be instrumented for Autotools—it doesn't really matter, because
autoscan is decidedly non-destructive. It will never alter any existing files in a
project.

The autoscan utility generates a warning message for each problem it discovers in an existing *configure.ac* file. In this example, autoscan noticed that
configure.ac should be using the Autoconf-provided AC_CHECK_HEADERS, AC_PREREQ,
AC_PROG_CC, and AC_PROG_INSTALL macros. It made these assumptions based on
information gleaned from the existing *Makefile.in* templates and from the C-
language source files, as you can see by the comments after the warning statements beginning at ❶. You can always see these messages (in even greater
detail) by examining the *autoscan.log* file.

NOTE *The notices you receive from autoscan and the contents of your* configure.ac *file may
differ slightly from mine, depending on the version of Autoconf you have installed. I
have version 2.64 of GNU Autoconf installed on my system (the latest, as of this writing).
If your version of autoscan is older (or newer), you may see some minor differences.*

Looking at the generated *configure.scan* file, I note that autoscan has added
more text to this file than was in my original *configure.ac* file. After looking it
over to ensure that I understand everything, I see that it's probably easiest for
me to overwrite *configure.ac* with *configure.scan* and then change the few bits
of information that are specific to Jupiter:

```
$ mv configure.scan configure.ac
$ cat configure.ac
#                                              -*- Autoconf -*-
# Process this file with autoconf to produce a configure script.

AC_PREREQ([2.64])
AC_INIT([FULL-PACKAGE-NAME], [VERSION], [BUG-REPORT-ADDRESS])
AC_CONFIG_SRCDIR([src/main.c])
AC_CONFIG_HEADERS([config.h])

# Checks for programs.
AC_PROG_CC
AC_PROG_INSTALL

# Checks for libraries.
```

```
# Checks for header files.
AC_CHECK_HEADERS([stdlib.h])

# Checks for typedefs, structures, and compiler characteristics.

# Checks for library functions.

AC_CONFIG_FILES([Makefile
                 src/Makefile])
AC_OUTPUT
$
```

My first modification involves changing the AC_INIT macro parameters for Jupiter, as illustrated in Listing 3-11.

```
#                                           -*- Autoconf -*-
# Process this file with autoconf to produce a configure script.

AC_PREREQ([2.64])
AC_INIT([Jupiter], [1.0], [jupiter-bugs@example.org])
AC_CONFIG_SRCDIR([src/main.c])
AC_CONFIG_HEADERS([config.h])
...
```

Listing 3-11: configure.ac: Tweaking the AC_INIT macro generated by autoscan

The autoscan utility does a lot of the work for you. The *GNU Autoconf Manual*[10] states that you should modify this file to meet the needs of your project before you use it, but there are only a few key issues to worry about (besides those related to AC_INIT). I'll cover each of these issues in turn, but first, let's take care of a few administrative details.

The Proverbial autogen.sh Script

Before autoreconf came along, maintainers passed around a short shell script, often named autogen.sh or bootstrap.sh, which would run all of the Autotools required for their projects in the proper order. The autogen.sh script can be fairly sophisticated, but to solve the problem of the missing install-sh script (see "Missing Required Files in Autoconf" on page 74), I'll just add a simple temporary autogen.sh script to the project root directory, as shown in Listing 3-12.

```
#!/bin/sh
autoreconf --install
❶ automake --add-missing --copy >/dev/null 2>&1
```

Listing 3-12: autogen.sh: A temporary bootstrap script that executes the required Autotools

The automake --add-missing option copies the required missing utility scripts into the project, and the --copy option indicates that true copies should be

---

10. See the Free Software Foundation's *GNU Autoconf Manual* at *http://www.gnu.org/software/autoconf/manual/index.html*.

made (otherwise, symbolic links are created that refer to the files where they're installed with the Automake package).[11]

MISSING REQUIRED FILES IN AUTOCONF

When I first tried to execute autoreconf on the *configure.ac* file in Listing 3-11, I discovered a minor problem related to using Autoconf *without* Automake. When I ran the configure script, it failed with an error: configure: error: cannot find install-sh or install.sh ...

Autoconf is all about portability and, unfortunately, the Unix install utility is not as portable as it could be. From one platform to another, critical bits of installation functionality are just different enough to cause problems, so the Autotools provide a shell script called install-sh (deprecated name: install.sh). This script acts as a wrapper around the system's own install utility, masking important differences between various versions of install.

autoscan noticed that I'd used the install program in my *src/Makefile.in* template, so it generated an expansion of the AC_PROG_INSTALL macro. The problem is that configure couldn't find the install-sh wrapper script anywhere in my project.

I reasoned that the missing file was part of the Autoconf package, and it just needed to be installed. I also knew that autoreconf accepts a command-line option to install such missing files into a project directory. The --install option supported by autoreconf is designed to pass tool-specific options down to each of the tools that it calls in order to install missing files. However, when I tried that, I found that the file was still missing, because autoconf doesn't support an option to install missing files.[1]

I could have manually copied install-sh from the Automake installation directory (usually */usr/(local/)share/automake-**), but looking for a more automated solution, I tried manually executing automake --add-missing --copy. This command generated a slew of warnings indicating that the project was not configured for Automake. However, I could now see that install-sh had been copied into my project root directory, and that's all I was after. Executing autoreconf --install didn't run automake because *configure.ac* was not configured for Automake.

Autoconf should ship with install-sh, since it provides a macro that requires it, but then autoconf would have to provide an --add-missing command-line option. Nevertheless, there is actually a quite obvious solution to this problem. The install-sh script is not really required by any code Autoconf generates. How could it be? Autoconf doesn't generate any makefile constructs—it only substitutes variables into your *Makefile.in* templates. Thus, there's really no reason for Autoconf to complain about a missing install-sh script.[2]

---

1. Worse still, the *GNU Autoconf Manual* that I was using at the time told me that "Autoconf comes with a copy of install-sh that you can use"—but it's really Automake and Libtool that come with copies of install-sh.

2. When I presented this problem on the Autoconf mailing list, I was told several times that autoconf has no business copying install-sh into a project directory, thus there is no install-missing-file functionality accessible from the autoconf command line. If this is indeed the case, then autoconf has no business complaining about the missing file, either!

---

11. The automake --add-missing option copies in the missing required utility scripts, and the --copy option indicates that true copies should be made—otherwise, symbolic links are created to the files where the automake package has installed them. This isn't as bad as it sounds, because when make dist generates a distribution archive, it creates true copies in the image directory. Therefore, links work just fine, as long as you (the maintainer) don't move your work area to another host. Note that automake provides a --copy option, but autoreconf provides just the opposite: a --symlink option. Thus, if you execute automake --add-missing and you wish to actually copy the files, you should pass --copy as well. If you execute autoreconf --install, --copy will be assumed and passed to automake by autoreconf.

NOTE *When* make dist *generates a distribution archive, it creates true copies in the image directory, so the use of symlinks causes no real problems, as long as you (the maintainer) don't move your work area to another host.*

We don't need to see the warnings from automake, so I've redirected the stderr and stdout streams to */dev/null* on the automake command line at ❶ in this script. In Chapter 5, we'll remove autogen.sh and simply run autoreconf --install, but for now, this will solve our missing file problems.

Updating Makefile.in

Let's execute autogen.sh and see what we end up with:

```
$ sh autogen.sh
$ ls -1p
autogen.sh
autom4te.cache/
❶ config.h.in
configure
configure.ac
❷ install-sh
Makefile.in
src/
$
```

We know from the file list at ❶ that *config.h.in* has been created, so we know that autoreconf has executed autoheader. We also see the new install-sh script at ❷ that was created when we executed automake in autogen.sh. Anything provided or generated by the Autotools should be copied into the archive directory so that it can be shipped with release tarballs. Therefore, we'll add cp commands for these two files to the $(distdir) target in the top-level *Makefile.in* template. Note that we don't need to copy the autogen.sh script because it's purely a maintainer tool—users should never need to execute it from a tarball distribution.

Listing 3-13 illustrates the required changes to the $(distdir) target in the top-level *Makefile.in* template.

```
...
$(distdir): FORCE
        mkdir -p $(distdir)/src
        cp $(srcdir)/configure.ac $(distdir)
        cp $(srcdir)/configure $(distdir)
        cp $(srcdir)/config.h.in $(distdir)
        cp $(srcdir)/install-sh $(distdir)
        cp $(srcdir)/Makefile.in $(distdir)
        cp $(srcdir)/src/Makefile.in $(distdir)/src
        cp $(srcdir)/src/main.c $(distdir)/src
...
```

Listing 3-13: Makefile.in: Additional files needed in the distribution archive image directory

If you're beginning to think that this could become a maintenance problem, then you're right. I mentioned earlier that the $(distdir) target was painful to maintain. Luckily, the distcheck target still exists and still works as designed. It would have caught this problem, because attempts to build from the tarball will fail without these additional files—and the check target certainly won't succeed if the build fails. When we discuss Automake in Chapter 5, we will clear up much of this maintenance mess.

Initialization and Package Information

Now let's turn our attention back to the contents of the *configure.ac* file in Listing 3-11. The first section contains Autoconf initialization macros. These are required for all projects. Let's consider each of these macros individually, because they're all important.

AC_PREREQ

The AC_PREREQ macro simply defines the earliest version of Autoconf that may be used to successfully process this *configure.ac* file:

```
AC_PREREQ(version)
```

The *GNU Autoconf Manual* indicates that AC_PREREQ is the only macro that may be used before AC_INIT. This is because it's good to ensure you're using a new enough version of Autoconf before you begin processing any other macros, which may be version dependent.

AC_INIT

The AC_INIT macro, as its name implies, initializes the Autoconf system. Here's its prototype, as defined in the *GNU Autoconf Manual*:[12]

```
AC_INIT(package, version, [bug-report], [tarname], [url])
```

It accepts up to five arguments (autoscan only generates a call with the first three): package, version, and optionally, bug-report, tarname, and url. The package argument is intended to be the name of the package. It will end up (in a canonical form) as the first part of the name of an Automake-generated release distribution tarball when you execute make dist.

NOTE *Autoconf uses a normalized form of the package name in the tarball name, so you can use uppercase letters in the package name, if you wish. Automake-generated tarballs are named* tarname-version.tar.gz *by default, but* tarname *is set to a normalized form of the package name (lowercase, with all punctuation converted to underscores). Bear this in mind when you choose your package name and version string.*

---

12. The square brackets used in the macro definition prototypes within this book (as well as the *GNU Autoconf Manual*) indicate optional parameters, not Autoconf quotes.

The optional bug-report argument is usually set to an email address, but any text string is valid. An Autoconf substitution variable called @PACKAGE_BUGREPORT@ is created for it, and that variable is also added to the *config.h.in* template as a C-preprocessor definition. The intent here is that you use the variable in your code to present an email address for bug reports at appropriate places—possibly when the user requests help or version information from your application.

While the version argument can be anything you like, there are a few commonly used OSS conventions that will make things a little easier for you. The most widely used convention is to pass in *major.minor* (e.g., 1.2). However, there's nothing that says you can't use *major.minor.revision*, and there's nothing wrong with this approach. None of the resulting VERSION variables (Autoconf, shell, or make) are parsed or analyzed anywhere—they're only used as place-holders for substituted text in various locations.[13] So if you wish, you may even add nonnumeric text into this macro, such as *0.15.alpha1*, which is occasionally useful.[14]

NOTE   *The RPM package manager, on the other hand, does care what you put in the version string. For the sake of RPM, you may wish to limit the version string text to only alpha-numeric characters and periods—no dashes or underscores.*

The optional url argument should be the URL for your project website. It's shown in the help text displayed by configure --help.

Autoconf generates the substitution variables @PACKAGE_NAME@, @PACKAGE_VERSION@, @PACKAGE_TARNAME@, @PACKAGE_STRING@ (a stylized concatena-tion of the package name and version information), @PACKAGE_BUGREPORT@, and @PACKAGE_URL@ from the arguments to AC_INIT.

AC_CONFIG_SRCDIR

The AC_CONFIG_SRCDIR macro is a sanity check. Its purpose is to ensure that the generated configure script knows that the directory on which it is being exe-cuted is actually the project directory.

More specifically, configure needs to be able to locate itself, because it generates code that executes itself, possibly from a remote directory. There are myriad ways to inadvertently fool configure into finding some other configure script. For example, the user could accidentally provide an incorrect --srcdir argument to configure. The $0 shell script parameter is unreliable, at best—it may contain the name of the shell, rather than that of the script, or it may be that configure was found in the system search path, so no path infor-mation was specified on the command line.

---

13. As far as M4 is concerned, all data is text; thus M4 macro arguments, including package and version, are treated simply as strings. M4 doesn't attempt to interpret any of this text as numbers or other data types.

14. A future version of Autoconf will support a public macro that allows lexicographical comparison of version strings, and certain internal constructs in current versions already use such functionality. Thus, it's good practice to form version strings that increase properly in a lexical fashion from version to version.

The configure script could try looking in the current or parent directories, but it still needs a way to verify that the configure script it locates is actually itself. Thus, AC_CONFIG_SRCDIR gives configure a significant hint that it's looking in the right place. Here's the prototype for AC_CONFIG_SRCDIR:

```
AC_CONFIG_SRCDIR(unique-file-in-source-dir)
```

The argument can be a path (relative to the project's configure script) to any source file you like. You should choose one that is unique to your project so as to minimize the possibility that configure is fooled into thinking some other project's configuration file is itself. I try to choose a file that sort of represents the project, such as a source file named for a feature that defines the project. That way, in case I ever decide to reorganize the source code, I'm not likely to lose it in a file rename. But it doesn't really matter, because both autoconf and configure will tell you and your users if it can't find this file.

The Instantiating Macros

Before we dive into the details of AC_CONFIG_HEADERS, I'd like to spend a little time on the file generation framework Autoconf provides. From a high-level perspective, there are four major things happening in *configure.ac*:

- Initialization
- Check request processing
- File instantiation request processing
- Generation of the configure script

We've covered initialization—there's not much to it, although there are a few more macros you should be aware of. Check out the *GNU Autoconf Manual* for more information—look up AC_COPYRIGHT, for an example. Now let's move on to file instantiation.

There are actually four so-called *instantiating macros*: AC_CONFIG_FILES, AC_CONFIG_HEADERS, AC_CONFIG_COMMANDS, and AC_CONFIG_LINKS. An instantiating macro accepts a list of tags or files; configure will generate these files from templates containing Autoconf substitution variables.

NOTE   *You might need to change the name of AC_CONFIG_HEADER (singular) to AC_CONFIG_HEADERS (plural) in your version of configure.scan. The singular version is the older name for this macro, and the older macro is less functional than the newer one.*[15]

The four instantiating macros have an interesting common signature. The following prototype can be used to represent each of them, with appropriate text replacing the *XXX* portion of the macro name:

```
AC_CONFIG_XXXS(tag..., [commands], [init-cmds])
```

---

15. This was a defect in autoscan that had not been fixed as of Autoconf version 2.61. However, version 2.62 of autoscan correctly generates a call to the newer, more functional AC_CONFIG_HEADERS.

For each of these four macros, the tag argument has the form OUT[:INLIST], where INLIST has the form INO[:IN1:...:INn]. Often, you'll see a call to one of these macros with only a single argument, as in the three examples below (note that these examples represent macro *calls*, not *prototypes*, so the square brackets are actually Autoconf quotes, not indications of optional parameters):

```
AC_CONFIG_HEADERS([config.h])
```

In this example, *config.h* is the OUT portion of the above specification. The default value for INLIST is the OUT portion with *.in* appended to it. So, in other words, the above call is exactly equivalent to:

```
AC_CONFIG_HEADERS([config.h:config.h.in])
```

What this means is that config.status contains shell code that will generate *config.h* from *config.h.in*, substituting all Autoconf variables in the process. You may also provide a list of input files in the INLIST portion. In this case, the files in INLIST will be concatenated to form the resulting OUT file:

```
AC_CONFIG_HEADERS([config.h:cfg0:cfg1:cfg2])
```

Here, config.status will generate *config.h* by concatenating cfg0, cfg1, and cfg2 (in that order), after substituting all Autoconf variables. The *GNU Autoconf Manual* refers to this entire OUT[:INLIST] construct as a *tag*.

Why not just call it a *file*? Well, this parameter's primary purpose is to provide a sort of command-line target name—much like makefile targets. It can also be used as a filesystem name if the associated macro generates files, as is the case with AC_CONFIG_HEADERS, AC_CONFIG_FILES, and AC_CONFIG_LINKS.

But AC_CONFIG_COMMANDS is unique in that it doesn't generate any files. Instead, it runs arbitrary shell code, as specified by the user in the macro's arguments. Thus, rather than name this first parameter after a secondary function (the generation of files), the *GNU Autoconf Manual* refers to it more generally, according to its primary purpose—as a command-line *tag* that may be specified on the config.status command line, in this manner:

```
$ ./config.status config.h
```

This config.status command line will regenerate the *config.h* file based on the macro call to AC_CONFIG_HEADERS in *configure.ac*. It will *only* regenerate *config.h*.

Enter ./config.status --help to see the other command-line options you can use when executing config.status:

```
$ ./config.status --help
'config.status' instantiates files from templates according to the
current configuration.
```

❶ Usage: ./config.status [OPTION]... [TAG]...

```
        -h, --help       print this help, then exit
        -V, --version    print version number and configuration settings, then exit
        -q, --quiet, --silent
                         do not print progress messages
        -d, --debug      don't remove temporary files
            --recheck    update config.status by reconfiguring in the same
    conditions
❷       --file=FILE[:TEMPLATE]
                         instantiate the configuration file FILE
            --header=FILE[:TEMPLATE]
                         instantiate the configuration header FILE

❸ Configuration files:
    Makefile src/Makefile

❹ Configuration headers:
    config.h

    Report bugs to <bug-autoconf@gnu.org>.
    $
```

Notice that config.status provides custom help about a project's
config.status file. It lists configuration files ❸ and configuration headers ❹
that we can use as tags on the command line where the usage specifies
[TAG]... at ❶. In this case, config.status will only instantiate the specified
objects. In the case of commands, it will execute the command set specified by
the tag passed in the associated expansion of the AC_CONFIG_COMMANDS macro.

Each of these macros may be used multiple times in a *configure.ac* file.
The results are cumulative, and we can use AC_CONFIG_FILES as many times as
we need to in *configure.ac*. It is also important to note that config.status supports the --file= option (at ❷). When you call config.status with tags on the
command line, the only tags you can use are those the help text lists as available configuration files, headers, links, and commands. When you execute
config.status with the --file= option, you're telling config.status to generate
a new file that's not already associated with any of the calls to the instantiating
macros found in *configure.ac*. This new file is generated from an associated
template using configuration options and check results determined by the
last execution of configure. For example, I could execute config.status in this
manner:

```
$ ./config.status --file=extra:extra.in
```

NOTE   *The default template name is the filename with a .in suffix, so this call could have
been made without using the :extra.in portion of the option. I added it here for clarity.*

Let's return to the instantiating macro signature at the bottom of
page 78. I've shown you that the tag... argument has a complex format,
but the ellipsis indicates that it also represents multiple tags, separated by
whitespace. The format you'll see in nearly all *configure.ac* files is shown in
Listing 3-14.

```
...
AC_CONFIG_FILES([Makefile
                src/Makefile
                lib/Makefile
                etc/proj.cfg])
...
```

Listing 3-14: Specifying multiple tags (files) in AC_CONFIG_FILES

Each entry here is one tag specification, which, if fully specified, would look like the call in Listing 3-15.

```
...
AC_CONFIG_FILES([Makefile:Makefile.in
                src/Makefile:src/Makefile.in
                lib/Makefile:lib/Makefile.in
                etc/proj.cfg:etc/proj.cfg.in])
...
```

Listing 3-15: Fully specifying multiple tags in AC_CONFIG_FILES

Returning to the instantiating macro prototype, there are two optional arguments that you'll rarely see used in these macros: commands and init-cmds. The commands argument may be used to specify some arbitrary shell code that should be executed by config.status just before the files associated with the tags are generated. It is unusual for this feature to be used within the file-generating instantiating macros. You will almost always see the commands argument used with AC_CONFIG_COMMANDS, which generates no files by default, because a call to this macro is basically useless without commands to execute![16] In this case, the tag argument becomes a way of telling config.status to execute a specific set of shell commands.

The init-cmds argument initializes shell variables at the top of config.status with values available in *configure.ac* and configure. It's important to remember that all calls to instantiating macros share a common namespace along with config.status. Therefore, you should try to choose your shell variable names carefully so they are less likely to conflict with each other and with Autoconf-generated variables.

The old adage about the value of a picture versus an explanation holds true here, so let's try a little experiment. Create a test version of your *configure.ac* file that contains only the contents of Listing 3-16.

```
AC_INIT([test], [1.0])
AC_CONFIG_COMMANDS([abc],
                   [echo "Testing $mypkgname"],
                   [mypkgname=$PACKAGE_NAME])
AC_OUTPUT
```

Listing 3-16: Experiment #1—a simple configure.ac *file*

---

16. The truth is that we don't often use AC_CONFIG_COMMANDS.

Now execute autoreconf, configure, and config.status in various ways to see what happens:

```
  $ autoreconf
❶ $ ./configure
  configure: creating ./config.status
  config.status: executing abc commands
  Testing test
  $
❷ $ ./config.status
  config.status: executing abc commands
  Testing test
  $
❸ $ ./config.status --help
  'config.status' instantiates files from templates according to the current
  configuration.
  Usage: ./config.status [OPTIONS]... [FILE]...
  ...
  Configuration commands:
   abc

  Report bugs to <bug-autoconf@gnu.org>.
  $
❹ $ ./config.status abc
  config.status: executing abc commands
  Testing test
  $
```

As you can see at ❶, executing configure caused config.status to be executed with no command-line options. There are no checks specified in *configure.ac*, so manually executing config.status, as we did at ❷, has nearly the same effect. Querying config.status for help (as we did at ❸) indicates that abc is a valid tag; executing config.status with that tag (as we did at ❹) on the command line simply runs the associated commands.

In summary, the important points regarding the instantiating macros are as follows:

- The config.status script generates all files from templates.

- The configure script performs all checks and then executes config.status.

- When you execute config.status with no command-line options, it generates files based on the last set of check results.

- You can call config.status to execute file generation or command sets specified by any of the tags given in any of the instantiating macro calls.

- config.status may generate files not associated with any tags specified in *configure.ac*, in which case it will substitute variables based on the last set of checks performed.

AC_CONFIG_HEADERS

As you've no doubt concluded by now, the `AC_CONFIG_HEADERS` macro allows you to specify one or more header files that `config.status` should generate from template files. The format of a configuration header template is very specific. A short example is given in Listing 3-17.

```
/* Define as 1 if you have unistd.h. */
#undef HAVE_UNISTD_H
```

Listing 3-17: A short example of a header file template

You can place multiple statements like this in your header template, one per line. The comments are optional, of course. Let's try another experiment. Create a new *configure.ac* file like that shown in Listing 3-18.

```
AC_INIT([test], [1.0])
AC_CONFIG_HEADERS([config.h])
AC_CHECK_HEADERS([unistd.h foobar.h])
AC_OUTPUT
```

Listing 3-18: Experiment #2—a simple configure.ac *file*

Create a template header file called *config.h.in* that contains the two lines in Listing 3-19.

```
#undef HAVE_UNISTD_H
#undef HAVE_FOOBAR_H
```

Listing 3-19: Experiment #2 continued—a simple config.h.in *file*

Now execute the following commands:

```
$ autoconf
$ ./configure
checking for gcc... gcc
...
❶ checking for unistd.h... yes
checking for unistd.h... (cached) yes
checking foobar.h usability... no
checking foobar.h presence... no
❷ checking for foobar.h... no
configure: creating ./config.status
❸ config.status: creating config.h
$
$ cat config.h
/* config.h.  Generated from ...  */
#define HAVE_UNISTD_H 1
❹ /* #undef HAVE_FOOBAR_H */
$
```

You can see at ❸ that config.status generated a *config.h* file from the simple *config.h.in* template we wrote. The contents of this header file are based on the checks executed by configure. Since the shell code generated by AC_CHECK_HEADERS([unistd.h foobar.h]) was able to locate a *unistd.h* header file (❶) in the system include directory, the corresponding #undef statement was converted into a #define statement. Of course, no *foobar.h* header was found in the system include directory, as you can also see by the output of configure at ❷; therefore, its definition was left commented out in the template, as shown at ❹.

Thus, you may add the sort of code shown in Listing 3-20 to appropriate C-language source files in your project.

```
#if HAVE_CONFIG_H
# include <config.h>
#endif

#if HAVE_UNISTD_H
# include <unistd.h>
#endif

#if HAVE_FOOBAR_H
# include <foobar.h>
#endif
```

Listing 3-20: Using generated CPP definitions in a C-language source file

Using autoheader to Generate an Include File Template

Manually maintaining a *config.h.in* template is more trouble than necessary. The format of *config.h.in* is very strict—for example, you can't have any leading or trailing whitespace on the #undef lines. Besides that, most of the information you need from *config.h.in* is available in *configure.ac*.

Fortunately, the autoheader utility will generate a properly formatted header file template for you based on the contents of *configure.ac*, so you don't often need to write *config.h.in* templates. Let's return to the command prompt for a final experiment. This one is easy—just delete your *config.h.in* template and then run autoheader and autoconf:

```
$ rm config.h.in
$ autoheader
$ autoconf
$ ./configure
checking for gcc... gcc
...
checking for unistd.h... yes
checking for unistd.h... (cached) yes
checking foobar.h usability... no
checking foobar.h presence... no
checking for foobar.h... no
```

```
configure: creating ./config.status
config.status: creating config.h
$
$ cat config.h
/* config.h. Generated from config.h.in... */
/* config.h.in. Generated from configure.ac... */
...
/* Define to 1 if you have... */
/* #undef HAVE_FOOBAR_H */
/* Define to 1 if you have... */
#define HAVE_UNISTD_H 1
/* Define to the address where bug... */
#define PACKAGE_BUGREPORT ""
/* Define to the full name of this package. */
#define PACKAGE_NAME "test"
/* Define to the full name and version... */
#define PACKAGE_STRING "test 1.0"
/* Define to the one symbol short name... */
#define PACKAGE_TARNAME "test"
/* Define to the version... */
#define PACKAGE_VERSION "1.0"
/* Define to 1 if you have the ANSI C... */
#define STDC_HEADERS 1
$
```

NOTE   *Again, I encourage you to use autoreconf, which will automatically run autoheader if it notices an expansion of AC_CONFIG_HEADERS in* configure.ac.

As you can see by the output of the cat command at ❶, an entire set of preprocessor definitions was derived from *configure.ac* by autoheader.

Listing 3-21 shows a much more realistic example of using a generated *config.h* file to increase the portability of your project source code. In this example, the AC_CONFIG_HEADERS macro call indicates that *config.h* should be generated, and the call to AC_CHECK_HEADERS will cause autoheader to insert a definition into *config.h*.

```
AC_INIT([test], [1.0])
AC_CONFIG_HEADERS([config.h])
AC_CHECK_HEADERS([dlfcn.h])
AC_OUTPUT
```

Listing 3-21: A more realistic example of using AC_CONFIG_HEADERS

The *config.h* file is intended to be included in your source code in locations where you might wish to test a configured option in the code itself using the C preprocessor. This file should be included first in source files so it can influence the inclusion of system header files later in the source.

NOTE   *The* config.h.in *template that autoheader generates doesn't contain an include-guard construct, so you need to be careful that it's not included more than once in a source file.*

It's often the case that every *.c* file in a project needs to include *config.h*. In this case, it might behoove you to include *config.h* at the top of an internal project header file that's included by all the source files in your project. You can (and probably should) also add an include-guard construct to this internal header file to protect against including it more than once.

Don't make the mistake of including *config.h* in a public header file if your project installs libraries and header files as part of your product set. For more detailed information on this topic, refer to "Item 1: Keeping Private Details out of Public Interfaces" on page 272.

Using the *configure.ac* file from Listing 3-21, the generated configure script will create a *config.h* header file with appropriate definitions for determining, at compile time, whether or not the current system provides the dlfcn interface. To complete the portability check, you can add the code from Listing 3-22 to a source file in your project that uses dynamic loader functionality.

```
#if HAVE_CONFIG_H
# include <config.h>
#endif

❶ #if HAVE_DLFCN_H
# include <dlfcn.h>
#else
# error Sorry, this code requires dlfcn.h.
#endif
...
❷ #if HAVE_DLFCN_H
    handle = dlopen("/usr/lib/libwhatever.so", RTLD_NOW);
#endif
...
```

Listing 3-22: A sample source file that checks for dynamic loader functionality

If you already had code that included *dlfcn.h*, autoscan would have generated a line in *configure.ac* to call AC_CHECK_HEADERS with an argument list containing *dlfcn.h* as one of the header files to be checked. Your job as maintainer is to add the conditional statements at ❶ and ❷ to your source code around the existing inclusions of the *dlfcn.h* header file and around calls to the *dlfcn* interface functions. This is the crux of Autoconf-provided portability.

Your project might prefer dynamic loader functionality, but could get along without it if necessary. It's also possible that your project requires a dynamic loader, in which case your build should terminate with an error (as this code does) if the key functionality is missing. Often, this is an acceptable stopgap until someone comes along and adds support to the source code for a more system-specific dynamic loader service.

NOTE   *If you have to bail out with an error, it's best to do so at configuration time rather than at compile time. The general rule of thumb is to bail out as early as possible.*

One obvious flaw in this source code is that *config.h* is only included if HAVE_CONFIG_H is defined in your compilation environment. You must define HAVE_CONFIG_H manually on your compiler command lines if you're writing your own makefiles. Automake does this for you in generated *Makefile.in* templates.

HAVE_CONFIG_H is part of a string of definitions passed on the compiler command line in the Autoconf substitution variable @DEFS@. Before autoheader and AC_CONFIG_HEADERS functionality existed, Automake added all of the compiler configuration macros to the @DEFS@ variable. You can still use this method if you don't use AC_CONFIG_HEADERS in *configure.ac*, but it's not recommended— mainly because a large number of definitions make for very long compiler command lines.

Back to Remote Builds for a Moment

As we wrap up this chapter, you'll notice that we've come full circle. We started out covering some preliminary information before we discussed how to add remote builds to Jupiter. Now we'll return to this topic for a moment, because I haven't yet covered how to get the C preprocessor to properly locate a generated *config.h* file.

Since this file is generated from a template, it will be at the same relative position in the build directory structure as its counterpart template file, *config.h.in*, is in the source directory structure. The template is located in the top-level *source* directory (unless you chose to put it elsewhere), so the generated file will be in the top-level *build* directory. Well, that's easy enough—it's always one level up from the generated *src/Makefile*.

Before we draw any conclusions then about header file locations, let's consider where header files might appear in a project. We might generate them in the current build directory, as part of the build process. We might also add internal header files to the current source directory. We know we have a *config.h* file in the top-level build directory. Finally, we might also create a top-level *include* directory for library interface header files our package provides. What is the order of priority for these various *include* directories?

The order in which we place *include directives* (-I*path* options) on the compiler command line is the order in which they will be searched, so the order should be based on which files are most relevant to the source file currently being compiled. Thus, the compiler command line should include -I*path* directives for the current build directory (.) first, followed by the source directory [$(srcdir)], then the top-level build directory (..), and finally, our project's *include* directory, if it has one. We impose this ordering by adding -I*path* options to the compiler command line, as shown in Listing 3-23.

```
...
jupiter: main.c
        $(CC) -I. -I$(srcdir) -I.. $(CPPFLAGS) $(CFLAGS) -o $@ main.c
...
```

Listing 3-23: src/Makefile.in: Adding proper compiler include directives

Now that we know this, we need to add another rule of thumb for remote builds to the list we created on page 69:

- Add preprocessor commands for the current build directory, the associated source directory, and the top-level build directories, in that order.

Summary

In this chapter, we covered just about all the major features of a fully functional GNU project build system, including writing a *configure.ac* file, from which Autoconf generates a fully functional configure script. We've also covered adding remote build functionality to makefiles with VPATH statements.

So what else is there? Plenty! In the next chapter, I'll continue to show you how you can use Autoconf to test system features and functionality before your users run make. We'll also continue enhancing the configuration script so that when we're done, users will have more options and understand exactly how our package will be built on their systems.

4

MORE FUN WITH AUTOCONF: CONFIGURING USER OPTIONS

*Hope is not the conviction that something will turn out well,
but the certainty that something makes sense,
regardless of how it turns out.*
—*Václav Havel*, Disturbing the Peace

In Chapter 3, we discussed the essentials of
Autoconf—how to bootstrap a new or existing project and how to understand some of
the basic aspects of *configure.ac* files. In this chapter, we'll cover some of the more complex Autoconf
macros. We'll begin by learning how to substitute our
own variables into template files (e.g., *Makefile.in*) and how to define our own
preprocessor definitions from within the configuration script. Throughout
this chapter, we'll continue to develop functionality in the Jupiter project by
adding important checks and tests. We'll cover the all-important AC_OUTPUT
macro, and we'll conclude by discussing the application of user-defined
project configuration options as specified in the *configure.ac* file.

In addition to all this, I'll present an analysis technique that you can
use to decipher the inner workings of macros. Using the somewhat complex
AC_CHECK_PROG macro as an example, I'll show you some ways to find out what's
going on under the hood. After all, when software is distributed in source
format, its secrets can't stay hidden forever.

Substitutions and Definitions

I'll begin this chapter by discussing three of the most important macros in the Autoconf suite: AC_SUBST and AC_DEFINE, along with the latter's twin brother, AC_DEFINE_UNQUOTED.

These macros provide the primary mechanisms for communication between the configuration process and the build and execution processes. Values that are *substituted* into generated files provide configuration information to the build process, while values *defined* in preprocessor variables provide configuration information at build time to the compiler and at runtime to the built programs and libraries. As a result, it's well worth becoming thoroughly familiar with AC_SUBST and AC_DEFINE.

AC_SUBST

You can use AC_SUBST to extend the variable substitution functionality that's such an integral part of Autoconf. Every Autoconf macro that has anything to do with substitution variables ultimately calls this macro to create the substitution variable from an existing shell variable. Sometimes the shell variables are inherited from the environment; other times, higher-level macros set the shell variables as part of their functionality before calling AC_SUBST. The signature of this macro is rather trivial (note that the square brackets in this prototype represent optional arguments, not Autoconf quotes):

```
AC_SUBST(shell_var[, value])
```

NOTE *If you choose to omit any trailing optional parameters when using M4 macro calls, you may also omit the trailing commas. However, if you omit any arguments from the middle of the list, you must show the commas as placeholders for the missing arguments.*

The first argument, shell_var, represents a shell variable whose value you wish to substitute into all files generated by config.status from templates. The optional second parameter is the value assigned to the variable. If it isn't specified, the shell variable's current value will be used, whether it's inherited or set by some previous shell code.

The substitution variable will have the same name as the shell variable, except that it will be bracketed with at signs (@) in the template files. Thus, a shell variable named my_var would become a substitution variable named @my_var@, and you could use it in any template file.

Calls to AC_SUBST in *configure.ac* should not be made conditionally; that is, they should not be called within conditional shell statements like if-then-else constructs. The reason becomes clear when you carefully consider the purpose of AC_SUBST: You've already hardcoded substitution variables into your template files, so you'd better use AC_SUBST for each variable unconditionally, or else your output files will retain the substitution variables, rather than the values that should have been substituted.

AC_DEFINE

The `AC_DEFINE` and `AC_DEFINE_UNQUOTED` macros define C-preprocessor macros, which can be simple or function-like macros. These are either defined in the *config.h.in* template (if you use `AC_CONFIG_HEADERS`) or passed on the compiler command line (via the `@DEFS@` substitution variable) in *Makefile.in* templates. Recall that if you don't write *config.h.in* yourself, autoheader will write it based on calls to these macros in your *configure.ac* file.

These two macro names actually represent four different Autoconf macros. Here are their prototypes:

```
AC_DEFINE(variable, value[, description])
AC_DEFINE(variable)
AC_DEFINE_UNQUOTED(variable, value[, description])
AC_DEFINE_UNQUOTED(variable)
```

The difference between the normal and the `UNQUOTED` versions of these macros is that the normal versions use, verbatim, the specified value as the value of the preprocessor macro. The `UNQUOTED` versions perform shell expansion on the value argument, and they use the result as the value of the preprocessor macro. Thus, you should use `AC_DEFINE_UNQUOTED` if the value contains shell variables that you want configure to expand. (Setting a C-preprocessor macro in a header file to an unexpanded shell variable makes no sense, because neither the C compiler nor the preprocessor will know what to do with it when the source code is compiled.)

The difference between the single- and multi-argument versions lies in the way the preprocessor macros are defined. The single-argument versions simply guarantee that the macro is *defined* in the preprocessor namespace, while the multi-argument versions ensure that the macro is defined with a specific value.

The optional third parameter, `description`, tells autoheader to add a comment for this macro to the *config.h.in* template. (If you don't use autoheader, it makes no sense to pass a description here—hence its optional status.) If you wish to define a preprocessor macro without a value and provide a `description`, you should use the multi-argument versions of these macros, but leave the value argument empty.

Checking for Compilers

The `AC_PROG_CC` macro ensures that the user's system has a working C-language compiler. Here's the prototype for this macro:

```
AC_PROG_CC([compiler-search-list])
```

If your code requires a particular flavor or brand of C compiler, you can pass a whitespace-separated list of program names in this argument. For example, if you use `AC_PROG_CC([cc cl gcc])`, the macro expands into shell code that searches for cc, cl, and gcc, in that order. Usually, the argument is omitted, allowing the macro to find the best compiler option available on the user's system.

You'll recall from "An Even Quicker Start with autoscan" on page 71 that when autoscan noticed C source files in the directory tree, it inserted a no-argument call to this macro into Jupiter's *configure.scan* file. Listing 4-1 reproduces the relevant portion of the generated *configure.scan* file:

```
...
# Checks for programs.
AC_PROG_CC
AC_PROG_INSTALL
...
```

Listing 4-1: configure.scan: Checking for compilers and other programs

NOTE   *If the source files in Jupiter's directory tree had been suffixed with .cxx or .C (an upper-case .C extension indicates a C++ source file), autoscan would have instead inserted a call to* AC_PROG_CXX, *as well as a call to* AC_LANG([C++]).

The AC_PROG_CC macro looks for gcc and then cc in the system search path. If it doesn't find either, it looks for other C compilers. When it finds a compatible compiler, the macro sets a well-known variable, CC, to the full path of the program, with options for portability as needed.

The AC_PROG_CC macro also defines the following Autoconf substitution variables, some of which you may recognize as *user variables* (listed in Table 2-2 on page 53):

- @CC@ (full path of compiler)
- @CFLAGS@ (e.g., -g -O2 for gcc)
- @CPPFLAGS@ (empty by default)
- @EXEEXT@ (e.g., *.exe*)
- @OBJEXT@ (e.g., *.o*)

AC_PROG_CC configures these substitution variables, but unless you use them in your *Makefile.in* templates, you're just wasting time running configure. Conveniently, we're already using them in our *Makefile.in* templates, because earlier in the Jupiter project, we added them to our compiler command line and then added a default value for CFLAGS that the user could override on the make command line.

The only thing left to do is ensure that config.status substitutes values for these substitution variables. Listing 4-2 shows the relevant portions of the *src* directory *Makefile.in* template and the changes necessary to make this happen.

```
...
# Tool-specific substitution variables
CC              = @CC@
```

```
CFLAGS        = @CFLAGS@
CPPFLAGS      = @CPPFLAGS@

...
jupiter: main.c
        $(CC) $(CFLAGS) $(CPPFLAGS) -I. -I$(srcdir) -I.. -o $@ main.c
...
```

Listing 4-2: src/Makefile.in: *Using Autoconf compiler and flag substitution variables*

Checking for Other Programs

Immediately following the call to AC_PROG_CC (see Listing 4-1) is a call to
AC_PROG_INSTALL. All of the AC_PROG_* macros set (and then substitute, using
AC_SUBST) various environment variables that point to the located utilities.
AC_PROG_INSTALL does the same thing for the install utility. To use this check,
you need to use the associated Autoconf substitution variables in your *Makefile.in*
templates, just as we did above with @CC@, @CFLAGS@, and @CPPFLAGS@. Listing 4-3
illustrates these changes.

```
...
# Tool-specific substitution variables
CC              = @CC@
CFLAGS          = @CFLAGS@
CPPFLAGS        = @CPPFLAGS@
INSTALL         = @INSTALL@
INSTALL_DATA    = @INSTALL_DATA@
INSTALL_PROGRAM = @INSTALL_PROGRAM@
INSTALL_SCRIPT  = @INSTALL_SCRIPT@

...
install:
        $(INSTALL) -d $(DESTDIR)$(bindir)/jupiter
        $(INSTALL_PROGRAM) -m 0755 jupiter $(DESTDIR)$(bindir)/jupiter
...
```

Listing 4-3: src/Makefile.in: *Substituting the* install *utility in your* Makefile.in *templates*

The value of @INSTALL@ is obviously the path of the located installation
script. The value of @INSTALL_DATA@ is ${INSTALL} -m 0644. Based on this, you
might think that the values of @INSTALL_PROGRAM@ and @INSTALL_SCRIPT@ would be
something like ${INSTALL} -m 0755, but they're not. These values are set simply
to ${INSTALL}.[1]

You might also need to test for other important utility programs, including lex, yacc, sed, awk, and so on. If your program requires one or more of these
tools, you can add calls to AC_PROG_LEX, AC_PROG_YACC, AC_PROG_SED, or AC_PROG_AWK.
autoscan will add calls to AC_PROG_YACC and AC_PROG_LEX to *configure.scan* if it detects
files in your project's directory tree with *.yy* or *.ll* extensions.

---

1. Was this an oversight? I doubt it. I'd guess this was the original intention, but it was found to
cause more problems than it solved, so -m 0755 was removed.

You can check for about a dozen different programs using these more specialized macros. If a program check fails, the resulting `configure` script will fail with a message indicating that the required utility could not be found and that the build cannot continue until it's been properly installed.

The program and compiler checks cause `autoconf` to substitute specially named variables into template files. You can find the names of the variables for each macro in the *GNU Autoconf Manual*. You should use these make variables in commands within your *Makefile.in* templates to invoke the tools they represent. The Autoconf macros will set the values of these variables according to the tools it finds installed on the user's system, *if the user has not already set them in the environment.*

This is a key aspect of Autoconf-generated `configure` scripts—the user can *always* override anything `configure` will do to the environment by exporting or setting an appropriate variable before executing `configure`.[2]

For example, if the user chooses to build with a specific version of `bison` installed in his home directory, he could enter the following command in order to ensure that `$(YACC)` refers to the correct version of `bison` and that the shell code `AC_PROG_YACC` generates does little more than substitute the existing value of `YACC` for `@YACC@` in your *Makefile.in* templates:

```
$ cd jupiter
$ ./configure YACC="$HOME/bin/bison -y"
...
```

NOTE *Passing the variable setting to `configure` as a parameter is functionally similar to setting the variable for the `configure` process on the command line in the shell environment (e.g., `YACC="$HOME/bin/bison -y" configure`). The advantage of using the syntax given in the example above is that `config.status --recheck` can then track the value and properly re-execute `configure` from the makefile with the options that were originally given to it. Thus, you should always use the parameter syntax, rather than the shell environment syntax, to set variables for `configure`.*

To check for the existence of a program not covered by these more specialized macros, you can call the generic `AC_CHECK_PROG` macro or write your own special-purpose macro (see Chapter 10).

The key points to take away here are as follows:

- `AC_PROG_*` macros check for the existence of programs.
- If they find a program, a substitution variable is created.
- You should use these substitution variables in your *Makefile.in* templates to execute associated utilities.

---

2. Since users are not Autoconf experts, it's good practice to add information about variables that affect your project's configuration to your project's *README* or *INSTALL* files.

A Common Problem with Autoconf

We should take this opportunity to address a particular problem that developers new to the Autotools consistently encounter. Here's the formal definition of AC_CHECK_PROG, as you will find it in the *GNU Autoconf Manual*:

AC_CHECK_PROG(variable, prog-to-check-for, value-if-found,
    [value-if-not-found], [path], [reject])

Check whether program *prog-to-check-for* exists in *path*. If it is found, set *variable* to *value-if-found*, otherwise to *value-if-not-found*, if given. Always pass over *reject* (an absolute filename) even if it is the first found in the search path; in that case, set *variable* using the absolute filename of the *prog-to-check-for* found that is not *reject*. If *variable* was already set, do nothing. Calls AC_SUBST for *variable*.[3]

This is pretty dense language, but after a careful reading, you can extract the following from this description:

- If prog-to-check-for is found in the system search path, then variable is set to value-if-found; otherwise, it's set to value-if-not-found.

- If reject is specified (as a full path), and it's the same as the program found in the system search path in the previous step, then skip it, and continue to the next matching program in the system search path.

- If reject is found first in path, and then another match (other than reject) is found, set variable to the absolute path name of the second (non-reject) match.

- If the user has already set variable in the environment, then variable is left untouched (thereby allowing the user to override the check by setting variable before running configure).

- AC_SUBST is called on variable to make it an Autoconf substitution variable.

Upon first reading this description, there appears to be a conflict: We see in the first item that variable will be set to one of two specified values, based on whether or not prog-to-check-for is found in the system search path. But then we see in the third item that variable will be set to the full path of some program if reject is found first and skipped.

Discovering the real functionality of AC_CHECK_PROG is as easy as reading a little shell script. While you could refer to the definition of AC_CHECK_PROG in Autoconf's *programs.m4* macro file, you'll be one level removed from the actual shell code that performs the check. Wouldn't it be better to just look at the shell script that AC_CHECK_PROG generates? We'll use Jupiter's *configure.ac* file to play with this concept. Modify your *configure.ac* file according to the changes highlighted in Listing 4-4.

---

3. See section 5.2.2, Generic Program and File Checks, in version 2.64 (July 26, 2009) of the *GNU Autoconf Manual* (*http://www.gnu.org/software/autoconf/manual/index.html*).

```
...
AC_PREREQ(2.59)
AC_INIT([Jupiter], [1.0], [jupiter-bugs@example.org])
AC_CONFIG_SRCDIR([src/main.c])
AC_CONFIG_HEADER([config.h])

# Checks for programs.
AC_PROG_CC
_DEBUG_START_
AC_CHECK_PROG([bash_var], [bash], [yes], [no],, [/usr/sbin/bash])
_DEBUG_END_
AC_PROG_INSTALL
...
```

Listing 4-4: A first attempt at using AC_CHECK_PROG

Now execute autoconf, open the resulting configure script, and search for _DEBUG_START_.

NOTE   *The _DEBUG_START_ and _DEBUG_END_ strings are known as* picket fences. *I added these to* configure.ac *for the sole purpose of helping me find the beginning and end of the shell code generated by the AC_CHECK_PROG macro. I chose these macros in particular because you're not likely to find them anywhere else in the generated* configure *script.[4]*

Listing 4-5 shows the portion of configure this macro generates.

```
...
_DEBUG_START_
❶ # Extract the first word of "bash", so it can be a program name with args.
set dummy bash; ac_word=$2
echo "$as_me:$LINENO: checking for $ac_word" >&5
echo $ECHO_N "checking for $ac_word... $ECHO_C" >&6
if test "${ac_cv_prog_bash_var+set}" = set; then
  echo $ECHO_N "(cached) $ECHO_C" >&6
else if test -n "$bash_var"; then
  # Let the user override the test.
  ac_cv_prog_bash_var="$bash_var"
else
  ac_prog_rejected=no
  as_save_IFS=$IFS; IFS=$PATH_SEPARATOR
  for as_dir in $PATH
  do
    IFS=$as_save_IFS
    test -z "$as_dir" && as_dir=.
    for ac_exec_ext in ''$ac_executable_extensions;
    do
      if $as_executable_p "$as_dir/$ac_word$ac_exec_ext"; then
❷       if test "$as_dir/$ac_word$ac_exec_ext" = "/usr/sbin/bash"; then
          ac_prog_rejected=yes
          continue
```

---

4. Don't be tempted to set these *picket-fence* tokens to a value in order to keep configure from complaining about them. If you do, configure *won't* complain about them, and you might just forget to remove them.

```
           fi
           ac_cv_prog_bash_var="yes"
           echo "$as_me:$LINENO: found $as_dir/$ac_word$ac_exec_ext" >&5
           break 2
         fi
       done
     done
❸   if test $ac_prog_rejected = yes; then
       # We found a bogon in the path, so make sure we never use it.
       set dummy $ac_cv_prog_bash_var
       shift
       if test $# != 0; then
         # We chose a different compiler from the bogus one. However,
         # it has the same basename, so the bogon will be chosen first
         # if we set bash_var to just the basename; use the full file name.
         shift
         ac_cv_prog_bash_var="$as_dir/$ac_word${1+' '}$@"
       fi
     fi
   test -z "$ac_cv_prog_bash_var" && ac_cv_prog_bash_var = "no"
 fi
 fi
 bash_var=$ac_cv_prog_bash_var
 if test -n "$bash_var"; then
   echo "$as_me:$LINENO: result: $bash_var" >&5
   echo "${ECHO_T}$bash_var" >&6
 else
   echo "$as_me:$LINENO: result: no" >&5
   echo "${ECHO_T}no" >&6
 fi
 _DEBUG_END_
 ...
```

Listing 4-5: A portion of configure generated by AC_CHECK_PROG

The opening comment at ❶ in this shell script is a clue that AC_CHECK_PROG
has some undocumented functionality. Apparently, you may pass in arguments
along with the program name in the prog-to-check-for parameter. Shortly,
we'll look at a situation in which you might want to do that.

Farther down in the script at ❷, you can see that the reject parameter
was added into the mix in order to allow configure to search for a particular
version of a tool. From the code at ❸, we can see that bash_var can have three
different values: Empty if the requested program is not found in the path,
the program specified if it's found, or the full path of the program specified
if reject is found first.

Where do you use reject? Well, for instance, on Solaris systems with
proprietary Sun tools installed, the default C compiler is often the Solaris C
compiler. But some users may want to use the GNU C compiler rather than
the Solaris C compiler. As maintainers, we don't know which compiler will be
found first in a user's search path. AC_CHECK_PROG allows us to ensure that gcc is
used with a full path if another C compiler is found first in the search path.

M4 macros are aware of the fact that arguments are given, empty, or missing, and they do different things based on these conditions. Many of the standard Autoconf macros are written to take full advantage of empty or unspecified optional arguments and generate entirely different shell code in each of these conditions. Autoconf macros may also optimize the generated shell code for these different conditions.

Given what we now know, we probably should have called AC_CHECK_PROG in this manner, instead:

```
AC_CHECK_PROG([bash_shell],[bash -x],[bash -x],,,[/usr/sbin/bash])
```

You can see in this example that the manual is technically accurate. If reject is not specified and bash is found in the system path, then bash_shell will be set to bash -x. If bash is *not* found in the system path, then bash_shell will be set to the empty string. If, on the other hand, reject *is* specified, and the undesired version of bash is found *first* in the path, then bash_shell will be set to the full path of the *next* version found in the path, along with the originally specified argument (-x). The reason the macro uses the full path in this case is to make sure that configure will avoid executing the version that was found first in the path—reject. The rest of the configuration script can now use the bash_shell variable to run the desired bash shell, as long as it doesn't test out empty.

Checks for Libraries and Header Files

The decision of whether or not to use an external library in a project is a tough one. On one hand, you want to reuse existing code to provide required functionality instead of writing it yourself. Reuse is one of the hallmarks of the open source software world. On the other hand, you don't want to depend on functionality that may not exist on all target platforms or that may require significant porting in order to make the libraries you need available where you need them.

Occasionally, library-based functionality can differ in minor ways between platforms. Although the functionality may be essentially equivalent, the libraries may have different package names or different API signatures. The POSIX threads (*pthreads*) library, for example, is similar in functionality to many native threading libraries, but the libraries' APIs are usually different in minor ways, and their package names are almost always different. Consider what would happen if we tried to build a multithreaded project on a system that didn't support *pthreads*; in a case like this, you might want to use the *libthreads* library on Solaris instead.

Autoconf library selection macros allow generated configuration scripts to intelligently select the libraries that provide the necessary functionality, even if those libraries are named differently between platforms. To illustrate the use of the Autoconf library selection macros, we'll add some trivial (and fairly contrived) multithreading capabilities to the Jupiter project that will allow jupiter to print its message using a background thread. We'll use the *pthreads* API as our base threading model. In order to accomplish this with our Autoconf-based configuration script, we need to add the *pthreads* library to our project build system.

NOTE *The proper use of multithreading requires the definition of additional substitution variables containing appropriate flags, libraries, and definitions. The* ACX_PTHREAD *macro does all of this for you. You can find the documentation for* ACX_PTHREAD *at the Autoconf Macro Archive website.[5] See "Doing Threads the Right Way" on page 210 for examples of using* ACX_PTHREAD.

First, let's tackle the changes to the source code. We'll modify *main.c* so that the message is printed by a secondary thread, as shown in Listing 4-6.

```
#include <stdio.h>
#include <stdlib.h>
#include <pthread.h>

static void * print_it(void * data)
{
    printf("Hello from %s!\n", (const char *)data);
    return 0;
}

int main(int argc, char * argv[])
{
    pthread_t tid;
    pthread_create(&tid, 0, print_it, argv[0]);
    pthread_join(tid, 0);
    return 0;
}
```

Listing 4-6: src/main.c: Adding multithreading to the Jupiter project source code

This is clearly a ridiculous use of a thread; nevertheless, it *is* the prototypical form of thread usage. Consider a hypothetical situation in which the background thread performs some long calculation, and main is doing other things while print_it is working. On a multiprocessor machine, using a thread in this manner could literally double a program's throughput.

Now all we need is a way to determine which libraries should be added to the compiler command line. If we weren't using Autoconf, we'd just add the library to our linker command line in the makefile, as shown in Listing 4-7.

```
program: main.c
        $(CC) ... -lpthread ...
```

Listing 4-7: Manually adding the pthreads library to the compiler command line

Instead, we'll use the Autoconf-provided AC_SEARCH_LIBS macro, an enhanced version of the basic AC_CHECK_LIB macro. The AC_SEARCH_LIBS macro allows us to test for required functionality within a list of libraries. If the functionality exists in one of the specified libraries, then an appropriate command-line

---

5. See *http://www.nongnu.org/autoconf-archive/acx_pthread.html.*

option is added to the @LIBS@ substitution variable, which we would then use in a *Makefile.in* template on the compiler (linker) command line. Here is the formal definition of AC_SEARCH_LIBS from the *GNU Autoconf Manual*:

```
AC_SEARCH_LIBS(function, search-libs,
    [action-if-found], [action-if-not-found], [other-libraries])
```

Search for a library defining *function* if it's not already available. This equates to calling 'AC_LINK_IFELSE([AC_LANG_CALL([], [*function*])])' first with no libraries, then for each library listed in *search-libs*.

Add '-l*library*' to LIBS for the first library found to contain *function*, and run *action-if-found*. If *function* is not found, run *action-if-not-found*.

If linking with *library* results in unresolved symbols that would be resolved by linking with additional libraries, give those libraries as the *other-libraries* argument, separated by spaces: e.g., '-lXt -lX11'. Otherwise, this macro fails to detect that *function* is present, because linking the test program always fails with unresolved symbols.[6]

Can you see why the generated configuration script is so large? When you pass a particular function in a call to AC_SEARCH_LIBS, linker command-line arguments are added to a substitution variable called @LIBS@. These arguments ensure that you will link with a library that contains the function passed in. If multiple libraries are listed in the second parameter, separated by whitespace, configure will determine which of these libraries are available on your user's system and use the most appropriate one.

Listing 4-8 shows how to use AC_SEARCH_LIBS in Jupiter's *configure.ac* file to find the library that contains the pthread_create function. AC_SEARCH_LIBS won't add anything to the @LIBS@ variable if it doesn't find pthread_create in the *pthreads* library.

```
...
# Checks for libraries.
AC_SEARCH_LIBS([pthread_create], [pthread])
...
```

Listing 4-8: configure.ac: Using AC_SEARCH_LIBS to check for the pthreads library on the system

As we'll discuss in detail in Chapter 7, naming patterns for libraries differ between systems. For example, some systems name libraries *lib*basename.*so*, while others use *lib*basename.*sa* or *lib*basename.*a*. AC_SEARCH_LIBS addresses this situation (quite elegantly) by using the compiler to calculate the actual name of the library from its *basename*; it does this by attempting to link a small test program with the requested function from the test library. Only -l*basename* is passed on the compiler command line—a near-universal convention among Unix compilers.

---

6. See section 5.4, Library Files in version 2.64 (July 26, 2009) of the *GNU Autoconf Manual* (*http://www.gnu.org/software/autoconf/manual/index.html*).

We'll have to modify *src/Makefile.in* again in order to properly use the now-populated @LIBS@ variable, as shown in Listing 4-9.

```
...
# Tool-related substitution variables
CC           = @CC@
LIBS         = @LIBS@
CFLAGS       = @CFLAGS@
CPPFLAGS     = @CPPFLAGS@

...
jupiter: main.c
        $(CC) $(CFLAGS) $(CPPFLAGS) -I. -I$(srcdir) -I.. -o $@ main.c $(LIBS)
...
```

Listing 4-9: src/Makefile.in: Using the @LIBS@ substitution variable

NOTE *I added $(LIBS) after the source files on the compiler command line because the linker cares about object file order—it searches files for required functions in the order they are specified on the command line.*

I want *main.c* to be the primary source of object code for jupiter, so I'll continue to add additional objects, including libraries, to the command line after this file.

Is It Right or Just Good Enough?

At this point, we've ensured that our build system will properly use *pthreads* on most systems.[7] If our system needs a particular library, that library's name will be added to the @LIBS@ variable and then subsequently used on the compiler command line. But we're not done yet.

This system *usually* works fine, but it still fails in corner cases. Because we want to provide an excellent user experience, we'll take Jupiter's build system to the next level. In doing this, we need to make a design decision: In case configure fails to locate a *pthreads* library on a user's system, should we fail the build process or build a jupiter program without multithreading?

If we choose to fail the build, the user will notice, because the build will stop with an error message. (Though it may not be a very user-friendly one—either the compile or link process will fail with a cryptic error message about a missing header file or an undefined symbol.) On the other hand, if we choose to build a single-threaded version of jupiter, we'll need to display some clear message that the program is being built without multithreading functionality, and explain why.

---

7. My choice of *pthreads* as an example is perhaps unfortunate, because adding multithreading to an application often requires more than simply adding a single library to the command line. Many platforms require additional compiler options (e.g., -mthreads, -pthreads, -qthreads, and so on), libraries, and C-preprocessor definitions in order to enable multithreading in an application. Some platforms even require a completely different compiler (for instance, AIX requires the use of the cc_r alias). The examples in this book happen to work fine, even on platforms that require these switches, only because they don't make extensive use of the standard C library.

One potential problem is that some users' systems may have a *pthreads* shared library installed, but they don't have the *pthread.h* header file installed—most likely because the *pthreads* executable (shared-library) package was installed, but the developer package wasn't. Shared libraries are often packaged independently of static libraries and header files, and while executables are installed as part of a dependency chain for higher-level applications, developer packages are typically installed directly by a user.[8] For this reason, Autoconf provides macros to test for the existence of both libraries and header files. We can use the AC_CHECK_HEADERS macro to ensure the existence of a particular header file.

Autoconf checks are very thorough. They usually not only ensure that a file exists but also that the file is the correct one, because they allow you to specify assertions about the file that the macro then verifies. The AC_CHECK_HEADERS macro doesn't just scan the filesystem for the requested header. Like AC_SEARCH_LIBS, AC_CHECK_HEADERS builds a short test program in the appropriate language and then compiles it to ensure that the compiler can both find and use the file. In essence, Autoconf macros try to test not just for the existence of specific features but for the functionality required from those features.

The AC_CHECK_HEADERS macro is defined in the *GNU Autoconf Manual* as follows:

```
AC_CHECK_HEADERS(header-file..., [action-if-found],
    [action-if-not-found], [includes = 'default-includes'])
```

For each given system header file *header-file* in the blank-separated argument list that exists, define HAVE_*header-file* (in all capitals). If *action-if-found* is given, it is additional shell code to execute when one of the header files is found. You can give it a value of 'break' to break out of the loop on the first match. If *action-if-not-found* is given, it is executed when one of the header files is not found.[9]

Normally, AC_CHECK_HEADERS is called only with a list of desired header files in the first argument. The remaining arguments are optional and are not often used, because the macro works pretty well without them.

We'll add a check for the *pthread.h* header file to *configure.ac* using AC_CHECK_HEADERS. As you may have noticed, *configure.ac* already calls AC_CHECK_HEADERS looking for *stdlib.h*. AC_CHECK_HEADERS accepts a list of file names, so we'll just add *pthread.h* to the list, using a space to separate the filenames, as shown in Listing 4-10.

```
...
# Checks for header files.
AC_CHECK_HEADERS([stdlib.h pthread.h])
...
```

Listing 4-10: configure.ac: Adding pthread.h to the AC_CHECK_HEADERS macro

---

8. The *pthreads* library is so important on most systems that the developer package is often installed by default, even on basic installations of Linux or other modern Unix operating systems.

9. See section 5.6.3, Generic Header Checks in version 2.64 (July 26, 2009) of the *GNU Autoconf Manual* (*http://www.gnu.org/software/autoconf/manual/index.html*).

In order to make this package available to as many people as possible, we'll use the dual-mode build approach, which will allow us to provide at least *some* form of the jupiter program to users without a *pthreads* library. In order to accomplish this, we need to add some conditional preprocessor statements to *src/main.c*, as shown in Listing 4-11.

```
#if HAVE_CONFIG_H
# include <config.h>
#endif

#include <stdio.h>
#include <stdlib.h>

#if HAVE_PTHREAD_H
# include <pthread.h>
#endif

static void * print_it(void * data)
{
    printf("Hello from %s!\n", (const char *)data);
    return 0;
}

int main(int argc, char * argv[])
{
#if HAVE_PTHREAD_H
    pthread_t tid;
    pthread_create(&tid, 0, print_it, argv[0]);
    pthread_join(tid, 0);
#else
    print_it(argv[0]);
#endif
    return 0;
}
```

Listing 4-11: src/main.c: Adding conditional code, based on the existence of pthread.h

In this version of *main.c*, we've added a couple of conditional checks for the header file. If the shell script generated by AC_CHECK_HEADERS locates the *pthread.h* header file, the HAVE_PTHREAD_H macro will be defined to the value 1 in the user's *config.h* file. If the shell script doesn't find the header file, the definition will be added as a comment in *config.h*. Because we rely on these definitions, we also need to include *config.h* at the top of *main.c*.

Recall that HAVE_CONFIG_H must be defined on the compiler command line and that Autoconf populates the @DEFS@ substitution variable with this definition if *config.h* is available. If you choose not to use the AC_CONFIG_HEADERS macro in *configure.ac*, then @DEFS@ will contain all the definitions generated by all the macros that call AC_DEFINE. In this example, we've used AC_CONFIG_HEADERS, so *config.h.in* will contain most of these definitions, and @DEFS@ will only contain HAVE_CONFIG_H. The *config.h.in* template method significantly shortens the compiler command line (and also makes it simple to take a snapshot of the template and modify it by hand for non-Autotools platforms). Listing 4-12 shows the required changes to the *src/Makefile.in* template.

```
...
# Tool-related substitution variables
CC            = @CC@
DEFS          = @DEFS@
LIBS          = @LIBS@
CFLAGS        = @CFLAGS@
CPPFLAGS      = @CPPFLAGS@

...
jupiter: main.c
        $(CC) $(CFLAGS) $(DEFS) $(CPPFLAGS) -I. -I$(srcdir) -I.. \
          -o $@ main.c $(LIBS)
...
```

Listing 4-12: src/Makefile.in: Adding the use of @DEFS@ to the src-level makefile

NOTE   *I've added $(DEFS) before $(CPPFLAGS), giving the end user the option to override any of my policy decisions on the command line.*

We now have everything we need to conditionally build the jupiter program. If the user's system has *pthreads* functionality installed, he'll automatically build a version of jupiter that uses multiple threads of execution; otherwise, he'll have to settle for serialized execution. The only thing left to do is to add some code to *configure.ac* that will display a message during configuration indicating that, if it can't find the *pthreads* library, it will build a program that uses serialized execution.

Now, consider the unlikely scenario of a user who has the header file installed but doesn't have the library. For example, if the user executes configure with CPPFLAGS=-I/usr/local/include but neglects to add LDFLAGS=-L/usr/local/lib, it will seem to configure that the header is available, but the library is missing. This condition is easily remedied by simply skipping the header file check entirely if configure can't find the library. Listing 4-13 shows the required changes to *configure.ac*.

```
...
# Checks for libraries.
have_pthreads=no
AC_SEARCH_LIBS([pthread_create], [pthread], [have_pthreads=yes])

# Checks for header files.
AC_CHECK_HEADERS([stdlib.h])

if test "x${have_pthreads}" = xyes; then
    AC_CHECK_HEADERS([pthread.h], [], [have_pthreads=no])
fi

if test "x${have_pthreads}" = xno; then
    AC_MSG_WARN([
```

```
    -----------------------------------------
    Unable to find pthreads on this system.
    Building a single-threaded version.
    -----------------------------------------])
fi
...
```

Listing 4-13: configure.ac: Adding code to indicate that multithreading is not available during configuration

Now, when we run autoreconf and configure, we'll see some additional output (highlighted here):

```
$ autoreconf
$ ./configure
checking for gcc... gcc
...
checking for library containing pthread_create... -lpthread
...
checking pthread.h usability... yes
checking pthread.h presence... yes
checking for pthread.h... yes
configure: creating ./config.status
config.status: creating Makefile
config.status: creating src/Makefile
config.status: creating config.h
$
```

If a user's system is missing the *pthreads* library, he'd see different output. To emulate this for testing purposes, we can rename the *pthreads* libraries (both shared and static), and then execute configure again. (Don't forget to restore their proper names after you've finished running this test.)

```
$ su
Password: ******
# mv /usr/lib/libpthread.so ...
# mv /usr/lib/libpthread.a ...
# exit
$ ./configure
checking for gcc... gcc
...
checking for library containing pthread_create... no
...
checking for stdint.h... yes
checking for unistd.h... yes
checking for stdlib.h... (cached) yes
configure: WARNING:
    -----------------------------------------
    Unable to find pthreads on this system.
    Building a single-threaded version.
    -----------------------------------------
configure: creating ./config.status
config.status: creating Makefile
```

```
config.status: creating src/Makefile
config.status: creating config.h
```

Had we chosen to fail the build if the *pthread.h* header file or the *pthreads* libraries were not found, then the source code would have been simpler; there would have been no need for conditional compilation. In that case, we could change *configure.ac* to look like Listing 4-14.

```
...
# Checks for libraries.
have_pthreads=no
AC_SEARCH_LIBS([pthread_create], [pthread], [have_pthreads=yes])

# Checks for header files.
AC_CHECK_HEADERS([stdlib.h])

if test "x${have_pthreads}" = xyes; then
    AC_CHECK_HEADERS([pthread.h], [], [have_pthreads=no])
fi

if test "x${have_pthreads}" = xno; then
    AC_MSG_ERROR([

-------------------------------------------
    The pthread library and header file
    required to build jupiter. Stopping...
    Check 'config.log' for more information.
-------------------------------------------])
fi
...
```

Listing 4-14: Failing the build if no pthreads library is found

NOTE *Autoconf macros generate shell code that checks for the existence of system features and sets variables based on these tests. However, it's up to you as maintainer to add shell code to* configure.ac *that makes functional decisions based on the contents of the resulting variables.*

Printing Messages

In the preceding examples, we used a few Autoconf macros to display messages to the user during configuration: AC_MSG_WARN and AC_MSG_ERROR. Here are the prototypes for the various AC_MSG_* macros provided by Autoconf:

```
AC_MSG_CHECKING(feature-description)
AC_MSG_RESULT(result-description)
AC_MSG_NOTICE(message)
AC_MSG_ERROR(error-description[, exit-status])
AC_MSG_FAILURE(error-description[, exit-status])
AC_MSG_WARN(problem-description)
```

The `AC_MSG_CHECKING` and `AC_MSG_RESULT` macros are designed to be used together. The `AC_MSG_CHECKING` macro prints a line indicating that it's checking for a particular feature, but it doesn't print a carriage return at the end of this line. Once the feature has been found (or not found) on the user's machine, the `AC_MSG_RESULT` macro prints the result at the end of the line, followed by a carriage return that completes the line started by `AC_MSG_CHECKING`. The *result* text should make sense in the context of the *checking* message. For instance, the message `Looking for a C compiler. . .` might be terminated either with the name of the compiler found or with the text `not found`.

The `AC_MSG_NOTICE` and `AC_MSG_WARN` macros simply print a string to the screen. The leading text for `AC_MSG_WARN` is `configure: WARNING:`, while that of `AC_MSG_NOTICE` is simply `configure:`.

The `AC_MSG_ERROR` and `AC_MSG_FAILURE` macros generate an error message, stop the configuration process, and return an error code to the shell. The leading text for `AC_MSG_ERROR` is `configure: error:`. `AC_MSG_FAILURE` prints a line indicating the directory in which the error occurred, the user-specified message, and then the line, `See 'config.log' for more details.`. The optional second parameter (`exit-status`) in these macros allows the maintainer to specify a particular status code to be returned to the shell. The default value is 1.

The text messages output by these macros are displayed to `stdout` and sent to the *config.log* file, so it's important to use these macros instead of simply using shell `echo` or `print` statements.

Supplying multiple lines of text in the first argument of these macros is especially important in the case of warning messages that merely indicate that the build is continuing with limitations. On a fast build machine in a large configuration process, a single-line warning message could zip right past without even being noticed by the user. This is less of a problem in cases where `configure` terminates with an error, because the user will easily discover the issue at the end of the output.[10]

Supporting Optional Features and Packages

I've discussed the different ways to handle situations when a *pthreads* library exists and when it doesn't. But what if a user wants to build a single-threaded version of jupiter when the *pthreads* library *is* installed? We certainly don't want to add a note to Jupiter's `README` file telling the user to rename his *pthreads* libraries!

---

10. There is a very strong sentiment on the Autoconf mailing list that you should *not* generate multiline messages. The reasons given are many and varied, but they ultimately all boil down to one: Many larger projects already generate thousands of lines of configuration output. Much work has gone into making Autoconf-generated configuration scripts as quiet as possible, but they're still not very quiet. My best advice is to use multiline messages in situations where there is simply no other way to effectively notify a user of an important issue, such as building on a platform with unexpected limitations. Many is the time I've finished a 15-minute build only to find that `configure` notified me in the first minute that the resulting binaries would be missing functionality that I needed.

Autoconf provides two macros for working with optional features and external software packages: AC_ARG_ENABLE and AC_ARG_WITH. Their prototypes are as follows:

```
AC_ARG_WITH(package, help-string, [action-if-given], [action-if-not-given])
AC_ARG_ENABLE(feature, help-string, [action-if-given], [action-if-not-given])
```

As with many Autoconf macros, these two may be used simply to set some environment variables:

- AC_ARG_WITH: ${withval} and ${with_*package*}
- AC_ARG_ENABLE: ${enableval} and ${enable_*feature*}

The macros can also be used in a more complex form, where the environment variables are used by shell script in the macros' optional arguments. In either case, the resulting variable must be used in *configure.ac*, or it will be pointless to perform the check.

The macros are designed to add the options --enable-*feature*[=yes|no] and --with-*package*[=arg] to the generated configuration script's command-line interface, along with appropriate help text to the output generated when the user enters configure --help. If the user gives these options, the macros set the above environment variables within the script. (The values of these variables may be used later in the script to set or clear various preprocessor definitions or substitution variables.)

AC_ARG_WITH controls your project's use of optional external software packages, while AC_ARG_ENABLE controls the inclusion or exclusion of optional software features. The choice to use one or the other is often a matter of perspective on the software you're considering, and sometimes it's simply a matter of preference, as these macros provide somewhat overlapping sets of functionality.

For instance, in the Jupiter project, it could be justifiably argued that Jupiter's use of *pthreads* constitutes the use of an external software package, so you'd use AC_ARG_WITH. However, it could also be said that *asynchronous processing* is a software feature that might be enabled via AC_ARG_ENABLE. In fact, both of these statements are true, and which option you use should be dictated by a high-level architectural perspective of the feature or package to which you're providing optional access. The *pthreads* library supplies more than just thread-creation functions—it also provides mutexes and condition variables, both of which may be used by a library package that doesn't create threads. If a project provides a library that needs to act in a thread-safe manner within a multithreaded process, then it will probably use mutex objects from the *pthreads* library, but it may never create a thread. Thus, a user may choose to disable asynchronous execution as a feature at configuration time, but the project will still need to link the *pthreads* library in order to access the mutex functionality. In such cases, it makes more sense to specify --enable-async-exec than --with-pthreads.

In general, you should use AC_ARG_WITH when the user needs to choose between implementations of a feature provided by different packages or internally within the project. For instance, if jupiter had some reason to encrypt a file, it might be written to use either an internal encryption algorithm or an external encryption library. The default configuration might use an internal algorithm, but the package might allow the user to override the default with a command-line option, --with-libcrypto. When it comes to security, the use of a widely understood library can really help your package gain community trust. Offering your users a choice like this can encourage them to try your package.

Coding Up the Feature Option

Having decided to use AC_ARG_ENABLE, how do we enable or disable the async-exec feature by default? The difference in how these two cases are encoded in *configure.ac* is limited to the help text and the shell script passed in the action-if-not-given argument. The help text describes the available options and the default value, and the shell script indicates what we want to happen if the option is *not* specified. (Of course, if it is specified, we don't need to assume anything.)

Say we decide that asynchronous execution is a risky or experimental feature that we want to disable by default. In this situation, we could add the code shown in Listing 4-15 to *configure.ac*.

```
...
AC_ARG_ENABLE([async-exec],
    [  --enable-async-exec      enable async exec],
    [async_exec=${enableval}], [async_exec=no])
...
```

Listing 4-15: Feature disabled by default

On the other hand, if we decide that asynchronous execution is fundamental to Jupiter, we should probably enable it by default, as in Listing 4-16.

```
...
AC_ARG_ENABLE([async-exec],
    [  --disable-async-exec     disable async exec],
    [async_exec=${enableval}], [async_exec=yes])
...
```

Listing 4-16: Feature enabled by default

Now, the question is, do we check for the library and header file regardless of the user's desire for this feature, or do we only check for them if the async-exec feature is enabled? In this case, it's a matter of preference, because we're using the *pthreads* library only for this feature. (If we were also using it for non-feature-specific reasons, we'd have to check for it in either case.)

In cases where we need the library even if the feature is disabled, we would add the AC_ARG_ENABLE macro call, as in the example above, and an additional call to AC_DEFINE to create a *config.h* definition specifically for this feature. Since we don't really want to enable the feature if the library or header file is missing—even if the user specifically requested it—we'll also add some shell code to turn the feature off if either is missing, as shown in Listing 4-17.

```
...
# Checks for command-line options
AC_ARG_ENABLE([async-exec],
    [  --disable-async-exec    disable async execution feature],
    [async_exec=${enableval}], [async_exec=yes])

have_pthreads=no
AC_SEARCH_LIBS([pthread_create], [pthread], [have_pthreads=yes])

if test "x${have_pthreads}" = xyes; then
    AC_CHECK_HEADERS([pthread.h], [], [have_pthreads=no])
fi

if test "x${have_pthreads}" = xno; then
❶    if test "x${async_exec}" = xyes; then
        AC_MSG_WARN([
    -----------------------------------------
    Unable to find pthreads on this system.
    Building a single-threaded version.
    -----------------------------------------])
    fi
    async_exec=no
fi

if test "x${async_exec}" = xyes; then
    AC_DEFINE([ASYNC_EXEC], 1, [async execution enabled])
fi
...
```

Listing 4-17: configure.ac: Properly managing an optional feature during configuration

Notice that at ❶ I've also added an additional test for a yes value in the async_exec variable, because this text really belongs to the feature test, not to the *pthreads* library test. Remember, we're trying to create a logical separation between testing for *pthreads* functionality and testing for the requirements of the async-exec feature itself.

Of course, now we also have to modify *src/main.c* to use the new definition, as shown in Listing 4-18.

```
...
#if HAVE_PTHREAD_H
# include <pthread.h>
#endif

static void * print_it(void * data)
{
    printf("Hello from %s!\n", (const char *)data);
    return 0;
}
```

```
int main(int argc, char * argv[])
{
#if ASYNC_EXEC
    pthread_t tid;
    pthread_create(&tid, 0, print_it, argv[0]);
    pthread_join(tid, 0);
#else
    print_it(argv[0]);
#endif
    return 0;
}
```

Listing 4-18: src/main.c: *Changing the conditional around async-exec–specific code*

Notice that we've left the HAVE_PTHREAD_H check around the inclusion of the header file in order to facilitate the use of *pthread.h* in ways besides those required by this feature.

In order to check for the library and header file only if the feature is enabled, we wrap the original check code in a test of async_exec, as shown in Listing 4-19.

```
...
if test "x${async_exec}" = xyes; then
    have_pthreads=no
    AC_SEARCH_LIBS([pthread_create], [pthread], [have_pthreads=yes])

    if test "x${have_pthreads}" = xyes; then
        AC_CHECK_HEADERS([pthread.h], [], [have_pthreads=no])
    fi

    if test "x${have_pthreads}" = xno; then
        AC_MSG_WARN([
-----------------------------------------
Unable to find pthreads on this system.
Building a single-threaded version.
-----------------------------------------])
        async_exec=no
    fi
fi

if test "x${async_exec}" = xyes; then
    AC_DEFINE([ASYNC_EXEC], 1, [async execution enabled])
fi
...
```

Listing 4-19: configure.ac: *Checking for the library and header file only if a feature is enabled*

This time, we've removed the test for async_exec from the echo statements by moving the original check from around the echo statements to around the entire set of checks.

Formatting Help Strings

We'll make one final change to our use of AC_ARG_ENABLE in Listing 4-17. Notice that in the second argument, there are exactly two spaces between the open square bracket and the start of the argument text. You'll also notice that the number of spaces between the argument and the description depends on the length of the argument text, because the description text is supposed to be presented to the user aligned with a particular column. There are four spaces between --disable-async-exec and the description, but there are five spaces after --enable-async-exec, because the word *enable* is one character shorter than the word *disable*.

But what if the Autoconf project maintainers decide to change the format of the help text for configuration scripts? Or what if you modify your option name but forget to adjust the indentation on your help text?

To solve this potential problem, we'll turn to an Autoconf helper macro called AS_HELP_STRING, whose prototype is as follows:

```
AS_HELP_STRING(left-hand-side, right-hand-side,
    [indent-column = '26'], [wrap-column = '79'])
```

This macro's sole purpose is to abstract away knowledge about the number of spaces that should be embedded in the help text at various places. To use it, replace the second argument in AC_ARG_ENABLE with a call to AS_HELP_STRING, as shown in Listing 4-20.

```
...
AC_ARG_ENABLE([async-exec],
    [AS_HELP_STRING([--disable-async-exec],
        [disable asynchronous execution @<:@default: no@:>@])],
    [async_exec=${enableval}], [async_exec=yes])
...
```

Listing 4-20: configure.ac: *Using AS_HELP_STRING*

Checks for Type and Structure Definitions

Now let's consider how we might test for system- or compiler-provided type and structure definitions. When writing cross-platform networking software, one quickly learns that the data sent between machines needs to be formatted in a way that doesn't depend on a particular CPU or operating system architecture. Some systems' native integer sizes are 32 bits, while others' are 64 bits. Some systems store integer values in memory and on disk from least-significant byte to most-significant byte, while others do the reverse.

Let's consider an example. When using C-language structures to format network messages, one of the first roadblocks you'll encounter is the lack of basic C-language types that have the same size from one platform to another. A CPU with a 32-bit machine word size would likely have a C compiler with 32-bit int and unsigned types. The sizes of the basic integer types in the C language are implementation defined. This is by design, in order to allow implementations to use sizes for char, short, int, and long that are optimal for each platform.

While this language feature is great for optimizing software designed to run on one platform, it's not very helpful when choosing types to move data *between* platforms. In order to address this problem, engineers have tried everything from sending network data as strings (think XML), to inventing their own sized types.

In an attempt to remedy this shortcoming in the language, the C99 standard provides the sized types int*N*_t and uint*N*_t, where *N* may be 8, 16, 32, or 64. Unfortunately, not all of today's compilers provide these types. (Not surprisingly, GNU C has been at the forefront for some time now, providing C99-sized types with the inclusion of the new *stdint.h* header file.)

To alleviate the pain to some extent, Autoconf provides macros for determining whether C99-specific standardized types exist on a user's platform, and defining them if they don't exist. For example, you can add a call to AC_TYPE_UINT16_T to *configure.ac* in order to ensure that uint16_t exists on your users' platforms, either as a system definition in *stdint.h* or (the non-standard but more prolific) *inttypes.h*, or as an Autoconf definition in *config.h*.

The compiler tests for such integer-based types are typically written by a generated configuration script as a bit of C code that looks like the code shown in Listing 4-21.

```
int main()
{
❶    static int test_array[1 - 2 * !((uint16_t) -1 >> (16 - 1) == 1)];
     test_array[0] = 1;
     return 0;
}
```

Listing 4-21: A compiler check for a proper implementation of uint16_t

You'll notice that the important line in Listing 4-21 is the one at ❶ in which test_array is declared. Autoconf is relying on the fact that all C compilers will generate an error if you attempt to define an array with a negative size. If uint16_t isn't exactly 16 bits of unsigned data on this platform, the array size will be negative.

Notice, too, that the bracketed expression in the listing is a compile-time expression.[11] Whether this could have been done with simpler syntax is anyone's guess, but this code does the trick on all the compilers Autoconf supports. The array is defined with a nonnegative size only if the following three conditions are met:

- uint16_t is defined in one of the included header files.
- The size of uint16_t is exactly 16 bits.
- uint16_t is unsigned on this platform.

---

11. It would have to be a compile-time expression, anyway, as C-language array sizes must be statically defined.

Follow the pattern shown in Listing 4-22 to use the definitions provided by this macro. Even on systems where *stdint.h* or *inttypes.h* are not available, Autoconf will add code to *config.h* that will define uint16_t if the system header files don't provide it, so you can use the type in your source code without additional tests.

```
#if HAVE_CONFIG_H
# include <config.h>
#endif

#if HAVE_STDINT_H
# include <stdint.h>
#elif HAVE_INTTYPES_H
# include <inttypes.h>
#endif
...
uint16_t x;
...
```

Listing 4-22: Source code that properly uses Autoconf's uint16_t definitions

Autoconf offers a few dozen type checks like AC_TYPE_UINT16_T, as detailed in Section 5.9 of the *GNU Autoconf Manual*. In addition, a generic type check macro, AC_CHECK_TYPES, allows you to specify a comma-separated list of questionable types that your project needs.

NOTE   *This list is comma-separated because some definitions (like struct fooble) may have embedded spaces. Since they are comma-delimited, you* must *use Autoconf's square-bracket quotes around this parameter if you list more than one type.*

Here is the formal declaration of AC_CHECK_TYPES:

```
AC_CHECK_TYPES(types, [action-if-found], [action-if-not-found],
    [includes = 'default-includes'])
```

If you don't specify a list of header files in the last parameter, the default headers will be used in the compiler test by way of the macro AC_INCLUDES_DEFAULT, which expands to the text shown in Listing 4-23.

```
#include <stdio.h>
#ifdef HAVE_SYS_TYPES_H
# include <sys/types.h>
#endif
#ifdef HAVE_SYS_STAT_H
# include <sys/stat.h>
#endif
#ifdef STDC_HEADERS
# include <stdlib.h>
# include <stddef.h>
```

```
#else
# ifdef HAVE_STDLIB_H
# include <stdlib.h>
# endif
#endif
#ifdef HAVE_STRING_H
# if !defined STDC_HEADERS && defined HAVE_MEMORY_H
# include <memory.h>
# endif
# include <string.h>
#endif
#ifdef HAVE_STRINGS_H
# include <strings.h>
#endif
#ifdef HAVE_INTTYPES_H
# include <inttypes.h>
#endif
#ifdef HAVE_STDINT_H
# include <stdint.h>
#endif
#ifdef HAVE_UNISTD_H
# include <unistd.h>
#endif
```

Listing 4-23: The definition of AC_INCLUDES_DEFAULT, as of Autoconf version 2.64

If you know that your type is not defined in one of these header files, you should specify one or more header files to be included in the test, as shown in Listing 4-24. This listing includes the default header files first, followed by the additional header files (which will often need some of the defaults anyway).

```
  AC_CHECK_TYPES([struct doodah], [], [], [
❶ AC_INCLUDES_DEFAULT
#include<doodah.h>
#include<doodahday.h>])
```

Listing 4-24: Using a non-default set of includes in the check for struct doodah

Notice at ❶ in Listing 4-24 that I've wrapped the last parameter of the macro over three lines in *configure.ac*, without indentation. This text is included verbatim in the test source file, and because some older compilers have a problem with placing the hash mark in a preprocessor statement anywhere other than the first column, it's a good idea to tell Autoconf to start each #include line in column one in this manner.

NOTE   *These are the sorts of things that developers complain about with regard to Autoconf. When you have problems with such syntax, check the* config.log *file for the complete source code for all failed tests, including the compiler output generated during compilation of the test. This information often provides the solution to your problem.*

The AC_OUTPUT Macro

Finally, we come to the AC_OUTPUT macro, which expands, within configure, into shell code that generates the config.status script based on the data specified in the previous macro expansions. All other macros must be used before AC_OUTPUT is expanded, or they will be of little value to your generated configure script. (Additional shell script may be placed in *configure.ac* after AC_OUTPUT, but it will not affect the configuration or file generation performed by config.status.)

Consider adding shell echo or print statements after AC_OUTPUT to tell the user how the build system is configured based on the specified command-line options. You can also use these statements to tell the user about additional useful targets for make. For example, one of my projects contains the code shown in Listing 4-25 after AC_OUTPUT in *configure.ac*.

```
...
AC_OUTPUT

echo \
"-------------------------------------------------

${PACKAGE_NAME} Version ${PACKAGE_VERSION}

Prefix: '${prefix}'.
Compiler: '${CC} ${CFLAGS} ${CPPFLAGS}'

Package features:
  Async Execution: ${async_exec}

Now type 'make @<:@<target>@:>@'
  where the optional <target> is:
    all                 - build all binaries
    install             - install everything

-------------------------------------------------"
```

Listing 4-25: configure.ac: Adding configuration summary text to the output of configure

Adding such output to the end of *configure.ac* is a handy project feature, because it tells the user, at a glance, exactly what happened during configuration. Since variables such as debug are set to on or off based on configuration, the user can see whether the configuration he asked for actually took place.

Summary

In this chapter, we've covered some of the more advanced constructs found in the *configure.ac* files for many projects. We started with the macros required to generate substitution variables. I refer to these as "advanced" macros because many of the higher-level Autoconf macros use AC_SUBST and AC_DEFINE internally, making them somewhat transparent to you. However, knowing about them helps you to understand how Autoconf works and also provides some of the background information necessary for helping you learn to write your own macros.

We covered checks for compilers and other tools, as well as checks for non-ubiquitous data types and structures on your users' systems. The examples in this chapter were designed to help you to understand the proper use of the Autoconf type- and structure-definition check macros, as well as others.

We also examined a technique for debugging the use of complex Autoconf macros: using picket fences around a macro call in *configure.ac* in order to quickly locate the associated generated text in `configure`. We looked at checks for libraries and header files, and we examined some of the details involved in the proper use of these Autoconf macros. We went into great detail about building a robust and user-friendly configuration process, including the addition of project-specific command-line options to generated `configure` scripts.

Finally, we discussed the proper placement of the `AC_OUTPUT` macro in *configure.ac*, as well as the addition of some summary-generation shell code designed to help your users understand what happened during the configuration of your project on their system.

The next chapter takes us away from Autoconf for a while, as we turn our attention to GNU Automake, an Autotools toolchain add-on that abstracts many of the details of creating very functional makefiles for open source projects.

5

AUTOMATIC MAKEFILES
WITH AUTOMAKE

If you understand, things are just as they are;
if you do not understand, things are just as they are.
—*Anonymous*

Shortly after Autoconf began its journey to
success, David MacKenzie started working
on a new tool for automatically generating
makefiles for a GNU project: Automake. During
early development of the *GNU Coding Standards*, it
became apparent to MacKenzie that because the *GCS*
is fairly specific about how and where a project's products should be built,
tested, and installed, much of a GNU project makefile was boilerplate material. Automake takes advantage of this fact to make maintainers' lives easier.

MacKenzie's work on Automake lasted almost a year, ending around
November 1994. A year later, in November 1995, Tom Tromey (of Red Hat
and Cygnus fame) took over the Automake project and played a significant
role in its development. Although MacKenzie wrote the initial version of
Automake in Bourne shell script, Tromey completely rewrote the tool in Perl
and continued to maintain and enhance Automake over the next five years.

By the end of 2000, Alexandre Duret-Lutz had essentially taken over maintenance of the Automake project. His role as project lead lasted until about mid-2007, and since then, the project has been maintained by Ralf Wildenhues,[1] with occasional input from Akim Demaille and Jim Meyering.

Most of the complaints I've seen about the Autotools are ultimately associated with Automake. The reasons are simple: Automake provides the highest level of abstraction over the build system, and imposes a fairly rigid structure on projects that use it. Automake's syntax is concise—in fact, it's terse, almost to a fault. One Automake statement represents a *lot* of functionality. But once you understand it, you can get a fairly complete, complex, and functionally correct build system up and running in short order—that is, in minutes, not hours or days.

In this chapter, I'll provide you with some insight into the inner workings of Automake. With such insight, you'll begin to feel comfortable not only with what Automake can do for you but also with extending it in areas where its automation falls short.

Getting Down to Business

Let's face it—getting a makefile right is often difficult. The devil, as they say, is in the details. Consider the following changes to the files in our project directory structure, as we continue to improve the project build system for Jupiter:

```
❶ $ rm autogen.sh Makefile.in src/Makefile.in
❷ $ echo "SUBDIRS = src" > Makefile.am
❸ $ echo "bin_PROGRAMS = jupiter
  > jupiter_SOURCES = main.c" > src/Makefile.am
❹ $ touch NEWS README AUTHORS ChangeLog
  $ ls -1
  AUTHORS
  ChangeLog
  configure.ac
  Makefile.am
  NEWS
  README
  src
  $
```

The rm command at ❶ deletes our hand-coded *Makefile.in* templates and the autogen.sh script we wrote to ensure that all the support scripts and files are copied into the root of our project directory. We won't need this script anymore, because we're upgrading Jupiter to Automake proper. (For the sake of brevity, I've used echo statements at ❷ and ❸ to write the new *Makefile.am* files; you can use a text editor if you wish.)

NOTE *There is a hard carriage return at the end of the line at ❸. The shell will continue to accept input after the carriage return until the quotation is closed.*

---

1. I owe many heartfelt thanks to Ralf for kindly answering so many seemingly trivial questions while I worked on this book.

I've used the touch command at ❹ to create new, empty versions of the *NEWS*, *README*, *AUTHORS*, and *ChangeLog* files in the project root directory. (The *INSTALL* and *COPYING* files are added by autoreconf -i.) These files are required by the GCS for all GNU projects. And although they're not required for non-GNU programs, they've become something of an institution in the OSS world; users have come to expect them.

NOTE *The* GNU Coding Standards *covers the format and contents of these files. Sections 6.7 and 6.8 cover the* NEWS *and* ChangeLog *files, respectively, and Section 7.3 covers the* README, INSTALL, *and* COPYING *files. The* AUTHORS *file is a list of people (names and optional email addresses) to whom attribution should be given.[2]*

Enabling Automake in configure.ac

To enable Automake within the build system, I've added a single line to *configure.ac*: a call to AM_INIT_AUTOMAKE between the calls to AC_INIT and AC_CONFIG_SRCDIR, as shown in Listing 5-1.

```
...
AC_INIT([Jupiter], [1.0], [jupiter-bugs@example.org])
AM_INIT_AUTOMAKE
AC_CONFIG_SRCDIR([src/main.c])
...
```

Listing 5-1: Adding Automake functionality to configure.ac

If your project has already been configured with Autoconf, this is the *only* line that's required to enable Automake, besides the normal requirements of an Autoconf input file. The AM_INIT_AUTOMAKE macro accepts an optional argument: a whitespace-separated list of option tags, which can be passed into this macro to modify the general behavior of Automake. For a detailed description of each option, see Chapter 17 of the *GNU Automake Manual*.[3] I will, however, point out a few of the most useful options here.

check-news

The check-news option causes make dist to fail if the project's current version (from *configure.ac*) doesn't show up in the first few lines of the *NEWS* file.

dist-bzip2, dist-lzma, dist-shar, dist-zip, dist-tarZ

You can use the dist-* options to change the default distribution package type. By default, make dist builds a *.tar.gz* file, but developers often want to distribute, for example, *.tar.bz2* packages instead. These options make the change quite easy. (Even without the dist-bzip2 option, you can override the current default by using make dist-bzip2, but using the option is simpler if you always want to build *.bz2* packages.)

---

2. This information is taken from the March 27, 2010 version of the *GNU Coding Standards* at *http://www.gnu.org/prep/standards/.*

3. See the Free Software Foundation's *GNU Automake Manual* at *http://www.gnu.org/software/automake/manual.*

readme-alpha

The `readme-alpha` option temporarily alters the behavior of the build and distribution processes during alpha releases of a project. Using this option causes a file named *README-alpha*, found in the project root directory, to be distributed automatically. The use of this option also alters the expected versioning scheme of the project.

-W*category*, --warnings=*category*

The `-W`*category* and `--warnings=`*category* options indicate that the project would like to use Automake with various warning categories enabled. Multiple such options can be used with different category tags. Refer to the *GNU Automake Manual* to find a list of valid categories.

silent-rules

The `silent-rules` feature causes Automake to generate makefiles that allow the user to specify that only the toolname and output filename are sent to `stdout` during the build. The resulting output looks something like this:

```
$ make
  CC     foo.o
  CXX    bar.o
  ...
  CXXLD  prog
$
```

parallel-tests

The `parallel-tests` feature allows checks to be executed in parallel in order to take advantage of multiprocessor machines during execution of the `check` target.

version

The *version* option is actually a placeholder for a version number that represents the lowest version of Automake that is acceptable for this project. For instance, if `1.11` is passed as an option tag, Automake will fail while processing *configure.ac* if its version is earlier than 1.11. This can be useful if you're trying to use features that only exist in the latest version of Automake.

With the new *Makefile.am* files in place and Automake enabled in *configure.ac*, let's run `autoreconf` with the `-i` option in order to add any new utility files that Automake may require for our project:

```
$ autoreconf -i
configure.ac:6: installing `./install-sh'
configure.ac:6: installing `./missing'
src/Makefile.am: installing `./depcomp'
Makefile.am: installing `./INSTALL'
Makefile.am: installing `./COPYING'
Makefile.am:    Consider adding the COPYING file to the version control
system
```

```
Makefile.am:      for your code, to avoid questions about which license your
project uses.
$
$ ls -1p
aclocal.m4
AUTHORS
autom4te.cache/
ChangeLog
config.h.in
configure
configure.ac
COPYING
depcomp
INSTALL
install-sh
Makefile.am
Makefile.in
missing
NEWS
README
src/
$
```

Adding the AM_INIT_AUTOMAKE macro to *configure.ac* causes autoreconf -i to now execute automake -i, which includes a few more new utility files: *aclocal.m4*, *install-sh*, *missing*, and *depcomp*. Additionally, Automake now generates *Makefile.in* from *Makefile.am*.

Automake also adds default *INSTALL* and *COPYING* text files containing boilerplate text that pertains specifically to the GNU project. You can modify these files for your projects as you see fit. I find the default *INSTALL* file text to be useful for general-purpose instructions related to Autotools-built projects, but I like to prepend some project-specific information to the top of this file before committing it to my repository. Automake's -i option won't overwrite these text files in a project that already contains them, so feel free to modify the default files as you see fit, once they've been added by autoreconf -i.

The *COPYING* file contains the text of the GPL, which may or may not apply to your package. If your project is released under GPL, just leave the text as is. If you're releasing under another license, such as the BSD, MIT, or Apache Commons licenses, replace the default text with text appropriate for that license.[4]

NOTE *You only need to use the -i option once in a newly checked-out work area or a newly created project. Once the missing utility files have been added, you can drop the -i option in future calls to autoreconf.*

The commands listed above create an Automake-based build system that contains everything we wrote into our original *Makefile.in* templates, except that this system is more correct and functionally complete according to the *GCS*. A glance at the resulting generated *Makefile.in* template shows that

---

4. See the Open Source Initiative website at *http://opensource.org/* for current license text for nearly all known open source licenses.

Automake has done a significant amount of work for us. The resulting top-level *Makefile.in* template is nearly 18KB, while the original, hand-coded makefiles were only a few hundred bytes long.

An Automake build system supports the following important make targets (derived from an Automake-generated *Makefile*):

all	distdir	install
install-strip	install-data	install-exec
uninstall	install-dvi	install-html
install-info	install-ps	install-pdf
installdirs	check	installcheck
mostlyclean	clean	distclean
maintainer-clean	dvi	pdf
ps	info	html
tags	ctags	dist
dist-bzip2	dist-gzip	dist-lzma
dist-shar	dist-zip	dist-tarZ

As you can see, this goes far beyond what we could provide in our hand-coded *Makefile.in* templates. Automake writes this base functionality into every project that uses it.

A Hidden Benefit: Automatic Dependency Tracking

In "Dependency Rules" on page 29 we discussed make dependency rules. These are rules we define in makefiles so that make is aware of the hidden relationships between C-language source files and included header files. Automake goes to a lot of trouble to ensure that you don't have to write such dependency rules for languages it understands, like C, C++, and Fortran. This is an important feature for projects containing more than a few source files.

Writing dependency rules by hand for dozens or hundreds of source files is both tedious and error prone. In fact, it's such a problem that compiler writers often provide a mechanism that enables the compiler to write these rules automatically based on its internal knowledge of the source files and the language. The GNU compilers, among others, support a family of -M options (i.e., -M, -MM, -MF, -MG, and so on) on the command line. These options tell the compiler to generate a make dependency rule for the specified source file. (Some of these options can be used on the normal compiler command line, so the dependency rule can be generated when the source file is being compiled.)

The simplest of these options is the basic -M option, which causes the compiler to generate a dependency rule for the specified source file on stdout and then terminate. This rule can be captured in a file, which is then included by the makefile so that the dependency information within this rule is incorporated into the directed graph that make builds.

But what happens on systems where the native compilers don't provide dependency generation options, or where they don't work together with the compilation process? In such cases, Automake provides a wrapper script called depcomp that executes the compiler twice: once for dependency information, and again to compile the source file. When the compiler lacks the options to generate *any* dependency information, another tool may be used to recursively determine which header files affect a given source file. On systems where none of these options are available, automatic dependency generation fails.

NOTE *For a more detailed description of the dependency-generating compiler options, see "Item 11: Using Generated Source Code" on page 302. For more on Automake dependency management, see the relevant sections of the* GNU Automake Manual.

What's in a Makefile.am File?

In Chapter 3 we discussed how Autoconf accepts as input a shell script sprinkled with M4 macros, and then generates the same shell script with those macros fully expanded. Likewise, Automake accepts as input a makefile sprinkled with Automake commands. Just as Autoconf's input files are simply enhanced shell scripts, Automake *Makefile.am* files are nothing more than standard makefiles with additional Automake-specific syntax.

One significant difference between Autoconf and Automake is that the only text Autoconf outputs is the existing shell script in the input file and any additional shell script resulting from the expansion of embedded M4 macros. Automake, on the other hand, assumes that all makefiles should contain a minimal infrastructure designed to support the *GCS*, in addition to any targets and variables that you specify.

To illustrate this point, create a *temp* directory in the root of the Jupiter project and add an empty *Makefile.am* file to it. Next, add this new *Makefile.am* to the project's *configure.ac* file with a text editor and reference it from the top-level *Makefile.am* file, like this:

```
  $ mkdir temp
  $ touch temp/Makefile.am
❶ $ echo "SUBDIRS = src temp" > Makefile.am
  $ vi configure.ac
  ...
  AC_CONFIG_FILES([Makefile
                  src/Makefile
❷                 temp/Makefile])
  ...
  $ autoreconf
  $ ./configure
  ...
  $ ls -1sh temp
  total 20K
❸  12K Makefile
     0 Makefile.am
❹ 8.0K Makefile.in
  $
```

I used an echo statement at ❶ to rewrite a new top-level *Makefile.am* file that has SUBDIRS reference both *src* and *temp*. I used vi to add *temp/Makefile* to the list of makefiles Autoconf will generate from templates (❷). As you can see, there is a certain amount of support code generated into every makefile that Automake considers indispensable. Even an empty *Makefile.am* file generates an 8KB *Makefile.in* template (❹), from which configure generates a 12KB *Makefile* (❸).[5]

Since the make utility uses a fairly rigid set of rules for processing makefiles, Automake takes some license with your additional make code. Specifically:

- make variables defined in *Makefile.am* files are placed at the top of the resulting *Makefile.in* template, immediately following any Automake-generated variable definitions.

- make rules specified in *Makefile.am* files are placed at the end of the resulting *Makefile.in* template, immediately after any Automake-generated rules.

- Most Autoconf variables substituted by config.status are converted to make variables and initialized to those substitution variables.

The make utility doesn't care where rules are in relation to each other, because it reads every rule into an internal database before processing any of them. Variables are treated similarly, as long as they are defined before the rules that use them. In order to avoid any variable binding issues, Automake places all variables at the top of the output file in the order in which they're defined in the input file.

Analyzing Our New Build System

Now let's look at what we put into those two simple *Makefile.am* files, beginning with the top-level *Makefile.am* file (shown in Listing 5-2).

```
SUBDIRS = src
```

Listing 5-2: Makefile.am: The top-level Makefile.am file contains only a subdirectory reference.

This single line of text tells Automake several things about our project:

- One or more subdirectories contain makefiles to be processed in addition to this file.[6]

- Directories in this space-delimited list should be processed in the order specified.

- Directories in this list should be recursively processed for all primary targets.

- Directories in this list should be treated as part of the project distribution, unless otherwise specified.

---

5. It's fairly instructive to examine the contents of this *Makefile.in* template to see the Autoconf substitution variables that are passed in, as well as the framework code that Automake generates.

6. I refer here to actual makefiles, not *Makefile.am* files. Automake determines the list of *Makefile.am* files to process from *configure.ac*'s AC_CONFIG_FILES list. The SUBDIRS list merely exists to tell make which directories to process from the current makefile, and in which order.

As with most Automake constructs, SUBDIRS is simply a make variable that has special meaning for Automake. The SUBDIRS variable may be used to process *Makefile.am* files within arbitrarily complex directory structures, and the directory list may contain any relative directory references (not just immediate subdirectories). You might say that SUBDIRS is kind of like the glue that holds makefiles together in a project's directory hierarchy.

Automake generates recursive make rules that implicitly process the current directory after those specified in the SUBDIRS list, but it's often necessary to build the current directory before some or all of the other directories in the list. You may change the default ordering by referencing the current directory with a dot anywhere in the SUBDIRS list. For example, to build the top-level directory before the *src* directory, you could change the SUBDIRS variable in Listing 5-2 as follows:

```
SUBDIRS = . src
```

Now let's turn to the *Makefile.am* file in the *src* directory, shown in Listing 5-3.

```
bin_PROGRAMS = jupiter
jupiter_SOURCES = main.c
```

Listing 5-3: src/Makefile.am: *The initial version of this* Makefile.am *file contains only two lines.*

The first line is a product list variable specification, and the second line is a product source variable specification.

Product List Variables

Products are specified in a *Makefile.am* file using a *product list variable (PLV)*, which (like SUBDIRS) is a class of make variables that have special meaning to Automake. The following template shows the general format of a PLV:

```
[modifier-list]prefix_PRIMARY = product1 product2 ... productN
```

The PLV name in the first line of Listing 5-3 consists of two components: the prefix (*bin*) and the primary (PROGRAMS), separated by an underscore (_). The value of the variable is a whitespace-separated list of products generated by this *Makefile.am* file.

Installation Location Prefixes

The *bin* portion of the product list variable shown in Listing 5-3 is an example of an *installation location prefix*. The *GCS* defines many common installation locations, and most are listed in Table 2-1 on page 46. However, any make variable ending in dir, whose value is a filesystem location, is a viable installation location variable and may be used as a prefix in an Automake PLV.

You reference an installation location variable in a PLV prefix by omitting the dir portion of the variable name. For example, in Listing 5-3, the $(bindir) make variable is referred to only as bin when it is used as an installation location prefix.

Automake also recognizes four installation location variables starting with the special prefix pkg: pkglibdir, pkgincludedir, pkgdatadir, and pkglibexecdir. These pkg versions of the standard libdir, includedir, datadir, and libexecdir variables indicate that the listed products should be installed in a subdirectory of these locations named after the package. For example, in the Jupiter project, products listed in a PLV prefixed with lib would be installed into $(libdir), while those listed in a PLV prefixed with pkglib would be installed into $(libdir)/*jupiter*.

Since Automake derives the list of valid installation locations and prefixes from all make variables ending in dir, you may provide your own PLV prefixes that refer to custom installation locations. To install a set of XML files into an *xml* directory within the system data directory, you could use the code in Listing 5-4 in your *Makefile.am* file.

```
xmldir = $(datadir)/xml
xml_DATA = file1.xml file2.xml file3.xml ...
```

Listing 5-4: Specifying a custom installation directory

Installation location variables will contain default values defined either by Automake-generated makefiles or by you in your *Makefile.am* files, but your users can always override these default values on their configure or make command lines. If you don't want certain products to be installed during a particular build, specify an empty value in an installation location variable on the command line; the Automake-generated rules will ensure that products intended for those directories aren't installed. For example, to install only documentation and shared data files for a package, you could enter make bindir='' libdir='' install.

Prefixes Not Associated with Installation

Certain prefixes are not related to installation locations. For example, noinst, check, and EXTRA are used (respectively) to indicate products that are not installed, used only for testing, or are optionally built. Here's a little more information about these three prefixes:

- The noinst prefix indicates that the listed products should be built but not installed. For example, a static so-called *convenience library* might be built as an intermediate product and then used in other stages of the build process to build final products. The noinst prefix tells Automake that the product should not be installed and that only a static library should be built. (After all, it makes no sense to build a shared library that won't be installed.)

- The check prefix indicates products that are to be built only for testing purposes and will thus not need to be installed. Products listed in PLVs prefixed with check are only built if the user enters make check.

- The EXTRA prefix is used to list programs that are conditionally built. Automake requires that all source files be specified statically within a *Makefile.am* file, as opposed to being calculated or derived during the build process, so that it can generate a *Makefile.in* template that will work for any possible command line. However, a project maintainer may elect to allow some products to be built conditionally based on configuration options given to the configure script. If products are listed in variables generated by the configure script, they should also be listed in a PLV, prefixed with EXTRA, within a *Makefile.am* file. This concept is illustrated in Listings 5-5 and 5-6.

```
AC_INIT(...)
...
optional_programs=
AC_SUBST([optional_programs])
...
if test "x$(build_opt_prog)" = xyes; then
❶    optional_programs=$(optional_programs) optprog
fi
...
```

Listing 5-5: A conditionally built program defined in a shell variable in configure.ac

```
❷ EXTRA_PROGRAMS = optprog
❸ bin_PROGRAMS = myprog $(optional_programs)
```

Listing 5-6: Using the EXTRA prefix to conditionally define products in Makefile.am

At ❶ in Listing 5-5, optprog is appended to an Autoconf substitution variable called optional_programs. The EXTRA_PROGRAMS variable at ❷ in Listing 5-6 lists optprog as a product that may or may not be build, based on end-user configuration choices, which determine whether $(optional_programs) at ❸ is empty or contains optprog.

While it may appear redundant to specify optprog in both *configure.ac* and *Makefile.am*, Automake needs the information in EXTRA_PROGRAMS because it cannot attempt to interpret the possible values of $(optional_programs), as defined in *configure.ac*. Hence, adding optprog to EXTRA_PROGRAMS in this example tells Automake to generate rules to build it, even if the value of the $(optional_programs) variable doesn't contain optprog during a particular build.

Primaries

Primaries are like product classes, and they represent types of products that might be generated by a build system. A primary defines the set of steps required to build, test, install, and execute a particular class of products. For example, programs and libraries are built using different compiler and linker commands, Java classes require a virtual machine to execute them, and Python programs require an interpreter. Some product classes, such as scripts, data, and headers, have no build, test, or execution semantics—only installation semantics.

The list of supported primaries defines the set of product classes that can be built automatically by an Automake build system. Automake build systems can still build other product classes, but the maintainer must define the make rules explicitly within the project's *Makefile.am* files.

A thorough understanding the Automake primaries is the key to properly using Automake. Some of the most important primaries are as follows.

PROGRAMS

When the PROGRAMS primary is used in a PLV, Automake generates make rules that use compilers and linkers to build binary executable programs for the listed products.

LIBRARIES / LTLIBRARIES

The use of the LIBRARIES primary causes Automake to generate rules that build static archives (libraries) using the system compiler and librarian. The LTLIBRARIES primary does the same thing, but the generated rules also build Libtool shared libraries and execute these tools (as well as the linker) through the libtool script. (I'll discuss the Libtool package in detail in Chapters 6 and 7.) Automake restricts the installation locations for the LIBRARIES and LTLIBRARIES primaries: They can only be installed in $(libdir) and $(pkglibdir).

PYTHON

Python is an interpreted language; the python interpreter converts a Python script, line by line, into Python byte code, executing it as it's converted, so (like shell scripts) Python source files are executable as written. The use of the PYTHON primary tells Automake to generate rules that precompile Python source files (*.py*) into standard (*.pyc*) and optimized (*.pyo*) byte-compiled versions using the py-compile utility. Because of the normally interpreted nature of Python sources, this compilation occurs at install time rather than at build time.

JAVA

Java is a virtual machine platform; the use of the JAVA primary tells Automake to generate rules that convert Java source files (*.java*) into Java class files (*.class*) using the javac compiler. While this process is correct, it's not complete. Java programs (of any consequence) generally contain more than one class file, which are usually packaged as *.jar* or *.war* files, both of which may also contain several ancillary text files. The JAVA primary is useful, but only just. (I'll discuss using—and extending—the JAVA primary in "Building Java Sources Using the Autotools" on page 230.)

SCRIPTS

Script, in this context, refers to any interpreted text file—whether it's shell, Perl, Python, Tcl/Tk, JavaScript, Ruby, PHP, Icon, Rexx, or some other. Automake allows a restricted set of installation locations for the SCRIPTS primary, including $(bindir), $(sbindir), $(libexecdir), and $(pkgdatadir). While Automake doesn't generate rules to build scripts, it also doesn't assume that a script is a static file in the project. Scripts are often generated by hand-written rules in *Makefile.am* files, sometimes by processing an input file with the sed or awk utilities. For this reason, scripts are not distributed automatically. If you have a static script in your project that you'd like Automake to add to your distribution tarball, you should prefix the SCRIPTS primary with the dist modifier as discussed in "PLV and PSV Modifiers" on page 132.

DATA

Arbitrary data files can be installed using the DATA primary in a PLV. Automake allows a restricted set of installation locations for the DATA primary, including $(datadir), $(sysconfdir), $(sharedstatedir), $(localstatedir), and $(pkgdatadir). Data files are not automatically distributed, so if your project contains static data files, use the dist modifier on the DATA primary as discussed in "PLV and PSV Modifiers" on page 132.

HEADERS

Header files are a form of source file. Were it not for the fact that some header files are installed, they could simply be listed with the product sources. Header files containing the public interface for installed library products are installed into either the $(includedir) or a package-specific subdirectory defined by $(pkgincludedir), so the most common PLVs for such installed headers are the include_HEADERS and pkginclude_HEADERS variables. Like other source files, header files are distributed automatically. If you have a generated header file, use the nodist modifier with the HEADERS primary as discussed in "PLV and PSV Modifiers" on page 132.

MANS

Man pages are UTF-8 text files containing troff markup, which is rendered by man when viewed by a user. Man pages can be installed using the man_MANS or man$N$_MANS product list variables, where N represents a single-digit section number between 0 and 9. Files in the man_MANS PLV should have a numeric extension indicating the man section to which they belong and their target directory. Files in the man$N$_MANS PLV may be named with either numeric extensions or a *.man* extension, which will be renamed to the associated numeric extensions when they're installed by make install. Project man pages are not distributed by default because man pages are often generated, so you should use the dist modifier as discussed in "PLV and PSV Modifiers" on page 132.

TEXINFOS

When it comes to Linux or Unix documentation, Texinfo[7] is the GNU project format of choice. The makeinfo utility accepts Texinfo source files (*.texinfo, .txi,* or *.texi*) and renders info files (*.info*) containing UTF-8 text annotated with Texinfo markup, which the info utility renders into formatted text for the user. The most common product list variable for use with Texinfo sources is info_TEXINFOS. The use of this PLV causes Automake to generate rules to build *.info, .dvi, .ps,* and *.html* documentation files. However, only the *.info* files are built with make all and installed with make install. In order to build the other types of files, you must specify the dvi, ps, pdf, html, install-dvi, install-ps, install-pdf, and install-html targets explicitly on the make command line. Since the makeinfo utility is not installed by default in many Linux distributions, the generated *.info* files are automatically added to distribution tarballs so your end users won't have to go looking for makeinfo.

---

7. See the Texinfo project website at *http://www.gnu.org/software/texinfo/*.

Product Source Variables

The second line in Listing 5-3 is an example of an Automake *product source variable (PSV)*. PSVs conform to the following template:

```
[modifier-list]product_SOURCES = file1 file2 ... fileN
```

Like PLVs, PSVs are comprised of multiple parts: the product name (jupiter in this case) and the SOURCES tag. The value of a PSV is a whitespace-separated list of source files from which *product* is built. The value of the PSV in the second line of Listing 5-3 is the list of source files used to build the jupiter program. Ultimately, Automake adds these files to various make rule dependency lists and commands in the generated *Makefile.in* templates.

Only characters that are allowed in make variables (letters, numbers, and the at sign) are allowed in the *product* tag of a PSV. As a result, Automake performs a transformation on product names listed in PLVs to render the *product* tags used in the associated PSVs. Automake converts illegal characters into underscores, as shown in Listing 5-7.

```
❶ lib_LIBRARIES = libc++.a
❷ libc___a_SOURCES = ...
```

Listing 5-7: Illegal make variable characters are converted to underscores in product tags.

Here, Automake converts *libc++.a* in the PLV at ❶ into the PSV *product* tag libc___a (that's three underscores) to find the associated PSV at ❷ in the *Makefile.am* file. You must know the transformation rules so you can write PSVs that match your products.

PLV and PSV Modifiers

The modifier-list portions of the PLV and PSV templates defined above contain a set of optional modifiers. The following BNF-like rule defines the format of the modifier-list element of these templates:

```
modifier-list = modifier_[modifier-list]
```

Modifiers change the normal behavior of the variable to which they are prepended. Some of the more important ones are dist, nodist, nobase, and notrans.

The dist modifier indicates a set of files that should be distributed (that is, that should be included in the distribution package that's built when make dist is executed). For example, assuming that some source files for a product should be distributed and some should not, the variables shown in Listing 5-8 might be defined in the product's *Makefile.am* file.

```
dist_myprog_SOURCES = file1.c file2.c
nodist_myprog_SOURCES = file3.c file4.c
```

Listing 5-8: Using the dist and nodist modifiers in a Makefile.am file

Automake normally strips relative path information from the list of header files in a HEADERS PLV. The nobase modifier is used to suppress the removal of path information from installed header files that are obtained from subdirectories by a *Makefile.am* file. For example, take a look at the PLV definition in Listing 5-9.

```
nobase_pkginclude_HEADERS = mylib.h sys/constants.h
```

Listing 5-9: Using the nobase PLV modifier in a Makefile.am *file*

In this line we can see that *mylib.h* is in the same directory as *Makefile.am*, but *constants.h* is located in a subdirectory called *sys*. Normally, both files would be installed into $(pkgincludedir) by virtue of the pkginclude installation location prefix. However, since we're using the nobase modifier, Automake will retain the *sys/* portion of the second file's path for installation, and *constants.h* will be installed into $(pkgincludedir)/*sys*. This is useful when you want the installation (destination) directory structure to be the same as the project (source) directory structure as files are copied during installation.

The notrans modifier may be used on man page PLVs for man pages whose names should not be transformed during installation. (Normally, Automake will generate rules to rename the extension on man pages from *.man* to *.N* (where *N* is *0, 1, . . . , 9*) as they're installed.)

You can also use the EXTRA prefix as a modifier. When used with a product source variable (such as jupiter_SOURCES), EXTRA specifies extra source files that are directly associated with the jupiter product, as shown in Listing 5-10.

```
EXTRA_jupiter_SOURCES = possibly.c
```

Listing 5-10: Using the EXTRA prefix with a product SOURCES variable

Here, *possibly.c* may or may not be compiled, based on some condition defined in *configure.ac*.

Unit Tests: Supporting make check

In Chapter 2 we added code to *src/Makefile* that executes the jupiter program and checks for the proper output string when the user makes the check target. I've duplicated the check target code in Listing 5-11.

```
...
check: all
        ./jupiter | grep "Hello from .*jupiter!"
        @echo "*** ALL TESTS PASSED ***"
...
```

Listing 5-11: The check target

Fortunately, Automake has solid support for unit tests. To add our simple grep test back into the new Automake-generated build system, we can add a few lines to the bottom of *src/Makefile.am*, as shown in Listing 5-12.

```
bin_PROGRAMS = jupiter
jupiter_SOURCES = main.c
```

❶ `check_SCRIPTS = greptest.sh`
❷ `TESTS = $(check_SCRIPTS)`

❸ `greptest.sh:`
```
        echo './jupiter | grep "Hello from .*jupiter!"' > greptest.sh
        chmod +x greptest.sh
```

❹ `CLEANFILES = greptest.sh`

Listing 5-12: src/Makefile.am*: Additional code required to support the check target*

The check_SCRIPTS line at ❶ is a PLV which refers to a script that is generated at build time. Since the prefix is check, we know that scripts listed in this line will only be built when the user enters make check. However, we must supply a make rule for building the script as well as a rule for cleaning up the file later, during execution of the clean target. We use the CLEANFILES variable at ❹ to extend the list of files that Automake deletes during make clean.

The TESTS line at ❷ is the important one in Listing 5-12 because it indicates which targets are executed when the user makes the check target. (Since the check_SCRIPTS variable contains a complete list of these targets, I've simply referenced it here.) In this particular case, check_SCRIPTS is redundant, because Automake generates rules to ensure that all the scripts listed in TESTS are built before the tests are executed. check_* PLVs become important when additional helper scripts or programs must be built before those listed in TESTS are executed.

Reducing Complexity with Convenience Libraries

Jupiter is fairly trivial as open source software projects go, so in order to highlight some more of Automake's key features, let's expand it a little. We'll first add a convenience library, and then modify jupiter to consume this library. A *convenience library* is a static library that's only used within the containing project. Such temporary libraries are generally used when multiple binaries in a project need to incorporate the same source code. I'll move the code in *main.c* to a library source file and call the function in the library from jupiter's main routine. Begin by executing the following commands from the top-level project directory:

```
$ mkdir common
$ touch common/jupcommon.h
$ copy src/main.c common/print.c
$ touch common/Makefile.am
$
```

Now add the highlighted text from Listings 5-13 and 5-14 to the *.h* and *.c* files, respectively, in the new *common* directory.

```
int print_routine(const char * name);
```

Listing 5-13: common/jupcommon.h: *The initial version of this file*

```
#if HAVE_CONFIG_H
# include <config.h>
#endif

#include "jupcommon.h"

#include <stdio.h>
#include <stdlib.h>

#if HAVE_PTHREAD_H
# include <pthread.h>
#endif

static void * print_it(void * data)
{
    printf("Hello from %s!\n", (const char *)data);
    return 0;
}

int print_routine(const char * name)
{
#if ASYNC_EXEC
    pthread_t tid;
    pthread_create(&tid, 0, print_it, (void*)name);
    pthread_join(tid, 0);
#else
    print_it(name);
#endif
    return 0;
}
```

Listing 5-14: common/print.c: *The initial version of this file*

As you can see, *print.c* is merely a copy of *main.c*, with a few small modifications (bolded in Listing 5-14). First, I renamed main to print_routine, and then I added the inclusion of the *jupcommon.h* header file after the inclusion of *config.h*. This header file provides print_routine's prototype to *src/main.c* where it's called from main. Next we modify *src/main.c*, as shown in Listing 5-15, then add the text in Listing 5-16 to *common/Makefile.am*.

```
#include "jupcommon.h"

int main(int argc, char * argv[])
{
    return print_routine(argv[0]);
}
```

Listing 5-15: src/main.c: *Required modifications to have main call into the new library*

```
noinst_LIBRARIES = libjupcommon.a
libjupcommon_a_SOURCES = jupcommon.h print.c
```

Listing 5-16: common/Makefile.am: Initial version of this file

Let's examine this new *Makefile.am* file. The first line indicates which products this file should build and install. The `noinst` prefix indicates that this library is designed solely to make using the source code in the common directory more convenient.

We're creating a static library called *libjupcommon.a*, also known as an *archive*. Archives are like *.tar* files that only contain object files (*.o*). They can't be executed or loaded into a process address space like shared libraries, but they can be added to a linker command line like object files. Linkers are smart enough to realize that such archives are merely groups of object files.

NOTE   *Linkers add to the binary product every object file specified explicitly on the command line, but they only extract from archives those object files that are actually referenced in the code being linked.*

The second line in Listing 5-16 is a product source variable that contains the list of source files associated with this library.[8]

Product Option Variables

Now we need to add some additional information to *src/Makefile.am* so that the generated *Makefile* can find the new library and header file we added to the *common* directory. Let's add two more lines to the existing *Makefile.am* file, as shown in Listing 5-17.

```
  bin_PROGRAMS = jupiter
  jupiter_SOURCES = main.c
❶ jupiter_CPPFLAGS = -I$(top_srcdir)/common
❷ jupiter_LDADD = ../common/libjupcommon.a
  ...
```

Listing 5-17: src/Makefile.am: Adding compiler and linker directives to Makefile.am files

Like the `jupiter_SOURCES` variable, these two new variables are derived from the program name. These *product option variables (POVs)* are used to specify product-specific options to tools that are used to build products from source code.

---

8. I chose to place both the header file and the source file in this list. I could have used a `noinst_HEADERS` PLV for the header file, but it isn't necessary, because the `libjupcommon_a_SOURCES` list works just as well. The appropriate time to use `noinst_HEADERS` is when you have a directory that contains no source files—such as an internal *include* directory. Since header files are associated with compilation only through include references within your source code, the only effect of using `noinst_HEADERS` is that the listed header files are simply added to the project's distribution file list. (You'd get exactly the same effect by listing such header files in the `EXTRA_DIST` variable.)

The `jupiter_CPPFLAGS` variable at ❶ adds product-specific C-preprocessor flags to the compiler command line for all source files that are compiled for the jupiter program. The `-I$(top_srcdir)/common` directive tells the C preprocessor to add `$(top_srcdir)`/*common* to its list of locations in which to look for header file references.[9]

The `jupiter_LDADD` variable at ❷ adds libraries to the `jupiter` program's linker command line. The file path *../common/libjupcommon.a* merely adds an object to the linker command line so that code in this library can become part of the final program. Adding a library to a *program*`_LDADD` or *library*`_LIBADD` variable is only necessary for libraries that are built as part of your own package. If you're linking your program with a library that's already installed on the user's system, a call to `AC_CHECK_LIB` or `AC_SEARCH_LIBS` in *configure.ac* will cause the generated `configure` script to add an appropriate reference to the linker command line via the `LIBS` variable.

The set of POVs supported by Automake are derived mostly from a subset of the standard user variables listed in Table 2-2 on page 53. You'll find a complete list of program and library option variables in the *GNU Autoconf Manual*, but here are some of the important ones.

product`_CPPFLAGS`

Use *product*`_CPPFLAGS` to pass flags to the C preprocessor on the compiler command line.

product`_CFLAGS`

Use *product*`_CFLAGS` to pass C-compiler flags on the compiler command line.

product`_LDFLAGS`

Use *product*`_LDFLAGS` to pass global and order-independent shared library and program linker configuration flags and options to the linker, including `-static`, `-version-info`, `-release`, and so on.

program`_LDADD`

Use *program*`_LDADD` to add Libtool objects (*.lo*) or libraries (*.la*) or non-Libtool objects (*.o*) or archives (*.a*) to the linker command line when linking a program.[10]

library`_LIBADD`

Use *library*`_LIBADD` to add non-Libtool linker objects and archives to non-Libtool archives on the ar utility command line. The ar utility will incorporate archives mentioned on the command line into the product archive, so you can use this variable to gather multiple archives together into one.

ltlibrary`_LIBADD`

Use *ltlibrary*`_LIBADD` to add Libtool linker objects (*.lo*) and Libtool static or shared libraries (*.la*) to a Libtool static or shared library.

---

9. The C preprocessor will search for header files referenced with angle brackets in the resulting include search path. It will also search for header files referenced with double quotes within the system include search path, but it will check the current directory first. Thus, you should use double quotes, rather than angle brackets, to reference header files that can be referenced relative to your project directory structure.

10. The file extensions on non-Libtool objects and archives are not standardized, so my use of *.o* and *.a* here are for example only.

You can use the last three option variables in this list to pass lists of order-dependent static and shared library references to the linker. You can also use these option variables to pass -L and -l options. The following are acceptable formats: -L*libpath*, -l*libname*, [*relpath/*]*archive*.a, [*relpath/*]*objfile*.$(OBJEXT), [*relpath/*]*ltobject*.lo, and [*relpath/*]*ltarchive*.la. (Note that the term *relpath* indicates a relative path within the project.)

Per-Makefile Option Variables

You'll often see the Automake variables AM_CPPFLAGS and AM_LDFLAGS used in a *Makefile.am* file. These per-makefile forms of these flags are used when the maintainer wants to apply the same set of flags to all products specified in the *Makefile.am* file.[11] For example, if you need to set a group of preprocessor flags for all products in a *Makefile.am* file and then add additional flags for a particular product (prog1), you could use the statements shown in Listing 5-18.

```
AM_CFLAGS = ... some flags ...
...
❶ prog1_CFLAGS = ... more flags ... $(AM_CFLAGS)
...
```

Listing 5-18: Using both per-product and per-file flags

The existence of a per-product variable overrides Automake's use of the per-makefile variable, so you need to add the per-makefile variable to the per-product variable in order to have the per-makefile variable affect that product, as shown in Listing 5-18 at ❶.

NOTE   *User variables, such as CFLAGS, are reserved for the end user and should never be modified by configuration scripts or makefiles. Automake will always append them to the appropriate utility command lines, thus allowing the user to override the options specified in the makefile.*

Building the New Library

Next, we need to edit the SUBDIRS variable in the top-level *Makefile.am* file in order to include the new *common* directory we just added. We also need to add the new makefile that was generated in the *common* directory to the list of files generated from templates in the AC_CONFIG_FILES macro call in *configure.ac*. These changes are shown in Listings 5-19 and 5-20.

```
SUBDIRS = common src
```

Listing 5-19: Makefile.am: Adding the common *directory to the SUBDIRS variable*

---

11. Using per-makefile flags can generate more compact makefiles, because per-product flags cause Automake to emit per-product rules, instead of more general suffix rules. When large file sets are involved, the difference is significant.

```
...
AC_CONFIG_FILES([Makefile
                common/Makefile
                src/Makefile])
...
```

Listing 5-20: configure.ac: Adding common/Makefile *to the* AC_CONFIG_FILES *macro*

Now let's give our updated build system a try. Add the -i option to the autoreconf command line so that it will install any additional missing files that might be required after these enhancements:

```
$ autoreconf -i
configure.ac:6: installing './install-sh'
configure.ac:6: installing './missing'
common/Makefile.am:1: library used but 'RANLIB' is undefined
❶ common/Makefile.am:1:   The usual way to define 'RANLIB' is to add
'AC_PROG_RANLIB'
common/Makefile.am:1:   to 'configure.ac' and run 'autoconf' again.
common/Makefile.am: installing './depcomp'
❷ src/Makefile.am:2: compiling 'main.c' with per-target flags requires
'AM_PROG_CC_C_O' in 'configure.ac'
autoreconf: automake failed with exit status: 1
$
```

Well, it looks like we're not quite done yet. Since we've added a new type of entity—static libraries—to our build system, automake (via autoreconf) tells us at ❶ that we need to add a new macro, AC_PROG_RANLIB, to the *configure.ac* file.[12] We're also told at ❷ that we need to add the Automake macro AM_PROG_CC_C_O, because this macro defines constructs in the resulting configure script that support the use of per-product flags like jupiter_CPPFLAGS. Specifically, the use of per-product flags requires the use of a wrapper script around compilers that can't handle -c (to name the input source file) and -o (to name the output object file) on the same command line.

Now add these two macros to *configure.ac*, as shown in Listing 5-21.

```
...
# Checks for programs.
AC_PROG_CC
AC_PROG_INSTALL
AC_PROG_RANLIB
AM_PROG_CC_C_O
...
```

Listing 5-21: configure.ac: Adding AC_PROG_RANLIB *and* AM_PROG_CC_C_O

---

12. There's a lot of history behind the use of the ranlib utility on archive libraries. I won't get into whether it's still useful with respect to modern development tools, but I will say that whenever you see it used in modern makefiles, there always seems to be a preceding comment about running ranlib "in order to add karma" to the archive, implying that the use of ranlib is somehow unnecessary. You be the judge.

Finally, enter autoreconf -i once more.

```
$ autoreconf -i
configure.ac:14: installing `./compile'
$
```

It seems that Automake has added yet another missing file; the compile script is a wrapper around some older compilers that do not understand the concurrent use of the -c and -o command-line options. When you use product-specific flags, Automake has to generate code that may compile source files multiple times with different flags for each file. Thus, it has to name the object files differently for each set of flags it uses. The requirement for the compile script actually comes from the inclusion of the AM_PROG_CC_C_O macro.

What Goes into a Distribution?

Automake usually determines automatically what should go into a distribution created with make dist, because it's very aware of every file's role in the build process. To this end, Automake wants to be told about every source file used to build a product and about every file and product installed. This means, of course, that all files must be specified at some point in one or more PLV and PSV variables.[13]

The Automake EXTRA_DIST variable contains a space-delimited list of files and directories that should be added to the distribution package when the dist target is made. For example:

```
EXTRA_DIST = windows
```

You could use the EXTRA_DIST variable to add a source directory to the distribution package that Automake would not automatically add—for example, a Windows-specific directory.

NOTE   *In this case,* windows *is a directory, not a file. Automake will automatically recursively add every file in this directory to the distribution package; this may include some files that you really didn't want there, such as hidden .svn or .CVS status directories. See "Automake -hook and -local Rules" on page 214 for a way around this problem.*

---

13. This bothers some developers—and with good reason. There are cases where dozens of installable files are generated by tools using long, apparently random, and generally unimportant naming conventions. Listing such generated files statically in a variable is painful, to say the least. Regardless, the current requirement is that all files must be specified. Don't bother trying to find a way around it. You'll end up hacking half the Automake source code to get it to work.

Maintainer Mode

Occasionally, timestamps on distribution source files will be newer than the current time setting of a user's system clock. Regardless of the cause, this inconsistency confuses make, causing it to think that every source file is out of date and needs to be rebuilt. As a result, it will re-execute the Autotools in an attempt to bring configure and the *Makefile.in* templates up to date. But as maintainers, we don't really expect our users to have the Autotools installed— or at least not the latest versions that we've installed on our systems.

This is where Automake's *maintainer mode* comes in. By default, Automake adds rules to makefiles that regenerate template files, configuration scripts, and generated sources from maintainer source files such as *Makefile.am* and *configure.ac*, as well as Lex and Yacc input files. However, we can use the Automake AM_MAINTAINER_MODE macro in *configure.ac* to disable the generation of these maintainer-level make rules.

For maintainers who want these rules in place to keep their build system properly updated after build system changes, the AM_MAINTAINER_MODE macro provides a configure script command-line option (--enable-maintainer-mode) that tells configure to generate *Makefile.in* templates that contain rules and commands to execute the Autotools as necessary.

Maintainers must be aware of the use of AM_MAINTAINER_MODE in their projects. They will need to use this command-line option when running configure in order to generate full build systems that will properly rebuild Autotools-generated files when their sources are modified.

NOTE *I also recommend mentioning the use of maintainer mode in the project* INSTALL *or* README *files so that end users are not surprised when they modify Autotools sources without effect.*

Although Automake's maintainer mode has its advantages, you should know that there are various arguments against using it. Most focus on the idea that make rules should never be purposely restricted, because doing so generates a build system that will always fail under certain circumstances. These are purist arguments, in my opinion. Using AM_MAINTAINER_MODE— especially when properly documented as mentioned above—provides an aspect of user-friendliness to the build process.

Cutting Through the Noise

The amount of noise generated by Autotools-based build systems has been one of the most controversial topics on the Automake mailing list. One camp appreciates quiet builds that just display important information, such as warnings and errors. The other side argues that valuable information is often embedded in this so-called "noise," so all of it is important and should be displayed. Occasionally, a new Autotools developer will post a question about how to reduce the amount of information displayed by make. This almost always spawns a heated debate that lasts for several days over a few dozen email messages. The old timers just laugh about it and often joke about how "someone has turned on the switch again."

The truth of the matter is that both sides have valid points. The GNU project is all about options, so the Automake maintainers have added the ability to allow you to optionally make silent rules available to your users. *Silent rules* in Automake makefiles are not really silent, they're just somewhat less noisy than traditional Automake-generated rules.

Instead of displaying the entire compiler or linker command line, silent rules display a short line indicating the tool and the name of the file being processed by that tool. Output generated by make is still displayed so the user knows which directory and target are currently being processed. Here is Jupiter's build output, with silent rules enabled:

```
$ configure --enable-silent-rules
...
$ make
make  all-recursive
make[1]: Entering directory '/home/jcalcote/dev/autotools/autotools/book/
jupiter-automake-ch5'
Making all in common
```

```
make[2]: Entering directory '/home/jcalcote/dev/autotools/autotools/book/
jupiter-automake-ch5/common'
  CC      print.o
  AR      libjupcommon.a
make[2]: Leaving directory '/home/jcalcote/dev/autotools/autotools/book/
jupiter-automake-ch5/common'
Making all in src
make[2]: Entering directory '/home/jcalcote/dev/autotools/autotools/book/
jupiter-automake-ch5/src'
  CC      jupiter-main.o
  CCLD    jupiter
make[2]: Leaving directory '/home/jcalcote/dev/autotools/autotools/book/
jupiter-automake-ch5/src'
make[2]: Entering directory '/home/jcalcote/dev/autotools/autotools/book/
jupiter-automake-ch5'
make[2]: Nothing to be done for 'all-am'.
make[2]: Leaving directory '/home/jcalcote/dev/autotools/autotools/book/
jupiter-automake-ch5'
make[1]: Leaving directory '/home/jcalcote/dev/autotools/autotools/book/
jupiter-automake-ch5'
$
```

As you can see, the use of silent rules doesn't make a lot of difference for Jupiter—Jupiter's build system spends a lot of time moving between directories and very little time actually building things. But in projects with hundreds of source files, you'd see long lists of CC *filename*.o lines, with an occasional indication that make is changing directories or the linker is building a product.

To enable silent rules in Automake-generated *Makefile.am* templates, you must do *one* of the following:

- Add the silent-rules option to the argument of AM_INIT_AUTOMAKE in *configure.ac*
- Call the AM_SILENT_RULES macro in *configure.ac*

The user sets the default verbosity for his build with --enable-silent-rules or --disable-silent-rules on the configure command line. The build will then either be "silent" or normal based on the configured default and on whether the user specifies V=0 or V=1 on the make command line.

NOTE *Neither configure option is required—silent rules are ultimately controlled by the V variable in the generated makefile. The configure option merely sets the default value of V.*

For smaller projects, I find Automake's silent rules to be less useful than simply redirecting stdout to */dev/null* on the make command line, in this manner:

```
$ make >/dev/null
print.c: In function 'print_routine':
print.c:24: warning: passing argument 4 of 'pthread_create' discards
qualifiers from pointer target type
$
```

As this example shows, warnings and errors are still displayed on `stderr`, along with enough information for you to determine where the problem is located.[14] Warning-free builds are truly silent in this case. You should use this technique to clean up compiler warnings in your source code every so often. Silent rules can help because warnings stand out in the build output.

Summary

In this chapter, we've discussed how to instrument a project for Automake using a project that had already been instrumented for Autoconf. (Newer projects are typically instrumented for both Autoconf and Automake at the same time.)

We covered the use of the `SUBDIRS` variable to tie *Makefile.am* files together, as well as the concepts surrounding product list, product source, and product option variables. Along with product list variables, I discussed Automake primaries—a concept at the very heart of Automake. Finally, I discussed the use of `EXTRA_DIST` to add additional files to distribution packages, the `AM_MAINTAINER_MODE` macro to ensure that users don't need to have the Auto-tools installed, and the use of Automake silent rules.

In Chapters 6 and 7 we'll examine adding Libtool to the Jupiter project, and in Chapters 8 and 9 we'll Autotool-ize a real-world project as we explore several other important aspects of Automake.

---

14. I caused this warning to be generated by removing the (`void*`) cast from the last argument to pthread_create in *print.c*.

6

BUILDING LIBRARIES
WITH LIBTOOL

The years teach much which the days never know.
—Emerson, "Experience"

 After too many bad experiences building shared libraries for multiple platforms without the help of GNU Libtool, I have come to two conclusions. First, the person who invented the concept of shared libraries should be given a raise . . . and a bonus. Second, the person who decided that shared library management interfaces and naming conventions should be left to the implementation should be flogged.

The very existence of Libtool stands as a witness to the truth of this sentiment. Libtool exists for only one reason—to provide a standardized, abstract interface for developers who want to create and access shared libraries in a portable manner. It abstracts both the shared-library build process and the programming interfaces used to dynamically load and access shared libraries at runtime.

Before I get into a discussion of the proper use of Libtool, I'll spend a few paragraphs on the features and functionality that shared libraries provide so you will understand the scope of the material I'm covering here.

The Benefits of Shared Libraries

Shared libraries provide a way to deploy reusable chunks of functionality in a convenient package. You can load shared libraries into a process address space either automatically at program load time, using the operating system loader, or manually via code in the application itself. The point at which an application binds functionality from a shared library is very flexible, and the developer determines it based on the program's design and the end user's needs.

The interfaces between the program executable and the modules defined as shared libraries must be reasonably well designed, because shared-library interfaces must be well specified. This rigorous specification promotes good design practices. When you use shared libraries, the system essentially forces you to be a better programmer.

Shared libraries may be (as their name implies) shared among processes. This sharing is very literal. The code segments for a shared library can be loaded once into physical memory pages. Those same memory pages can then be mapped into the process address spaces of multiple programs. The data pages must, of course, be unique for each process, but global data segments are often small compared to the code segments of a shared library. This is true efficiency.

It is easy to update shared libraries during program upgrades. Even if the base program doesn't change between two revisions of a software package, you can replace an old version of a shared library with a new one, as long as the new version's interfaces have not been changed. If interfaces *have* changed, two versions of the same shared library may reside together within the same directory, because the versioning schemes used by shared libraries (and supported by Libtool) on various platforms allow multiple versions of a library to be named differently in the filesystem but treated as the same library by the operating system loader. Older programs will continue to use older versions of the library, while newer programs are free to use the newer versions.

If a software package specifies a well-defined plug-in interface, then shared libraries can be used to implement user-configurable loadable functionality. This means that additional functionality can become available to a program after it's been released, and third-party developers can even add functionality to your program, if you publish a document describing your plug-in interface specification (or if they're smart enough to figure it out on their own).

There are a few widely known examples of these types of systems. Eclipse, for instance, is almost a pure plug-in framework. The base executable supports little more than a well-defined plug-in interface. Most of the functionality in an Eclipse application comes from library functions. Eclipse is written in Java and uses Java class libraries and *.jar* files, but the principle is the same, regardless of the language or platform.

How Shared Libraries Work

The specifics of how POSIX-compliant operating systems implement shared libraries vary from platform to platform, but the general idea is the same.

Shared libraries provide chunks of executable code that the operating system can load into a program's address space and execute. The following discussion applies to shared-library references that the linker resolves when a program is built and the operating system loader resolves when the program is loaded.

Dynamic Linking at Load Time

As a program executable image is being built, the linker (formally called a *link editor*) maintains a table of symbols—function entry points and global data addresses. Each symbol referenced within the accumulating body of object code is added to this table as the linker finds it. As symbol definitions are located, the linker resolves symbol references in the table to their addresses. At the end of the linking process, all object files (or simply *objects*) containing referenced symbol definitions are linked together and become part of the program executable image. Objects found in static libraries that contain no referenced symbol definitions are discarded, but objects linked explicitly are added to the binary image even if they contain no referenced symbol definitions. If there are outstanding references in the symbol table after all the objects have been analyzed, the linker exits with an error message. On success, the final executable image may be loaded and executed by a user. The image is now entirely self-contained, depending on no external binary code.

Assuming that all undefined references are resolved during the linking process, if the list of objects to be linked contains one or more shared libraries, the linker will build the executable image from all *non-shared* objects specified on the linker command line. This includes all individual object files (*.o*) and all objects contained in static library archives (*.a*). However, it will add two tables to the binary image header. The first is the outstanding *external reference table*—a table of references to symbol definitions found only in shared libraries during the linking process. The second is the *shared-library table*, containing the list of shared-library names and versions in which the outstanding undefined references were found.

When the operating system loader attempts to load the program, it must resolve the remaining outstanding references in the external reference table to symbols imported from the shared libraries named in the shared-library table. If the loader can't resolve all of the references, then a load error occurs and the process is terminated with an operating system error message. Note that these external symbols are not tied to a specific shared library. As long as they're found in any one of the searched libraries, they're accepted.

NOTE *This process differs slightly from the way a Windows operating system loader resolves symbols in Dynamic Link Libraries (DLLs). On Windows, the linker ties a particular symbol to a specifically named DLL at program build time.[1]*

---

1. Windows is not the only system to use hard references in this manner. Modern Windows operating systems are based on the *Common Object File Format (COFF)* system. COFF is also used by other operating systems, such as IBM's AIX. Many Unix (and all Linux) systems today are based on the *Executable and Linking Format (ELF)* system, which promotes the use of soft references, which don't need to be fully resolved until the program is executed.

Using free-floating external references has both pros and cons. On some operating systems, unbound symbols can be satisfied by a library specified by the user. That is, a user can entirely replace a library (or a portion of a library) at runtime by simply preloading one that contains the same symbols. On BSD and Linux-based systems, for example, a user can use the LD_PRELOAD environment variable to inject a shared library into a process address space. Since the loader loads these libraries before any other libraries, the loader will locate symbols in the preloaded libraries when it tries to resolve external references. The program author's intended libraries will not even be checked, because the symbols provided by these libraries have already been resolved by the preloaded libraries.

In the following example, the Linux df utility is executed with an environment containing the LD_PRELOAD variable. This variable has been set to a path referring to a library that presumably contains a heap manager that's compatible with the C *malloc* interface. This technique can be used to debug problems in your programs. By preloading your own heap manager, you can capture memory allocations in a logfile—in order to debug memory block overruns, for instance. This sort of technique is used by such widely known debugging aids as the *valgrind* package.[2]

In the following example, the LD_PRELOAD environment variable is set on the same command line used to execute the df program. This shell code causes only the df child process environment to contain the LD_PRELOAD variable, set to the specified value:

```
$ LD_PRELOAD=$HOME/lib/libmymalloc.so /bin/df
...
```

Unfortunately, free-floating symbols can also lead to problems. For instance, two libraries can provide the same symbol name, and the dynamic loader can inadvertently bind an executable to a symbol from the wrong library. At best, this will cause a program crash when the wrong arguments are passed to the mismatched function. At worst, it can present security risks because the mismatched function might be used to capture passwords and security credentials passed by the unsuspecting program.

C-language symbols do not include parameter information, so it's rather likely that symbols will clash in this manner. C++ symbols are a bit safer, in that the entire function signature (minus the return type) is encoded into the symbol name. However, even C++ is not immune to hackers that purposely replace security functions with their own versions of those functions (assuming, of course, that they have access to your runtime shared-library search path).

Automatic Dynamic Linking at Runtime

The operating system loader can also use a very late form of binding, often referred to as *lazy binding*. In this situation, the external reference table entries

---

2. For more information on the Valgrind tool suite, see the Valgrind Developers' website at *http://valgrind.org/*.

in the program header are initialized so that they refer to code within the dynamic loader itself.

When a program first calls a *lazy entry*, the call is routed to the loader, which will then (potentially) load the proper shared library, determine the actual address of the function, reset the entry point in the jump table, and finally, redirect the processor to the shared-library function (which is now available). The next time this happens, the jump table entry will have already been correctly initialized, and the program will jump directly to the called function. This is very efficient because the overhead for the jump after fix-up is no more than a normal indirect function call, and the cost of the initial load and link is amortized over many calls to the function during the lifetime of the process.

This lazy binding mechanism makes program startup very fast because shared libraries whose symbols are not bound until they're needed aren't even loaded until the application program first references them. But, consider this—the program may *never* reference them. And that means they may never be loaded, saving both time and space. A good example of this sort of situation might be a word processor with a thesaurus feature implemented in a shared library. How often do you use your thesaurus? If the program is using automatic dynamic linking, chances are that the shared library containing the thesaurus code will never be loaded in most word processing sessions.

As good as this system appears to be, there can be problems. While using automatic runtime dynamic linking can give you faster load times, better performance, and more efficient use of space, it can also cause your application to terminate abruptly and without warning. In the event that the loader can't find the requested symbol—perhaps the required library is missing—it has no recourse except to abort the process.

Why not ensure that all symbols exist when the program is loaded? Because if the loader resolved all symbols at load time, it might as well populate the jump table entries at that point, too. After all, it had to load all the libraries to ensure that the symbols actually exist, so this entirely defeats the purpose of using lazy binding. Furthermore, even if the loader did check all external references when the program was first started, there's nothing to stop someone from deleting one or more of these libraries before the program uses them, while the program is still running.[3] Thus, even the pre-check is defeated.

The moral of this story is that there's no free lunch. If you don't want to pay the insurance premium for longer up-front load times and more space consumed (even if you may never really need it), then you may have to take the hit of a missing symbol at runtime, causing a program crash.

Manual Dynamic Linking at Runtime

One possible solution to the aforementioned problem is to take personal responsibility for some of the system loader's work. Then, when things don't go right, you have a little more control over the outcome. In the case of the

---

3. Unix-like (POSIX) systems will retain deleted files for which outstanding file handles exist within running processes. From the filesystem user's perspective, the file appears to be gone, but the file remains intact until the last file handle is closed. Thus, this argument is not conclusive. As an aside, Windows operating systems simply disallow the delete operation on open files.

thesaurus module, was it really necessary to terminate the program if the thesaurus library could not be loaded or didn't provide the correct symbols? Of course not—but the operating system loader can't know that. Only the software programmer can make such judgment calls.

When a program manages dynamic linking manually at runtime, the linker is left out of the equation entirely, and the program doesn't call any exported shared-library functions directly. Rather, shared-library functions are referenced through function pointers that the program itself populates at runtime.

Here's how it works: A program calls an operating system function (dlopen) to manually load a shared library into its own process address space. This function returns a *handle*, or an opaque value representing the loaded library. The program then calls another loader function (dlsym) to import a symbol from the library to which the handle refers. If all goes well, the operating system returns the address of the requested function or data item from the desired library. The program may then call the function, or access the global data item, through this pointer.

If something goes wrong in this process—the symbol isn't found within the library or the library isn't found—then it becomes the responsibility of the program to define the results, perhaps by displaying an error message indicating that the program was not configured correctly. In the example of the word processor above, a simple dialog indicating that the thesaurus is unavailable would be entirely sufficient.

This is a little nicer than the way automatic dynamic runtime linking works; while the loader has no option but to abort, the application has a higher-level perspective and can handle the problem much more gracefully. The drawback, of course, is that you as the programmer have to manage the process of loading libraries and importing symbols within your application code. However, this process is not very difficult, as I'll demonstrate later in this chapter.

Using Libtool

An entire book could be written about the details of shared libraries and how they're implemented on various systems. The short primer you just read should suffice for our immediate needs, so I'll now move on to how you can use Libtool to make a package maintainer's life a little easier.

The Libtool project was started in 1996 by Gordon Matzigkeit. It was designed to extend Automake, but you can use it independently within hand-coded makefiles, as well. The Libtool project is currently maintained by Bob Friesenhahn, Peter O'Gorman, Gary Vaughan, and Ralf Wildenhues. As of this writing, the latest version of Libtool is version 2.2.6.

Abstracting the Build Process

First, let's look at how Libtool helps during the build process. Libtool provides a script (ltmain.sh) that config.status consumes in a Libtool-enabled project. The config.status script converts configure test results and the ltmain.sh script into a custom version of the libtool script, specifically tailored to your project.[4] Your project's makefiles then use this libtool script to build the shared libraries listed in any Automake product list variables defined with the Libtool-specific LTLIBRARIES primary. The libtool script is really just a fancy wrapper around the compiler, linker, and other tools. You should ship the ltmain.sh script in a distribution tarball, as part of your end-user build system. Automake-generated rules ensure that this happens properly.

The libtool script insulates the author of the build system from the nuances of building shared libraries on different platforms. This script accepts a well-defined set of options, converting them to appropriate platform- and linker-specific options on the target platform and toolset. Thus, the maintainer doesn't need to worry about the specifics of building shared libraries on each platform—he only needs to understand the available libtool script options. These options are well specified in the *GNU Libtool Manual*,[5] and I'll cover many of them in this chapter.

On systems that don't support shared libraries at all, the libtool script uses appropriate commands and options to build and link only static archive libraries. Furthermore, the maintainer doesn't have to worry about the differences between building shared libraries and building static libraries when using Libtool. You can emulate building your package on a static-only system by using the --disable-shared option on the configure command line for your Libtool-enabled project. This option causes Libtool to assume that shared libraries cannot be built on the target system.

Abstraction at Runtime

You can also use Libtool to abstract the programming interfaces the operating system supplies for loading libraries and importing symbols. If you've ever dynamically loaded a library on a Linux system, you're familiar with the standard POSIX shared-library API, including the dlopen, dlsym, and dlclose functions. A system-level shared library, usually called simply *dl*, provides these functions. This translates to a binary image file named *libdl.so* (or something similar on systems that use different library-naming conventions).

Unfortunately, not all Unix systems that support shared libraries provide the *libdl.so* library or functions using these names. To address these differences, Libtool provides a shared library called *ltdl*, which exports a clean, portable, library-management interface, very similar to the POSIX *dl* interface. The use of this library is optional, of course, but it is highly recommended because it provides more than just a common API across shared-library platforms—it also provides an abstraction for manual dynamic linking between shared-library and non–shared-library platforms.

---

4. Libtool also offers the option of generating the project-specific libtool script when configure is executed. This is done with the LT_OUTPUT macro within *configure.ac*. You may wish to do this if you find you have a need to execute libtool from within configure—for example, to test certain link-related features of your user's environment. In this case, you will need libtool to exist before you execute it for these checks.

5. See the Free Software Foundation's *GNU Libtool Manual*, version 2.2.6 (August 2008) at *http://www.gnu.org/software/libtool/manual/*.

What?! How can that work?! On systems that don't support shared libraries, Libtool actually creates internal symbol tables within the executable that contain all the symbols you would otherwise find within shared libraries (on systems that support shared libraries). By using such symbol tables on these platforms, the lt_dlopen and lt_dlsym functions can make your code appear to be loading libraries and importing symbols, when in fact, the library load function does nothing more than return a handle to the appropriate internal symbol table, and the import function merely returns the address of code that's been statically linked into the program itself. On these systems, a project's shared-library code is linked directly into the programs that would normally load them at runtime.

Installing Libtool

If you want to make use of the latest version of Libtool while developing your packages, you may find that you either have to download, build, and install it manually or look for an updated *libtool* package from your distribution provider.

Downloading, building, and installing Libtool is really trivial, as you'll see here. However, you should check the GNU Libtool website[6] before executing these steps in order to ensure you're getting the most recent package:

```
$ wget ftp.gnu.org/gnu/libtool/libtool-2.2.6a.tar.gz
...
$ tar xzf libtool-2.2.6a.tar.gz
$ cd libtool-2.2.6a
$ ./configure && make
...
$ sudo make install
...
```

Be aware that the default installation location (as with most of the GNU packages) is */usr/local*. If you wish to install Libtool into the */usr* hierarchy, you'll need to use the --prefix=/usr option on the configure command line. The recommended practice is to install distribution-provided packages into the */usr* hierarchy and user-built packages into the */usr/local* tree, but if you're trying to get a hand-built version of Libtool to interoperate with distribution-provided versions of Autoconf and Automake, you may have to install Libtool into the */usr* hierarchy. The simplest way to avoid problems with package inter-dependencies is to install hand-built versions of all three packages into */usr/local*.

Adding Shared Libraries to Jupiter

Now that I've presented the background information, let's take a look at how we might add a Libtool shared library to the Jupiter project. First, let's consider what functionality we could add to Jupiter using a shared library. Perhaps we wish to provide our users with some library functionality that their own

_____

6. See *http://www.gnu.org/software/libtool/*.

applications could use. Or we might have several applications in a package that need to share the same functionality. A shared library is a great tool for both of these scenarios because you get to reuse code and save memory—the cost of the memory used by shared code is amortized across multiple applications, both internal and external to the project.

Let's add a shared library to Jupiter that provides Jupiter's printing functionality. We can do this by having the new shared library call into the *libjupcommon.a* static library. Remember that calling a routine in a static library has the same effect as linking the object code for the called routine right into the calling program. The called routine ultimately becomes an integral part of the calling binary image (program or shared library).[7]

Additionally, we'll provide a public header file from the Jupiter project that will allow external applications to call this same functionality. This will allow other applications to display stuff in the same quaint manner that the jupiter program does. (This would be significantly cooler if we were doing something useful in jupiter, but you get the idea.)

Using the LTLIBRARIES Primary

Automake has built-in support for Libtool; it's the Automake package, rather than the Libtool package that provides the LTLIBRARIES primary. Libtool doesn't really qualify as a pure Automake extension, but rather more of an add-on package for Automake, where Automake provides the necessary infrastructure for this specific add-on package. You can't access Automake's LTLIBRARIES primary functionality without Libtool, because the use of this primary generates make rules that call the libtool build script.

Libtool ships separately, rather than as part of Automake, because you can use Libtool quite effectively independently of Automake. If you want to try Libtool by itself, I'll refer you to the *GNU Libtool Manual*; the opening chapters describe the use of the libtool script as a stand-alone product. It's as simple as modifying your makefile commands so that the compiler, linker, and librarian are called through the libtool script and then modifying some of your command-line parameters as required by Libtool.

Public Include Directories

A project subdirectory named *include* should only contain public header files—those that expose a public interface in your project. We're now going to add just such a header file to the Jupiter project, so we'll create a directory called *include* in the project root directory.

---

7. Many of you more experienced Autotools (or simply Unix) programmers may be cringing at my engineering choices here. For instance, linking a Libtool library against a traditional static archive is inappropriate for several reasons, which will become clear as we continue. During the process, we'll see that there is a significant difference between a traditional static archive and a Libtool convenience library (on some platforms). Please remember that Jupiter is a learning experience and a work in progress. I promise we'll work out the kinks by the end of the chapter.

If we had multiple shared libraries, we'd have a choice to make: Do we create separate *include* directories, one in each library source directory, or do we add a single, top-level *include* directory? I usually use the following rule of thumb to make my decision: If the libraries are designed to work together as a group, and if consuming applications generally use the libraries together, then I use a single, top-level *include* directory. If, on the other hand, the libraries can be effectively used independently, and if they offer fairly autonomous sets of functionality, then I provide individual *include* directories in the libraries' own directories.

In the end, it doesn't really matter much, because the header files for these libraries will be installed in directory structures that are entirely different from the ones where they exist within your project. In fact, you should make sure you don't inadvertently use the same filename for public headers in two different libraries in your project—if you do, you'll have problems installing these files. They generally end up all together in the $(prefix)/*include* directory, although you can override this default by using either the includedir variable or the pkginclude prefix in your *Makefile.am* files.

The includedir variable allows you to specify where you want your header files to be installed by defining the exact value of Automake's $(includedir) variable, the usual value of which is $(prefix)/*include*. The use of the pkginclude prefix indicates to Automake that you want your header files to be in a private, package-specific directory, beneath the directory indicated by $(includedir), called $(includedir)/$(PACKAGE).

We'll also add another root-level directory (*libjup*) for Jupiter's new shared library, *libjupiter*. These changes require you to add references to the new directories to the top-level *Makefile.am* file's SUBDIRS variable, and then add corresponding makefile references to the AC_CONFIG_FILES macro in *configure.ac*. We'll start by creating the directories and adding a new *Makefile.am* file to the *include* directory:

```
$ mkdir libjup
$ mkdir include
❶ $ echo "include_HEADERS = libjupiter.h" > include/Makefile.am
$
```

The *include* directory's *Makefile.am* file is trivial—it contains only a single line, in which an Automake HEADERS primary refers to the public header file *libjupiter.h*. Note at ❶ that we're using the include prefix on this primary. You'll recall that this prefix indicates that files specified in this primary are destined to be installed in the $(includedir) directory (e.g., */usr/(local/)include*). The HEADERS primary is similar to the DATA primary in that it specifies a set of files that are to be treated simply as data to be installed without modification or preprocessing. The only really tangible difference is that the HEADERS primary restricts the possible installation locations to those that make sense for header files.

The *libjup/Makefile.am* file is a bit more complex, containing four lines as opposed to just one or two. This file is shown in Listing 6-1.

```
❶ lib_LTLIBRARIES = libjupiter.la
❷ libjupiter_la_SOURCES = jup_print.c
❸ libjupiter_la_CPPFLAGS = -I$(top_srcdir)/include -I$(top_srcdir)/common
❹ libjupiter_la_LIBADD = ../common/libjupcommon.a
```

Listing 6-1: libjup/Makefile.am: The initial version of this file

Let's analyze this file, line by line. The line at ❶ is the primary specification, and it contains the usual prefix for libraries: lib. The products this prefix references will be installed in the $(libdir) directory. (We could have also used the pkglib prefix to indicate that we wanted our libraries installed into $(libdir)/*jupiter*.) Here, we're using the LTLIBRARIES primary, rather than the original LIBRARIES primary. The use of LTLIBRARIES tells Automake to generate rules that use the libtool script, rather than calling the compiler (and possibly the librarian) directly to generate the products.

The line at ❷ lists the sources that are to be used for the first (and only) product.

The line at ❸ indicates a set of C-preprocessor flags that are to be used on the compiler command line for locating the associated shared-library header files. These options indicate that the preprocessor should search the top-level *include* and *common* directories for header files referenced in the source code.

The last line (at ❹) indicates a set of linker options for this product. In this case, we're specifying that the *libjupcommon.a* static library should be linked into (i.e., become part of) the *libjupiter.so* shared library.

NOTE *The more experienced Autotools library developer will notice a subtle flaw in this* Makefile.am *file. Here's a hint: It's related to linking Libtool libraries against non-Libtool libraries. This concept presents a major stumbling block for many newcomers, so I've written the initial version of this file to illustrate the error. Not to worry, however—we'll correct the flaw later in this chapter as we work through this issue in a logical fashion.*

There is an important concept regarding the *_LIBADD variables that you should strive to understand completely: Libraries that are consumed within, and yet built as part of, the same project should be referenced internally using relative paths within the *build* directory hierarchy. Libraries that are external to a project generally don't need to be referenced explicitly at all, because the project's configure script should already have added appropriate -L and -l options for those libraries into the $(LIBS) environment variable when it processed the code generated by the AC_CHECK_LIB or AC_SEARCH_LIBS macros.

Next, we'll hook these new directories into the project's build system. To do so, we need to modify the top-level *Makefile.am* and *configure.ac* files. These changes are shown in Listings 6-2 and 6-3.

```
SUBDIRS = common include libjup src
```

Listing 6-2: Makefile.am: Adding include *and* libjup *to the SUBDIRS variable*

```
...
AC_PREREQ([2.61])
AC_INIT([Jupiter], [1.0], [bugs@jupiter.org])
AM_INIT_AUTOMAKE
❶ LT_PREREQ([2.2])
  LT_INIT([dlopen])
  ...
  AC_PROG_CC
  AC_PROG_INSTALL
❷ # AC_PROG_RANLIB
  AM_PROG_CC_C_O
  ...
  AC_CONFIG_FILES([Makefile
                  common/Makefile
❸                 include/Makefile
                  libjup/Makefile
                  src/Makefile])
  ...
```

Listing 6-3: configure.ac: Adding the include *and* libjup *directory makefiles*

Three unrelated changes were required in *configure.ac*. The first is the addition at ❶ of the Libtool setup macros LT_PREREQ and LT_INIT. The LT_PREREQ macro works just like Autoconf's AC_PREREQ macro (used a few lines higher). It indicates the earliest version of Libtool that can correctly process this project. You should choose the lowest reasonable values for the arguments in both of these macros, because higher values needlessly restrict you and your co-maintainers to more recent versions of the Autotools.[8] The LT_INIT macro initializes the Libtool system for this project.

The second change is just as interesting. I commented out the use of the AC_PROG_RANLIB macro at ❷. (And after all we went through to put it there in the first place!) Because Libtool is now building all of the project libraries, and Libtool understands all aspects of the library build process, we no longer need to instruct Autoconf to make sure ranlib is available. In fact, if you leave this macro in, you'll get a warning when you execute autoreconf -i. I've simply commented it out in Listing 6-3, but you can go ahead and delete it, if you wish.

The last change is found at ❸ in the argument to the AC_CONFIG_FILES macro call, where we've added references to the two new *Makefile.am* files that we added to the *include* and *libjup* directories.

---

8. I don't mean to state that you should only use older functionality provided by the Autotools in order to cater to your users that don't want to upgrade. Remember that those who care what versions of the Autotools you're using are the developers working on your project. This is a significantly smaller audience than the users who will be building your distribution tarballs. Choose version numbers that reflect the oldest versions of the Autotools that support the functionality you use in your *configure.ac* file. If you use the latest features, then set the version numbers accordingly and don't lose any sleep over it.

Customizing Libtool with LT_INIT Options

You can specify default values for enabling or disabling static and shared libraries in the argument list passed into the LT_INIT macro. LT_INIT accepts a single, optional argument: a whitespace-separated list of keywords. The following are the most important keywords allowed in this list, along with an explanation of their proper use.

dlopen

> This option enables checking for dlopen support. The *GNU Libtool Manual* states that this option should be used if the package makes use of the -dlopen and -dlpreopen libtool flags; otherwise, libtool will assume that the system does not support *dl-opening*. There's only one reason for using the -dlopen or -dlpreopen flags: You intend to dynamically load and import shared-library functionality at runtime by calling into the *ltdl* library within your project's source code. Additionally, these two options do very little unless you intend to use the *ltdl* library (rather than directly using the *dl* library) to manage your runtime dynamic linking. Thus, you should use this option only if you intend to use the *ltdl* library.

disable-fast-install

> This option changes the default behavior for LT_INIT to disable optimization for fast installation on systems where it matters. The concept of fast installation exists because uninstalled programs and libraries may need to be executed from within the build tree (during make check, for example). On some systems, installation location affects the final linked binary image, so Libtool must either relink programs and libraries on these systems when make install is executed or else relink programs and libraries for make check. Libtool chooses to relink for make check by default, allowing the original binaries to be installed quickly without relinking during make install. The user can override this default, depending on platform support, by specifying --enable-fast-install to configure.

shared and disable-shared

> These two options change the default behavior for creating shared libraries. The effects of the shared option are default behavior on all systems where Libtool knows how to create shared libraries. The user may override the default shared library–generation behavior by specifying either --disable-shared or --enable-shared on the configure command line.

static and disable-static

> These two options change the default behavior for creating static libraries. The effects of the static option are default behavior on all systems where shared libraries have been disabled and on most systems where shared libraries have been enabled. If shared libraries are enabled, the user may override this default by specifying --disable-static on the configure command line. Libtool will always generate static libraries on systems without shared libraries. Hence, you can't (effectively) use the disable-shared and disable-static arguments to LT_INIT or the --disable-shared

and `--disable-static` command-line options for configure at the same time. (Note, however, that you may use the shared and static `LT_INIT` options or the `--enable-shared` and `--enable-static` command-line options together.)

pic-only and no-pic

These two options change the default behavior for creating and using PIC object code. The user may override the defaults set by these options by specifying `--without-pic` or `--with-pic` on the configure command line. I'll discuss the meaning of PIC object code in "So What Is PIC, Anyway?" on page 164.

NOTE *I've omitted the description for the `win32-dll` option. I mention it here for completeness.*

Now that we've finished setting up the build system for the new library, we can move on to discussing the source code. Listing 6-4 shows the contents of the new *jup_print.c* source file that's referenced in the second line of *libjup/ Makefile.am*. Listing 6-5 shows the contents of the new *include/libjupiter.h* library header file.

```
#include <libjupiter.h>
#include <jupcommon.h>

int jupiter_print(const char * name)
{
    print_routine(name);
}
```

Listing 6-4: libjup/jup_print.c: The initial contents of the shared-library source file

```
#ifndef LIBJUPITER_H_INCLUDED
#define LIBJUPITER_H_INCLUDED

int jupiter_print(const char * name);

#endif /* LIBJUPITER_H_INCLUDED */
```

Listing 6-5: include/libjupiter.h: The initial contents of the shared-library public header file

This leads us to another general software engineering principle. I've heard it called by many names, but the one I tend to use the most is the *DRY principle*—the acronym stands for *don't repeat yourself.* C function prototypes are very useful because, when used correctly, they enforce the fact that the public's view of a function is identical to the package maintainer's view. All too often, I've seen source files that don't include their corresponding header files. It's easy to make a small change in a function or prototype and then not duplicate it in the other location—unless you've included the public header file within the source file. When you do this consistently, the compiler catches any inconsistencies for you.

We also need to include the static library header file (*jupcommon.h*), because we call its function (*print_routine*) from within the public library function. You may have also noticed that I placed the public header file first—there's a good

Chapter 6

reason for this. By placing the public header file first in the source file, we ensure that the use of this header file doesn't depend on any other files in the project.

For example, let's say the public header file has a hidden dependency on some construct (such as a type definition, structure, or preprocessor definition) defined in an internal header like *jupcommon.h*. If we include the public header file after *jupcommon.h*, the dependency would be hidden when the compiler begins to process the public header file, because the required construct is already available in the *translation unit* (the source file combined with all of the included header files).

I'd like to make one final point about the contents of Listing 6-5. The preprocessor conditional construct is commonly called an *include guard*. It is a mechanism for preventing your header files from inadvertently being included multiple times within the same translation unit. I use include guards routinely in all my header files, and it's good practice to do so. A good optimizing compiler (e.g., gcc) will recognize include guards in header files and skip the file entirely on subsequent inclusions within the same translation unit.

Since a public header file will be consumed by foreign source code, it's even more critical that you use include guards religiously in these header files. While you can control your own code base, you have no say in the code that one of your library consumers writes. What I'm advocating here is that you assume you're the best programmer you know, and everyone else is a little below your skill level. You can do this nicely by not mentioning it to anyone, but you should *act* like it's a fact when you write your public header files.

Next, we'll modify the `jupiter` application's `main` function so that it calls into the shared library instead of the common static library. These changes are shown in Listing 6-6.

```
#include <libjupiter.h>

int main(int argc, char * argv[])
{
    jupiter_print(argv[0]);
    return 0;
}
```

Listing 6-6: src/main.c: Changing main to call the shared-library function

Here, we've changed the print function from `print_routine`, found in the static library, to `jupiter_print`, as provided by the new shared library. We've also changed the header file included at the top from *libjupcommon.h* to *libjupiter.h*.

My choices of names for the public function and header file were arbitrary but based on a desire to provide a clean, rational, and informational public interface. The name *libjupiter.h* very clearly indicates that this header file specifies the public interface for *libjupiter.so*. I try to name library interface functions to make it clear that that they are part of an interface. How you choose to name your public interface members—files, functions, structures, type definitions, preprocessor definitions, global data, and so on—is up to you, but you should consider using a similar philosophy. Remember, the goal is to provide a great end-user experience. Intuitive naming should be a significant part of your strategy. For example, it is a good general practice to choose a common prefix for your program and library symbols.[9]

Finally, we must also modify the *src/Makefile.am* file to use our new shared library, rather than the *libjupcommon.a* static library. These changes are shown in Listing 6-7.

```
  bin_PROGRAMS = jupiter
  jupiter_SOURCES = main.c
❶ jupiter_CPPFLAGS = -I$(top_srcdir)/include
❷ jupiter_LDADD = ../libjup/libjupiter.la
  ...
```

Listing 6-7: src/Makefile.am: Adding shared-library references to the src directory makefile

Here, we've changed the `jupiter_CPPFLAGS` statement at ❶ so that it refers to the new top-level *include* directory, rather than the *common* directory. We've also changed the `jupiter_LDADD` statement at ❷ so that it refers to the new Libtool shared-library object, rather than the *libjupcommon.a* static library. All else remains the same. The syntax for referring to a Libtool library is identical to that for referring to an older, static library—only the library extension is different. The Libtool library extension *.la* stands for *libtool archive.*

Let's take a step back for a moment. Do we actually need to make this change? No, of course not. The `jupiter` application will continue to work just fine the way we originally wrote it. Linking the code for the static library's `print_routine` directly into the application works just as well as calling the new shared-library routine (which ultimately contains the same code, anyway). In fact, there is slightly more overhead in calling a shared-library routine because of the extra level of indirection when calling through a shared-library jump table.

In a real project, you might actually leave it the way it was. Because both public entry points, `main` and `jupiter_print`, call exactly the same function (`print_routine`) in *libjupcommon.a,* their functionality is identical. Why add even the slight overhead of a call through the public interface? Well, one reason is that you can take advantage of shared code. By using the shared-library function, you're not duplicating code—neither on disk nor in memory. This is the DRY principle at work.

Another reason is to exercise the interface you're providing for users of your shared library. You'll catch bugs in your public interfaces more quickly if your project code uses your shared libraries exactly the way you expect other programs to use them.

In this situation, you might now consider simply moving the code from the static library into the shared library, thereby removing the need for the static library entirely. However, I'm going to beg your indulgence with my contrived example. In a more complex project, I might very well have a need

---

9. This is especially relevant on ELF systems, where it can be difficult to determine which of your library symbols might conflict with symbols from other libraries.

for this sort of configuration. Common code is often gathered together into static convenience libraries, and more often than not, only a portion of this common code is reused in shared libraries. I'm going to leave it the way it is here for the sake of its educational value.

Reconfigure and Build

Since we've added a major new component to our project build system (Libtool), we'll clean up the work area and add the -i option to the autoreconf command line to ensure that all of the proper files are installed into the project root directory:

```
$ autoreconf -i
❶ libtoolize: putting auxiliary files in '.'.
  libtoolize: copying file './ltmain.sh'
  libtoolize: Consider adding 'AC_CONFIG_MACRO_DIR([m4])' to configure.ac and
  libtoolize: rerunning libtoolize, to keep the correct libtool macros in-tree.
  libtoolize: Consider adding '-I m4' to ACLOCAL_AMFLAGS in Makefile.am.
❷ configure.ac:16: installing './compile'
  configure.ac:8: installing './config.guess'
  configure.ac:8: installing './config.sub'
  configure.ac:6: installing './install-sh'
  configure.ac:6: installing './missing'
  common/Makefile.am: installing './depcomp'
  Makefile.am: installing './INSTALL'
  Makefile.am: installing './COPYING'
$
```

Because we completely removed all generated and copied files from our project directory, most of these notifications have to do with replacing files we've already discussed. However, there are a few noteworthy exceptions.

First, notice the comments from libtoolize at ❶. Most of them are simply suggesting that we move to the new Autotools convention of adding M4 macro files to a directory called *m4* in the project root directory. We're going to ignore these comments for now, but in Chapters 8 and 9, we'll actually do this for a real project.

As you can see at ❷, it appears that the addition of Libtool has caused a few new files to be added to our project—namely, the ltmain.sh, config.guess, and config.sub files. configure uses ltmain.sh to build a project-specific version of libtool for the Jupiter project. I'll describe the config.guess and config.sub scripts later.

Let's go ahead and execute configure and see what happens:

```
$ ./configure
...
checking for ld used by gcc... /usr/x86_64-suse-linux/bin/ld
checking if the linker (/usr/x86_64-suse-linux/bin/ld) is GNU ld... yes
checking for BSD- or MS-compatible name lister (nm)... /usr/bin/nm -B
checking the name lister (/usr/bin/nm -B) interface... BSD nm
checking whether ln -s works... yes
checking the maximum length of command line arguments... 1572864
```

```
checking whether the shell understands some XSI constructs... yes
checking whether the shell understands "+="... yes
checking for /usr/x86_64-suse-linux/bin/ld option to reload object files... -r
checking for objdump... objdump
checking how to recognize dependent libraries... pass_all
checking for ar... ar
checking for strip... strip
checking for ranlib... ranlib
checking command to parse /usr/bin/nm -B output from gcc object... ok
...
checking for shl_load... no
checking for shl_load in -ldld... no
checking for dlopen... no
checking for dlopen in -ldl... yes
checking whether a program can dlopen itself... yes
checking whether a statically linked program can dlopen itself... no
checking whether stripping libraries is possible... yes
checking if libtool supports shared libraries... yes
checking whether to build shared libraries... yes
checking whether to build static libraries... yes
...
configure: creating ./config.status
config.status: creating Makefile
config.status: creating common/Makefile
config.status: creating include/Makefile
config.status: creating libjup/Makefile
config.status: creating src/Makefile
config.status: creating config.h
config.status: executing depfiles commands
config.status: executing libtool commands
$
```

The first thing to note is that Libtool adds *significant* overhead to the configuration process. I've only shown the output lines here that are *new* since we added Libtool. All we've added to the *configure.ac* file is the reference to the LT_INIT macro, and we've nearly doubled our configure script output. This should give you some idea of the number of system characteristics that must be examined to create portable shared libraries. Fortunately, Libtool does a lot of the work for you.

Now, let's run the make command and see what sort of output we get.

NOTE *In the following examples, I've presented only the output lines that are relevant to our discussion, and I've added blank lines between lines for readability. I've used ellipses to indicate omitted output lines.*

```
$ make
...
❶ /bin/sh ../libtool --tag=CC   --mode=compile gcc -DHAVE_CONFIG_H -I. -I..
  -I../include -I../common   -g -O2 -MT libjupiter_la-jup_print.lo -MD -MP -MF
  .deps/libjupiter_la-jup_print.Tpo -c -o libjupiter_la-jup_print.lo `test -f
  'jup_print.c' || echo './'`jup_print.c
```

❷ libtool: compile: gcc -DHAVE_CONFIG_H -I. -I.. -I../include -I../common -g -O2 -MT libjupiter_la-jup_print.lo -MD -MP -MF .deps/libjupiter_la-jup_print.Tpo -c jup_print.c -fPIC -DPIC -o .libs/libjupiter_la-jup_print.o

❸ libtool: compile: gcc -DHAVE_CONFIG_H -I. -I.. -I../include -I../common -g -O2 -MT libjupiter_la-jup_print.lo -MD -MP -MF .deps/libjupiter_la-jup_print.Tpo -c jup_print.c -o libjupiter_la-jup_print.o >/dev/null 2>&1

❹ mv -f .deps/libjupiter_la-jup_print.Tpo .deps/libjupiter_la-jup_print.Plo

❺ /bin/sh ../libtool --tag=CC   --mode=link gcc -g -O2   -o libjupiter.la -rpath /usr/local/lib libjupiter_la-jup_print.lo ../common/libjupcommon.a -lpthread

❻ *** Warning: Linking the shared library libjupiter.la against the
   *** static library ../common/libjupcommon.a is not portable!

   libtool: link: gcc -shared .libs/libjupiter_la-jup_print.o   ../common/libjupcommon.a -lpthread   -Wl,-soname -Wl,libjupiter.so.0 -o .libs/libjupiter.so.0.0.0

❼ /usr/lib64/gcc/x86_64-suse-linux/4.3/../../../../x86_64-suse-linux/bin/ld: ../common/libjupcommon.a(print.o): relocation R_X86_64_32 against 'a local symbol' can not be used when making a shared object; recompile with -fPIC

   ../common/libjupcommon.a: could not read symbols: Bad value

   collect2: ld returned 1 exit status

   make[2]: *** [libjupiter.la] Error 1
   ...

We seem to have some errors to fix. The first point of interest is that the libtool script is being called at ❶ with a --mode=compile option, which causes libtool to act as a wrapper script around a somewhat modified version of a standard gcc command line. You can see the effects of this statement in the next two compiler command lines at ❷ and ❸. *Two compiler commands?* That's right. It appears that libtool is running the compiler twice against our source file.

A careful comparison of these two command lines shows that the first compiler command is using two additional flags, -fPIC and -DPIC. The first line also appears to be directing the output file to a *.libs* subdirectory, whereas the second line is saving it in the current directory. Finally, both the stdout and stderr output are redirected to */dev/null* in the second line.

NOTE   *Occasionally, you may run into a situation where a source file compiles fine in the first compilation, but it fails in the second due to a PIC-related source code defect. These sorts of problems are rare, but they can be a real pain when they occur because make halts the build with an error but doesn't give you any error messages to explain the problem! When you see this situation, simply pass the -no-suppress flag in the CFLAGS variable on the make command line in order to tell Libtool not to redirect output from the second compilation to /dev/null.*

This double-compile feature has caused a fair amount of anxiety on the Libtool mailing list over the years. Mostly, this is due to a lack of understanding of what Libtool is trying to do and why it's necessary. Using Libtool's various configure script command-line options, you can force a single compilation, but doing so brings a certain loss of functionality, which I'll explain here shortly.

The line at ❹ renames the dependency file from *.Tpo to *.Plo. You might recall from Chapters 2 and 5 that dependency files contain make rules that declare dependencies between source files and referenced header files. The C preprocessor generates these rules when you use the -MT compiler option. However, the overarching concept to understand here is that one Libtool command may (and often does) execute a group of shell commands.

The line at ❺ is another call to the libtool script, this time using the --mode=link option. This option generates a call to execute the compiler in *link mode*, passing all of the libraries and linker options specified in the *Makefile.am* file.

And finally, at ❻ we come to the first problem—a portability warning about linking a shared library against a static library. Specifically, this warning is about linking a *Libtool* shared library against a *non-Libtool* static library. Notice that this is not an error. Were it not for additional errors we'll encounter later, the library would be built in spite of this warning.

After the portability warning, libtool attempts to link the requested objects together into a shared library named *libjupiter.so.0.0.0*. But here the script runs into the real problem: at ❼ a linker error indicates that somewhere from within *libjupcommon.a*—and more specifically, within *print.o*—an x86_64 object relocation cannot be performed because the original source file (*print.c*) was apparently not compiled correctly. The linker is kind enough to tell me exactly what I need to do to fix the problem (bolded in the example): I need to compile the source code using a -fPIC compiler option.

Now, if you were to encounter this error and didn't know anything about the -fPIC option, you'd be wise to open the man page for gcc and study it before inserting compiler and linker options willy-nilly until the warning or error disappears (unfortunately, a common practice of inexperienced programmers). Software engineers should understand the meaning and nuances of every command-line option used by the tools in their build systems. Otherwise, they don't really know what they have when their build completes. It may work the way it should, but if it does, it's by luck rather than by design. Good engineers know their tools, and the best way to learn is to study error messages and their fixes until the problem is well understood before moving on.

So What Is PIC, Anyway?

When operating systems create new process address spaces, they typically load program executable images at the same memory address. This magic address is system specific. Compilers and linkers understand this, and they know what the magic address is on any given system. Therefore, when they generate internal references to function calls or global data, they can generate those references as *absolute* addresses. If you were somehow able to load the executable at a different location in memory, it would simply not work properly because the absolute addresses within the code would not be correct. At the very least, the program would crash when the processor jumped to the wrong location during a function call.

Consider Figure 6-1 for a moment. Assume we have a system whose magic executable load address is 0x10000000; this diagram depicts two process address spaces within that system. In the process on the left, an executable image is loaded correctly at address 0x10000000. At some point in the code, a jmp instruction tells the processor to transfer control to the absolute address 0x10001000, where it continues executing instructions in another area of the program.

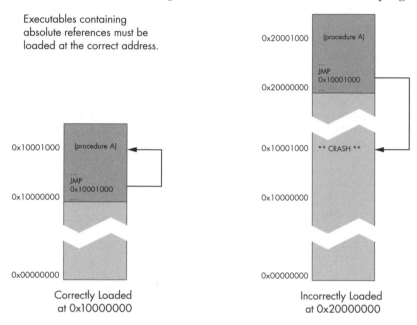

Figure 6-1: Absolute addressing in executable images

In the process on the right, the program is loaded incorrectly at address 0x20000000. When that same branch instruction is encountered, the processor jumps to address 0x10001000, because that address is hardcoded into the program image. This, of course, fails—often spectacularly by crashing, but sometimes with more subtle and dastardly ramifications.

That's how things work for program images. However, when a *shared library* is built for certain types of hardware (x86 and amd64 included), neither the compiler nor linker know beforehand where the library will be loaded. This is because many libraries may be loaded into a process, and the order in which they are loaded depends on how the *executable* is built, not the library. Furthermore, who's to say which library owns location A and which one owns location B? The fact is, a library may be loaded *anywhere* into a process where there is space for it at the time it's loaded. Only the operating system loader knows where it will finally reside—and even then, it only knows just before the library is actually loaded.

As a result, shared libraries can only be built from a special class of object files called PIC objects. *PIC* is an acronym that stands for *position-independent code*, and it implies that references within the object code are not absolute, but *relative*. When you use the -fPIC option on the compiler command line, the compiler will use somewhat less efficient relative addressing in branching instructions. Such position-independent code may be loaded anywhere.

Figure 6-2 depicts the concept of relative addressing as used when generating PIC objects. When using relative addressing, addresses work correctly regardless of where the image is loaded, because they're always encoded relative to the current instruction pointer. In Figure 6-2, the diagrams indicate a shared library loaded at the same addresses as those in Figure 6-1 above—that is, 0x10000000 and 0x20000000. In both cases, the dollar sign used in the jmp instruction represents the current instruction pointer (IP), so $ + 0xC74 tells the processor that it should jump to the instruction starting 0xC74 bytes ahead of the current position of the instruction pointer.

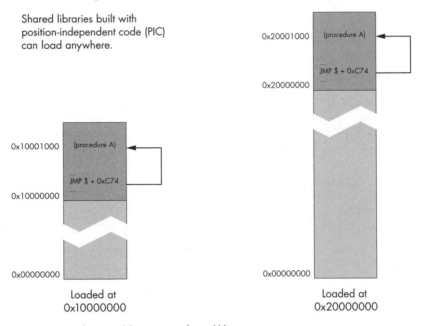

Figure 6-2: Relative addressing in shared-library images

There are various nuances to generating and using position-independent code, and you should become familiar with all of them before using them so you can choose the option that is most appropriate for your situation. For example, the GNU C compiler also supports a -fpic option (lowercase), which uses a slightly quicker but more limited mechanism to generate relocatable object code.[10]

---

10. Wikipedia has a very informative page on position-independent code although I find its treatment of Windows DLLs to be somewhat outdated. See *http://en.wikipedia.org/wiki/ Position-independent_code/*.

Fixing the Jupiter PIC Problem

From what we now understand, one way to fix our linker error is to add the
-fPIC option to the compiler command line for the source files that comprise
the *libjupcommon.a* static library. Listing 6-8 illustrates the changes required
to the *common/Makefile.am* file.

```
noinst_LIBRARIES = libjupcommon.a
libjupcommon_a_SOURCES = jupcommon.h print.c
libjupcommon_a_CFLAGS = -fPIC
```

*Listing 6-8: common/Makefile.am: Changes required for generation of PIC objects in a
static library*

And now let's retry the build:

```
$ autoreconf
$ ./configure
...
$ make
...
/bin/sh ../libtool --tag=CC   --mode=link gcc  -g -O2   -o libjupiter.la
-rpath /usr/local/lib libjupiter_la-jup_print.lo ../common/libjupcommon.a
-lpthread
```
❶ *** Warning: Linking the shared library libjupiter.la against the
*** static library ../common/libjupcommon.a is not portable!

```
libtool: link: gcc -shared  .libs/libjupiter_la-jup_print.o   ../common/
libjupcommon.a -lpthread     -Wl,-soname -Wl,libjupiter.so.0 -o .libs/
libjupiter.so.0.0.0

libtool: link: (cd ".libs" && rm -f "libjupiter.so.0" && ln -s
"libjupiter.so.0.0.0" "libjupiter.so.0")

libtool: link: (cd ".libs" && rm -f "libjupiter.so" && ln -s
"libjupiter.so.0.0.0" "libjupiter.so")

libtool: link: ar cru .libs/libjupiter.a ../common/libjupcommon.a
libjupiter_la-jup_print.o

libtool: link: ranlib .libs/libjupiter.a

libtool: link: ( cd ".libs" && rm -f "libjupiter.la" && ln -s "../
libjupiter.la" "libjupiter.la" )
...
```

We now have a shared library built properly with position-independent
code, as per system requirements. However, we still have that strange warning
at ❶ about the portability of linking a Libtool library against a static library.
The problem here is not in *what* we're doing, but rather *how* we're doing it.
You see, the concept of PIC does not apply to all hardware architectures. Some

CPUs don't support any form of absolute addressing in their instruction sets. As a result, native compilers for these platforms don't support a -fPIC option—it has no meaning for them.

If we tried, for example, to compile this code on an IBM RS/6000 system using the native IBM compiler, it would hiccup when it came to the -fPIC option on the linker command line. This is because it doesn't make sense to support such an option on a system where all code is generated as position-independent code.

One way we could get around this problem would be to make the -fPIC option conditional in *Makefile.am,* based on the target system and the tools we're using. But that's exactly the sort of problem that Libtool was designed to address! We'd have to account for all the different Libtool target system types and toolsets in order to handle the entire set of conditions that Libtool already handles. Additionally, some systems and compilers may require different command-line options to accomplish the same goal.

The way around this portability problem, then, is to let Libtool generate the static library, as well. Libtool makes a distinction between static libraries that are installed as part of a developer's kit and static libraries that are only used internally within a project. It calls such internal static libraries *convenience libraries,* and whether or not a convenience library is generated depends on the prefix used with the LTLIBRARIES primary. If the noinst prefix is used, then Libtool assumes we want a convenience library, because there's no point in generating a shared library that will never be installed. Thus, convenience libraries are always generated as static archives, which have no value unless they're linked to other code within the project.

The reason for distinguishing between convenience libraries and other forms of static libraries is that convenience libraries are always built, whereas installed static libraries are only built if the --enable-static option is specified on the configure command line, or conversely, if the --disable-static option is *not* specified, and the default library type has been set to static. The conversion from an older static library to a newer Libtool convenience library is simple enough—all we have to do is add LT to the primary name and remove the -fPIC option and the CFLAGS variable (since there were no other options being used in that variable). Note also that I've changed the library extension from *.a* to *.la.* Don't forget to change the prefix on the SOURCES variable to reflect the new name of the library—*libjupcommon.la.* These changes are highlighted in Listings 6-9 and 6-10.

```
noinst_LTLIBRARIES = libjupcommon.la
libjupcommon_la_SOURCES = jupcommon.h print.c
```

Listing 6-9: common/Makefile.am: *Changing from a static library to a Libtool static library*

```
...
libjupiter_la_LIBADD = ../common/libjupcommon.la
```

Listing 6-10: libjup/Makefile.am: *Changing from a static library to a Libtool static library*

Now when we try to build, here's what we get:

```
$ autoreconf
$ ./configure
...
$ make
...
/bin/sh ../libtool --tag=CC   --mode=compile gcc -DHAVE_CONFIG_H -I. -I..
-I../include -I../common   -g -O2 -MT libjupiter_la-jup_print.lo -MD -MP -MF
.deps/libjupiter_la-jup_print.Tpo -c -o libjupiter_la-jup_print.lo 'test -f
'jup_print.c' || echo './''jup_print.c
...
❶ /bin/sh ../libtool --tag=CC   --mode=link gcc  -g -O2   -o libjupiter.la -
❷ rpath /usr/local/lib libjupiter_la-jup_print.lo ../common/libjupcommon.la
-lpthread

libtool: link: gcc -shared  .libs/libjupiter_la-jup_print.o  -Wl,--whole-
archive ../common/.libs/libjupcommon.a -Wl,--no-whole-archive  -lpthread
-Wl,-soname -Wl,libjupiter.so.0 -o .libs/libjupiter.so.0.0.0
...
❸ libtool: link: ar cru .libs/libjupiter.a  libjupiter_la-jup_print.o  .libs/
libjupiter.lax/libjupcommon.a/print.o
...
```

You can see at ❸ that the common library is now built as a static convenience library, because the ar utility builds *libjupcommon.a*. Libtool also seems
to be building files with new and different extensions—a closer look will
reveal extensions such as *.la* and *.lo* (at ❶ and ❷, respectively). If you examine
these files, you'll find that they're actually descriptive text files containing
object and library metadata. Listing 6-11 shows the partial contents of *common/
libjupcommon.la*.

```
# libjupcommon.la - a libtool library file
# Generated by ltmain.sh (GNU libtool) 2.2.6a
#
# Please DO NOT delete this file!
# It is necessary for linking the library.
# The name that we can dlopen(3).
dlname=''
# Names of this library.
❶ library_names=''
# The name of the static archive.
❷ old_library='libjupcommon.a'
# Linker flags that can not go in dependency_libs.
inherited_linker_flags=''
# Libraries that this one depends upon.
❸ dependency_libs=' -lpthread'
...
```

Listing 6-11: common/libjupcommon.la: Textual metadata found in a library archive (.la) file

The various fields in these files help the linker—or rather the libtool wrapper script—to determine certain options that the maintainer would otherwise have to remember and manually pass to the linker on the command line. For instance, the library's shared and static names are documented at ❶ and ❷ here, as well as any library dependencies required by these libraries (at ❸).

In this library, we can see that *libjupcommon.a* depends on the *pthreads* library. But, by using Libtool, we don't have to pass a -lpthread option on the libtool command line, because libtool can detect from the contents of this metadata file (the line at ❸) that the linker will need this option, and it passes the option for us.

Making these files human readable was a minor stroke of genius, as they can tell us a lot about Libtool libraries at a glance. These files are designed to be installed on an end user's machine with their associated binaries, and in fact, the make install rules that Automake generates for Libtool libraries do just this.

Summary

In this chapter, I outlined the basic rationale for shared libraries. As an exercise, we added a shared library to Jupiter that incorporates functionality from the convenience library we created earlier. We began with a more or less intuitive approach to incorporating a static library into a Libtool shared library, and in the process, discovered a more portable and correct way to do this using Libtool convenience libraries.

As with the other packages in the Autotools toolchain, Libtool gives you a lot of functionality and flexibility. But as you've probably noticed, with this degree of functionality and flexibility comes a price—complexity. The size of Jupiter's configuration script increased dramatically with the addition of Libtool, and the time required to compile and link our project increased accordingly.

In the next chapter, we're going to continue our discussion of Libtool by looking at library versioning issues and Libtool's solution to the portability problems presented by manual dynamic runtime library management.

7

LIBRARY INTERFACE VERSIONING AND RUNTIME DYNAMIC LINKING

*Occasionally he stumbled over the truth, but hastily
picked himself up and hurried on as if nothing had happened.*
—*Sir Winston Churchill,*
quoted in The Irrepressible Churchill

In the last chapter, I explained the concepts of dynamically loadable shared libraries. I also showed you how easy it is to add Libtool-shared-library functionality and flexibility to your projects, whether your projects provide shared libraries, static libraries, convenience archives, or some mixture of these. There are still two major Libtool topics we need to cover. The first is library versioning, and the second involves using the Libtool *ltdl* library to portably build dynamically loadable modules within your projects.

When I talk about the version of a library, I'm referring specifically to the version of the library's public interface, but I need to clearly define the term *interface* in this context. A *shared-library interface* refers to all aspects of a shared library's connections with the outside world. Besides the function and data signatures that a library exports, these connections include files and file formats, network connections and wire data formats, IPC channels and protocols, and so on. When considering whether to assign a new version to a shared library, you should carefully examine all aspects of the library's interactions with the world to determine if a change will cause the library to act differently from a user's perspective.

Libtool's attempts to hide the differences among shared-library platforms are so well conceived that if you've always used Libtool to build shared libraries, you may not even realize that the way shared libraries are versioned is significantly different between platforms.

System-Specific Versioning

Let's examine how shared-library versioning works on a few different systems to put the Libtool abstraction into context.

Shared-library versioning can be done either internally or externally. *Internal versioning* means that the library name does not reflect its version in any way. Thus, internal versioning implies that some form of executable header information provides the linker with the appropriate function calls for the requested *application binary interface (ABI)*. This also implies that all function calls for all versions of the library are maintained within the same shared-library file. Libtool supports internal versioning where it's mandated by platform requirements, but it prefers to use external versioning. With *external versioning*, version information is specified in the filename itself.

In addition to library-level versioning, wherein a particular version number or string refers to the entire library interface, many Unix systems also support a form of export- or symbol-level versioning, wherein a shared library exports multiple named or numbered versions of the same function or global data item. While Libtool does not hinder the use of such export-level versioning schemes on a per-system basis, it does not provide any specific portability support for them, either. Therefore, I won't go into great detail on this subject.

Linux and Solaris Library Versioning

Modern Linux borrows much of its library versioning system from more recent versions of Sun Microsystem's Solaris operating system.[1] These systems use a form of external library versioning in which version information is encoded in the shared-library filename, following a specific pattern or template. Let's look at a partial directory listing for the */usr/lib* directory on a typical (32-bit) Linux system:

```
$ ls -lr /usr/lib
...
❶ -rwxr-xr-x ... libname.so.X.Y
❷ lrwxrwxrwx ... libname.so.X -> libname.so.X.Y
❸ lrwxrwxrwx ... libname.so -> libname.so.X
❹ -rw-r--r-- ... libname.a
...
$
```

1. Note that older Solaris systems and the original Linux shared-library system used the older, so-called *a.out* scheme, in which libraries were managed quite differently. In the a.out scheme, all binary code had to be manually mapped into memory using a mapping file that had the same base name as the library and ended in the *.sa* extension. The mapping file had to be manually edited to ensure that the program and all shared libraries were mapped into non-overlapping regions of the process address space. This system was eventually replaced with PIC code, wherein the loader can determine the position of code in memory at runtime.

The *lib*name.*so*.X.Y entry at ❶ is the actual shared-library binary file. The *X.Y* portion of the filename represents the version information, where *X* is the major version number and *Y* is the minor version number. The general rule is that changes in *X* represent non–backward compatible changes to the library's ABI, while changes in *Y* represent backward-compatible modifications, including isolated additions to the library's interface and non-intrusive bug fixes.

The *lib*name.*so*.X entry at ❷ is referred to as a library's *shared object name (soname)*[2] and is actually a soft link that points to the binary file. The soname is the format that consuming programs and libraries reference internally. The link is created by the ldconfig utility, which (among other things) ensures that an appropriate soname can locate the latest minor version of an installed library. Notice how this versioning scheme allows multiple sonames for different major versions and multiple binaries with different major and minor versions to all co-exist within a single directory.

Most libraries are installed with a so-called *linker name* entry (at ❸) as well. This is a soft link ending only in *.so* that usually refers to the soname with the highest major version number. The linker name is the name by which a library is referred to on the linker command line. The installation process, not ldconfig, creates the linker name; this allows you to run programs on your system that are linked against the latest version of a library but develop against an older version of that library, or vice versa.

The entry at ❹ refers to the static archive form of the library, which has a *.a* extension on Linux and Solaris systems.

Occasionally, you'll see what appears to be a third numbered component:

```
-rwxr-xr-x ... libname.so.X.Y.Z
```

In this example, *Y.Z* is really just a two-part minor version number. Such additional numeric information in the minor version number is sometimes referred to as the library's *patch level.*[3]

From here on out, the waters become muddied by a strange array of external and internal shared-library versioning techniques. Each of these less-than-intuitive systems is designed to overcome some of the fundamental problems that have been discovered in the Solaris system over the years.[4] Let's look at a few of them.

IBM AIX Library Versioning

Traditionally, IBM's AIX used a form of internal versioning, storing all library code within a single archive file that follows the pattern *lib*name.*a*.

---

2. Soname is pronounced "ess-oh-name."

3. According to legend, the entire minor version number can really be any alpha-numeric text, though it's usually limited to dot-separated numbers—if only to maintain the sanity of the user. The *GNU Libtool Manual* claims that the ldconfig utility will honor the patch level when it creates the soname link, automatically selecting the highest value found. If this value can be any alpha-numeric text, then it's difficult to see how this statement can be true; perhaps the utility uses some heuristic (such as lexicographical value) to attempt to isolate the more "recent" version of the library.

4. In my humble opinion, the additional problems caused by these "enhancements" aren't really justified by the solutions they provide.

This file may actually contain both static and shared forms of code, as well as 32-bit and 64-bit code. Internally, all shared-library code is stored in a single, logical, shared-object file within the archive file, while static library objects are stored as individual logical object files within the archive.

I said "traditionally" because more recent versions of AIX (including all 64-bit versions) now support the concept of loading shared-library code directly from physical *.so* files.

Libtool generates shared-library code on AIX using both of these schemes. If the AIX `-brtl` native linker flag is specified on the command line, Libtool generates shared libraries with *.so* extensions. Otherwise, it generates combined libraries following the older, single-file scheme.[5]

When using the *.so* file scheme on AIX, Libtool generates libraries named in the Linux/Solaris pattern in order to maintain a degree of alliance with these more popular platforms. Regardless of the shared-library extension used, however, version information is still not stored in the filename; it is stored internally, within the library and consuming executables. As far as I can tell, Libtool ensures that the correct internal structures are created to reflect the proper versioning information within the shared-library header. It does this by passing appropriate flags to the native linker with embedded version information derived from the Libtool version string.

Executables on most Unix systems also support the concept of an embedded runtime library search path (called a *LIBPATH* on AIX), which usually specifies a set of colon-separated filesystem paths to be searched for shared-library dependencies. You can use Libtool's `-R` command-line option to specify a library search path for both programs and libraries. Libtool will translate this option to the appropriate GNU or native linker option on any given system.

I say executables *usually* support this option because on AIX, there are a few nuances. If all of the directories specified in the LIBPATH are real directories, everything works as expected—that is, the LIBPATH acts purely as a library search path. However, if the first segment of the LIBPATH is not a real filesystem entry, it acts as a so-called *loader domain*, which is basically a namespace for a particular shared library. Thus, multiple shared libraries of the same name can be stored within the same AIX archive (*.a*) file, each assigned (by linker options) to a different loader domain. The library that matches the loader domain specified in the LIBPATH is loaded from the archive. This can have nasty side effects if you assign a loader domain via the LIBPATH that later becomes (by chance) a real filesystem entry. On the other hand, you could also specify a search directory in the LIBPATH that happens to match a loader domain in a shared library. If that directory is removed later, then you'll unintentionally begin to use the loader domain. As you can imagine, strange behavior ensues. Most of these issues have been solved by AIX developers by ensuring that loader domain strings look nothing like filesystem paths.

---

5. The `-brtl` flag tells the native AIX linker to generate load-time resolved shared objects, wherein external symbol references are resolved at the time the library is loaded, as opposed to the default link-time resolved objects, wherein external symbol references are resolved at link time. Resolving objects at load time is more similar to how objects are treated on Linux and Solaris or, more generally, on ELF systems.

MICROSOFT DLL VERSIONING

Consider Microsoft Windows *dynamic link libraries (DLLs)*. These are shared libraries in every sense of the word, and they provide a proper application programming interface. But unfortunately, Microsoft has, in the past, provided no integrated DLL interface versioning scheme. As a result, Windows developers have often referred to DLL versioning issues (tongue-in-cheek, I'm sure) as *DLL Hell*.

As a sort of band-aid fix to this problem, DLLs on Windows systems can be installed into the same directory as the program that uses them. The Windows operating system loader will always attempt to use the local copy before searching for a copy in the system path. This alleviates a part of the problem because it allows you to install a specific version of the library with the package that requires it. While this is a fair solution, it's not really a good solution, because one of the major benefits of shared libraries is that they can be shared—both on disk and in memory. If every application has its own copy of a different version of the library, then this benefit of shared libraries is lost—both on disk and in memory.

Since the introduction of this partial solution years ago, Microsoft hasn't paid much attention to DLL-sharing efficiency issues. The reasons for this include both a cavalier attitude regarding the cost of disk space and RAM and a technical issue regarding the implementation of Windows DLLs. Instead of generating position-independent code, Microsoft system architects chose to link DLLs with a specific base address and then list all of the absolute address references in a base table in the library image header. When a DLL can't be loaded at the desired base address (because of a conflict with another DLL), the loader *rebases* the DLL by picking a new base address and changing all of the absolute addresses in the code segment that are referred to in the base table. When a DLL is rebased in this manner, it can only be shared with processes that happen to rebase the DLL to the same address. The odds of accidentally encountering such a scenario—especially among applications with many DLL components—are pretty slim.

Recently, Microsoft invented the concept of the *side-by-side cache* (sometimes referred to as *SxS*), which allows developers to associate a unique identification value (a GUID, in fact) with a particular version of a DLL installed in a system location. The location directory name is derived from the DLL name and the version identifier. Applications built against SxS-versioned libraries have metadata stored in their executable headers indicating the specifically versioned DLLs that they require. If the right version is found (by newer OS loaders) in the SxS cache, then it is loaded. Based on policy in the EXE header's metadata, the loader can revert to the older scheme of looking for a local, and then a global, copy of the DLL. This is a vast improvement over earlier solutions, and it provides a very flexible versioning system.

The side-by-side cache effectively moves the Windows DLL architecture a step closer to the Unix way of managing shared libraries. Think of the SxS as a system installation location for libraries—much like the */usr/lib* directory on Unix systems. Also similar to Unix, multiple versions of the same DLL may be co-installed in the side-by-side cache.

Regardless of the similarities, since DLLs use the rebasing technique as opposed to PIC code, the side-by-side cache is still a fairly benign efficiency improvement with respect to applications that manage dozens of shared libraries. SxS is really intended for system libraries that many applications are likely to consume. These are generally based at different addresses, so that the odds of clashing (and thus rebasing) are decreased but not entirely eliminated.

The entire based approach to shared libraries has the major drawback that the program address space may become fairly fragmented as the system loader honors randomly chosen base addresses throughout a 32-bit address space. 64-bit addressing helps tremendously in this area, so you may find the side-by-side cache to be much more effective with respect to improving memory-use efficiency on 64-bit Windows systems.

On AIX systems, all code, whether static or shared, is compiled as position-independent code because AIX has only ever been ported to PowerPC and RS/6000 processors. The architectures of these processors only allow for PIC code, so AIX compilers can't generate non-PIC code.

HP-UX/AT&T SVR4 Library Versioning

Hewlett Packard's version of Unix (since HP-UX version 10.0) adds a form of library-level versioning that's very similar to the versioning used in AT&T UNIX System V Release 4. For our purposes, you can consider these two types of systems to work nearly the same way.

The native linker looks for libraries specified by their base name with a *.sl* extension. However, consuming programs and libraries contain a reference to that library's *internal name*. The internal name is assigned to the library by a linker command-line option and should contain the library's interface version number.

The actual library is named with only the major interface version as an extension, and a soft link is created with a *.sl* extension pointing to the library. Thus, a shared library on these systems will follow this pattern:

```
libname.X
libname.sl -> libname.X
```

The only version information we have to work with is a major version number, which should be used to indicate non-backward-compatible changes from one version to the next. Since there's no minor version number, as on Linux or Solaris, we can't keep multiple revisions of a particular interface version around. The only option is to replace version zero of a library with an updated version zero if bug fixes or backward-compatible enhancements (e.g., non-intrusive additions to the interface) are made.

However, we can still have multiple major versions of the library coinstalled, and Libtool takes full advantage of what's available on these systems.

The Libtool Library Versioning Scheme

The authors of Libtool tried hard to provide a versioning scheme that could be mapped to any of the schemes used by any Libtool platform. The Libtool versioning scheme is designed to be flexible enough to be forward compatible with reasonable future changes to existing Libtool platforms and even to new Libtool platforms.

Nevertheless, it's not a panacea. When extending Libtool for a new type of shared-library platform, situations have occurred (and continue to occur) that require some serious and careful evaluation. No one can be an expert on all systems, so the Libtool developers rely heavily on outside contributions to create proper mappings from the Libtool versioning scheme to the schemes of new or would-be Libtool platforms.

Library Versioning Is Interface Versioning

You should consciously avoid thinking of library version numbers (either Libtool's or those of a particular platform) as product *major*, *minor*, and *revision* values. In fact, these values have very specific meaning to the operating system loader, and they must be updated properly for each new library version in order to keep from confusing the loader. A confused loader could load the wrong version of a library based on incorrect version information assigned to the library.

Several years ago, I was working with my company's corporate versioning committee to come up with a software-versioning policy for the company as a whole. The committee wanted the engineers to ensure that the version numbers incorporated into our shared-library names were in alignment with the corporate software versioning strategy. It took me the better part of a day to convince them that a shared-library version was not related to a product version in any way, nor should such a relationship be established or enforced by them or by anyone else.

Here's why: The version number on a shared library is not really a library version but an interface version. The *interface* I'm referring to here is the application binary interface presented by a library to the user, another programmer desiring to call functions presented by the interface. An executable program has a single, well-defined, standard entry point (usually called `main` in the C language). But a shared library has multiple entry points that are generally not standardized in a manner that is widely understood. This makes it much more difficult to determine whether or not a particular version of a library is interface compatible with another version of the same library.

In Libtool's versioning scheme, shared libraries are said to support a range of interface versions, each identified by a unique integer value. If any publicly visible aspect of an interface changes between public releases, it can no longer be considered the same interface; it therefore becomes a new interface, identified by a new integer identifier. Each public release of a library in which the interface has changed simply acquires the next consecutive interface version number. Libraries that change in a backward-compatible manner between releases are said to support both the old and the new interface; thus a particular release of a library may support interface versions 2–5, for example.

Libtool library version information is specified on the `libtool` command line with the `-version-info` option, as shown in Listing 7-1.

```
libname_la_LDFLAGS = -version-info 0:0:0
```

Listing 7-1: Setting shared-library version information in a Makefile.am file

The Libtool developers wisely chose the colon separator over the period in an effort to keep developers from trying to directly associate Libtool version string values with the version numbers appended to the end of shared-library files on various platforms. The three values in the version string are respectively called the interface *current*, *revision*, and *age* values.

The *current* value represents the current interface version number. This is the value that changes when a new interface version must be declared because the interface has changed in some publicly visible way since the last public release of the library. The first interface in a library is given a version number of zero by convention. Consider a shared library in which the developer has added a new function to the set of functions exposed by this library since the last public release. The interface can't be considered the same in this new version because there's one additional function. Thus, its *current* number must be increased from zero to one.

The *age* value represents the number of back versions supported by the shared library. In mathematical terms, the library is said to support the interface range, *current − age* through *current*. In the example I just gave, a new function was added to the library, so the interface presented in this version of the library is not the same as it was in the previous version. However, the previous version is still fully supported, because the previous interface is a proper subset of the current interface. Therefore, the *age* value should also be incremented from zero to one.

The *revision* value merely represents a serial revision of the current interface. That is, if no publicly visible changes are made to a library's interface between releases—perhaps only an internal function was optimized—then the library name should change in some manner, if only to distinguish between the two releases. But both the *current* and *age* values would be the same, because the interface has not changed from the user's perspective. Therefore, the *revision* value is incremented to reflect the fact that this is a new release of the same interface. In the previous example, the *revision* value would be left at zero, because one or both of the other values was incremented.

To simplify the release process for shared libraries, the Libtool versioning algorithm should be followed step-wise for each new version of a library that is about to be publicly released:[6]

1. Start with version information 0:0:0 for each new Libtool library. (This is done automatically if you simply omit the -version-info option from the list of linker flags passed to the libtool script.) For existing libraries, start with the previous public release's version information.

2. If the library source code has changed at all since the last update, then increment *revision* (*c:r.a* becomes *c:r+1:a*).

3. If any exported functions or data have been added, removed, or changed since the last update, increment *current* and set *revision* to 0.

4. If any exported functions or data have been added since the last public release, increment *age*.

5. If any exported functions or data have been removed since the last public release, set *age* to 0.

---

6. See the Free Software Foundation's *GNU Libtool Manual* at *http://www.gnu.org/software/libtool/manual/*.

Keep in mind that this is an algorithm, and as such, it's designed to be followed step by step as opposed to jumping directly to the steps that appear to apply to your case. For example, if you removed an API function from your library since the last release, you would not simply jump to the last step and set *age* to zero. Rather, you would follow all of the steps until you reached the last step, and *then* set *age* to zero.

NOTE *Remember to update the version information only immediately before a public release of your software. More frequent updates are unnecessary and only guarantee that the current interface number becomes larger faster.*

Let's look at an example. Assume that this is the second release of a library, and the first release used a `-version-info` string of `0:0:0`. One new function was added to the library interface during this development cycle, and one existing function was deleted. The effect on the version information string for this new release of the library would be as follows:

1. Begin with the previous version information: `0:0:0`
2. `0:0:0` becomes `0:1:0` (the library's source was changed)
3. `0:1:0` becomes `1:0:0` (the library's interface was modified)
4. `1:0:0` becomes `1:0:1` (one new function was added)
5. `1:0:1` becomes `1:0:0` (one old function was removed)

It should be clear by now that there is no *direct* correlation between Libtool's *current*, *revision*, and *age* values and Linux's major, minor, and optional patch-level values. Instead, mapping rules are used to transform the values in one scheme to values in the other.

Returning to the above example, wherein a second release of a library added one function and removed one function, we ended up with a new Libtool version string of `1:0:0`. The version string `1:0:0` indicates that the library is not backward compatible with the previous version (*age* is zero), so the Linux shared-library file would be named *lib*name.*so.1.0.0*. This looks suspiciously like the Libtool version string—but don't be fooled. This fairly common coincidence is perhaps one of the most confusing aspects of the Libtool versioning abstraction.

Let's modify our example just a little to say that we've added a new library interface function but haven't removed anything. Start again with the original version information of `0:0:0` and follow the algorithm:

1. Begin with the previous version information: `0:0:0`
2. `0:0:0` becomes `0:1:0` (the library's source was changed)
3. `0:1:0` becomes `1:0:0` (the library's interface was modified)
4. `1:0:0` becomes `1:0:1` (one new function was added)
5. Not applicable (nothing was removed)

This time, we end up with a Libtool version string of 1:0:1, but the resulting Linux or Solaris shared-library filename is *lib*name.*so.0.1.0.* Consider for a moment what it means, in the face of major, minor, and patch-level values, to have a nonzero *age* value in the Libtool version string. An *age* value of one (as in this case) means that we are effectively still supporting a Linux major value of zero, because this new version of the library is 100-percent backward compatible with the previous version. The minor value in the shared-library filename has been incremented from zero to one to indicate that this is, in fact, an updated version of the soname, *lib*name.*so.0.* The patch-level value remains at zero because this value indicates a bug fix to a particular minor revision of an soname.

Once you fully understand Libtool versioning, you'll find that even this algorithm does not cover all possible interface modification scenarios. Consider, for example, version information of 0:0:0 for a shared library that you maintain. Now assume you add a new function to the interface for the next public release. This second release properly defines version information of 1:0:1 because the library supports both interface versions 0 and 1. However, just before the third release of the library, you realize that you didn't really need that new function after all, so you remove it. This is the only publicly visible change made to the library interface in this release. The algorithm would have set the version information string to 2:0:0. But in fact, you've merely removed the second interface and are now presenting the original interface once again. Technically, this library would be properly configured with a version information string of 0:1:0 because it presents a second release of version 0 of the shared-library interface. The moral of this story is that you need to fully understand the way Libtool versioning works, and then decide, based on that understanding, what the proper next-version values should be.

I'd also like to point out that the *GNU Libtool Manual* makes little effort to describe the myriad ways an interface can be different from one version of a library to another. An interface version indicates functional semantics as well as API syntax. If you change the way a function works semantically but leave the function signature untouched, you've still changed the function. If you change the network wire format of data sent by a shared library, then it's not really the same shared library from the perspective of consuming code. All the operating system loader really cares about when attempting to determine which library to load is: *Will this library work just as well as that one?* In these cases, the answer would have to be no, because even though the API interface is identical, the publicly visible way the two libraries do things is not the same.

When Library Versioning Just Isn't Enough

These types of changes to a library's interface are so complex that project maintainers will often simply rename the library, thereby skirting library versioning issues entirely. One excellent way to rename your library is to use Libtool's -release flag. This flag adds a separate class of library versioning information into the base name of the library, effectively making it an entirely new library from the perspective of the operating system loader. The -release flag is used in the manner shown in Listing 7-2.

```
libname_la_LDFLAGS = -release 2.9.0 -version-info 0:0:0
```

Listing 7-2: Setting shared-library release information in a Makefile.am file

In this example, I used -release and -version-info in the same set of Libtool flags, just to show you that they can be used together. You'll note here that the release string is specified as a series of dot-separated values. In this case, the final name of your Linux or Solaris shared library will be *lib*name-*2.9.0.so.0.0.0*.

Another reason developers choose to use release strings is to provide some sort of correlation between library versions across platforms. As demonstrated above, a particular Libtool version information string will probably result in different library names across platforms because Libtool maps version information into library names differently from platform to platform. Release information remains stable across platforms, but you should carefully consider how you wish to use release strings and version information in your shared libraries, because the way you choose to use them will affect binary compatibility between releases of your libraries. The OS loader will not consider two versions of a library to be compatible if they have different release strings, regardless of the values of those strings.

Using libltdl

Now let's move on to a discussion of Libtool's *ltdl* library. Once again, I'm going to have to add some functionality to the Jupiter project in order to illustrate these concepts. The goal here is to create a plug-in interface that the jupiter program can use to modify output based on end-user policy choices.

Necessary Infrastructure

Currently, jupiter prints *Hello, from jupiter!* (Actually, the name printed is more likely, at this point, to be a long, ugly path containing some Libtool directory garbage and some derivation of the name *jupiter*, but just pretend it prints *jupiter* for now.) We're going to add an additional parameter named salutation to the common static library method, print_routine. This parameter will also be of type pointer-to-char and will contain the leading word or phrase— the salutation—in jupiter's greeting.

Listings 7-3 and 7-4 indicate the changes that we need to make to files in the *common* subdirectory.

```
...
static void * print_it(void * data)
{
    const char ** strings = (const char **)data;
    printf("%s from %s!\n", strings[0], strings[1]);
    return 0;
}
```

```
int print_routine(const char * salutation, const char * name)
{
    const char * strings[] = {salutation, name};
#if ASYNC_EXEC
    pthread_t tid;
    pthread_create(&tid, 0, print_it, strings);
    pthread_join(tid, 0);
#else
    print_it(strings);
#endif
    return 0;
}
```

Listing 7-3: common/print.c: Adding a salutation to the print_routine *function*

```
int print_routine(const char * salutation, const char * name);
```

Listing 7-4: common/jupcommon.h: Adding a salutation to the print_routine *prototype*

Listings 7-5 and 7-6 show the changes we need to make to files in the *libjup* and *include* subdirectories.

```
...
int jupiter_print(const char * salutation, const char * name)
{
    print_routine(salutation, name);
}
```

Listing 7-5: libjup/jup_print.c: Adding a salutation to the jupiter_print *function*

```
...
int jupiter_print(const char * salutation, const char * name);
...
```

Listing 7-6: include/libjupiter.h: Adding a salutation to the jupiter_print *prototype*

And finally, Listing 7-7 shows what we need to do to *main.c* in the *src* directory.

```
...
#define DEFAULT_SALUTATION "Hello"

int main(int argc, char * argv[])
{
    const char * salutation = DEFAULT_SALUTATION;
    jupiter_print(salutation, argv[0]);
    return 0;
}
```

Listing 7-7: src/main.c: Passing a salutation to jupiter_print

To be clear, all we've really done here is parameterize the salutation throughout the print routines. That way, we can indicate from main which salutation we'd like to use. I've set the default salutation to *Hello*, so that nothing will have changed from the user's perspective. Thus, the overall effect of these changes is benign. Note also that these are all source code changes—we've made no changes to the build system. I wanted to compartmentalize these changes so as to not confuse this necessary refactoring with what we're doing to the build system to add the new module-loading functionality.

After making these changes, should you update the version number of this shared library? That depends on whether you've already shipped this library (i.e., posted a tarball) before you made the changes. The point of versioning is to maintain some semblance of control over your public interface—but if you're the only one who's ever seen it, then there's no point in changing the version number.

Adding a Plug-In Interface

I'd like to make it possible to change the salutation displayed by simply changing which plug-in module is loaded at runtime. All the changes we'll need to make to the code and build system to add this functionality will be limited to the *src* directory and its subdirectories.

First, we need to define the actual plug-in interface. We'll do this by creating a new private header file in the *src* directory called *module.h*. This file is shown in Listing 7-8.

```
#ifndef MODULE_H_INCLUDED
#define MODULE_H_INCLUDED

❶ #define GET_SALUTATION_SYM "get_salutation"

❷ typedef const char * get_salutation_t(void);
❸ const char * get_salutation(void);

#endif  /* MODULE_H_INCLUDED */
```

Listing 7-8: src/module.h: The initial contents of this file

This header file has a number of interesting aspects. First, let's look at the preprocessor definition, GET_SALUTATION_SYM at ❶. This string represents the name of the function you need to import from the plug-in module. I like to define these in the header file so all the information that needs to be reconciled exists in one place. In this case, the symbol name, the function type definition, and the function prototype must all be in alignment, and you can use this single definition for all three.

Another interesting item is the type definition at ❷. If we don't provide one, the user is going to have to invent one, or else use a complex typecast on the return value of the dlsym function. Therefore, we'll provide it here for consistency and convenience.

Finally, look at the function prototype at ❸. This isn't so much for the caller as it is for the module itself. Modules providing this function should include this header file so the compiler can catch potential misspellings of the function name.

Doing It the Old-Fashioned Way

For this first attempt, let's use the *dl* interface provided by the Solaris/Linux *libdl.so* library. In the next section, we'll convert this code over to the Libtool *ltdl* interface for greater portability. To do this right, we need to add checks to *configure.ac* to look for both the *libdl* library and the *dlfcn.h* header file. These changes to *configure.ac* are highlighted in Listing 7-9.

```
...
# Checks for header files (2).
❶ AC_CHECK_HEADERS([stdlib.h dlfcn.h])

# Checks for libraries.
# Checks for typedefs, structures, and compiler...
# Checks for library functions.
❷ AC_SEARCH_LIBS([dlopen], [dl])
...
echo \
"------------------------------------------------

 ${PACKAGE_NAME} Version ${PACKAGE_VERSION}

 Prefix: '${prefix}'.
 Compiler: '${CC} ${CFLAGS} ${CPPFLAGS}'
❸ Libraries: '${LIBS}'
...
```

Listing 7-9: configure.ac: Adding checks for the dl library and public header file

At ❶, I added the *dlfcn.h* header file to the list of files passed to the AC_CHECK_HEADERS macro, and then at ❷ I added a check for the dlopen function in the *dl* library. Note here that the AC_SEARCH_LIBS macro searches a list of libraries for a function, so this call goes in the "Checks for library functions" section rather than the "Checks for libraries" section. To help us see which libraries we're actually linking against, I've also added a line to the echo statement at the end of the file. The Libraries: line at ❸ displays the contents of the LIBS variable, which is modified by the AC_SEARCH_LIBS macro.

NOTE   *The LT_INIT macro also checks for the existence of the* dlfcn.h *header file, but I do it here explicitly so it's obvious to observers that I wish to use this header file. This is a good rule of thumb to follow, as long as it doesn't negatively affect performance too much.*

Adding a module requires several changes, so we'll make them all here, beginning with the following command sequence:

```
$ cd src
$ mkdir -p modules/hithere
$
```

I've created two new subdirectories. The first is *modules*, beneath *src*, and the second is *hithere*, beneath *modules*. Each new module added to this project will have its own directory beneath *modules*. The *hithere* module will provide the salutation *Hi there*.

Listing 7-10 illustrates how to add a SUBDIRS variable to the *src/Makefile.am* file to ensure that the build system processes the *modules/hithere* directory.

```
❶ SUBDIRS = modules/hithere

   bin_PROGRAMS = jupiter
❷ jupiter_SOURCES = main.c module.h
   ...
   greptest.sh:
❸         echo './jupiter | grep ".* from .*jupiter!"' > greptest.sh
   ...
```

Listing 7-10: src/Makefile.am: Adding a SUBDIRS variable to this Makefile.am file

The way I've used SUBDIRS at ❶ presents a new concept. Until now, Automake has only processed direct descendants of the current directory, but this is not strictly necessary, as you can see. In fact, for Jupiter, the *modules* directory will only contain additional subdirectories, so it makes little sense to provide a *modules/Makefile.am* file just so you can reference its subdirectories.

While you're editing the file, you should add the new *module.h* header file to the SOURCES variable at ❷. If you don't do this, jupiter will still compile and build correctly for you as the maintainer, but the distcheck target will fail because none of the *Makefile.am* files will have mentioned *module.h*.

We also need to change the way the greptest.sh shell script is built so it can test for any type of salutation. A simple modification of the regular expression at ❸ will suffice.

I created a *Makefile.am* file in the new *hithere* subdirectory that contains instructions on how to build the *hithere.c* source file, and then I added the *hithere.c* source file to this directory. These files are shown in Listings 7-11 and 7-12, respectively.

```
   pkglib_LTLIBRARIES = hithere.la
   hithere_la_SOURCES = hithere.c
❶ hithere_la_LDFLAGS = -module -avoid-version
```

Listing 7-11: src/modules/hithere/Makefile.am: The initial version of this file

```
#include "../../module.h"

const char * get_salutation(void)
{
    return "Hi there";
}
```

Listing 7-12: src/modules/hithere/hithere.c: *The initial version of this file*

The *hithere.c* source file includes the semi-private *module.h* header file using a double-quoted relative path. Since Automake automatically adds -I$(srcdir) to the list of *include* paths used, the C preprocessor will properly sort out the relative path. The file then defines the get_salutation function, whose prototype is in the *module.h* header file. This implementation simply returns a pointer to a static string, and as long as the library is loaded, the caller can access the string. However, callers must be aware of the scope of data references returned by plug-in modules; otherwise, the program may unload a module before a caller is done using it.

The last line of *hithere/Makefile.am* (at ❶ in Listing 7-11) requires some explanation. Here, we're using a -module option on the hithere_la_LDFLAGS variable. This is a Libtool option that tells Libtool you want to call your library *hithere*, and not *libhithere*. The *GNU Libtool Manual* makes the statement that modules do not need to be prefixed with *lib*. And since your code will be loading these modules manually, it should not have to be concerned with determining and properly using a platform-specific library prefix.

If you don't care to use module versioning on your dynamically loadable (dlopen-ed) modules, try using the Libtool -avoid-version option. This option causes Libtool to generate a shared library whose name is *lib*name.*so*, rather than *lib*name.*so.0.0.0*. It also suppresses generation of the *lib*name.*so.0* and *lib*name.*so* soft links that refer to the binary image. Because I'm using both options, my module will simply be named *hithere.so*.

In order to get this module to build, we'll need to add the new *hithere* module's makefile to the AC_CONFIG_FILES macro in *configure.ac*, as shown in Listing 7-13.

```
...
AC_CONFIG_FILES([Makefile
                common/Makefile
                include/Makefile
                libjup/Makefile
                src/Makefile
                src/modules/hithere/Makefile])
...
```

Listing 7-13: configure.ac: *Adding the* hithere *directory makefile to* AC_CONFIG_FILES

Finally, in order to use the module, we'll need to modify *src/main.c* so that it loads the module, imports the symbol, and calls it. These changes to *src/main.c* are highlighted in bold in Listing 7-14.

```
        #include <libjupiter.h>
❶ #include "module.h"

❷ #if HAVE_CONFIG_H
   # include <config.h>
   #endif

❸ #if HAVE_DLFCN_H
   # include <dlfcn.h>
   #endif

   #define DEFAULT_SALUTATION "Hello"

   int main(int argc, char * argv[])
   {
       const char * salutation = DEFAULT_SALUTATION;

❹ #if HAVE_DLFCN_H
       void * module;
       get_salutation_t * get_salutation_fp = 0;

❺     module = dlopen("./module.so", RTLD_NOW);
       if (module != 0)
       {
           get_salutation_fp = (get_salutation_t *)
                   dlsym(module, GET_SALUTATION_SYM);
           if (get_salutation_fp != 0)
               salutation = get_salutation_fp();
       }
   #endif

       jupiter_print(salutation, argv[0]);

❻ #if HAVE_DLFCN_H
       if (module != 0)
           dlclose(module);
   #endif

       return 0;
   }
```

Listing 7-14: src/main.c: Using the new plug-in module from the main function

I'm including the new private *module.h* header file at ❶, and I added pre-processor directives to conditionally include *config.h* at ❷ and *dlfcn.h* at ❸. Finally, I added two sections of code, one before and one after the original call to jupiter_print (at ❹ and ❻, respectively). Both are conditionally compiled based on the existence of a dynamic loader, allowing the code to build and run correctly on systems that do not provide the *libdl* library.

The general philosophy I use when deciding whether or not code should be conditionally compiled is this: If configure fails because a library or header file is missing, then I don't need to conditionally compile the code that uses the item `configure` checks for. If I check for a library or header file in `config-` `ure` but allow it to continue if it's missing, then I'd better use conditional compilation.

There are just a few more minor points to bring up regarding the use of *dl* interface functions. First, at ❺ `dlopen` accepts two parameters: a filename or *path* (absolute or relative) and a *flags* word, which is the bitwise composite of your choice of several flag values defined in *dlfcn.h*. Check the man page for `dlopen` to learn more about these `flag` bits. If you use a path, then `dlopen` honors that path verbatim, but if you use a filename, the library search path is searched in an attempt to locate your module. By prefixing the name with *./*, we're telling `dlopen` not to search the library path.

We want to be able to configure which module `jupiter` uses, so we're loading a generic name, *module.so*. In fact, the built module is located several directories below the *src* directory in the build tree, so we'll need to create a soft link in the current directory called *module.so* that points to the module we wish to load. This is a rather shabby form of configuration for Jupiter, but it works. In a real application, you would define the desired module to load using policy defined in some sort of configuration file, but in this example, I'm simply ignoring these details for the sake of simplicity.

The following command sequence shows our loadable module in action:

```
$ autoreconf
$ ./configure && make
...
$ cd src
$ ./jupiter
Hello from ...jupiter!
$
$ ln -s modules/hithere/.libs/hithere.so module.so
$ ./jupiter
Hi there from ...jupiter!
$
```

Converting to Libtool's *ltdl* Library

Libtool provides a wrapper library called *ltdl* that abstracts and hides some of the portability issues surrounding the use of shared libraries across many different platforms. Most applications ignore the *ltdl* library because of the added complexity involved in using it, but there are really only a few issues to deal with. I'll enumerate them here and then cover them in detail later.

- The *ltdl* functions follow a naming convention based on the *dl* library. The rule of thumb is that *dl* functions in the *ltdl* library have the prefix `lt_`. For example, `dlopen` is named `lt_dlopen`.

- Unlike the *dl* library, the *ltdl* library must be initialized and terminated at appropriate locations within a consuming application.

- Applications should be built using the -dlopen *modulename* option on the linker command line (in the *_LDFLAGS variable). This tells Libtool to link the code for the module into the application when building on platforms without shared libraries or when linking statically.

- The LTDL_SET_PRELOADED_SYMBOLS() macro should be used at an appropriate location within your program source code to ensure that module code can be accessed on non–shared library platforms or when building static-only configurations.

- Shared-library modules designed to be dlopen-ed using *ldtl* should use the -module option (and optionally, the -avoid-version option) on the linker command line (in the *_LDFLAGS variable).

- The *ltdl* library provides extensive functionality beyond the *dl* library; this can be intimidating, but know that all of this other functionality is optional.

Let's look at what we need to do to the Jupiter project build system in order to use the *ltdl* library. First, we need to modify *configure.ac* to look for the *ltdl.h* header and search for the lt_dlopen function. This means modifying references to *dlfcn.h* and the *dl* library in the AC_CHECK_HEADERS and AC_SEARCH_LIBS macros, as shown in bold in Listing 7-15.

```
...
# Checks for header files (2).
AC_CHECK_HEADERS([stdlib.h ltdl.h])

# Checks for libraries.
# Checks for typedefs, structures, and compiler...
# Checks for library functions.
AC_SEARCH_LIBS([lt_dlopen], [ltdl])
...
```

Listing 7-15: configure.ac: Switching from dl to ltdl in configure.ac

Even though we're using Libtool, we need to check for *ltdl.h* and *libltdl*, because *ltdl* is a separate library that must be installed on the end user's system. It should be treated the same as any other required third-party library. By searching for these installed resources on the user's system and failing configuration if they're not found, or by properly using preprocessor definitions in your source code, you can provide the same sort of configuration experience with *ltdl* that I've presented throughout this book when using other third-party resources.

I'd like you to recognize that this is the first time we've seen the requirement for the user to install an Autotools package on his system—and this is the very reason most people avoid using *ltdl*. The *GNU Libtool Manual* provides a detailed description of how to package the *ltdl* library with your project so it is built and installed on the user's system when your package is built and installed.[7]

---

7. In fact, the tutorial in the *GNU Libtool Manual* is a great example of adding subprojects to an Autotools build system.

Interestingly, shipping the source code for the *ltdl* library with your package is the only way to get your program to *statically* link with the *ltdl* library. Linking statically with *ltdl* has the side effect of not requiring the user to install the *ltdl* library on his system, since the library becomes part of the project's executable images. There are a few caveats, however. If your project also uses a third-party library that dynamically links to *ltdl*, you'll have a symbol conflict between the shared and static versions of the *ltdl* libraries.[8]

The next major change we need to make is in the source code—it is limited, in this case, to *src/main.c* and highlighted in bold in Listing 7-16.

```c
#include <libjupiter.h>
#include "module.h"

#if HAVE_CONFIG_H
# include <config.h>
#endif

#if HAVE_LTDL_H
# include <ltdl.h>
#endif

#define DEFAULT_SALUTATION "Hello"

int main(int argc, char * argv[])
{
    const char * salutation = DEFAULT_SALUTATION;

#if HAVE_LTDL_H
    int ltdl;
❶  lt_dlhandle module;
    get_salutation_t * get_salutation_fp = 0;

❷  LTDL_SET_PRELOADED_SYMBOLS();

❸  ltdl = lt_dlinit();
    if (ltdl == 0)
    {
❹      module = lt_dlopen("modules/hithere/hithere.la");
        if (module != 0)
        {
            get_salutation_fp = (get_salutation_t *)
                    lt_dlsym(module, GET_SALUTATION_SYM);
            if (get_salutation_fp != 0)
                salutation = get_salutation_fp();
        }
    }
#endif

    jupiter_print(salutation, argv[0]);
```

---

8. Given how rarely *ltdl* is currently used, this is an unlikely scenario these days, but this could change in the future if more packages begin to use *ltdl*.

```
#if HAVE_LTDL_H
    if (ltdl == 0)
    {
        if (module != 0)
            lt_dlclose(module);
        lt_dlexit();
    }
#endif

    return 0;
}
```

Listing 7-16: src/main.c: Switching from dl to ltdl in source code

These changes are very symmetrical with respect to the original code. Mostly, items that previously referred to DL or dl now refer to LTDL or lt_dl. For example, #if HAVE_DL_H becomes #if HAVE_LTDL_H, and so forth.

One important change is that the *ltdl* library must be initialized at ❸ with a call to lt_dlinit, whereas the *dl* library did not require initialization. In a larger program, the overhead of calling lt_dlinit and lt_dlexit would be amortized over a much larger code base.

Another important detail is the addition of the LTDL_SET_PRELOADED_SYMBOLS macro at ❷. This macro configures global variables required by the lt_dlopen and lt_dlsym functions on systems that don't support shared libraries or in cases in which the end user has specifically requested static libraries. It's benign on systems that use shared libraries.

One last detail is that the return type of dlopen is void *, or a generic pointer, whereas the return type of lt_dlopen is lt_dlhandle. (See ❶ and ❹.) This abstraction exists so *ltdl* can be ported to systems that use return types that are incompatible with a generic pointer.

When a system doesn't support shared libraries, Libtool actually links all of the modules that might be loaded right into the program. Thus, the jupiter program's linker (libtool) command line must contain some form of reference to these modules. This is done using the -dlopen *modulename* construct, as shown in Listing 7-17.

```
...
jupiter_LDADD = ../libjup/libjupiter.la -dlopen modules/hithere/hithere.la
...
```

Listing 7-17: src/Makefile.am: Adding a -dlopen option to the LDADD line

If you forget this addition to *src/Makefile.am,* you'll get a linker error about an undefined symbol. If it doesn't detect any modules being linked into the application, Libtool won't clutter your program's global symbol space with symbols that will never be referenced; the symbols required by the *ltdl* library will be missing if the symbol table is empty.

It appears that *ltdl* is not quite as flexible as *dl* regarding the sort of path information you can specify in lt_dlopen to reference a module. In order to fix this problem, I hard wired the proper relative path (*modules/hithere/hithere.la*) into *main.c*. A real program would undoubtedly use a more robust method of configuration, such as a configuration file containing the desired module name.[9]

Preloading Multiple Modules

If Libtool links multiple modules into a program on a system without shared-library support, and if those modules each provide their own version of get_salutation, then there will be a conflict of public symbols within the program's global symbol space. This is because all of these modules' symbols become part of the program's global symbol space, and the linker generally won't allow two symbols of the same name to be added to the executable symbol table. Which module's get_salutation function should be honored? Unfortunately, there's no good heuristic to resolve this conflict. The *GNU Libtool Manual* provides for this condition by defining a convention for maintaining symbol-naming uniqueness:

- All exported interface symbols should be prefixed with *modulename*_LTX_ (e.g., hithere_LTX_get_salutation).
- All remaining non-static symbols should be reasonably unique. The method Libtool suggests is to prefix them with _*modulename*_ (e.g., _jupiter_*somefunction*).
- Modules should be named differently even if they're built in different directories.

Although it's not explicitly stated in the manual, the lt_dlsym function first searches for the specified symbol as *modulename*_LTX_*symbolname*, and then, if it can't find a prefixed version of the symbol, for exactly *symbolname*. You can see that this convention is necessary, but only for cases in which Libtool may statically link such loadable modules directly into the application on systems that don't support shared libraries. The price you have to pay for Libtool's illusion of shared libraries on systems that don't support them is pretty high, but it's the going rate for getting the same loadable module functionality on all platforms.

To fix the *hithere* module's source code so that it conforms to this convention, we need to make one change to *hithere.c*, shown in Listing 7-18.

---

9. When I tried the same soft-link trick we used earlier to configure the desired module, lt_dlopen failed to find the module. You see, while the filesystem will happily hand lt_dlopen the properly dereferenced filesystem entry (*modules/hithere/hithere.la*), when lt_dlopen parses this text file, it tries to append the relative path it finds there onto the containing directory of the *link* rather than onto the *hithere.la* file to which the filesystem resolved that link.

```
❶ #define get_salutation hithere_LTX_get_salutation
❷ #include "../../module.h"

  const char * get_salutation(void)
  {
      return "Hi there";
  }
```

Listing 7-18: src/modules/hithere/hithere.c: Ensuring public symbols are unique when using ltdl

By defining the replacement for get_salutation at ❶ before the inclusion of the *module.h* header file at ❷, we're also able to change the prototype in the header file so that it matches the modified version of the function name. Because of the way the C preprocessor works, this substitution only affects the function prototype in *module.h*, not the quoted symbol string or the type definition. At this point, you may wish to go back and examine the way *module.h* is written to prove to yourself that this actually works.

Checking It All Out

You can test your program and modules for both static and dynamic shared-library systems by using the --disable-shared option on the configure command line, like this:

```
  $ autoreconf
  $ ./configure --disable-shared && make
  ...
  $ cd src
  $ ls -1p modules/hithere/.libs
❶ hithere.a
  hithere.la
  hithere.lai
  $
  $ ./jupiter
❷ Hi there, from ./jupiter!
  $
  $ cd ..
  $ make clean
  ...
  $ ./configure && make
  $ cd src
  $ ls -1p modules/hithere/.libs
  hithere.a
  hithere.la
  hithere.lai
  hithere.o
  hithere.so
  $
  $ ./jupiter
❸ Hi there, from .../jupiter!
  $
```

As you can see, the output at ❷ and ❸ contains the *hithere* module's salutation in both configurations, and yet the file listing at ❶ shows us that, in the `--disable-shared` version, the shared library doesn't even exist. It appears that *ltdl* is doing its job.

The Jupiter code base has become rather fragile, because I've ignored the issue of where to find shared libraries at runtime. As I've already mentioned, you would ultimately have to fix this problem in a real program. But given that I've finished my task of showing you how to properly use the Libtool *ltdl* library, and I've taken the *Hello, world!* concept *much* farther than anyone has a right to, I think I'll just leave that to you.

Summary

The decision to use shared libraries brings with it a whole truckload of issues, and if you're interested in maximum portability, you must deal with each of them. The *ltdl* library is not a solution to every problem. It solves some problems but brings others to the surface. Suffice it to say that using *ltdl* has trade-offs, but if you don't mind the extra maintenance effort, it's a good way to add maximum portability to your loadable-module project.

I hope that by spending some time going through the exercises in this book, you've been able to get your head around the Autotools enough to know how they work and what they're doing for you. At this point, you should be very comfortable *autotool-izing* your own projects—at least at the basic level. In the next two chapters, we'll dig even deeper into the Autotools by converting a much larger project to Autoconf, Automake, and Libtool.

8

FLAIM: AN AUTOTOOLS EXAMPLE

*Uncle Abner said . . . a person that started in to carry
a cat home by the tail was gitting knowledge
that was always going to be useful to him. . . .*
—*Mark Twain*, Tom Sawyer Abroad

 So far in this book, I've taken you on a whirl-wind tour of the main features of Autoconf, Automake, and Libtool. I've done my best to explain them in a manner that is not only simple to digest, but also easy to retain—especially if you've had the time and inclination to follow along with my examples on your own. I've always believed that no form of learning comes anywhere close to the learning that happens while doing.

In this chapter and the next, we'll continue learning about the Autotools by studying the process I used to convert an existing, real-world, open source project from a hand-coded makefile to a complete GNU Autotools build system. The examples I provide in these chapters illustrate the decisions I had to make during the conversion process, as well as concrete examples of Autotools features, including a few that I haven't yet presented in previous chapters. These two chapters will round out our study of the Autotools by presenting real solutions to real problems that I faced.

The project I chose to convert is called *FLAIM*, which stands for *FLexible Adaptable Information Management.*

What Is FLAIM?

FLAIM is a highly scalable database-management library written in C++ and built on its own thin portability layer called the FLAIM toolkit. Some readers may recognize FLAIM as the database used by both Novell eDirectory and the Novell GroupWise server. FLAIM originated at WordPerfect in the late 1980s, and it became part of Novell's software portfolio during the Novell/WordPerfect merger in 1994. Novell eDirectory uses a recent spin-off of the current version of FLAIM to manage directory information bases that contain over a billion objects, and GroupWise uses a much earlier spin-off to manage various server-side databases.

Novell made the FLAIM source code available as an open source project licensed under the GNU Lesser General Public License (LGPL) version 2[1] in 2006. The FLAIM project[2] is currently hosted by SourceForge.net, and it is the result of 25 years of development and hardening in various WordPerfect and Novell products and projects.[3]

Why FLAIM?

While FLAIM is far from a mainstream OSS project, it has several qualities that make it a perfect example for showing how to convert a project to use the Autotools. For one, FLAIM is currently built using a hand-coded GNU makefile that contains over 2,000 lines of complex make script. The FLAIM makefile contains a number of GNU make–specific constructs, and thus, you can only process this makefile using GNU make. Individual (but nearly identical) makefiles are used to build the *flaim*, *xflaim*, and *flaimsql* database libraries, and the FLAIM toolkit (*ftk*), as well as several utility and sample programs on Linux, various flavors of Unix, Windows, and NetWare.

The existing FLAIM build system targets several different flavors of Unix, including AIX, Solaris, and HP-UX, as well as Apple's OS X. It also targets multiple compilers on these systems. These features make FLAIM ideal for this sample conversion project because I can show you how to handle differences in operating systems and toolsets in the new *configure.ac* files.

The existing build system also contains rules for many of the standard Autotools targets, such as distribution tarballs. Additionally, it provides rules for building binary installation packages, as well as RPMs for systems that can build and install RPM packages. It even provides targets for building Doxygen[4] description files, which it then uses to build source documentation. I'll spend a few paragraphs showing you how you can add these types of targets to the infrastructure provided by Automake.

---

1. See the website for the GNU Lesser General Public License, version 2.1 at *http://www.gnu.org/licenses/lgpl-2.1.html/*.

2. See "FLAIM Introduction" on the FLAIM project wiki at *http://flaim.sourceforge.net/*.

3. You can read more about the history and development of FLAIM at *http://sourceforge.net/projects/flaim/*.

4. See *http://www.doxygen.org/*.

The FLAIM toolkit is a portability library that third-party projects can incorporate and consume independently. We can use the toolkit to demonstrate Autoconf's ability to manage separate subprojects as optional subdirectories within a project. If the user already has the FLAIM toolkit installed on his build machine, he can use the installed version or, optionally, override it with a local copy. On the other hand, if the toolkit is not installed, then the local, subdirectory-based copy will be used by default.

The FLAIM project also provides code to build both Java and C# language bindings, so I'll delve into those esoteric realms a bit. I won't go into great detail on building either Java or C# applications, but I will cover how to write *Makefile.am* files that generate both Java and C# programs and language-binding libraries.

The FLAIM project makes good use of unit tests. These are built as individual programs that run without command-line options, so I can easily show you how to add unit tests to the new FLAIM Autotools build system using Automake's trivial test framework.[5]

The FLAIM project and its original build system employ a reasonably modular directory layout, making it rather simple to convert to the Autotools. Because one of my goals is ultimately to submit this build system back to the project maintainers, it's nice not to have to rearrange too much of the source code. A simple pass of the `diff` utility over the directory tree should suffice.

An Initial Look

Let me start by saying that converting FLAIM from GNU makefiles to an Autotools build system is not a trivial project. It took me a couple of weeks, and much of that time was spent determining exactly what to build and how to do it—in other words, analyzing the legacy build system. Another significant portion of my time was spent converting aspects that lay on the outer fringes of Autotools functionality. For example, I spent *much* more time converting build system rules for building C# language bindings than I did converting rules for building the core C++ libraries.

The first step in this conversion project is to analyze FLAIM's existing directory structure and build system. What components are actually built, and which components depend on which others? Can individual components be built, distributed, and consumed independently? These types of component-level relationships are important because they'll often determine how you'll lay out your project directory structure.

The FLAIM project is actually several small projects under one umbrella project within its Subversion repository. There are three separate and distinct database products: *flaim*, *xflaim*, and *flaimsql*. The flaim subproject is the original FLAIM database library used by eDirectory and GroupWise. The xflaim project is a hierarchical XML database developed for internal projects at Novell; it is optimized for path-oriented, node-based access. The flaimsql project is an SQL layer on top of the FLAIM database. It was written as a sepa-

---

5. Autoconf supplies a more extensive test framework called Autotest. However, Autotest is still somewhat experimental, so I've decided not to cover it here.

rate library in order to optimize the lower-level FLAIM API for SQL access. This project was an experiment which, frankly, isn't quite finished (but it does compile).

The point is that all three of these database libraries are separate and unrelated to each other, with no inter-library dependencies. Since they may easily be used independently of one another, they can actually be shipped as individual distributions. You could consider each an open source project in its own right. This, then, will become one of my primary goals: to allow the FLAIM open source project to be easily broken up into smaller open source projects, which may be managed independently of one another.

The FLAIM toolkit is also an independent project. While it's tailored specifically for the FLAIM database libraries, providing just the system service abstractions required for a DBMS, it depends on nothing but itself, and thus, it may easily be used as the basis for portability within other projects without dragging along any unnecessary database baggage.[6]

The existing FLAIM project is laid out in its Subversion repository as shown in Listing 8-1.

```
trunk
  flaim
    java
    csharp
    flaim
      sample
      src
      util
    ftk
      src
      util
    sql
      src
    xflaim
      csharp
      java
      sample
      src
      util
```

Listing 8-1: The FLAIM project directory tree

The complete tree is fairly broad and somewhat deep in places, including significant utilities, tests, and other such binaries that are built by the legacy build system. At some point during the trek down into this hierarchy, I simply had to stop and consider whether it was worth converting that additional utility or layer. (If I hadn't done that, this chapter would be twice as long and half as useful.) To this end, I've decided to convert the following elements:

- The database libraries
- The unit and library interface tests

_____
6. As you might guess, the FLAIM toolkit's file I/O abstraction is highly optimized.

- The utilities and other such high-level programs found in various *util* directories
- The Java and C# language bindings found in the *xflaim* library

I'll also convert the C# unit tests, but I won't go into the Java unit tests, because I'm already converting the Java language bindings using Automake's JAVA primary. Since Automake provides no help for C#, I have to provide everything myself anyway, so I'll convert the entire C# code base. This will provide an example of writing the code for an entirely unsupported Automake product class.

Getting Started

As stated above, my first true design decision was how to organize the original FLAIM project into subprojects. As it turns out, the existing directory layout is almost perfect. I've created a master *configure.ac* file in the top-level *flaim* directory, which is just under the Subversion repository *trunk* directory. This top-most *configure.ac* file acts as a sort of Autoconf control file for each of the four lower-level projects: ftk, flaim, flaimsql, and xflaim.

I've managed the database library dependencies on the FLAIM toolkit by treating the toolkit as a pure external dependency defined by the make variables FTKINC and FTKLIB. I've conditionally defined these variables to point to one of a few different sources, including installed libraries and even locations given in user-specified configuration script options.

Adding the configure.ac Files

In the directory layout shown in Listing 8-2, I've used an annotation column to indicate the placement of individual *configure.ac* files. Each of these files represents a project that may be packaged and distributed independently.

```
trunk
  flaim         configure.ac (flaim-projects)
    flaim       configure.ac (flaim)
      sample
      src
      util
    ftk         configure.ac (ftk)
      src
      util
    sql         configure.ac (flaimsql)
      src
    xflaim      configure.ac (xflaim)
      csharp
      java
      sample
      src
      util
        java
```

Listing 8-2: An annotated update of the FLAIM project directory tree

My next task was to create these *configure.ac* files. The top-level file was trivial, so I created it by hand. The project-specific files were more complex, so I allowed the autoscan utility to do the bulk of the work for me. Listing 8-3 shows the top-level *configure.ac* file.

```
#                                              -*- Autoconf -*-
# Process this file with autoconf to produce a configure script.

AC_PREREQ([2.61])
❶ AC_INIT([flaim-projects], [1.0])
❷ AM_INIT_AUTOMAKE([-Wall -Werror foreign])
❸ LT_PREREQ([2.2])
  LT_INIT([dlopen])

❹ AC_CONFIG_MACRO_DIR([m4])
❺ AC_CONFIG_SUBDIRS([ftk flaim sql xflaim])
  AC_CONFIG_FILES([Makefile])
  AC_OUTPUT
```

Listing 8-3: configure.ac: *The umbrella project Autoconf input file*

This file is short and simple because it doesn't do much; nevertheless, there are some new and important concepts here. I invented the name *flaim-projects* and the version number *1.0*. These are not likely to change unless really dramatic changes take place in the project directory structure or the maintainers decide to ship a complete bundle of the subprojects.

The most important aspect is the AC_CONFIG_SUBDIRS macro at ❺, which I have yet to cover in this book. The argument is a whitespace-separated list of the subprojects to be built, where each is a complete *GCS*-compliant project in its own right. Here's the prototype for this macro:

```
AC_CONFIG_SUBDIRS(dir1[ dir2 ... dirN])
```

This macro allows the maintainer to set up a hierarchy of projects in much the same way that Automake SUBDIRS configures the directory hierarchy for Automake within a single project.

Because the four subprojects contain all of the actual build functionality, this *configure.ac* file acts merely as a control file, passing all specified configuration options to each of the subprojects in the order they're given in the macro's argument. The FLAIM toolkit project must be built first since the other projects depend on it.

Automake in the Umbrella Project

Automake usually requires the existence of several text files in the top-level project directory, including the *AUTHORS, COPYING, INSTALL, NEWS, README,* and *ChangeLog* files. It would be nice not to have to deal with these files in the umbrella project. One way to accomplish this is to simply not use Automake. I'd either have to write my own *Makefile.in* template for this directory or use Automake just once to generate a *Makefile.in* template that I could then check in to the repository as part of the project, along with the *install-sh* and *missing* scripts added by `automake --add-missing` (or `autoreconf -i`). Once these files were in place, I could remove `AM_INIT_AUTOMAKE` from the master *configure.ac* file.

Another option would be to keep Automake and simply use the `foreign` option at ❷ in the macro's optional parameter. This parameter contains a string of whitespace-separated options that tell Automake how to act in lieu of specific Automake command-line options. When Automake parses the *configure.ac* file, it notes these options and enables them as if they'd been passed on the command line to `automake`. The `foreign` option tells Automake that the project will not follow GNU standards, and thus, Automake will not require the usual GNU project text files.

I chose the latter of the two methods because I might wish to alter the list of subordinate projects at some point in the future, and I don't want to have to tweak a generated *Makefile.in* template by hand. I've also passed at ❷ the `-Wall` and `-Werror` options, which indicate that Automake should enable all Automake-specific warnings and report them as errors. These options have nothing to do with the user's compilation environment—only Automake processing.

Why Add the Libtool Macros?

Why include those expensive Libtool macros at ❸? Well, even though I don't do anything with Libtool in the umbrella project, the lower-level projects expect a containing project to provide all the necessary scripts, and the `LT_INIT` macro provides the `ltmain.sh` script. If you don't initialize Libtool in the umbrella project, tools like `autoreconf`, which actually look in the *parent* directory to determine if the current project is itself a subproject, will fail when they can't find scripts that the current project's *configure.ac* file requires.

For instance, `autoreconf` expects to find a file called *../ltmain.sh* within the ftk project's top-level directory. Note the reference to the parent directory here: `autoreconf` noticed, by examining the parent directory, that ftk was actually a subproject of a larger project. Rather than install all of the auxiliary scripts multiple times, the Autotools generate code that looks for scripts in the parent project's directory. This is done in an effort to reduce the number of copies of these scripts that are installed into multiproject packages.[7] If I don't use `LT_INIT` in the umbrella project, I can't successfully run `autoreconf` in the sub-projects, because the `ltmain.sh` script won't be in the parent project's top-level directory.

Adding a Macro Subdirectory

The `AC_CONFIG_MACRO_DIR` macro at ❹ indicates the name of a subdirectory in which the `aclocal` utility can find all project-specific M4 macro files. Here's the prototype:

```
AC_CONFIG_MACRO_DIR(macro-dir)
```

---

7. I don't think it's worth breaking hierarchical modularity in this manner, and to this degree, just to manage this strange child-to-parent relationship. `libtoolize` could have easily created and consumed these files within each project, and the space the files consume is hardly worth the effort that the Autotools go through to ensure there is only one copy of them in a distribution archive.

The *.m4* macro files in this directory are ultimately referenced with an M4 include statement in the aclocal-generated *aclocal.m4* file, which autoconf reads. This macro replaces the original *acinclude.m4* file with a directory containing individual macros or smaller sets of macros, each defined in their own *.m4* files.[8]

I've indicated by the parameter to AC_CONFIG_MACRO_DIR that all of the local macro files to be added to *aclocal.m4* are in a subdirectory called *m4*. As a bonus, when autoreconf -i is executed, and then when it executes the required Autotools with their respective add-missing options, these tools will note the use of this macro in *configure.ac* and add any required system macro files that are missing to the *m4* directory.

The reason I chose to use AC_CONFIG_MACRO_DIR here is that Libtool will not add its additional macro files to the project if you haven't enabled the macro directory option in this manner. Instead, it will complain that you should add these files to *acinclude.m4* yourself.[9]

Since this is a fairly complex project, and I wanted the Autotools to do this job for me, I decided to use this macro-directory feature. Future releases of the Autotools will likely require this form because it's considered the more modern way of adding macro files to *aclocal.m4*, as opposed to using a single user-generated *acinclude.m4* file.

The Top-Level Makefile.am File

The only other point to be covered regarding the umbrella project is the top-level *Makefile.am* file, shown in Listing 8-4.

```
❶ ACLOCAL_AMFLAGS = -I m4

❷ EXTRA_DIST = README.W32 tools win32

❸ SUBDIRS = ftk flaim sql xflaim

❹ rpms srcrpm:
          for dir in $(SUBDIRS); do \
            (cd $$dir && $(MAKE) $(AM_MAKEFLAGS) $@) || exit 1; \
          done

❺ dist-hook:
          rm -rf `find $(distdir) -name .svn`

  .PHONY: rpms srcrpm
```

Listing 8-4: Makefile.am: *The umbrella project Automake input file*

---

8. This entire system of combining M4 macro files into a single *aclocal.m4* file is a band-aid for a system that was not originally designed for more than one macro file. In my opinion, it could use a major overhaul by doing away with aclocal entirely and having Autoconf simply read the macro files in the specified (or defaulted) macro directory, along with other macro files found in system locations.

9. I found that my project didn't require any of the macros in the Libtool system macro files, but Libtool complained anyway.

The `ACLOCAL_AMFLAGS` variable at ❶ is required when you're using a macro subdirectory. According to the Automake documentation, this variable should be defined in the top-level *Makefile.am* file of any project that uses `AC_CONFIG_MACRO_DIR` in its *configure.ac* file. The flags specified on this line tell aclocal where it should look for macro files when it's executed by rules defined in *Makefile.am*. The format of this option is similar to that of a C-compiler command-line include (`-I`) directive; you can specify other aclocal command-line options as well.

The Autotools use this variable in two unrelated places. The first is in a make rule generated to update the *aclocal.m4* file from all of its various input sources. This rule and its supporting variable definitions are shown in Listing 8-5, which is a code snippet copied from an Autotools-generated makefile.

```
ACLOCAL_M4 = $(top_srcdir)/aclocal.m4
ACLOCAL=${SHELL} .../flaim-ch8-10/missing --run aclocal-1.10
ACLOCAL_AMFLAGS = -I m4
$(ACLOCAL_M4): $(am__aclocal_m4_deps)
        cd $(srcdir) && $(ACLOCAL) $(ACLOCAL_AMFLAGS)
```

Listing 8-5: The make rule and the variables used to update aclocal.m4 *from its various dependencies*

The `ACLOCAL_AMFLAGS` definition is also used during execution of autoreconf, which scans the top-level *Makefile.am* file for this definition and passes the value text directly to aclocal on the command line. Be aware that autoreconf does no variable expansion on this string, so if you add shell or make variable references to the text, they won't be expanded when autoreconf executes aclocal.

In Listing 8-4, I've used the `EXTRA_DIST` variable at ❷ to ensure that a few additional top-level files get distributed—these are files and directories that are specific to the Windows build system. This isn't critical to the umbrella project, since I don't intend to create distributions at this level, but I like to be complete.

The `SUBDIRS` variable at ❸ duplicates the information in the *configure.ac* file's `AC_CONFIG_SUBDIRS` macro.

The `rpms` and `srcrpm` targets at ❹ allow the end user to build RPM packages for RPM-based Linux systems. The code in this rule simply passes the commands down to each of the lower-level projects in succession.

When passing control to lower-level makefiles in the manner shown in the commands for these RPM targets, you should strive to follow this pattern. Passing the expansion of AM_MAKEFLAGS allows lower-level makefiles access to the same make flags defined in the current or parent makefile. However, you can add additional functionality to such recursive make code. To see how Automake passes control down to lower-level makefiles for its own targets, open an Automake-generated *Makefile.in* template and search for the text "`$(RECURSIVE_TARGETS):`". The code beneath this target shows exactly how Automake does it. While it looks complex at first glance, the code performs only two additional tasks. First, it ensures that continuation-after-error functionality (`make -k`) works properly, and second, it ensures that the current directory (`.`) is handled properly if found in the `SUBDIRS` variable.

This brings me to my final point about this code: If you choose to write your own recursive targets in this manner (and we'll see other examples of this later when we discuss conversion of the flaim build system), you should either avoid using a dot in the `SUBDIRS` variable or enhance the shell code to handle this special case. If you don't, your users will likely find themselves in an endless recursion loop when they attempt to make one of these targets. For a more extensive treatise on this topic, see "Item 2: Implementing Recursive Extension Targets" on page 276.

I'll discuss the `dist-hook` target at ❺ in "Automake -hook and -local Rules" on page 214.

The FLAIM Subprojects

I used `autoscan` to generate a starting point for the ftk project. The `autoscan` utility is a bit finicky when it comes to where it will look for information. If your project doesn't contain a makefile named exactly *Makefile*, or if your project already contains an Autoconf *Makefile.in* template, `autoscan` will not add any information about required libraries to the *configure.scan* output file. It has no way of determining this information except to look into your old build system, and it won't do this unless conditions are just right.

Given the complexity of the ftk project's legacy makefile, I was quite impressed with `autoscan`'s ability to parse it for library information. Listing 8-6 shows a portion of the resulting *configure.scan* file.

```
...
AC_PREREQ([2.61])
AC_INIT(FULL-PACKAGE-NAME, VERSION, BUG-REPORT-ADDRESS)
AC_CONFIG_SRCDIR([util/ftktest.cpp])
AC_CONFIG_HEADERS([config.h])

# Checks for programs.
AC_PROG_CXX
AC_PROG_CC
AC_PROG_INSTALL

# Checks for libraries.
# FIXME: Replace `main' with a function in `-lc':
AC_CHECK_LIB([c], [main])
# FIXME: Replace `main' with a function in...
AC_CHECK_LIB([crypto], [main])
...
AC_CONFIG_FILES([Makefile])
AC_OUTPUT
```

Listing 8-6: A portion of the output from autoscan when run over the ftk project directory structure

The FLAIM Toolkit configure.ac File

After modifying and renaming this *configure.scan* file, the resulting *configure.ac* file contains many new constructs, which I'll discuss in the next few sections. In order to facilitate the discussion, I split this file into two parts, the first half of which is shown in Listing 8-7.

```
#                                                    -*- Autoconf -*-
# Process this file with autoconf to produce a configure script.

AC_PREREQ([2.61])
❶ AC_INIT([FLAIMTK], [1.2], [flaim-users@lists.sourceforge.net])
❷ AM_INIT_AUTOMAKE([-Wall -Werror])
LT_PREREQ([2.2])
LT_INIT([dlopen])

❸ AC_LANG([C++])

❹ AC_CONFIG_MACRO_DIR([m4])
❺ AC_CONFIG_SRCDIR([src/flaimtk.h])
AC_CONFIG_HEADERS([config.h])

# Checks for programs.
AC_PROG_CXX
AC_PROG_INSTALL

# Checks for optional programs.
❻ FLM_PROG_TRY_DOXYGEN

# Configure options: --enable-debug[=no].
❼ AC_ARG_ENABLE([debug],
    [AS_HELP_STRING([--enable-debug],
      [enable debug code (default is no)])],
    [debug="$withval"], [debug=no])

# Configure option: --enable-openssl[=no].
AC_ARG_ENABLE([openssl],
    [AS_HELP_STRING([--enable-openssl],
      [enable the use of openssl (default is no)])],
    [openssl="$withval"], [openssl=no])

# Create Automake conditional based on the DOXYGEN variable
❽ AM_CONDITIONAL([HAVE_DOXYGEN], [test -n "$DOXYGEN"])
❾ AM_COND_IF([HAVE_DOXYGEN], [AC_CONFIG_FILES([docs/doxyfile])])
#AS_IF([test -n "$DOXYGEN"], [AC_CONFIG_FILES([docs/doxyfile])])
...
```

Listing 8-7: ftk/configure.ac: The first half of the ftk project's configure.ac *file*

At ❶, you will see that I substituted real values for the placeholders autoscan left in the AC_INIT macro. I added calls to AM_INIT_AUTOMAKE, LT_PREREQ, and LT_INIT at ❷, and I also added a call to AC_CONFIG_MACRO_DIR at ❹.

NOTE *I didn't use the foreign keyword in* AM_INIT_AUTOMAKE *this time. Since it's a real open source project, the FLAIM developers will (or at least, should) want these files. I used the* touch *command to create empty versions of the GNU project text files,[10] except for* COPYING *and* INSTALL, *which autoreconf adds.*

A new construct at ❸ is the AC_LANG macro, which indicates the programming language (and thus, the compiler) that Autoconf should use when generating compilation tests in configure. I've passed C++ as the parameter so Autoconf will compile these tests using the C++ compiler via the CXX variable, rather than the default C compiler via the CC variable. I then deleted the AC_PROG_CC macro call, since the source code for this project is written entirely in C++.

I changed the AC_CONFIG_SRCDIR file argument at ❺ to one that made more sense to me than the one randomly chosen by autoscan.

The FLM_PROG_TRY_DOXYGEN macro at ❻ is a custom macro that I wrote. Here's the prototype:

```
FLM_PROG_TRY_DOXYGEN(["quiet"])
```

I'll cover the details of how this macro works in Chapter 10. For now, just know that it manages a *precious* variable called DOXYGEN. If the variable is already set, this macro does nothing; if the variable is not set, it scans the system search path for a doxygen program, setting the variable to the program name if it finds one. I'll explain Autoconf precious variables when we get to the xflaim project.

At ❼, I added a couple of configuration options to configure's command-line parser with AC_ARG_ENABLE. I'll discuss the details of these calls more completely as we come to other new constructs that use the variables these macros define.

Automake Configuration Features

Automake provides the AM_CONDITIONAL macro I used at ❽; it has the following prototype:

```
AM_CONDITIONAL(variable, condition)
```

The variable argument is an Automake conditional name that you can use in your *Makefile.am* files to test the associated condition. The condition argument is a *shell condition*—a bit of shell script that could be used as the condition in a shell if-then statement. In fact, this is exactly how the macro uses the condition argument internally, so it must be formatted as a proper if-then statement condition expression:

```
if condition; then...
```

---

10. Of course, it's silly to distribute empty GNU text files. The thought here is that the project maintainer will fill these files with appropriate information about building, installing, and using the project. If you never intend to populate these files with quality instructions, then you're better off simply using the foreign option to disable them entirely.

The AM_CONDITIONAL macro always defines two Autoconf substitution variables named *variable*_TRUE and *variable*_FALSE. If the condition is true, *variable*_TRUE is empty and *variable*_FALSE is defined as a hash mark (#), which indicates the beginning of a comment in a makefile. If the condition is false, the definitions of these two substitution variables are reversed; that is, *variable*_FALSE is empty, and *variable*_TRUE becomes the hash mark. Automake uses these variables to conditionally comment out portions of your makefile script that are defined within Automake conditional statements.

This instance of AM_CONDITIONAL defines the conditional name HAVE_DOXYGEN, which you can use in the project's *Makefile.am* files to do something conditionally, based on whether or not doxygen can be executed successfully (via the DOXYGEN variable). Any lines of make script found within a test for truth in *Makefile.am* are prefixed with @*variable*_TRUE@ in the Automake-generated *Makefile.in* template. Conversely, any lines found within an Automake conditional test for falseness are prefixed with @*variable*_FALSE@. When config.status generates *Makefile* from *Makefile.in*, these lines are either commented out (prefixed with hash marks) or not, depending on the truth or falseness of the condition.

There's just one caveat with using AM_CONDITIONAL: You cannot call it conditionally (e.g., within a shell if-then-else statement) in the *configure.ac* file. You can't define substitution variables conditionally—you can define their contents differently based on the specified condition, but the variables themselves are either defined or not at the time Autoconf creates the configure script. Since Automake-generated template files are created long before the user executes configure, Automake must be able to rely on the existence of these variables, regardless of how they're defined.

Within the configure script, you may wish to perform other Autoconf operations based on the value of Automake conditionals. This is where the Automake-provided AM_COND_IF macro at ❾ comes into play.[11] Its prototype is as follows:

```
AM_COND_IF(conditional-variable, [if-true], [if-false])
```

If conditional-variable is defined as true by a previous call to AM_CONDITIONAL, the if-true shell script (including any Autoconf macro calls) is executed. Otherwise, the if-false shell script is executed.

Now let's say, for example, that you wish to conditionally build a portion of your project directory structure—say the *xflaim/docs/doxygen* directory—based on the Automake conditional HAVE_DOXYGEN. Perhaps you are appending the subdirectory in question onto the SUBDIRS variable within an Automake conditional statement in your *Makefile.am* file (I'm actually doing this, as you'll see in "The FLAIM Toolkit Makefile.am File" on page 212). Since make won't be building this portion of the project directory structure if the condition is false,

---

11. The AM_COND_IF macro was introduced in Automake 1.11, but there was a merge error in the 1.10.2 branch of Automake that caused information about AM_COND_IF to be inadvertently added to the documentation for version 1.10.2. If you have a version of Automake older than 1.11, you will not be able to use this macro, even though the 1.10.2 documentation shows that it is available. The code shown in the ftk project's *configure.ac* file is a reasonable work-around.

there's certainly little reason to have config.status process the *doxyfile.in* template within that directory during configuration. Therefore, you might use the code shown in Listing 8-8 in your *configure.ac* file.

```
...
AM_CONDITIONAL([HAVE_DOXYGEN], [test -n "$DOXYGEN"])
AM_COND_IF([HAVE_DOXYGEN], [AC_CONFIG_FILES([docs/doxyfile])])
...
```

Listing 8-8: ftk/configure.ac: Using AM_COND_IF to conditionally configure a template

With this code in place, configure simply will not process the *doxyfile.in* template at all within the *docs* directory if doxygen isn't installed on the user's system.

NOTE *The* doc/Makefile.in *template should not be included here because the* dist *target must be able to process all directories in the project—whether or not they're conditionally built—during execution of build targets such as* all *or* clean. *Thus, you should never conditionally process* Makefile.in *templates within* configure.ac. *However, you can certainly process other types of templates conditionally.*

Listing 8-9 shows the second half of ftk's *configure.ac* file.

```
...
# Configure for large files, even in 32-bit environments
❶ AC_SYS_LARGEFILE

# Check for pthreads
❷ ACX_PTHREAD(
   [AC_DEFINE([HAVE_PTHREAD], [1],
     [Define if you have POSIX threads libraries and header files.])
    LIBS="$PTHREAD_LIBS $LIBS"
    CFLAGS="$CFLAGS $PTHREAD_CFLAGS"
    CXXFLAGS="$CXXFLAGS $PTHREAD_CXXFLAGS"
    CC="$PTHREAD_CC"
    CXX="$PTHREAD_CXX"])

❸ # Checks for libraries.
  AC_SEARCH_LIBS([initscr], [ncurses])
  AC_CHECK_LIB([rt], [aio_suspend])
  AS_IF([test "x$openssl" = xyes],
❹  [AC_DEFINE([FLM_OPENSSL], [1], [Define to use openssl])
    AC_CHECK_LIB([ssl], [SSL_new])
    AC_CHECK_LIB([crypto], [CRYPTO_add])
    AC_CHECK_LIB([dl], [dlopen])
    AC_CHECK_LIB([z], [gzopen])])

❺ # Checks for header files.
  AC_HEADER_RESOLV
  AC_CHECK_HEADERS([arpa/inet.h fcntl.h limits.h malloc.h netdb.h netinet/in.h
  stddef.h stdlib.h string.h strings.h sys/mount.h sys/param.h sys/socket.h sys/
  statfs.h sys/statvfs.h sys/time.h sys/vfs.h unistd.h utime.h])
```

```
# Checks for typedefs, structures, and compiler characteristics.
AC_HEADER_STDBOOL
AC_C_INLINE
AC_TYPE_INT32_T
AC_TYPE_MODE_T
AC_TYPE_PID_T
AC_TYPE_SIZE_T
AC_CHECK_MEMBERS([struct stat.st_blksize])
AC_TYPE_UINT16_T
AC_TYPE_UINT32_T
AC_TYPE_UINT8_T

# Checks for library functions.
AC_FUNC_LSTAT_FOLLOWS_SLASHED_SYMLINK
AC_FUNC_MALLOC
AC_FUNC_MKTIME
AC_CHECK_FUNCS([atexit fdatasync ftruncate getcwd gethostbyaddr gethostbyname
gethostname gethrtime gettimeofday inet_ntoa localtime_r memmove memset mkdir
pstat_getdynamic realpath rmdir select socket strchr strrchr strstr])

# Configure DEBUG source code, if requested.
```
❻ `AS_IF([test "x$debug" = xyes],`
```
    [AC_DEFINE([FLM_DEBUG], [1], [Define to enable FLAIM debug features])])
```

❼ `...`

❽ `AC_CONFIG_FILES([Makefile`
```
                  docs/Makefile
                  obs/Makefile
                  obs/flaimtk.spec
                  src/Makefile
                  util/Makefile])

AC_OUTPUT
```

❾ `echo "`
```
  FLAIM toolkit ($PACKAGE_NAME) version $PACKAGE_VERSION
  Prefix.........: $prefix
  Debug Build....: $debug
  Using OpenSSL..: $openssl
  C++ Compiler...: $CXX $CXXFLAGS $CPPFLAGS
  Linker.........: $LD $LDFLAGS $LIBS
  Doxygen........: ${DOXYGEN:-NONE}
  "
```

Listing 8-9: ftk/configure.ac: The second half of the ftk project's configure.ac file

At ❶, I've called the AC_SYS_LARGEFILE macro. If the user has a 32-bit system, this macro ensures that appropriate C-preprocessor definitions (and possibly compiler options) that force the use of 64-bit file addressing (also called *large files*) are added to the *config.h.in* template. With these variables in place, C-library large-address-aware file I/O functions become available to the project source code. FLAIM, as a database system, cares very much about this feature.

Doing Threads the Right Way

There is another new construct, `ACX_PTHREAD`, at ❷. In the Jupiter project, I simply linked the jupiter program with the *pthreads* library via the `-lpthread` linker flag. But frankly, this is the wrong way to use *pthreads*.

In the presence of multiple threads of execution, you must configure many of the standard C-library functions to act in a thread-safe manner. You can do this by ensuring that one or more preprocessor definitions are visible to all of the standard library header files as they're being compiled into the program. These C-preprocessor definitions must be defined on the compiler command line, and they're not standardized between compiler vendors.

Some vendors provide entirely different standard libraries for building single-threaded versus multithreaded programs, because adding thread safety to a library reduces performance to a degree. Compiler vendors believe (correctly) that they're doing you a favor by giving you different versions of the standard library for these purposes. In this scenario, it's necessary to tell the linker to use the correct runtime libraries.

Unfortunately, every vendor does multithreading in its own way, from compiler options to library names to preprocessor definitions. But there is a reasonable solution to the problem: The Autoconf Macro Archive[12] provides a macro called `ACX_PTHREAD` that checks out a user's compiler and provides the correct flags and options for a wide variety of platforms.

Since the `ACX_PTHREAD` macro was originally written for C, I had to modify it slightly to make it work with C++, but this was not too difficult. I just had to ensure that the flags and options were placed in the `CXXFLAGS` variable along with the `CFLAGS` variable and that a `PTHREAD_CXX` variable was defined, in addition to the original `PTHREAD_CC` variable. This macro is very simple to use:

```
ACX_PTHREAD(action-if-found[, action-if-not-found])
```

It sets several environment variables, including `PTHREAD_CC`, `PTHREAD_CXX`, `PTHREAD_CFLAGS`, `PTHREAD_CXXFLAGS`, and `PTHREAD_LIBS`. It's up to the caller to use these variables properly by adding shell code to the `action-if-found` argument. If all of your project's code is multithreaded, things are simpler: You need only append these variables to, or consume them from within, the standard `CFLAGS`, `CXXFLAGS`, `CC`, `CXX`, and `LIBS` variables. The FLAIM project code base is completely multithreaded, so I chose to do this.

If you examine the contents of the *acx_pthread.m4* file in the *ftk/m4* directory, you might expect to find a large case statement that sets options for every compiler and platform combination known to man—but that's not the Autoconf way.

Instead, the macro incorporates a long list of known *pthreads* compiler options, and the generated configure script uses the host compiler to compile a small *pthreads* program with each one of these options in turn. The flags that are recognized by the compiler, and that therefore properly build the test program, are added to the `PTHREAD_CFLAGS` and `PTHREAD_CXXFLAGS` variables.

---

12. See *http://www.nongnu.org/autoconf-archive/*.

This way, `ACX_PTHREAD` stands a good chance of continuing to work properly, even in the face of significant changes to compiler options in the future—and this *is* the Autoconf way.

Getting Just the Right Libraries

I deleted the *FIXME* comments (see *configure.scan* in Listing 8-6 on page 204) above each of the `AC_CHECK_LIB` macro calls at ❸ in Listing 8-9. I started to replace the `main` placeholders in these macros with actual library function names, but then I began to wonder if all of those libraries were really necessary. I wasn't as concerned about autoscan's abilities as I was about the veracity of the original makefile. In hand-coded build systems, I've occasionally noticed that the author will cut and paste sets of library names from one makefile to another until the program builds without missing symbols.[13]

Instead of blindly continuing this trend, I chose to simply comment out all of the calls to `AC_CHECK_LIB` to see how far I could get in the build, adding them back in one at a time as required to resolve missing symbols. Unless your project consumes literally hundreds of libraries, this will only take a few extra minutes. I like to link only the libraries that are necessary for my project; it speeds up the link process, and when done religiously, provides a good form of project-level documentation.

The *configure.scan* file contained 14 such calls to `AC_CHECK_LIB`. As it turned out, the FLAIM toolkit on my 64-bit Linux system only required three of them: pthread, ncurses, and rt, so I deleted the remaining entries and swapped out the placeholder parameters for real functions in the ncurses and rt libraries.

I also converted the ncurses `AC_CHECK_LIB` call to `AC_SEARCH_LIBS` because I suspect that future FLAIM platforms may use different library names for *curses* functionality. I'd like to prepare the build system to have additional libraries searched on these platforms.

In retrospect, it appears that my gambit paid off rather handsomely, because I dropped from 14 libraries to 2. The third library was the POSIX Thread (*pthreads*) library, which is added via the `ACX_PTHREAD` macro I discussed in the previous section.

Maintainer-Defined Command-Line Options

The next four libraries are checked within an Autoconf conditional statement at ❹. This statement is based on the end user's use of the `--enable-openssl` command-line argument, which `AC_ARG_ENABLE` provides (see ❼ in Listing 8-7 on page 205).

The `AS_IF` macro works like a shell `if-then` statement. The first parameter is the condition, and the second parameter is the code to be executed if the condition is true. I use `AS_IF` instead of a shell `if-then` statement because, if any of the macros called within the conditional statement require additional macros to be expanded in order to operate correctly, `AS_IF` will ensure that these dependencies are expanded first, outside of the conditional statement. The `AS_IF` macro is part of the Autoconf auto-dependency framework (discussed in detail in Chapter 10).

---

13. For some reason, this activity is especially prevalent when libraries are being built, although programs are not immune to it.

In this case, the `openssl` variable is defined to either yes or no based on the default value given to `AC_ARG_ENABLE` and the end user's command-line choices.

The `AC_DEFINE` macro, called in the first argument of `AS_IF`, ensures that the C-preprocessor variable `FLM_OPENSSL` is defined in the *config.h* header file. The `AC_CHECK_LIB` macros then ensure that `-lssl`, `-lcrypto`, `-ldl`, and `-lz` strings are added to the `LIBS` variable, but *only* if the `openssl` variable is set to yes. We don't want to insist that the user have those libraries installed unless he asked for features that need them.

You can get as sophisticated as you want when dealing with maintainer-defined command-line options such as `--enable-openssl`. But be careful: Some levels of automation can surprise your users. For instance, automatically enabling the option because your checks found that the OpenSSL libraries were installed and accessible can be a bit disconcerting.

I left all the header file and library function checks at ❺ as specified by autoscan, because a simple text scan through the source code for header files and function names is probably pretty accurate.

At ❻, we see the conditional (`AS_IF`) use of `AC_DEFINE` based on the contents of the `debug` variable. This is another environment variable that's conditionally defined based on the results of a command-line parameter given to `configure`. The `--enable-debug` option sets the the `debug` variable to yes, which ultimately enables the `FLM_DEBUG` C-preprocessor definition within *config.h*. Both `FLM_OPENSSL` and `FLM_DEBUG` were already used within the FLAIM project source code. Using `AC_DEFINE` in this manner allows the end user to determine which features are compiled into the libraries.

I left out a fairly large chunk of code at ❼ dealing with compiler and tool optimizations, which I'll present in the next chapter. This code is identical in all of the projects' *configure.ac* files.

Finally, I added references to *src/Makefile* and *util/Makefile* at ❽ to the `AC_CONFIG_FILES` macro call, and then I added my usual echo statement at ❾ near the bottom for some visual verification of my configuration status.

The FLAIM Toolkit Makefile.am File

Ignoring the commands for Doxygen- and RPM-specific targets (for now), the *ftk/Makefile.am* file is fairly trivial. Listing 8-10 shows the entire file.

```
ACLOCAL_AMFLAGS = -I m4

EXTRA_DIST = GNUMakefile README.W32 debian netware win32

❶ if HAVE_DOXYGEN
      DOXYDIR = docs
   Endif

   SUBDIRS = src util obs $(DOXYDIR)

❷ doc_DATA = AUTHORS ChangeLog COPYING INSTALL NEWS README
```

```
        RPM = rpm

❸  rpms srcrpm: dist
           (cd obs && $(MAKE) $(AM_MAKEFLAGS) $@) || exit 1
           rpmarch=`$(RPM) --showrc | \
             grep "^build arch" | sed 's/\(.*: \)\(.*\)/\2/'`; \
           test -z "obs/$$rpmarch" || \
             ( mv obs/$$rpmarch/* . && rm -rf obs/$$rpmarch )
           rm -rf obs/$(distdir)

❹  dist-hook:
           rm -rf `find $(distdir) -name .svn`

    .PHONY: srcrpm rpms
```

Listing 8-10: ftk/Makefile.am: The entire contents of the FLAIM toolkit's top-level makefile

In this file you'll find the usual ACLOCAL_AMFLAGS, EXTRA_DIST, and SUBDIRS variable definitions, but you can also see the use of an Automake conditional at ❶. The if statement allows me to append another directory (*docs*) to the SUBDIRS list, but only if the doxygen program is available (according to configure). I used a separate variable here (DOXYDIR), but the Automake conditional could just as well have surrounded a statement that directly appends the directory name (doc) to the SUBDIRS variable using the Automake += operator.

NOTE   *Don't confuse Automake conditionals with make conditionals, which use the keywords ifeq, ifneq, ifdef, and ifndef. If you try to use an Automake conditional in* Makefile.am *without a corresponding AM_CONDITIONAL statement in* configure.ac, *Automake will complain about it. When used properly, Automake converts this construct to something that make understands before make sees it.*

Another new construct (at least in a top-level *Makefile.am* file) is the use of the doc_DATA variable at ❷. The FLAIM toolkit provides some extra documentation files in its top-level directory that I'd like to have installed. By using the doc prefix on the DATA primary, I'm telling Automake that I'd like these files to be installed as data files in the $(docdir) directory, which ultimately resolves to the $(prefix)/*share/doc* directory, by default.

Files mentioned in DATA variables that don't already have special meaning to Automake are not automatically distributed (that is, they're not added to distribution tarballs), so you have to manually distribute them by adding them to the files listed in the EXTRA_DIST variable.

NOTE   *I did not have to list the standard GNU project text files in EXTRA_DIST because they're always distributed automatically. However, I did have to mention theses files in the doc_DATA variable, because Automake makes no assumptions about which files you want to install.*

I'll defer a discussion of the RPM targets at ❸ to the next chapter.

Automake -hook and -local Rules

Automake recognizes two types of integrated extensions, which I call -local targets and -hook targets. Automake recognizes and honors -local extensions for the following standard targets:

all	info	dvi
ps	pdf	html
check	install-data	install-dvi
install-exec	install-html	install-info
install-pdf	install-ps	uninstall
installdirs	installcheck	mostlyclean
clean	distclean	maintainer-clean

Adding a -local to any of these in your *Makefile.am* files will cause the associated commands to be executed *before* the standard target. Automake does this by generating the rule for the standard target so that the -local version is one of its dependencies (if it exists).[14] In "Cleaning Your Room" on page 226, I'll show an example of this concept using a clean-local target.

The -hook targets are a bit different in that they are executed *after* the corresponding standard target is executed.[15] Automake does this by adding another command to the end of the standard target command list. This command merely executes $(MAKE) on the containing makefile, with the -hook target as the command-line target. Thus, the -hook target is executed at the end of the standard target commands in a recursive fashion.

The following standard Automake targets support -hook versions:

install-data	install-exec	uninstall
dist	distcheck	

Automake automatically adds all existing -local and -hook targets to the .PHONY rule within the generated makefile.

I use the dist-hook target at ❹ in *Makefile.am* to adjust the distribution directory after it's built but before make builds a tarball from its contents. The rm command removes extraneous files and directories that become part of the distribution directory as a result of my adding entire directories to the EXTRA_DIST variable. When you add directory names to EXTRA_DIST (*debian*, *netware*, and *win32*, in this case), everything in those directories is added to the distribution—even hidden Subversion control files and directories.

Listing 8-11 is a portion of the generated *Makefile* that shows how Automake incorporates dist-hook into the final makefile. The relevant portions are bolded.

---

14. Automake -local targets can be somewhat problematic when using parallel make (make -j), because parallel make cannot guarantee that dependencies are processed in the order in which they're listed: They may be executed in parallel. This is arguably a design flaw in Automake, but it's far too late to fix it at this point.

15. There are exceptions to this rule. In fact, the dist-hook target is actually executed after the distdir target, rather than after the dist target. Basically, the hook rules are executed where they make the most sense.

```
...
distdir: $(DISTFILES)
        ... # copy files into distdir
        $(MAKE) $(AM_MAKEFLAGS) top_distdir="$(top_distdir)" \
           distdir="$(distdir)" dist-hook
        ... # change attributes of files in distdir
...
dist dist-all: distdir
        tardir=$(distdir) && $(am__tar) | GZIP=$(GZIP_ENV) gzip -c \
          >$(distdir).tar.gz
        $(am__remove_distdir)
...
.PHONY: ... dist-hook ...
...
dist-hook:
        rm -rf `find $(distdir) -name .svn`
...
```

Listing 8-11: ftk/Makefile: The results of defining the dist-hook target in ftk/Makefile.am

This brings me to a bit of advice: Don't be afraid to dig into the generated makefiles to see exactly what Automake is doing with your code. Many people take one look at an Automake-generated makefile and immediately give up. While there is a fair amount of ugly shell code in the make commands, most of it is safe to ignore. You're usually more interested in the make rules that Automake is generating, and it's easy to separate these out. Once you understand the purpose of the rules (and you should by now), you are well on your way to becoming an Automake expert.

Designing the ftk/src/Makefile.am File

I now need to create *Makefile.am* files in the *src* and *utils* directories for the FLAIM toolkit project. I want to ensure that all of the original functionality is preserved from the old build system as I'm creating these files. Basically, this includes:

- Properly building the ftk shared and static libraries
- Properly specifying installation locations for all installed files
- Setting the ftk shared-library version information correctly
- Ensuring that all remaining unused files are distributed
- Ensuring that platform-specific compiler options are used

The template shown in Listing 8-12 should cover most of these points, so I'll be using it for all of the FLAIM library projects, with appropriate additions and subtractions, based on the needs of each individual library.

```
EXTRA_DIST = ...

lib_LTLIBRARIES = ...
include_HEADERS = ...

xxxxx_la_SOURCES = ...
xxxxx_la_LDFLAGS = -version-info x:y:z
```

Listing 8-12: A framework for the src *and* utils *directory* Makefile.am *files*

The original GNU makefile told me that the library was named *libftk.so*. This is a bad name for a library on Linux, because most of the three-letter library names are already taken. Thus, I made an executive decision and renamed the *ftk* library to *flaimtk*.

Listing 8-13 shows most of the final *ftk/src/Makefile.am* file.

```
❶ EXTRA_DIST = ftknlm.h

❷ pkgconfigdir = $(libdir)/pkgconfig
   pkgconfig_DATA = libflaimtk.pc

❸ lib_LTLIBRARIES = libflaimtk.la

❹ include_HEADERS = flaimtk.h
❺ libflaimtk_la_SOURCES = \
   ftkarg.cpp \
   ftkbtree.cpp \
   ftkcmem.cpp \
   ftkcoll.cpp \
   ...
   ftksys.h \
   ftkunix.cpp \
   ftkwin.cpp \
   ftkxml.cpp

❻ libflaimtk_la_LDFLAGS = -version-info 0:0:0
```

Listing 8-13: ftk/src/Makefile.am: *The entire file contents, minus a few dozen source files*

I added the Libtool library name, *libflaimtk.la*, to the lib_LTLIBRARIES list at ❸ and changed the *xxxxx* portions of the remaining macros in Listing 8-13 to libflaimtk. I could have entered all the source files by hand, but I noticed while reading the original makefile that it used the GNU make function macro $(wildcard src/*.cpp) to build the file list from the contents of the *src* directory. This tells me that all of the *.cpp* files within the *src* directory are required (or at least consumed) by the library. To get the file list into *Makefile.am*, I used a simple shell command to concatenate it to the end of the *Makefile.am* file (assuming I'm in the *ftk/src* directory):

```
$ ls *.cpp >> Makefile.am
```

This leaves me with a single-column, alphabetized list of all of the *.cpp* files in the *ftk/src* directory at the bottom of *ftk/src/Makefile.am*. I moved the list up to just below the `libflaimtk_la_SOURCES` line at ❺ and added backslash characters after the equal sign and each of the files except the last one. Another formatting technique is to simply wrap the line with a backslash and a carriage return approximately every 70 characters, but I prefer to put each file on a separate line, especially early in the conversion process, so I can easily extract or add files to the lists as needed.

I had to manually examine each header file in the *src* directory in order to determine its use in the project. There were only four header files, and as it turns out, the only one the FLAIM toolkit does *not* use on Unix and Linux platforms is *ftknlm.h*, which is specific to the NetWare build. I added this file to the `EXTRA_DIST` list at ❶ so it would be distributed; just because the build doesn't use it doesn't mean that users won't want or need it.[16]

The (newly renamed) *flaimtk.h* file is the only public header file, so I moved it into the `include_HEADERS` list at ❹. The other two files are used internally in the library build, so I left them in the `libflaimtk_la_SOURCES` list. Had this been my own project, I would have moved *flaimtk.h* into an *include* directory off the project root directory, but remember that one of my goals here was to limit changes to the directory structure and the source code. Moving this header file is a philosophical decision that I decided to leave to the maintainers.

Finally, I noticed in the original makefile that the last release of the *ftk* library published an interface version of *4.0*. However, since I changed the name of the library from *libftk* to *libflaimtk*, I reset this value to *0.0* because it's a different library. I replaced *x:y:z* with `0:0:0` in the -version-info option at ❻ within the `libflaimtk_la_LDFLAGS` variable.

NOTE   *A version string of 0:0:0 is the default, so I could have removed the argument entirely and achieved the same result. However, including it gives new developers some insight into how to change the interface version in the future.*

I added the `pkgconfigdir` and `pkgconfig_DATA` variables at ❷ in order to provide support for installing pkg-config metadata files for this project. (For more on the pkg-config system, see "Item 9: Using pkg-config with Autotools" on page 299.)

Moving On to the ftk/util Directory

Properly designing *Makefile.am* for the *util* directory requires examining the original makefile again for more products. A quick glance at the *ftk/util* directory showed that there was only one source file: *ftktest.cpp*. This appeared to be some sort of testing program for the *ftk* library, but I know that the FLAIM developers use it all the time in various ways besides simply for testing a build. So I had a design decision to make here: Should I build this as a normal program or as a check program?

---

16. I could have simply added this header file to the `libflaimtk_la_SOURCES` variable, because header files added to `SOURCES` variables are merely added to the distribution. But doing so would have hidden from observers the fact that this header file is not used in the Unix build in any way.

Check programs are only built when make check is executed, and they're never installed. If I want ftktest built as a regular program, but not installed, I have to use the noinst prefix rather than the usual bin prefix in the program list variable.

In either case, I probably want to add ftktest to the list of tests that are executed during make check, so the two questions here are (1) whether I want to automatically run ftktest during make check, and (2) whether I want to install the ftktest program. Given that the FLAIM toolkit is a mature product, I opted to build ftktest during make check and leave it uninstalled.

Listing 8-14 shows my final *ftk/util/Makefile.am* file.

```
FTK_INCLUDE = -I$(top_srcdir)/src
FTK_LTLIB = ../src/libflaimtk.la

check_PROGRAMS = ftktest

ftktest_SOURCES = ftktest.cpp
ftktest_CPPFLAGS = $(FTK_INCLUDE)
ftktest_LDADD = $(FTK_LTLIB)

TESTS = ftktest
```

Listing 8-14: ftk/util/Makefile.am: The final contents of this file

I hope that by now you can see the relationship between TESTS and check_PROGRAMS. To be blunt, there really is *no* relationship between the files listed in check_PROGRAMS and those listed in TESTS. The check target simply ensures that check_PROGRAMS are built before the TESTS programs and scripts are executed. TESTS can refer to anything that can be executed without command-line parameters. This separation of duties makes for a very clean and flexible system.

And that's it for the FLAIM toolkit library and utilities. I don't know about you, but I'd much rather maintain this small set of short files than a single 2,200-line makefile!

Designing the XFLAIM Build System

Now that I've finished with the FLAIM toolkit, I'll move on to the xflaim project. I'm choosing to start with xflaim, rather than flaim, because it supplies the most build features that can be converted to the Autotools, including the Java and C# language bindings (which I won't actually discuss in detail until Chapter 9). After xflaim, covering the remaining database projects would be redundant, because the processes are identical, if not a little simpler. However, you can find the other build system files in this book's downloadable companion source archive.

I generated the *configure.ac* file using autoscan once again. It's important to use autoscan in each of the individual projects, because the source code for each project is different and will thus cause different macros to be written into each *configure.scan* file. I then used the same techniques I used on the FLAIM toolkit to create xflaim's *configure.ac* file.

The XFLAIM configure.ac File

After hand-modifying the generated *configure.scan* file and renaming it *configure.ac*, I found it to be similar in many ways to the toolkit's *configure.ac* file. It's fairly long, so I'll show you only the most significant differences in Listing 8-15.

```
...
❶ # Checks for optional programs.
FLM_PROG_TRY_CSC
FLM_PROG_TRY_CSVM
FLM_PROG_TRY_JNI
FLM_PROG_TRY_JAVADOC
FLM_PROG_TRY_DOXYGEN

❷ # Configure variables: FTKLIB and FTKINC.
AC_ARG_VAR([FTKLIB], [The PATH wherein libflaimtk.la can be found.])
AC_ARG_VAR([FTKINC], [The PATH wherein flaimtk.h can be found.])
...
❸ # Ensure that both or neither are specified.
if (test -n "$FTKLIB" && test -z "$FTKINC") || \
   (test -n "$FTKINC" && test -z "$FTKLIB"); then
  AC_MSG_ERROR([Specify both FTK library and include paths, or neither.])
fi

# Not specified? Check for FTK in standard places.
if test -z "$FTKLIB"; then
❹   # Check for FLAIM toolkit as a subproject.
  if test -d "$srcdir/ftk"; then
    AC_CONFIG_SUBDIRS([ftk])
    FTKINC='$(top_srcdir)/ftk/src'
    FTKLIB='$(top_builddir)/ftk/src'
  else
❺     # Check for FLAIM toolkit as a superproject.
    if test -d "$srcdir/../ftk"; then
      FTKINC='$(top_srcdir)/../ftk/src'
      FTKLIB='$(top_builddir)/../ftk/src'
    fi
  fi
fi

❻ # Still empty? Check for *installed* FLAIM toolkit.
if test -z "$FTKLIB"; then
  AC_CHECK_LIB([flaimtk], [ftkFastChecksum],
    [AC_CHECK_HEADERS([flaimtk.h])
     LIBS="-lflaimtk $LIBS"],
    [AC_MSG_ERROR([No FLAIM toolkit found. Terminating.])])
fi

❼ # AC_SUBST command line variables from FTKLIB and FTKINC.
if test -n "$FTKLIB"; then
  AC_SUBST([FTK_LTLIB], ["$FTKLIB/libflaimtk.la"])
  AC_SUBST([FTK_INCLUDE], ["-I$FTKINC"])
fi
```

```
❽ # Automake conditionals
AM_CONDITIONAL([HAVE_JAVA], [test "x$flm_prog_have_jni" = xyes])
AM_CONDITIONAL([HAVE_CSHARP], [test -n "$CSC"])
AM_CONDITIONAL([HAVE_DOXYGEN], [test -n "$DOXYGEN"])
AC_COND_IF([HAVE_DOXYGEN], [AC_CONFIG_FILES([docs/doxygen/doxyfile])])
#AS_IF([test -n "$DOXYGEN"], [AC_CONFIG_FILES([docs/doxygen/doxyfile])])
...
echo "
  ($PACKAGE_NAME) version $PACKAGE_VERSION
  Prefix.........: $prefix
  Debug Build....: $debug
  C++ Compiler...: $CXX $CXXFLAGS $CPPFLAGS
  Linker.........: $LD $LDFLAGS $LIBS
  FTK Library....: ${FTKLIB:-INSTALLED}
  FTK Include....: ${FTKINC:-INSTALLED}
  CSharp Compiler: ${CSC:-NONE} $CSCFLAGS
  CSharp VM......: ${CSVM:-NONE}
  Java Compiler..: ${JAVAC:-NONE} $JAVACFLAGS
  JavaH Utility..: ${JAVAH:-NONE} $JAVAHFLAGS
  Jar Utility....: ${JAR:-NONE} $JARFLAGS
  Javadoc Utility: ${JAVADOC:-NONE}
  Doxygen........: ${DOXYGEN:-NONE}
"
```

Listing 8-15: xflaim/configure.ac: *The most significant portions of this Autoconf input file*

First, notice that I've invented a few more `FLM_PROG_TRY_*` macros at ❶. Here I'm checking for the existence of the following programs: a C# compiler, a C# virtual machine, a Java compiler, a JNI header and stub generator, a Java-doc generation tool, a Java archive tool, and doxygen. I've written separate macro files for each of these checks and added them to my *xflaim/m4* directory.

As with the `FLM_PROG_TRY_DOXYGEN` macro used in the toolkit, each of these macros attempts to locate the associated program, but these macros don't fail the configuration process if they can't find the program. I want to be able to use these programs if they're available, but I don't want to require the user to have them in order to build the base libraries.

You'll find a new macro, `AC_ARG_VAR`, at ❷. Like the `AC_ARG_ENABLE` and `AC_ARG_WITH` macros, `AC_ARG_VAR` allows the project maintainer to extend the command-line interface of the configure script. This macro is different, how-ever, in that it adds a public variable, rather than a command-line option, to the list of public variables that configure cares about. In this case, I'm adding two public variables, `FTKINC` and `FTKLIB`. These will show up in the configure script's help text under the section "Some influential environment variables." The *GNU Autoconf Manual* calls these variables *precious.* All of my `FLM_PROG_TRY_*` macros use the `AC_ARG_VAR` macro internally to make the associated variables both public and precious.[17]

---

17. These variables are also automatically substituted into the *Makefile.in* templates that Automake generates. However, I don't really need this substitution functionality, because I'm going to build other variables out of these ones, and I'll want the derived variables, instead of the public variables, to be substituted.

The large chunk of code beginning at ❸ actually uses these variables to set other variables used in the build system. The user can set the public variables in the environment or he can specify them on the `configure` script's command line in this manner:

```
$ ./configure FTKINC="$HOME/dev/ftk/include" ...
```

First, I'll check to see that either both or neither of the `FTKINC` and `FTKLIB` variables are specified. If only one of them is given, I have to fail with an error. The user isn't allowed to tell me where to find only *half* the toolkit; I need both the header file and the library. If neither of these variables is specified, I search for them at ❹ by looking for a subdirectory of the xflaim project directory called *ftk*. If I find one, I'll configure that directory as a subproject to be processed by Autoconf, using the `AC_CONFIG_SUBDIRS` macro.[18] I'll also set both of these variables to point to the appropriate relative locations within the ftk project.

If I don't find *ftk* as a subdirectory, I'll look for it in the parent directory at ❺. If I find it there, I'll set the variables appropriately. This time, I don't need to configure the located *ftk* directory as a subproject, because I'm assuming that the xflaim project is itself a subproject of the umbrella project. If I don't find *ftk* as either a subproject or a sibling project, I'll use the standard `AC_CHECK_LIB` and `AC_CHECK_HEADERS` macros at ❻ to see if the user's host has the toolkit library installed. In that case, I need only add `-lflaimtk` to the `LIBS` variable. Also in that case, the header file will be in the standard location: usually */usr(/local)/include*. The default functionality of the optional third argument to `AC_CHECK_LIB` would automatically add the library reference to the `LIBS` variable, but since I've overridden this default functionality, I have to add the toolkit library reference to `LIBS`.

If I don't find the library, I give up with an error message indicating that xflaim can't be built without the FLAIM toolkit. However, after making it through all these checks, if the `FTKLIB` variable is no longer empty, I use `AC_SUBST` at ❼ to publish the `FTK_INCLUDE` and `FTK_LTLIB` variables, which contain derivations of `FTKINC` and `FTKLIB` appropriate for use as command-line options to the preprocessor and the linker.

NOTE   *Chapter 10 converts the large chunk of code between ❸ and ❽ into a custom M4 macro called* `FLM_FTK_SEARCH`. *You'll find calls to this macro in the source archive versions of the project's various* configure.ac *files, instead of the code in Listing 8-15. Copies of the macro file, named* flm_ftk_search.m4, *can be found in each of the flaim, flaimsql, and xflaim projects'* m4 *directories.*

The remaining code at ❽ calls `AM_CONDITIONAL` for Java, C#, and Doxygen in a manner similar to the way I handled Doxygen in the ftk project. These macros are configured to generate warning messages indicating that the Java or C# portions of the xflaim project will not be built if those tools can't be found, but I allow the build to continue in any case.

---

18. You can use this macro conditionally and multiple times within the same *configure.ac* file.

Creating the xflaim/src/Makefile.am File

I'm skipping the *xflaim/Makefile.am* file, because it's nearly identical to *ftk/ Makefile.am*. Instead, we'll move on to *xflaim/src/Makefile.am*, which I wrote by following the same design principles used with the *ftk/src* version. It looks very similar to its ftk counterpart, with one exception: According to the original build system makefile, the Java native interface (JNI) and C# native language binding sources are compiled and linked right into the *xflaim* shared library.

This is not an uncommon practice, and it's quite useful because it alleviates the need for extra library objects built specifically for these languages. Essentially, the *xflaim* shared library exports native interfaces for these languages that are then consumed by their corresponding native wrappers.[19]

I'm going to ignore these language bindings for now, but later, when I'm finished with the entire xflaim project, I'll turn my attention back to properly hooking them into the library. With this exception then, the *Makefile.am* file shown in Listing 8-16 looks almost identical to its ftk counterpart.

```
if HAVE_JAVA
  JAVADIR = java
  JNI_LIBADD = java/libxfjni.la
endif

if HAVE_CSHARP
  CSDIR = cs
  CSI_LIBADD = cs/libxfcsi.la
endif

SUBDIRS = $(JAVADIR) $(CSDIR)

lib_LTLIBRARIES = libxflaim.la
include_HEADERS = xflaim.h

libxflaim_la_SOURCES = \
 btreeinfo.cpp \
 f_btpool.cpp \
 f_btpool.h \
 ...
 rfl.h \
 scache.cpp \
 translog.cpp

libxflaim_la_CPPFLAGS = $(FTK_INCLUDE)
libxflaim_la_LIBADD = $(JNI_LIBADD) $(CSI_LIBADD) $(FTK_LTLIB)
libxflaim_la_LDFLAGS = -version-info 3:2:0
```

Listing 8-16: xflaim/src/Makefile.am: The xflaim project src directory Automake input file

---

19. There are a few platform-specific problems to be aware of when you're building JNI libraries into native libraries in this manner. Apple's OS X version 10.4 and older seem to require that JNI libraries be named with a *.jnilib* extension; if they aren't, the JVM won't load these files, so the xflaim Java bindings won't work correctly on these systems. However, since the release of 10.6, 10.4 has been moved to end-of-life status.

I've conditionally defined the contents of the SUBDIRS variable here based on variables defined by corresponding Automake conditional statements in *configure.ac.* When make all is executed, the SUBDIRS variable conditionally recurses into the *java* and *cs* subdirectories. But when make dist is executed, a hidden DIST_SUBDIRS variable (which is created by Automake from *all of the possible contents* of the SUBDIRS variable) references all directories appended, either conditionally or unconditionally, to SUBDIRS.[20]

NOTE   *The library interface version information was extracted from the original makefile.*

Turning to the xflaim/util Directory

The *util* directory for xflaim is a bit more complex. According to the original makefile, it generates several utility programs as well as a convenience library that is consumed by these utilities.

It was somewhat more difficult to find out which source files belong to which utilities and which were not used at all. Several of the files in the *xflaim/ util* directory are not used by any of the utilities. Do we distribute these extra source files? I chose to do so, because they were already being distributed by the original build system, and adding them to the EXTRA_DIST list makes it obvious to later observers that they aren't used.

Listing 8-17 shows a portion of the *xflaim/util/Makefile.am* file; the parts that are missing are redundant.

```
EXTRA_DIST = dbdiff.cpp dbdiff.h domedit.cpp diffbackups.cpp xmlfiles

XFLAIM_INCLUDE = -I$(top_srcdir)/src
XFLAIM_LDADD = ../src/libxflaim.la

❶ AM_CPPFLAGS = $(XFLAIM_INCLUDE) $(FTK_INCLUDE)
LDADD = libutil.la $(XFLAIM_LDADD)

## Utility Convenience Library

noinst_LTLIBRARIES = libutil.la

libutil_la_SOURCES = \
 flm_dlst.cpp \
 flm_dlst.h \
 flm_lutl.cpp \
 flm_lutl.h \
 sharutil.cpp \
 sharutil.h

## Utility Programs

bin_PROGRAMS = xflmcheckdb xflmrebuild xflmview xflmdbshell
```

20. When you think about it, I believe you'll agree that this is some pretty tricky code. Automake has to unravel the values of the make variables used in SUBDIRS, which are defined within Automake conditional statements.

```
xflmcheckdb_SOURCES = checkdb.cpp
xflmrebuild_SOURCES = rebuild.cpp

xflmview_SOURCES = \
 viewblk.cpp \
 view.cpp \
 ...
 viewmenu.cpp \
 viewsrch.cpp

xflmdbshell_SOURCES = \
 domedit.h \
 fdomedt.cpp \
 fshell.cpp \
 fshell.h \
 xshell.cpp

## Check Programs

check_PROGRAMS = \
 ut_basictest \
 ut_binarytest \
 ...
 ut_xpathtest \
 ut_xpathtest2
❷ check_DATA = copy-xml-files.stamp
 check_HEADERS = flmunittest.h

 ut_basictest_SOURCES = flmunittest.cpp basictestsrv.cpp
❸ ...
 ut_xpathtest2_SOURCES = flmunittest.cpp xpathtest2srv.cpp

## Unit Tests

TESTS = \
 ut_basictest \
 ...
 ut_xpathtest2

## Miscellaneous rules required by Check Programs

❹ copy-xml-files.stamp:
        cp $(srcdir)/xmlfiles/*.xml .
        echo Timestamp > $@

❺ clean-local:
        rm -rf ix2.*
        rm -rf bld.*
        rm -rf tst.bak
        rm -f *.xml
        rm -f copy-xml-files.stamp
```

Listing 8-17: xflaim/util/Makefile.am: *The xflaim project's* util *directory Automake input file*

In this example, you can see by the ellipses that I left out several long lists of files and products. This makefile builds 22 unit tests, but because they're all identical, except for naming differences and the source files from which they're built, I only left the descriptions for two of them (at ❸).

I've defined the file-global AM_CPPFLAGS and LDADD variables at ❶ in order to associate the XFLAIM and FTK include and library files with each of the projects listed in this *Makefile.am* file. This way, I don't have to explicitly append this information to each product.

Notice that the AM_CPPFLAGS variable uses both the XFLAIM_INCLUDE and FTK_INCLUDE variables. The xflaim utilities clearly require information from both sets of header files, but the LDADD variable doesn't reference the *ftk* library, because Libtool manages intermediate library dependencies for you. Because I reference *libxflaim.la* through XFLAIM_LDADD, and because *libxflaim.la* lists *libflaimtk.la* as a dependency, Libtool is able to provide the transitive reference for me on the utility programs' linker command lines.

For a clearer picture of this, examine the contents of *libxflaim.la* (in your build directory under *xflaim/src*). You'll find a few lines near the middle of the file that look very much like the contents of Listing 8-18.

```
...
# Libraries that this one depends upon.
dependency_libs=' .../flaim/build/ftk/src/libflaimtk.la -lrt -lncurses'
...
```

Listing 8-18: The portion of xflaim/src/libxflaim.la *that shows dependency libraries*

The path information for *libflaimtk.la* is listed here; thus we don't have to specify it in the LDADD statement for the xflaim utilities.[21]

Stamp Targets

In creating this makefile, I ran across another minor problem that I hadn't anticipated. At least one of the unit tests seemed to require that some XML data files be present in the directory from which the test is executed. The test failed, and when I dug into it, I noticed that it failed while trying to open these files. Looking around a bit lead me to the *xflaim/util/xmldata* directory, which contained several dozen XML files.

I needed to copy those files into the build hierarchy's *xflaim/util* directory before I could run the unit tests. I know that products prefixed with check are built before TESTS are executed, so it occurred to me that I might list these files at ❷ in a check_DATA PLV. The check_DATA variable refers to a file called *copy-xml-files.stamp*, which is a special type of file target called a *stamp* target. Its purpose is to replace a group of unspecified files, or a non–file-based operation, with one single, representative file. This stamp file is used to indicate to the build system that all the XML data files have been copied into the *util* directory. Automake often uses stamp files in its own generated rules.

---

21. When *libxflaim.la* is installed, Libtool modifies the installed version of this file so it references the installed versions of the libraries rather than the libraries in the build directory structure.

The rule for generating the stamp file at ❹ also copies the XML data files into the test execution directory. The echo statement simply creates a file named *copy-xml-files.stamp* that contains a single word: *Timestamp*. The file may contain anything (or nothing at all). The important point here is that the file exists and has a time and date associated with it. The make utility uses this information to determine whether the copy operation needs to be executed. In this case, since *copy-xml-files.stamp* has no dependencies, its mere existence indicates to make that the operation has already been done. Delete the stamp file to get make to perform the copy operation on the next build.

This is a sort of hybrid between a true file-based rule and a phony target. Phony targets are always executed—they aren't real files, so make has no way of determining whether the associated operation should be performed based on file attributes. The timestamps of file-based rules can be checked against their dependency lists to determine whether they should be re-executed. Stamp rules like this are executed only if the stamp file is missing, because there are no dependencies against which the target's time and date should be compared.[22]

Cleaning Your Room

All files placed in the build directory should be cleaned up when the user enters make clean at the command prompt. Since I placed XML data files into the build directory, I also need to clean them up. Files listed in DATA variables are not cleaned up automatically, because DATA files are not necessarily generated. Sometimes the DATA primary is used to list static project files that need to be installed. I "created" a bunch of XML files and a stamp file, so I needed to remove these during make clean. To this end, I added the clean-local target at ❺, along with its associated rm commands.

NOTE *Be careful when deleting files copied from the source tree into the corresponding location in the build tree—you may inadvertently delete source files when building from within the source tree. You can compare $(srcdir) to "." within make commands to see if the user is building in the source tree.*

There is another way to ensure that files created using your own make rules get cleaned up during execution of the clean target. You can define the CLEANFILES variable to contain a whitespace-separated list of files (or wild-card specifications) to be removed. I used a clean-local target in this case, because the CLEANFILES variable has one caveat: It won't remove directories, only files. Each of the rm commands that removes a wild-card file specification refers to at least one directory. I'll show you a proper use of CLEANFILES shortly.

---

22. Stamp files have the inherent problem of not properly specifying the true relationship between targets and their dependencies—a critical requirement of a proper update. Regardless, a stamp file is sometimes the only reasonable way to accomplish a task within a makefile. One special case is to properly handle rules that generate multiple output or product files. GNU make has special pattern rule syntax for dealing with situations where multiple output files are generated by a single rule, but Automake tries hard not to depend on GNU make extensions. The use of stamp files in this case represents a work-around for a missing feature of make. Automake also uses stamp files when not doing so would cause a very large file set to become part of a target's dependency list. Since there are inherent negative side effects associated with stamp files, Automake reserves their use for these sorts of special cases.

Regardless of how well your unit tests clean up after themselves, you still might wish to write `clean` rules that attempt to clean up intermediary test files. That way, your makefiles will clean up droppings from interrupted tests and debug runs.[23] Remember that the user may be building in the source directory. Try to make your wild cards as specific as possible so you don't inadvertently remove source files.

I use the Automake-supported `clean-local` target here as a way to extend the `clean` target. The `clean-local` target is executed as a dependency of (and thus executed before) the `clean` target, if it exists. Listing 8-19 shows the corresponding code from the Automake-generated *Makefile*, so you can see how this infrastructure is wired up. The interesting bits are bolded.

```
...
clean: clean-am
❶ clean-am: clean-binPROGRAMS clean-checkPROGRAMS \
        clean-generic clean-libtool clean-local \
        clean-noinstLTLIBRARIES mostlyclean-am
...
❷ .PHONY: ... clean-local ...
...
clean-local:
        rm -rf ix2.*
        rm -rf bld.*
        rm -rf tst.bak
        rm -f *.xml
        rm -f copy-xml-files.stamp
...
```

Listing 8-19: Makefile: The clean rules generated by Automake from xflaim/util/Makefile.am

Automake noted that I had a target named `clean-local` in *Makefile.am*, so it added `clean-local` to the dependency list for `clean-am` at ❶ and then added it to the `.PHONY` variable at ❷. Had I not written a `clean-local` target, these references would have been missing from the generated *Makefile*.

Summary

Well, those are the basics. If you've followed along and understood what we did in this chapter, then you should be able to convert nearly any project to use an Autotools-based build system. For more details on the topics covered here, I refer you to the Autotools manuals. Often just knowing the name of a concept so you can easily find it in the manual is worth a great deal.

In the next chapter, I'll cover the stranger aspects of converting this project, including the details of building Java and C# code, adding compiler-specific optimization flags and command-line options, and even building RPM packages using user-defined make targets in your *Makefile.am* files.

---

23. You might also provide a debug option or environment variable that causes your tests to leave these droppings behind so they can be examined during debugging.

9

FLAIM PART II: PUSHING THE ENVELOPE

What we do in college is to get over our little-mindedness.
Education—to get it you have to hang around till you catch on.
—Robert Lee Frost[1]

It's a well-understood principle that no matter how many books you read, or how many lectures you attend, or how many queries you present on mailing lists, you'll still be left with unanswered questions. It's estimated that a quarter of the world's population has access to the Internet today.[2] There are hundreds of terabytes of information available from your desktop. Nevertheless, it seems every project has one or two issues that are just different enough from all others that even Internet searches are fraught with futility.

To reduce the potential frustration of learning the Autotools, this chapter continues with the FLAIM build system conversion project by tackling some of the less common features of FLAIM's build-system requirements. My hope is that by presenting solutions to some of these less common problems, you'll become familiar with the underlying framework provided by the Autotools.

---

1. Jay Parini, *Robert Frost: A Life*, p 185, (noted in his journals), citation from endnote 12.
2. See World Internet Usage Statistics News and World Population Stats at *http://www.internetworldstats.com/stats.htm/*.

Such familiarity provides the insight needed to bend the Autotools to your own unique requirements.

The *xflaim* library provides Java and C# language bindings. Automake provides rudimentary support for building Java sources, but currently provides no built-in support for building C# sources. In this chapter, I'll show you how to use Automake's built-in Java support to build the Java language bindings in xflaim, and then I'll show you how to write your own make rules for the C# language bindings.

We'll round out this chapter, and finish up the FLAIM conversion project, with discussions of using native compiler options, building generated documentation, and adding your own top-level recursive make targets.

Building Java Sources Using the Autotools

The *GNU Automake Manual* presents information on building Java sources in two different ways. The first is the traditional and widely understood method of compiling Java source code into Java byte code, which can then be executed within the Java Virtual Machine (JVM). The second way is the lesser-known method of compiling Java source code directly into native machine code using the GNU Compiler for Java (gcj) front end to the GNU compiler tool suite. The object files containing this machine code can then be linked together into native executable programs using the standard GNU linker.[3]

In this chapter, I'll focus on building Java class files from Java source files using the Automake built-in JAVA primary. We'll also explore the necessary extensions required to build and install *.jar* files.

Autotools Java Support

Autoconf has little, if any, built-in support for Java. For example, it provides no macros that locate Java tools in the end user's environment.[4] Automake's support for building Java classes is minimal, and getting it to work is not really that difficult if you're willing to dig in a bit. The biggest stumbling block is conceptual, more than functional. You have to work a little to align your understanding of the Java build process with that of the Automake designers.

Automake provides a built-in primary (JAVA) for building Java sources but it does not provide any preconfigured installation location prefixes for installing Java classes. However, the usual place to install Java classes and *.jar* files is in the $(datadir)/*java* directory, so creating a proper prefix is as simple as using the Automake prefix extension mechanism of defining a variable suffixed with *dir*, as shown in Listing 9-1.

---

3. The way the Automake manual organizes information on building Java sources may seem a bit strange when first encountered. Section 8.15, entitled "Java Support" discusses the use of gcj to build native executables from Java source files, while instructions for the more traditional operation of building Java byte code files are presented in section 10, "Other GNU Tools." The reason for this is that section 8 is about building programs and libraries, which is what the Autotools are all about.

4. The Autoconf Macro Archive (*http://www.nongnu.org/autoconf-archive/*) has plenty of user-contributed macros that can help your configuration process set you up to build Java applications from Automake scripts.

```
...
javadir = $(datadir)/java
java_JAVA = file_a.java file_b.java ...
...
```

Listing 9-1: Defining a Java installation directory in a Makefile.am file

Now, you don't often want to install Java sources, which is what you will accomplish when you define your JAVA primary with this sort of prefix. Rather, you want the *.class* files to be installed, or more likely a *.jar* file containing all of your *.class* files. It's generally more useful to define the JAVA primary with the noinst prefix. Additionally, files in the JAVA primary list are not distributed by default, so you may even want to use the dist super-prefix, as shown in Listing 9-2.

```
dist_noinst_JAVA = file_a.java file_b.java...
```

Listing 9-2: Defining a list of non-installed Java files that are distributed

When you define a list of Java source files in a variable containing the JAVA primary, Automake generates a make rule that builds that list of files all in one command, using the syntax shown in Listing 9-3.[5]

```
...
JAVAROOT = $(top_builddir)
JAVAC = javac
CLASSPATH_ENV = CLASSPATH=$(JAVAROOT):$(srcdir)/$(JAVAROOT):$$CLASSPATH
...
classdist_noinst.stamp: $(dist_noinst_JAVA)
        @list1='$?'; list2=; \
        if test -n "$$list1"; then \
          for p in $$list1; do \
            if test -f $$p; \
              then d=; \
              else d="$(srcdir)/"; \
            fi; \
            list2="$$list2 $$d$$p"; \
          done; \
          echo '$(CLASSPATH_ENV) $(JAVAC) -d $(JAVAROOT) $(AM_JAVACFLAGS) \
            $(JAVACFLAGS) '"$$list2"; \
❶       $(CLASSPATH_ENV) $(JAVAC) -d $(JAVAROOT) $(AM_JAVACFLAGS) \
            $(JAVACFLAGS) $$list2; \
        else :; fi
❷       echo timestamp > classdist_noinst.stamp
...
```

Listing 9-3: This long shell command was taken from a Makefile generated by Automake.

---

5. It's difficult to design a set of make rules to build individual *.class* files from corresponding *.java* files. The reasons for this include the fact that the name of a particular class file can't be determined without parsing the corresponding source file. Additionally, due to inner and anonymous class definitions, multiple class files, whose names are based on class names, can be generated from a single Java source file. Fortunately, it's orders of magnitude faster to compile an entire set of Java source files on one command line than to compile Java sources individually, based on individual source file time stamps.

Most of the stuff you see in these commands exists solely to prepend the $(srcdir) prefix onto each file in the user-specified list of Java sources in order to properly support VPATH builds. This code uses a shell for statement to split the list into individual files, prepend the $(srcdir), and then reassemble the list.[6]

The part that actually does the work of building the Java sources is found in two lines (one wrapped line, actually) near the bottom at ❶.

Automake uses a stamp file at ❷ because the single $(JAVAC) command generates several *.class* files from the *.java* files. Rather than choosing one of these files at random, Automake generates and uses a stamp file as the target of the rule which causes make to ignore the relationships between individual *.class* files and their corresponding *.java* files. That is, if you delete a *.class* file, the rules in the makefile will not cause it to be rebuilt. The only way to cause the re-execution of the $(JAVAC) command is to either modify one or more of the *.java* files, thereby causing their timestamps to become newer than that of the stamp file, or to delete the stamp file entirely.

The variables used in the build environment and on the command line include JAVAROOT, JAVAC, JAVACFLAGS, AM_JAVACFLAGS, and CLASSPATH_ENV. Each variable may be specified in the *Makefile.am* file. If a variable is not specified, the defaults shown in Listing 9-3 are used instead.

All *.java* files specified in a JAVA primary variable are compiled using a single command line, which may pose a problem on systems with limited command-line lengths. If you encounter such a problem, you can either break up your Java project into multiple Java source directories, or develop your own make rules for building Java classes. (When I discuss building C# code in "Building the C# Sources" on page 239, I demonstrate how to write such customs rules.)

The CLASSPATH_ENV variable sets the Java CLASSPATH environment variable so that it contains $(JAVAROOT), $(srcdir)/$(JAVAROOT), and then any class path that may have been configured in the environment by the end user.

The JAVAROOT variable is used to specify the location of the project's Java root directory within the project's build tree, where the Java compiler will expect to find the start of generated package directory hierarchies belonging to your project.

The JAVAC variable contains javac by default, with the assumption that javac can be found in the system path. The AM_JAVACFLAGS variable may be set in *Makefile.am*, though the non-Automake version of this variable (JAVACFLAGS) is considered a user variable, and thus shouldn't be set in makefiles.

This is all fine as far as it goes, but it doesn't go nearly far enough. In this relatively simple Java project, we still need to generate Java Native Interface (JNI) header files using the javah utility, and a *.jar* file from the *.class* files built from the Java sources. Unfortunately, Automake-provided Java support doesn't even begin to handle these tasks so we'll do the rest with hand-coded make rules. We'll begin with Autoconf macros to ensure that we have a good Java build environment.

---

6. It's interesting to note that this file list munging process could have been done in a half-line of GNU-make-specific code, but Automake is designed to generate makefiles that can be executed by many older make programs.

Using ac-archive Macros

The Autoconf Macro Archive supplies Autoconf macros that come close to what we need in order to ensure that we have a good Java development environment. In this particular case I downloaded the latest source package, and just hand-installed the *.m4* files that I needed into the *xflaim/m4* directory.

Then I modified the files (including their names) to work the way my FLM_PROG_TRY_DOXYGEN macro works. I wanted to locate any existing Java tools, but also be able to continue without them if necessary. Given the politics surrounding the existence of Java tools in Linux distributions, this is probably a wise approach.

I created the following macros within corresponding *.m4* files:

- FLM_PROG_TRY_JAVAC is defined in *flm_prog_try_javac.m4*
- FLM_PROG_TRY_JAVAH is defined in *flm_prog_try_javah.m4*
- FLM_PROG_TRY_JAVADOC is defined in *flm_prog_try_javadoc.m4*
- FLM_PROG_TRY_JAR is defined in *flm_prog_try_jar.m4*
- FLM_PROG_TRY_JNI is defined in *flm_prog_try_jni.m4*
- FLM_PROG_TRY_CSC is defined in *flm_prog_try_csc.m4*
- FLM_PROG_TRY_CSVM is defined in *flm_prog_try_csvm.m4*

With a bit more effort, I was also able to create the C# macros I needed to accomplish the same tasks for the C# language bindings. Listing 9-4 shows the portion of the xflaim *configure.ac* file that consumes these Java and C# macros.

```
...
# Checks for optional programs.
FLM_PROG_TRY_CSC
FLM_PROG_TRY_CSVM
FLM_PROG_TRY_JNI
FLM_PROG_TRY_JAVADOC
...
# Automake conditionals.
AM_CONDITIONAL([HAVE_JAVA], [test "x$ac_prog_have_jni" = xyes])
AM_CONDITIONAL([HAVE_CSHARP], [test -n "$CSC"])
...
```

Listing 9-4: xflaim/configure.ac: The portion of this file that searches for Java and C# tools

These macros set the CSC, CSVM, JAVAC, JAVAH, JAVADOC and JAR variables to the location of their respective C# and Java tools, and then substitute them into the xflaim project's *Makefile.in* templates using AC_SUBST. If any of these variables are already set in the user's environment when the configure script is executed, their values are left untouched, thus allowing the user to override the values that would have been set by the macros.

(I discuss the internal operation of these macros in Chapter 10.)

Canonical System Information

The only nonobvious bit of information you need to know about using macros from the Autoconf Macro Archive is that many of them rely on the built-in Autoconf macro, AC_CANONICAL_HOST. Autoconf provides a way to automatically expand any macros used internally by a macro definition right before the definition, so that required macros are made available immediately. However, if AC_CANONICAL_HOST is not used before certain macros (including LT_INIT), autoreconf will generate about a dozen warning messages.

To eliminate these warnings, I added AC_CANONICAL_SYSTEM to my xflaim-level *configure.ac* file, immediately after the call to AC_INIT. This macro, and those that it calls (AC_CANONICAL_BUILD, AC_CANONICAL_HOST, and AC_CANONICAL_TARGET), are designed to ensure that the $build, $host, and $target environment variables are defined by configure to contain appropriate values describing the user's build, host, and target systems.

These variables contain canonical values for the build, host, and target CPU, vendor, and operating system. Values like these are very useful to extension macros. If a macro can assume these variables are set properly, then it saves quite a bit of code duplication in the macro definition.

The values of these variables are calculated using the helper scripts config.guess and config.sub, which are distributed with Autoconf. The config .guess script uses a combination of uname commands to ferret out information about the build system, and then uses that information to derive a set of canonical values for CPU, vendor, and operating system. The config.sub script is used to reformat build, host, and target information specified by the user on the configure command line into a canonical value. The host and target values default to that of the build, unless you override them with command-line options to configure. Such an override might be used when cross-compiling. (See "Item 6: Cross-Compiling" on page 287, for a more detailed explanation of cross-compiling within the Autotools framework.)

The xflaim/java Directory Structure

The original xflaim source layout had the Java JNI and C# native sources located in directory structures outside of *xflaim/src*. The JNI sources were in *xflaim/java/jni*, and the C# native sources were in *xflaim/csharp/xflaim*. While Automake can generate rules for accessing files outside the current directory hierarchy, it seems silly to put these files so far away from the only library they can really belong to. Thus, in this case I broke my own rule about not rearranging files and moved the contents of these two directories beneath *xflaim/src*. I named the JNI directory *xflaim/src/java* and the C# native sources directory *xflaim/src/cs*. The following diagram illustrates this new directory hierarchy.

```
flaim
  xflaim
    src
      cs
      java
        wrapper
          xflaim
```

As you can see, I also added a *wrapper* directory beneath the *java* directory, in which I rooted the xflaim wrapper package hierarchy. Since the Java xflaim wrapper classes are part of the Java xflaim package, they must be located in a directory called *xflaim*. Nevertheless, the build happens in the wrapper directory. There are no build files found in the *wrapper/xflaim* directory, or any directories below that point.

NOTE *No matter how deep your package hierarchy is you will still build the Java classes in the* wrapper *directory, which is the* JAVAROOT *directory for this project. Autotools Java projects consider the* JAVAROOT *directory to be the build directory for the java package.*

The xflaim/src/Makefile.am File

At this point the *configure.ac* file is doing about all it can to ensure that I have a good Java build environment, in which case my build system will be able to generate my JNI wrapper classes and header files, and build my C++ JNI sources. If my end user's system doesn't provide these tools, he simply won't be able to build or link the JNI language bindings to the *xflaim* library on that host.

Have a look at the *xflaim/src/Makefile.am* file shown in Listing 9-5, and examine the portions that are relevant to building the Java and C# language bindings.

```
if HAVE_JAVA
  JAVADIR = java
  JNI_LIBADD = java/libxfjni.la
endif

if HAVE_CSHARP
  CSDIR = cs
  CSI_LIBADD = cs/libxfcsi.la
endif

SUBDIRS = $(JAVADIR) $(CSDIR)
...
libxflaim_la_LIBADD = $(JNI_LIBADD) $(CSI_LIBADD) $(FTK_LTLIB)
...
```

Listing 9-5: xflaim/src/Makefile.am: The portion of this makefile that builds Java and C# sources

I've already explained the use of the conditionals to ensure that the *java* and *cs* directories are only built if the proper conditions are met. You can now see how this fits into the build system I've created so far.

Notice that I'm conditionally defining two new library variables. If I can build the Java language bindings, the *java* subdirectory will be built, and the JNI_LIBADD variable will refer to the library that is built in the *java* directory. If I can build the C# language bindings, the *cs* subdirectory will be built, and the CSI_LIBADD variable will refer to the library that is built in the *cs* directory. In either case, if the required tools are not found by configure, the corresponding variable will remain undefined. When an undefined make variable is referenced, it expands to nothing, so there's no harm in using it in libxflaim_la_LIBADD.

Building the JNI C++ Sources

Now turn your attention to the *xflaim/src/java/Makefile.am* file shown in Listing 9-6.

```
SUBDIRS = wrapper

XFLAIM_INCLUDE = -I$(srcdir)/..

noinst_LTLIBRARIES = libxfjni.la

libxfjni_la_SOURCES = \
 jbackup.cpp \
 jdatavector.cpp \
 jdb.cpp \
 jdbsystem.cpp \
 jdomnode.cpp \
 jistream.cpp \
 jniftk.cpp \
 jniftk.h \
 jnirestore.cpp \
 jnirestore.h \
 jnistatus.cpp \
 jnistatus.h \
 jostream.cpp \
 jquery.cpp

libxfjni_la_CPPFLAGS = $(XFLAIM_INCLUDE) $(FTK_INCLUDE)
```

Listing 9-6: xflaim/src/java/Makefile.am: This makefile builds the JNI sources.

Again, I want the *wrapper* directory to be built first, before the *xflaim* library, because the *wrapper* directory will build the class files and JNI header files required by the JNI convenience library sources. Building this directory is not conditional. If I've made it this far into the build hierarchy, I know I have all the Java tools I need. This *Makefile.am* file simply builds a convenience library containing my JNI C++ interface functions.

Because of the way Libtool builds both shared and static libraries from the same sources, this convenience library will become part of both the *xflaim* shared and static libraries. The original build system makefile accounted for this by linking the JNI and C# native interface objects only into the shared library (where they make sense).

NOTE *The fact that these libraries are added to both the shared and static* xflaim *libraries is not really a problem. Objects in a static library remain unused in applications or libraries linking to the static library, as long as functions and data in those objects remain unreferenced, though this is a bit of a wart on my new build system.*

The Java Wrapper Classes and JNI Headers

Finally, *xflaim/src/java/wrapper/Makefile.am* takes us to the heart of the matter. I've tried many different configurations for building Java JNI wrappers, and this one always comes out on top. Listing 9-7 shows the wrapper directory's Automake input file.

```
JAVAROOT = .

❶ jarfile = $(PACKAGE_TARNAME)jni-$(PACKAGE_VERSION).jar
❷ jardir = $(datadir)/java
  pkgpath = xflaim
  jhdrout = ..

  $(jarfile): classdist_noinst.stamp
          $(JAR) cf $(JARFLAGS) $@ $(pkgpath)/*.class

❸ jar_DATA = $(jarfile)
  java-headers.stamp: $(dist_noinst_JAVA)
          @list=`echo $(dist_noinst_JAVA) | \
            sed -e 's|\.java||g' -e 's|/|.|g'`; \
          echo "$(JAVAH) -cp . -jni -d $(jhdrout) $(JAVAHFLAGS) $$list"; \
          $(JAVAH) -cp . -jni -d $(jhdrout) $(JAVAHFLAGS) $$list; \
❹         @echo "JNI headers generated" > java-headers.stamp

❺ all-local: java-headers.stamp

  CLEANFILES = $(jarfile) $(pkgpath)/*.class java-headers.stamp \
❻ $(jhdrout)/xflaim_*.h

  dist_noinst_JAVA = \
   $(pkgpath)/BackupClient.java \
   $(pkgpath)/Backup.java \
   ...
   $(pkgpath)/XFlaimException.java \
   $(pkgpath)/XPathAxis.java
```

Listing 9-7: xflaim/src/java/wrapper/Makefile.am: The wrapper directory's Makefile.am file

At the top of the file, I've set the JAVAROOT variable to dot (.), because I want Automake to be able to tell the Java compiler that this is where the package hierarchy begins. The default value for JAVAROOT is $(top_builddir), which would incorrectly have the wrapper class belong to the *xflaim.src.java.wrapper.xflaim* package.

I create a variable at ❶ called jarfile, which derives its value from $(PACKAGE_TARNAME) and $(PACKAGE_VERSION). (Recall from Chapter 2 that this is also how the destdir variable is derived, from which the name of the tarball comes.) A make rule indicates how the *.jar* file should be built. Here, I'm using the JAR variable, whose value was calculated by the FLM_PROG_TRY_JNI macro in the configure script.

I define a new installation variable at ❷ called jardir where *.jar* files are to be installed and I use that variable as the prefix for a DATA primary at ❸. Automake considers files that fit the Automake *where_HOW* scheme (with a defined *where*dir) as either architecture-independent data files or platform-specific executables. Installation location variables (those ending in dir) that begin with bin, sbin, libexec, sysconf, localstate, lib, or pkglib, or that contain the string "exec" are considered platform-specific executables, and are installed during execution of the install-exec target. Automake considers files installed in any other locations data files. These are installed during execution of the install-data target. The well-known installation locations such as *bindir*, *sbindir*, and so on are already taken, but if you wish to install custom architecture-dependent executable files, just ensure that your custom installation location variable contains the string "exec," as in myspecialexecdir.

I use another stamp file at ❹ in the rule that builds the JNI header files from the *.class* files for the same reasons that Automake used a stamp file in the rule that it uses to build *.class* files from *.java* source files.

This is the most complex part of this makefile, so I'll break it into smaller pieces.

The rule states that the stamp file depends on the source files listed in the dist_noinst_JAVA variable. The command is a bit of complex shell script that strips the *.java* extensions from the file list, and converts all the slash characters into periods. The reason for this is that the javah utility wants a list of class names, not a list of file names. The $(JAVAH) command then accepts this entire list as input in order to generate a corresponding list of JNI header files. The last line, of course, generates the stamp file.

Finally at ❺, I hook my java-headers.stamp target into the all target by adding it as a dependency to the all-local target. When the all target (the default for all Automake-generated makefiles) is executed in this makefile, *java-headers.stamp* will be built, along with the JNI headers.

NOTE   *It's a good idea to add custom rule targets as dependencies to the Automake-provided hook and local targets, rather than directly associating commands with these hook and local targets. By doing this, the commands for individual tasks on those targets remain isolated, and thus, easier to maintain.*

I add the *.jar* file, all of the *.class* files, the *java-headers.stamp* file, and all of the generated JNI header files to the CLEANFILES variable at ❻, so that Automake will clean them up when make clean is executed. Again, I can use the CLEANFILES variable here because I'm not trying to delete any directories.

The final step in writing any such custom code is to ensure that the distcheck target still works, because when we generate our own products, we have to ensure that the clean target properly removes them all.

A Caveat About Using the JAVA Primary

The one important caveat to using the JAVA primary is that you may define only one JAVA primary variable per *Makefile.am* file. The reason for this is that multiple classes may be generated from a single *.java* file, and the only way to know which classes came from which *.java* file would be for Automake to parse the *.java* files (which is ridiculous, and arguably the primary reason why build tools like *Apache Ant* were developed). Rather than do this, Automake allows only one JAVA primary per file, so all *.class* files generated within a given build directory are installed in the location specified by the single JAVA primary variable prefix.[7]

NOTE *The system I've designed above will work fine for this case, but it's a good thing I don't need to install my JNI header files because I have no way of knowing what they're called from within my* Makefile.am *file!*

You should by now be able to see the problems that the Autotools have with Java. In fact, these problems are not so much related to the design issues in the Autotools, as they are to design issues within the Java language itself, as you'll see in the next section.

Building the C# Sources

Returning to the *xflaim/src/cs* directory brings us to a discussion of building sources for a language for which Automake has no support: C#. Listing 9-8 shows the *Makefile.am* file that I wrote for the *cs* directory.

```
SUBDIRS = wrapper

XFLAIM_INCLUDE = -I$(srcdir)/..

noinst_LTLIBRARIES = libxfcsi.la

libxfcsi_la_SOURCES = \
 Backup.cpp \
 DataVector.cpp \
 Db.cpp \
```

---

7. It seems that I've broken this rule by assuming in my java-headers.stamp rule that the source for class information is the list of files specified in the dist_noinst_JAVA variable. In reality, I should probably be looking in the current build directory for all *.class* files found after the rules for the JAVA primary are executed. However, this goes against the general Autotools philosophy of only building or using pre-specified sources for a build step, thus, we'll live with what we have for the present.

```
DbInfo.cpp \
DbSystem.cpp \
DbSystemStats.cpp \
DOMNode.cpp \
IStream.cpp \
OStream.cpp \
Query.cpp

libxfcsi_la_CPPFLAGS = $(XFLAIM_INCLUDE) $(FTK_INCLUDE)
```

Listing 9-8: xflaim/src/cs/Makefile.am: *The contents of the* cs *directory's Automake input file*

Not surprisingly, this looks almost identical to the *Makefile.am* file found in the *xflaim/src/java* directory because I'm building a simple convenience library from C++ source files found in this directory, just as I did in the *java* directory. As in the Java version, this makefile first builds a subdirectory called *wrapper*.

Listing 9-9 shows the full contents of the *wrapper/Makefile.am* file.

```
EXTRA_DIST = xflaim cstest sample xflaim.ndoc

xfcs_sources = \
 xflaim/BackupClient.cs \
 xflaim/Backup.cs \
 ...
 xflaim/RestoreClient.cs \
 xflaim/RestoreStatus.cs

cstest_sources = \
 cstest/BackupDbTest.cs \
 cstest/CacheTests.cs \
 ...
 cstest/StreamTests.cs \
 cstest/VectorTests.cs

TESTS = cstest_script

AM_CSCFLAGS = -d:mono -nologo -warn:4 -warnaserror+ -optimize+
#AM_CSCFLAGS += -debug+ -debug:full -define:FLM_DEBUG
```

❶ `all-local: xflaim_csharp.dll`

```
clean-local:
        rm -f xflaim_csharp.dll xflaim_csharp.xml
        rm -f cstest_script cstest.exe libxflaim.so
        rm -f Output_Stream
        rm -rf abc backup test.*

install-exec-local:
        test -z "$(libdir)" || \
         $(MKDIR_P) "$(DESTDIR)$(libdir)"
        $(INSTALL_PROGRAM) xflaim_csharp.dll\
        "$(DESTDIR)$(libdir)"
```

```
        install-data-local:
                test -z "$(docdir)" || \
                 $(MKDIR_P) "$(DESTDIR)$(docdir)"
                $(INSTALL_DATA) xflaim_csharp.xml\
                  "$(DESTDIR)$(docdir)"

        uninstall-local:
                rm "$(DESTDIR)$(libdir)/xflaim_csharp.dll"
                rm "$(DESTDIR)$(docdir)/xflaim_csharp.xml"

❷ xflaim_csharp.dll: $(xfcs_sources)
                @list1='$(xfcs_sources)'; list2=; \
                if test -n "$$list1"; then \
                  for p in $$list1; do \
                    if test -f $$p; then d=; \
                    else d="$(srcdir)/"; fi; \
                    list2="$$list2 $$d$$p"; \
                  done; \
                  echo '$(CSC) -target:library\
                   $(AM_CSCFLAGS) $(CSCFLAGS) -out:$@\
                   -doc:$(@:.dll=.xml) '"$$list2"; \
                  $(CSC) -target:library $(AM_CSCFLAGS)\
                   $(CSCFLAGS) -out:$@ -doc:$(@:.dll=.xml)\
                   $$list2; \
                else :; fi

    check_SCRIPTS = cstest.exe cstest_script

❸ cstest.exe: xflaim_csharp.dll $(cstest_sources)
                @list1='$(cstest_sources)'; \
                 list2=; if test -n "$$list1"; then \
                  for p in $$list1; do \
                    if test -f $$p; then d=; \
                    else d="$(srcdir)/"; fi; \
                    list2="$$list2 $$d$$p"; \
                  done; \
                  echo '$(CSC) $(AM_CSCFLAGS) $(CSCFLAGS)\
                   -out:$@ '"$$list2"'\
                   -reference:xflaim_csharp.dll'; \
                  $(CSC) $(AM_CSCFLAGS) $(CSCFLAGS) -out:$@ $$list2 \
                    -reference:xflaim_csharp.dll; \
                else :; fi

❹ cstest_script: cstest.exe
                echo "#!/bin/sh" > cstest_script
                echo "$(top_builddir)/libtool --mode=execute \
❺                -dlopen=../../libxflaim.la $(CSVM) cstest.exe" >> cstest_script
                chmod 0755 cstest_script
```

Listing 9-9: xflaim/src/cs/wrapper/Makefile.am: The full contents of the C# makefile

The default target for *Makefile.am* is all, the same as that of a normal non-Automake makefile. Again, I've hooked my code into the all target by implementing the all-local target, which depends on a file named *xflaim_csharp.dll.*[8]

The C# sources are built by the commands under the *xflaim_csharp.dll* target at ❷ and the *xflaim_csharp.dll* binary depends on the list of C# source files specified in the xfcs_sources variable. The commands in this rule are copied from the Automake-generated *java/wrapper/Makefile*, and slightly modified to build C# binaries from C# source files (as highlighted in the listing). This isn't intended to be a lesson in building C# sources; the point here is that the default target is automatically built by creating a dependency between the all-local target and your own targets at ❶.

This *Makefile.am* file also builds a set of unit tests in C# that test the C# language bindings. The target of this rule is *cstest.exe* (❸), which ultimately becomes a C# executable. The rule states that *cstest.exe* depends on *xflaim_csharp.dll*, and the source files. I've again copied the commands from the rule for building *xflaim_csharp.dll* (as highlighted), and modified them for building the C# programs.

Ultimately, upon building the check target, the Automake-generated makefile will attempt to execute the scripts or executables listed in the TESTS variable. The idea here is to ensure that all necessary components are built before these files are executed. I've tied into the check target by defining check-local, and making it depend upon my test code targets.

The cstest_script at ❹ is a shell script built solely to execute the *cstest.exe* binary within the C# virtual machine. The C# virtual machine is found in the CSVM variable which was defined in configure by the code generated by the FLM_PROG_TRY_CSVM macro.

The cstest_script depends only on the cstest.exe program. However, the *xflaim* library must either be present in the current directory, or it must be in the system library search path. We gain maximum portability here by using Libtool's *execute* mode to add the *xflaim* library to the system library search path before executing the C# virtual machine at ❺.

Manual Installation

Since in this example I'm doing everything myself, I have to write my own installation rules. Listing 9-10 reproduces only the installation rules in the *Makefile.am* file from Listing 9-9.

```
...
install-exec-local:
        test -z "$(libdir)" || $(MKDIR_P) "$(DESTDIR)$(libdir)"
        $(INSTALL_PROGRAM) xflaim_csharp.dll "$(DESTDIR)$(libdir)"
```

---

8. This executable file name may be a bit confusing to those who are new to C#. In essence, Microsoft, the creators of C#, designed the C# virtual machine to execute Microsoft native (or almost native) binaries. In porting the C# virtual machine to Unix, the Mono team (the Linux C# compiler project) decided against breaking Microsoft's naming conventions, so that Microsoft-generated portable C# programs could be executed by the Mono C# virtual machine implementation. Nevertheless, C# still suffers from problems that need to be managed occasionally by name-mapping configuration files.

```
install-data-local:
        test -z "$(docdir)" || $(MKDIR_P) "$(DESTDIR)$(docdir)"
        $(INSTALL_DATA) xflaim_csharp.xml "$(DESTDIR)$(docdir)"

uninstall-local:
        rm -f "$(DESTDIR)$(libdir)/xflaim_csharp.dll"
        rm -f "$(DESTDIR)$(docdir)/xflaim_csharp.xml"
...
```

Listing 9-10: xflaim/src/cs/wrapper/Makefile.am: *The installation rules of this makefile*

According to the rules defined in the *GNU Coding Standards*, the installation targets do not depend on the binaries they install, so if the binaries haven't been built yet, I may have to exit from *root* to my user account to build the binaries with make all first.

Automake distinguishes between installing programs and installing data. However, there's only one uninstall target. The rationale seems to be that you might wish to do an install-exec operation per system in your network, but only one shared install-data operation. Uninstalling a product requires no such separation, because uninstalling data multiple times is typically harmless.

Cleaning Up Again

As usual, things must be cleaned up properly. The clean-local target handles this nicely as shown in Listing 9-11.

```
...
clean-local:
        rm -f xflaim_csharp.dll xflaim_csharp.xml
        rm -f cstest_script cstest.exe libxflaim.so
        rm -f Output_Stream
        rm -rf abc backup test.*
...
```

Listing 9-11: xflaim/src/cs/wrapper/Makefile.am: *The clean rules defined in this makefile*

Configuring Compiler Options

The original GNU make build system provided a number of command-line build options. By specifying a list of auxiliary targets on the make command line, the user could indicate that he wanted a debug or release build, force a 32-bit build on a 64-bit system, generate generic SPARC code on a Solaris system, and so on—a turnkey approach to build systems that is quite common in commercial code.

In open source projects, and particularly in Autotools-based build systems, the more common practice is to omit much of this rigid framework, allowing the user to set his own options in the standard user variables, CC, CPP, CXX, CFLAGS, CXXFLAGS, CPPFLAGS, and so on.[9]

Probably the most compelling argument for the Autotools approach to option management is that it's policy-driven, and the rigid frameworks used by commercial software vendors can easily be implemented in terms of the much more flexible policy-driven Autotools framework. For example, a *config.site* file might be used to provide site-wide options for all Autotools-based builds done at a particular site. A simple script can be used to configure various environment-based options before calling configure, or these options may even be passed to configure or make directly within such a script. The Autotools policy-driven approach offers the flexibility to be as configurable as a developer might wish, or as tight as required by management.

Ultimately, we'd like to have FLAIM project options conform to the Autotools policy-driven approach, however, I didn't want to lose the research effort involved in determining the hardcoded native compiler options specified in the original makefile. To this end, I've added back in *some* of the options to the *configure.ac* file that were supported by the original build system, but I've left others out as shown in Listing 9-12. This code enables various native compiler options, optimizations, and debugging features on demand, based on the contents of some of the user variables.

```
...
# Configure supported platforms' compiler and li...
❶ case $host in
    sparc-*-solaris*)
      LDFLAGS="$LDFLAGS -R /usr/lib/lwp"
      case $CXX in
        *g++*) ;;
        *)
          if "x$debug" = xno; then
            CXXFLAGS="$CXXFLAGS -xO3"
          fi
          SUN_STUDIO=`$CXX -V | grep "Sun C++"`
          if "x$SUN_STUDIO" = "xSun C++"; then
            CXXFLAGS="$CXXFLAGS -errwarn=%all -errtags\
              -erroff=hidef,inllargeuse,doubunder"
          fi ;;
      esac ;;

    *-apple-darwin*)
      AC_DEFINE([OSX], [],
        [Define if building on Apple OSX.]) ;;
```

9. The strange thing is that commercial software is developed by industry experts, while open source software is often built and consumed by hobbyists. And yet the *experts* are the ones using the menu-driven rigid-options framework, while the hobbyists have the flexibility to manually configure their compiler options the way they want. I suppose the most reasonable explanation for this is that commercial software relies on carefully crafted builds that must be able to be duplicated—usually by people who didn't write the original build system. Open source hobbyists would rather not give up the flexibility afforded by a more policy-driven approach.

```
  *-*-aix*)
    case $CXX in
      *g++*) ;;
      *) CXXFLAGS="$CXXFLAGS -qthreaded -qstrict" ;;
    esac ;;

  *-*-hpux*)
    case $CXX in
      *g++*) ;;
      *)
        # Disable "Placement operator delete
        # invocation is not yet implemented" warning
        CXXFLAGS="$CXXFLAGS +W930" ;;
    esac ;;
esac
...
```

Listing 9-12: xflaim/configure.ac: The portion of this file that enables compiler-specific options

Remember that this code depends on the earlier use of the `AC_CANONICAL_SYSTEM` macro which sets build, host, and target environment variables to canonical string values that indicate CPU, vendor, and operating system.

In Listing 9-12 I used the host variable in the case statement at ❶ to determine the type of system for which I'm building. This case statement determines if the user is building on Solaris, Apple Darwin, AIX, or HP/UX by looking for substrings in host that are common to all variations of these platforms. The config.guess and config.sub files are your friends here. If you need to write code like this for your project, examine these files to find common traits for the processes and systems for which you'd like to set various compiler and linker options.

NOTE   *In each of these cases (except for the definition of the OSX preprocessor variable on Apple Darwin systems), I'm really only setting flags for native compilers. The GNU compiler tools seem to be able to handle any code without the need for additional compiler options.*

Hooking Doxygen into the Build Process

I want to generate documentation as part of my build process, if possible. That is, if the user has doxygen installed, the build system will use it to build Doxygen documentation as part of the make all process.

The original build system has both static and generated documentation. The static documentation should always be installed, but the Doxygen documentation can only be built if the doxygen program is available on the host. Thus, I always build the *docs* directory, but I use the `AM_CONDITIONAL` macro to conditionally build the *docs/doxygen* directory.

Doxygen uses a configuration file (often called *doxyfile*) to configure literally hundreds of Doxygen options. This configuration file contains some information that is known to the configuration script. This sounds like the perfect opportunity to use an Autoconf-generated file. To this end, I've written an Autoconf template file called *doxyfile.in* that contains most of what a normal

Doxygen input file would contain, as well as a few Autoconf substitution variable references. The relevant lines in this file are shown in Listing 9-13.

```
...
PROJECT_NAME              = @PACKAGE_NAME@
...
PROJECT_NUMBER            = @PACKAGE_VERSION@
...
STRIP_FROM_PATH           = @top_srcdir@
...
INPUT                     = @top_srcdir@/src/xflaim.h
...
```

Listing 9-13: xflaim/docs/doxygen/doxyfile.in: The lines in this file that contain Autoconf variables

There are many other lines in this file, but they are all identical to the output file, so I've omitted them for the sake of space and clarity. The key here is that config.status will replace these substitution variables with their values as defined in *configure.ac*, and by Autoconf itself. If these values change in *configure.ac*, the generated file will be rewritten with the new values. I've added a conditional reference for *xflaim/docs/doxygen/doxyfile* to the AC_CONFIG_FILES list in xflaim's *configure.ac* file. That's all it takes.

Listing 9-14 shows the *xflaim/docs/doxygen/Makefile.am* file.

❶ docpkg = $(PACKAGE_TARNAME)-doxy-$(PACKAGE_VERSION).tar.gz

❷ doc_DATA = $(docpkg)

❸ $(docpkg): doxygen.stamp
        tar chof - html | gzip -9 -c >$@

doxygen.stamp: doxyfile
        $(DOXYGEN) $(DOXYFLAGS) $<
        echo Timestamp > $@

❹ install-data-hook:
        cd $(DESTDIR)$(docdir) && tar xf $(docpkg)

uninstall-data-hook:
        cd $(DESTDIR)$(docdir) && rm -rf html

❺ CLEANFILES = doxywarn.txt doxygen.stamp $(docpkg)

clean-local:
        rm -rf html

Listing 9-14: xflaim/docs/doxygen/Makefile.am: The full contents of this makefile

Here, I create a package name at ❶ for the tarball that will contain the Doxygen documentation files. This is basically the same as the distribution tarball for the xflaim project, except that it contains the text *-doxy* after the package name.

I define a doc_DATA variable at ❷ that contains the name of the Doxygen tarball. This file will be installed in the $(docdir) directory, which by default is $(datarootdir)/*doc*/$(PACKAGE_TARNAME), and $(datarootdir) is configured by Automake as $(prefix)/*share*, by default.

NOTE *The* DATA *primary brings with it significant Automake functionality—installation is managed automatically. While I must build the Doxygen documentation package, the* DATA *primary automatically hooks the* all *target for me, so that my package is built when the user executes* make *or* make all.

I use another stamp file at ❸ because Doxygen generates literally hundreds of .*html* files from the source files in my project. Rather than attempt to figure out a rational way to assign dependencies, I've chosen to generate one stamp file, and then use that to determine whether the documentation is out of date.[10]

I also decided that it would be nice to unpack the documentation archive into the package *doc* directory. Left up to Automake, the tarball would make it into the proper directory at installation time, but that's as far as it would go. I needed to be able to hook the installation process to do this, and this is the perfect use for an Automake -hook target. I use the install-data-hook target at ❹ because the -hook targets allow you to perform extra user-defined shell commands after the operation that's being hooked has completed. Likewise, I use uninstall-hook to remove the *html* directory created when the .*tar* file was extracted during installation. (There is no distinction between uninstalling platform-specific and platform-independent files, so there is only one hook for uninstalling files.)

To clean my generated files, I use a combination of the CLEANFILES variable at ❺ and a clean-local rule just to demonstrate that it can be done.

Adding Nonstandard Targets

Adding a new nonstandard target is a little different than hooking an existing target. In the first place, you don't need to use AM_CONDITIONAL and other Autoconf tests to see if you have the tools you need. Instead, you can do all conditional testing from the *Makefile.am* file because you control the entire command set associated with the target, although this isn't recommended practice. (It's always preferable to ensure that the build environment is configured correctly from the configure script.) In cases were make targets can only be expected to work under certain conditions, or on certain platforms, it's a good idea to provide checks within the target to ensure that the operation requested can actually be performed.

---

10. In fact, the only source file in this project that currently contains Doxygen markup is the *xflaim.h* header file but that could easily change, and it certainly won't hold true for all projects. Additionally, Doxygen generates hundreds of .*html* files, and this entire set of files represents the target of a rule to build the documentation. The stamp file stands in for these files as the target of the rule.

To start with, I create a directory within each project root directory called *obs* to contain the *Makefile.am* file for building RPM package files. (*OBS* is an acronym for *openSUSE Build Service*, an online package building service.)[11]

Building RPM package files is done using a configuration file, called a *spec* file, which is very much like the *doxyfile* used to configure Doxygen for a specific project. As with the *doxyfile*, the RPM spec file references information that configure knows about the package. So, I wrote an *xflaim.spec.in* file, adding substitution variables where appropriate, and then I added another file reference to the AC_CONFIG_FILES macro. This allows configure to substitute information about the project into the spec file. Listing 9-15 shows the relevant portion of the *xflaim.spec.in* file in bold.

```
Name: @PACKAGE_TARNAME@
BuildRequires: gcc-c++ libstdc++-devel flaimtk-devel gcc-java gjdoc fastjar
mono-core doxygen
Requires: libstdc++ flaimtk mono-core java >= 1.4.2
Summary: XFLAIM is an XML database library.
URL: http://sourceforge.net/projects/flaim/
Version: @PACKAGE_VERSION@
Release: 1
License: GPL
Vendor: Novell, Inc.
Group: Development/Libraries/C and C++
Source: %{name}-%{version}.tar.gz
BuildRoot: %{_tmppath}/%{name}-%{version}-build
...
```

Listing 9-15: xflaim/obs/xflaim.spec.in: *The portion of this file that illustrates using Autoconf variables*

Notice the use of the variables @PACKAGE_TARNAME@ and @PACKAGE_VERSION@ in this listing. Although the tar name is not likely to change much over the life of this project, the version will change often. Without the Autoconf substitution mechanism, I'd have to remember to update this version number whenever I updated the version in the *configure.ac* file. Listing 9-16 shows the *xflaim/obs/Makefile.am* file, which actually does the work of building the RPMs.

```
rpmspec = $(PACKAGE_TARNAME).spec

rpmmacros =\
 --define="_rpmdir $${PWD}"\
 --define="_srcrpmdir $${PWD}"\
 --define="_sourcedir $${PWD}/.."\
 --define="_specdir $${PWD}"\
 --define="_builddir $${PWD}"
```

---

11. See *http://build.opensuse.org/*. This is a service that I fell in love with almost as soon as it came out. I've had some experience building distro packages, and I can tell you, it's far less painful with the OBS than it is using more traditional techniques. Furthermore, packages built with the OBS can be published automatically on the OBS website (*http://software.opensuse.org/search/*) for public consumption immediately after they're built.

```
RPMBUILD = rpmbuild
RPMFLAGS = --nodeps --buildroot="$${PWD}/_rpm"

❶ rpmcheck:
        if [ which $(RPMBUILD) &> /dev/null ]; then \
          echo "*** This make target requires an rpm-based Linux
distribution."; \
          (exit 1); exit 1; \
        fi

srcrpm: rpmcheck $(rpmspec)
        $(RPMBUILD) $(RPMFLAGS) -bs $(rpmmacros) $(rpmspec)

rpms: rpmcheck $(rpmspec)
        $(RPMBUILD) $(RPMFLAGS) -ba $(rpmmacros) $(rpmspec)

.PHONY: rpmcheck srcrpm rpms
```

Listing 9-16: xflaim/obs/Makefile.am: *The complete contents of this makefile*

Building RPM packages is rather simple, as you can see. The targets provided by this makefile include srcrpm and rpms. The rpmcheck target at ❶ is used internally to verify that RPMs can be built in the end user's environment.

In order to find out which targets in a lower-level *Makefile.am* file are supported by a top-level build, look at the top-level *Makefile.am* file. As Listing 9-17 shows, if the target is not passed down, that target must be intended for internal use only, within the lower-level directory.

```
...
RPM = rpm

rpms srcrpm: dist
❶       (cd obs && $(MAKE) $(AM_MAKEFLAGS) $@) || exit 1
        rpmarch=`$(RPM) --showrc | grep "^build arch" | \
          sed 's/\(.*: \)\(.*\)/\2/'`; \
        test -z "obs/$$rpmarch" || \
          ( mv obs/$$rpmarch/* . && rm -rf /obs/$$rpmarch )
        rm -rf obs/$(distdir)
...
.PHONY: srcrpm rpms
```

Listing 9-17: xflaim/Makefile.am: *If the target is not passed down, then it's an internal target.*

As you can see from the command at ❶ in Listing 9-17, when a user targets rpms or srcrpm from the top-level build directory, the commands are recursively passed down to *obs/Makefile*. The remaining commands simply remove droppings left behind by the RPM build process that are simpler to remove at this level. (Try building an RPM package some time, and you'll see what I mean!)

Notice too that both of these top-level makefile targets depend on the dist target because the RPM build process requires the distribution tarball. Adding the tarball as a dependency of the rpms target simply ensures that the distribution tarball is there when the rpmbuild utility needs it.

Summary

While using the Autotools, there are many details to manage, most of which, as they say in the open source software world, *can wait for the next release!* Even as I committed this code to the FLAIM project repository, I noticed details that could be improved. The take-away lesson here is that a build system is never really finished. It should be incrementally improved over time, as you find time in your schedule to work on it. And it can be rewarding to do so.

I've shown you a number of new features that have not been covered in earlier chapters, and there are many more features that I cannot begin to cover in this book. Study the Autotools manuals to become truly proficient. At this point, it should be pretty simple for you to pick up that additional information yourself.

10

USING THE M4 MACRO PROCESSOR WITH AUTOCONF

By the time you've sorted out a complicated idea into little steps that even a stupid machine can deal with, you've learned something about it yourself.
—Douglas Adams,
Dirk Gently's Holistic Detective Agency

The M4 macro processor is simple to use, and yet hard to comprehend. The simplicity comes from the fact that it does just one thing very well. I'll wager that you or I could write the base functionality of M4 in a C program in just a few hours. At the same time, two aspects of M4 make it rather difficult to understand immediately.

First, the exceptions introduced by *special cases* that M4 deals with when it processes input text make it hard to grasp all of its rules immediately, though this complexity is easily mastered with time, patience, and practice. Second, the stack-based, pre-order recursive nature of M4's text processing model is difficult for the human mind to comprehend. Humans tend to process information breadth first, comprehending complete levels of a problem or data set, one level at a time, whereas M4 processes text in a depth-first fashion.

This chapter covers what I consider to be the bare minimum that you need to know to write Autoconf input files. I can't do justice to M4 in a single chapter of this book, so I'll cover the highlights. For more detail read the

GNU M4 Manual.[1] If you've already had some experience with M4, try the examples in that manual, and then try solving a few text problems of your own using M4. A small amount of such experimentation will vastly improve your understanding of M4.

M4 Text Processing

Like many other classic Unix tools, M4 is written as a standard input/output (stdio) filter. That is, it accepts input from standard input (stdin), processes it, and then sends it to standard output (stdout). Input text is read in as a stream of bytes and converted to *tokens* before processing. Tokens consist of comments, names, quoted strings, and single characters that are not part of a comment, name, or quoted string.

The *default* quote characters are the backtick (`) and the single quote ('). Use the backtick to start a quoted string, and the single quote character to terminate one:

```
`A quoted string'
```

M4 comments are similar to quoted strings in that each one is processed as a single token. Each comment is delimited by a hash mark (#) and a newline (\n) character. Thus, all text following an *unquoted* hash mark, up to and including the next newline character, is considered part of a comment.

Comments are not stripped from the output as they are in other computer language preprocessors, such as the C-language preprocessor. Rather, they are simply passed through without further processing.

The following example contains five tokens: a name token, a space character token, another name token, a second space character token, and finally, a single comment token:

```
Two names # followed by a comment
```

Names are any sequence of letters, digits, and underscore characters that do not begin with a digit. Thus, the first line of the following example contains two digit character tokens, followed by a name token, whereas the second line contains only a single name token:

```
88North20th_street
_88North20th_street
```

Note that whitespace characters (horizontal and vertical tabs, form feeds, carriage returns, spaces, and newlines) are specifically not part of a name, so whitespace characters may (and often do) act as name- or other-token delimiters. However, such whitespace delimiters are not discarded by M4, as they

---

1. See the Free Software Foundation's *GNU M4 – GNU Macro Processor* at *http://www.gnu.org/ software/m4/manual/*.

often are within a computer language compiler's parser. They're simply passed through from the input stream directly to the output stream without further modification.

Defining Macros

M4 provides a variety of built-in macros, many of which are critical to the proper use of this tool. For instance, it would be very difficult to get any useful functionality out of M4 if it didn't provide a way of defining macros. M4's macro definition macro is called define.

The define macro is simple to describe:

```
define(macro[, expansion])
```

The define macro expects at least one parameter, even if it's empty. If you supply only one parameter, then instances of the macro name that are found in the input text are simply deleted from the output text:

```
$ m4
define(`macro')

Hello macro world!
❶ Hello  world!
<ctrl-d>$
```

Note in the output text at ❶ that there are two spaces between Hello and world! All tokens except names that map to defined macros are passed from the input stream to the output stream without modification with one exception: Whenever any quoted text outside of comments is read from the input stream, one level of quotes is removed.

Another subtle aspect of the define macro is that its expansion is the empty string. Thus, the output of the definition above is simply the trailing carriage return after the definition in the input string.

Names, of course, are candidates for macro expansion. If a name token is found in the symbol table, it is replaced with the macro definition, as shown in the following example:

```
$ m4
❶ define(`macro', `expansion')
❷
  macro ``quoted' string'
❸ expansion `quoted' string
  <ctrl-d>$
```

The second output line at ❸ shows us that the first token (the name macro) is expanded, and the outer level of quotes around ``quoted' string' are removed by M4. The blank line at ❷ following the macro definition comes from the newline character I entered into the input stream when I pressed the ENTER key after the macro definition at ❶. Since this newline character is not part of the macro definition, M4 simply passes it through to the output stream. This can be a problem when defining macros in input text because you could end up with a slew of blank lines in the output text, one for each macro defined in the input text. Fortunately, there are ways around this problem. For example, I could simply not enter that newline character, as shown here:

```
$ m4
define(`macro', `expansion')macro
expansion
<ctrl-d>$
```

That solves the problem but it doesn't take a genius to see that this can lead to some readability issues. If you have to define your macros in this manner so that they don't affect your output text, you'll have a few run-on sentences in your input text!

M4 provides another built-in macro called dnl,[2] which causes all input text up to and including the next newline character to be discarded. It's common to find dnl used in *configure.ac*, but it's even more common to find it used in *.m4* macro definition files consumed by Autoconf while processing *configure.ac* files.

Here's an example of the proper use of dnl:

```
$ m4
define(`macro', `expansion')dnl
macro
expansion
<ctrl-d>$
```

There are a few dozen built-in M4 macros, all of which provide functionality that can't be obtained in any other way within M4. Some redefine fundamental behavior in M4.

For example, the changequote macro is used to change the default quote characters from backtick and single quote to whatever you wish. Autoconf uses a line like this near the top of the input stream to change the M4 quotes to the left and right square bracket characters like so:

```
changequote(`[',`]')dnl
```

Why would the Autoconf designers do this? Well, it's quite common in shell code to find unbalanced pairs of single quote characters. You'll recall from Chapter 3 that the input text to Autoconf is shell script, which means that there's a good chance that Autoconf will run into an unbalanced pair of M4 quotes in every input file it reads. This can lead to errors that are very difficult to track down, because they have more to do with M4 than they do with Autoconf.

---

2. The dnl macro name is actually an acronym that stands for discard to next line.

It's far less likely that the input shell script will contain an unbalanced pair of square bracket characters.

Macros with Arguments

Macros may also be defined to accept arguments, which may be referenced in the expansion text with $1, $2, $3, and so on. The number of arguments passed can be found in the variable $#. When using arguments in a macro call, there can be no intervening whitespace between the macro name and the opening parenthesis. Here's an example of a macro that's defined and then called in various ways:

```
$ m4
define(`with2args', `The arguments are $1 and $2.')dnl
❶ with2args
The arguments are  and .
with2args()
The arguments are  and .
❷ with2args(`arg1')
The arguments are arg1 and .
with2args(`arg1', `arg2')
The arguments are arg1 and arg2.
with2args(`arg1', `arg2', `arg3')
The arguments are arg1 and arg2.
❸ with2args (`arg1', `arg2')
The arguments are  and . (arg1, arg2)
<ctrl-d>$
```

In this example, the first and second calls starting at ❶ are macro calls without arguments. Such calls treat the parameters as if empty arguments were actually passed.[3] In both cases the macro expands to "The arguments are and " (note the double space between the last two words, as well as the trailing space). The next three calls beginning at ❷ pass one, two, and three arguments, respectively. As you can see by the resulting outputs of these three calls, parameters in the expansion text that reference missing arguments are treated as empty, while arguments passed without corresponding references are simply ignored.

The last call at ❸ is a bit different. Notice that it contains a space between the macro name and the opening parenthesis. The initial output of this call was similar to that of the first two calls, but following that initial output we find what appears to be a minor variation on the originally intended argument list (the quotes are missing). This is a macro call *without arguments*. Since it's not actually part of the macro call, M4 treats the argument list simply as text on the input stream. Thus, it's copied directly to the output stream, minus one level of quotes.

---

3. Actually, in the call without parentheses, $# will be zero, if used in the macro definition to determine the number of arguments passed, while in the call with empty parentheses, $# will be one. However, in both cases, both referenced parameters ($1 and $2) will still contain the empty string.

Whitespace Around Arguments

When passing arguments in macro calls, be aware of whitespace around arguments. The rules are simple: Unquoted *leading* whitespace is removed from arguments, and *trailing* whitespace is always preserved, whether quoted or not. Of course, *whitespace* here refers to carriage returns and newline characters as well as spaces and tabs. Here's an example of calling a macro with variations in leading and trailing whitespace:

```
$ m4
define(`with3args', `The three arguments are $1, $2, and $3.')dnl
❶ with3args(arg1,
           arg2,
           arg3)
The three arguments are arg1, arg2, and arg3.
❷ with3args(arg1
           ,arg2
           ,arg3
           )
The three arguments are arg1
           , arg2
           , and arg3
           .
<ctrl-d>$
```

In this example, I purposely omitted the quotes around the macro arguments in the calls at ❶ and ❷ in order to reduce confusion. The call at ❶ has only leading whitespace in the form of newlines and tab characters, while the call at ❷ has only trailing whitespace. I'll cover quoting rules shortly, at which point you'll see clearly how quoting affects whitespace in macro arguments.

The Recursive Nature of M4

Now we consider the recursive nature of the M4 input stream. Whenever a name token is expanded by a macro definition, the expansion text is pushed back onto the input stream for complete reprocessing. This recursive reprocessing continues to occur as long as there are macro calls found in the input stream that generate text.

For example:

```
$ m4
define(`macro', `expansion')dnl
macro ``quoted' text'
expansion `quoted' text
<ctrl-d>$
```

Here, I define a macro called *macro*, and then present this macro name on the input stream, followed by additional text, some of which is quoted, and some of which is double quoted.

The process used by M4 to parse this example is shown in Figure 10-1.

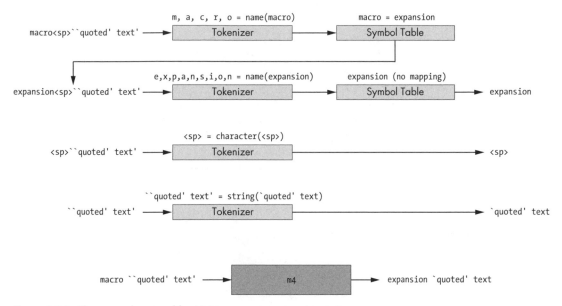

Figure 10-1: The procedure used by M4 to process an input text stream

In the bottom line of the figure, M4 is generating a stream of output text (expansion `quoted' text) from a stream of input text (macro ``quoted' text').

The diagram above this line shows how M4 actually generates the output text from the input text. When the first token (macro) is read in the top line, M4 finds a matching symbol in the symbol table, pushes it onto the input stream on the second line, and then restarts the input stream. Thus, the very next token read is another name token (expansion). Since this name is not found in the symbol table, the text is sent directly to the output stream. The third line sends the next token from the input stream (a space character) directly to the output stream. Finally, in the fourth line, one level of quotes is removed from the quoted text (``quoted' text'), and the result (`quoted' text) is sent to the output stream.

As you might guess, there are some potentially nasty side effects of this process. For example, you can accidentally define a macro that is infinitely recursive. The expansion of such a macro would lead to a massive amount of unwanted output, followed by a stack overflow. This is easy to do:

```
$ m4
define(`macro', `This is a macro')dnl
macro
This is a This is a This is a This is a This is a This is a...<ctrl-c>
$
```

This happens because the macro name expands into text containing the macro's own name, which is then pushed back onto the input stream for reprocessing. Consider the following scenario: *What would have been the result if I'd left the quotes off of the expansion text in the macro definition?* To help you discover the answer, let's turn next to M4 quoting rules.

Quoting Rules

Proper quoting is critical. You have probably encountered situations where your invocations of Autoconf macros didn't work as you expected. The problem is often a case of under-quoting, which means you omitted a required level of quotes around some text.

You see, each time text passes through M4, a layer of quotes is stripped off. Quoted strings are not names and are thus not subject to macro expansion, but if a quoted string passes through M4 twice, the second time through, it's no longer quoted. As a result, individual words within that string are no longer part of a string, but instead are parsed as name tokens, which are subject to macro expansion. To illustrate, enter the following text at a shell prompt:

```
$ m4
❶ define(`abc', `def')dnl
abc
def
❷ define(`abc', ``def'')dnl
abc
def
❸ define(`abc', ```def''')dnl
abc
`def'
<ctrl-d>$
```

In this example, the first time abc is defined (at ❶), it's quoted once. As M4 processes the macro definition, it removes a layer of quotes. Thus, the expansion text is stored in the symbol table without quotes, and we would expect the output of abc to be simply def, which it is.

As you can see, the second definition of abc (at ❷) is double quoted, so when the definition is processed, and the outer layer of quotes is stripped off, we would expect the expansion text in the symbol table to contain at least one set of quotes, and it does. Then why don't we see quotes around the output text? Remember that when macros are expanded, the expansion text is pushed onto the front of the input stream and reparsed using the usual rules. Thus, while the text of the second definition is stored quoted in the symbol table, as it's reprocessed upon use, the second layer of quotes is removed between the input and output streams.

The difference between ❶ and ❷ in this example is that the expansion text of ❷ is treated as quoted text by M4, rather than as a potential macro name. The quotes are removed during definition, but the enclosed text is not considered for further expansion because it's still quoted.

In the third definition of abc (at ❸), we finally see the result we were trying to obtain: a quoted version of the output text. The expansion text is entered into the symbol table double quoted, because the outermost set of quotes is stripped off during processing of the definition. Then, when the macro is used, the expansion text is reprocessed and the second set of quotes is stripped off, leaving one set in the final output text.

If you keep these rules in mind as you work with macros within Autoconf (including both definitions and calls), you'll find it easier to understand why things may not work the way you think they should. The *GNU M4 Manual* provides a simple rule of thumb for using quotes in macro calls: For each layer of nested parentheses in a macro call, use one layer of quotes.

Autoconf and M4

The autoconf program is a rather simple shell script. About 80 percent of the shell code in the script exists simply to ensure that the shell is functional enough to perform the required tasks. The remaining 20 percent parses command-line options. The last line of the script executes the autom4te program, a Perl script that acts as a wrapper around the m4 utility. Ultimately, autom4te calls m4 like this:

```
$ /usr/bin/m4 --nesting-limit=1024 --include=/usr/share/autoconf \
--debug=aflq --fatal-warning --error-output=autom4te.cache/traces.0t \
--trace=AC_CANONICAL_BUILD ... --trace=sinclude \
--reload-state=/usr/.../autoconf/autoconf.m4f aclocal.m4 configure.ac
```

As you can see, the three files that M4 is processing are */usr/.../autoconf/ autoconf.m4f*, *aclocal.m4*, and *configure.ac*, in that order.

NOTE *The .m4f extension on the master Autoconf macro file signifies a frozen M4 input file—a sort of precompiled version of the original .m4 file. When a frozen macro file is processed, it must be specified after a* --reload-state *option, in order to make M4 aware that it's not a normal input file. State is built cumulatively within M4 over all input files, so any macros defined by* aclocal.m4, *for instance, are available during the processing of* configure.ac.

The ellipsis between the two --trace options in the command line above is a placeholder for more than 100 such --trace options. It's a good thing the shell can handle long command lines!

The master Autoconf macro file, *autoconf.m4*, merely includes (using the m4_include macro) the other dozen or so Autoconf macro files, in the correct order, and then does a small amount of housekeeping before terminating. The *aclocal.m4* file is our project's macro file, built originally by the aclocal utility or handwritten for projects that don't use Automake. By the time *configure.ac* is processed, the M4 environment has been configured with hundreds of Autoconf macro definitions, which may be called as needed by *configure.ac*. This environment includes not only the recognized AC_* macros but also a few lower layers of Autoconf-provided macros that you may use to write your own macros.

One such lower layer is *m4sugar*,[4] which provides a nice clean namespace in which to define all of the Autoconf macros, as well as several improvements and additions to the existing M4 macros.

---

4. This is a hybrid palindromic acronym: *Readability And Greater Understanding Stands 4 M4Sugar.*

The Autoconf M4 Environment

Autoconf modifies the M4 environment in a few ways. First, as mentioned earlier, it changes the default quote characters from the backtick and single quote characters to the open and close square bracket characters. In addition, it configures M4 built-in macros such that most are prefixed with m4_, thereby creating a unique namespace for M4 macros. Thus, the M4 define macro becomes m4_define, and so on.[5]

Autoconf provides its own version of m4_define called AC_DEFUN. You should use AC_DEFUN instead of m4_define because it ensures that certain environmental constraints important to Autoconf are in place when your macro is called. The AC_DEFUN macro supports a prerequisite framework, so you can specify which macros are required to have been called before your macro may be called. This framework is accessed by using the AC_REQUIRE macro to indicate your macro's requirements at the beginning of your macro definition, like so:

```
# Test for option A
# -----------------
AC_DEFUN([TEST_A],
[AC_REQUIRE([TEST_B])dnl
test "$A" = "yes" && options="$options A"])
```

The rules for writing Autoconf macros using AC_DEFUN and the prerequisite framework are outlined in Chapter 9 of the *GNU Autoconf Manual*. Before you write your own macros, read Chapters 8 and 9 of that manual.

Writing Autoconf Macros

Why would we want to write Autoconf macros in the first place? One reason is that a project's *configure.ac* file might contain several instances of similar sets of code and we need the configure script to perform the same set of high-level operations on multiple directories or file sets. By converting the process into a macro, we reduce the number of lines of code in the *configure.ac* file, thereby reducing the number of possible points of failure. Another reason might be that an easily encapsulated bit of *configure.ac* code could be useful in other projects, or even to other people.

NOTE *The Autoconf Macro Archive provides many sets of related macros to solve common Autoconf problems. Anyone may contribute to the archive by emailing their macros to the project maintainer. There are frequent tarball releases available for free from the project website.[6]*

Simple Text Replacement

The simplest type of macro is one that replaces text verbatim, with no substitutions. An excellent example of this is found in the flaim project, where the flaim, xflaim, and sql projects' configure scripts attempt to locate the ftk

---

5. A notable exception is dnl. This macro is thankfully not renamed to m4_dnl.
6. See the Autoconf Macro Archive at *http://www.nongnu.org/autoconf-archive/*.

(FLAIM toolkit) project library and header file. Since I already discussed the operation of this code in Chapter 8, I'll only cover it briefly here as it relates to writing Autoconf macros, but I provide the relevant bit of *configure.ac* code in Listing 10-1 for convenience.

```
...
# Configure variables: FTKLIB and FTKINC.
AC_ARG_VAR([FTKLIB], [The PATH wherein libflaimtk.la can be found.])
AC_ARG_VAR([FTKINC], [The PATH wherein flaimtk.h can be found.])

# Ensure that both or neither FTK paths were specified.
if { test -n "$FTKLIB" && test -z "$FTKINC"; } ||
   { test -z "$FTKLIB" && test -n "$FTKINC"; }; then
  AC_MSG_ERROR([Specify both FTKINC and FTKLIB, or neither.])
fi

# Not specified? Check for FTK in standard places.
if test -z "$FTKLIB"; then
  # Check for FLAIM toolkit as a subproject.
  if test -d "$srcdir/ftk"; then
    AC_CONFIG_SUBDIRS([ftk])
    FTKINC='$(top_srcdir)/ftk/src'
    FTKLIB='$(top_builddir)/ftk/src'
  else
    # Check for FLAIM toolkit as a superproject.
    if test -d "$srcdir/../ftk"; then
      FTKINC='$(top_srcdir)/../ftk/src'
      FTKLIB='$(top_builddir)/../ftk/src'
    fi
  fi
fi

# Still empty? Check for *installed* FLAIM toolkit.
if test -z "$FTKLIB"; then
  AC_CHECK_LIB([flaimtk], [ftkFastChecksum],
    [AC_CHECK_HEADERS([flaimtk.h])
     LIBS="-lflaimtk $LIBS"],
    [AC_MSG_ERROR([No FLAIM toolkit found. Terminating.])])
fi

# AC_SUBST command line variables from FTKLIB and FTKINC.
if test -n "$FTKLIB"; then
  AC_SUBST([FTK_LTLIB], ["$FTKLIB/libflaimtk.la"])
  AC_SUBST([FTK_INCLUDE], ["-I$FTKINC"])
fi
...
```

Listing 10-1: xflaim/configure.ac: The ftk search code from the xflaim project

This code is identical in flaim, xflaim, and sql, though it may be modified in the future for one reason or another, so keeping it embedded in all three *configure.ac* files is redundant and error prone.

Even if we were to convert this code to a macro, we'd still have to put a copy of the macro file into each of the projects' *m4* directories. However, we could later edit only one of these macro files and copy it from the authoritative location into the other projects' *m4* directories. This would still be a better solution than having all of the code embedded in all three *configure.ac* files.

By converting this code to a macro, we can keep it in one place where portions of it cannot be confused for code that is not related to the process of locating the FLAIM toolkit library and header file. This happens quite often during later maintenance of a project's *configure.ac* file, as additional code designed for other purposes is dropped between chunks of code belonging to sequences like this.

Let's try converting this code into a macro. Our first attempt might look like Listing 10-2. (I've omitted a large chunk in the middle that is identical to the original code, for the sake of brevity.)

```
AC_DEFUN([FLM_FTK_SEARCH],
[# Configure variables: FTKLIB and FTKINC.
AC_ARG_VAR([FTKLIB], [The PATH wherein libflaimtk.la can be found.])
AC_ARG_VAR([FTKINC], [The PATH wherein flaimtk.h can be found.])
...
# AC_SUBST command line variables from FTKLIB and FTKINC.
if test -n "$FTKLIB"; then
  AC_SUBST([FTK_LTLIB], ["$FTKLIB/libflaimtk.la"])
  AC_SUBST([FTK_INCLUDE], ["-I$FTKINC"])
fi])
```

Listing 10-2: xflaim/m4/flm_ftk_search.m4: A first attempt at encapsulating ftk search code

In this pass, I've simply cut and pasted the entire *configure.ac* code sequence verbatim into the macro-body argument of a call to AC_DEFUN. The AC_DEFUN macro is defined by Autoconf and provides some additional functionality over the m4_define macro provided by M4. This additional functionality is strictly related to the prerequisite framework provided by Autoconf.

NOTE   *Be aware that AC_DEFUN must be used (rather than m4_define) in order for the macro definition to be found by aclocal in your external macro definition files. You must use AC_DEFUN if your macro definitions are in external files, but for simple macros defined within* configure.ac *itself you can use m4_define.*

Notice the use of M4 quoting around both the macro name (FLM_FTK_SEARCH) and the entire macro body. To illustrate the problems with not using these quotes in this example, consider how M4 would process the macro definition without the quotes. If the macro name were left unquoted, not much damage would be done, unless the macro happened to already be defined. If the macro were already defined, M4 would treat the macro name as a call with no parameters, and the existing definition would replace the macro name as M4 was reading the macro definition. (In this case, because of the unique name of the macro, there's not much chance that it's already defined, so I could have left the macro name unquoted with little effect, but it's good to be consistent.)

On the other hand, the macro body contains a fair amount of text and even Autoconf macro calls. Had we left the body unquoted, these macro calls would be expanded during the reading of the definition rather than during the later use of the macro, as we had intended.

Because the quotes are present, M4 stores the macro body as provided, with no additional processing during the reading of the definition other than to remove the outermost layer of quotes. Later, when the macro is called, the body text is inserted into the input stream in place of the macro call, and only then are the embedded macros expanded.

This macro requires no arguments because the same text is used identically in all three *configure.ac* files. The effect on *configure.ac* is to replace the entire chunk of code with the name of the macro, as shown in Listing 10-3.

```
...
FLM_PROG_TRY_DOXYGEN

❶ # Configure FTKLIB, FTKINC, FTK_LTLIB, and FTK_INCLUDE
FLM_FTK_SEARCH

# Check for Java compiler.
...
```

Listing 10-3: xflaim/configure.ac: Replacing the ftk search code with the new macro call

When writing a macro from existing code, consider the inputs to the existing chunk of code and the outputs provided by the code. Inputs will become possible macro arguments and outputs will become documented effects. In Listing 10-3, we have no inputs so we have no arguments, but what are the documentable effects of this code?

The comment at ❶ over the macro call in Listing 10-3 alludes to these effects. The FTKLIB and FTKINC variables are defined, and the FTK_LTLIB and FTK_INCLUDE variables are defined and substituted using AC_SUBST.

Documenting Your Macros

A proper macro definition provides a header comment that documents possible arguments, results, and potential side effects of the macro, as shown in Listing 10-4.

```
# FLM_FTK_SEARCH
# ----------------
# Define AC_ARG_VAR (user variables), FTKLIB, and FTKINC,
# allowing the user to specify the location of the FLAIM toolkit
# library and header file. If not specified, check for these files:
#   1. As a subproject.
#   2. As a super-project (sibling to the current project).
#   3. As installed components on the system.
# If found, AC_SUBST FTK_LTLIB and FTK_INCLUDE variables with
# values derived from FTKLIB and FTKINC user variables.
```

```
# FTKLIB and FTKINC are file locations, whereas FTK_LTLIB and
# FTK_INCLUDE are linker and preprocessor command-line options.
AC_DEFUN([FLM_FTK_SEARCH],
...
```

Listing 10-4: xflaim/m4/flm_ftk_search.m4: Adding a documentation header to the macro definition

This header comment documents both the effects of this macro and the way it operates, giving the user a clear picture of the sort of functionality he'll get when he calls it. The *GNU Autoconf Manual* indicates that such macro definition header comments are stripped from the final output; if you search the configure script for some text in the comment header, you'll see that it's missing.

Regarding coding style, the *GNU Autoconf Manual* suggests that it is good macro definition style to place the macro body's closing square-bracket quote and the closing parenthesis alone on the last line of the macro definition, along with a comment containing only the name of the macro being defined, as shown in Listing 10-5.

```
...
  AC_SUBST([FTK_INCLUDE], ["-I$FTKINC"])
❶ fi[]dnl
])# FLM_FTK_SEARCH
```

Listing 10-5: xflaim/m4/flm_ftk_search.m4: Suggested macro body closing style

The *GNU Autoconf Manual* also suggests that if you don't like the extra carriage return that the use of this format adds to the generated configure script, you can append the text []dnl to the last line of the macro body as at ❶ in Listing 10-5. The use of dnl causes the trailing carriage return to be ignored, and the open and close square brackets are simply empty Autoconf quotes that are stripped out during processing of later macro calls. The brackets are used to separate fi and dnl so they're recognized by M4 as two separate words.

NOTE   *The* GNU Autoconf Manual *defines a very complete naming convention for macros and their containing files. I've chosen simply to prefix all macro names and their containing files that are strictly related to the project with a project-specific prefix—in this case, FLM_ (flm_).*

M4 Conditionals

Now that you know how to write basic M4 macros we'll consider what it means to allow M4 to decide which text should be used to replace your macro call, based on arguments passed in the call.

Take a look at Listing 10-6; my first attempt at writing the FLM_PROG_ TRY_DOXYGEN macro that was first used in Chapter 8. This macro was designed with an optional argument, which isn't apparent from its use in Chapter 8 because the FLAIM code called the macro without arguments. Let's examine the definition of this macro. In the process we'll discover what it means to call it with and without arguments.

```
# FLM_PROG_TRY_DOXYGEN(["quiet"])
# -----------------------------
# FLM_PROG_TRY_DOXYGEN tests for an existing doxygen source
# documentation program. It sets or uses the environment
# variable DOXYGEN.
#
# If no arguments are given to this macro, and no doxygen
# program can be found, it prints a warning message to standard output
# and to the config.log file. If the "quiet" argument is passed,
# then only the normal "check" line is displayed.
#
# Makes the DOXYGEN variable precious to Autoconf. You can
# use the DOXYGEN variable in your Makefile.in files with
# @DOXYGEN@.
#
# NOTE: Currently, passing any value in the first argument has
#        the same effect as passing "quiet", however, you should
#        not rely on this, as all other words are reserved.
#
# Author:    John Calcote <john.calcote@gmail.com>
# Modified: 2009-04-23
# License:  AllPermissive
#
AC_DEFUN([FLM_PROG_TRY_DOXYGEN],
❶ [AC_ARG_VAR([DOXYGEN], [Doxygen source doc generation program])dnl
❷ AC_CHECK_PROGS([DOXYGEN], [doxygen])
❸ m4_ifval([$1],,
❹ [if test -z "$DOXYGEN"; then
    AC_MSG_WARN([doxygen not found - continuing without Doxygen support])
fi])
])# FLM_PROG_TRY_DOXYGEN
```

Listing 10-6: ftk/m4/flm_prog_try_doxygen.m4: A first attempt at FLM_PROG_TRY_DOXYGEN

First, we see a call to the AC_ARG_VAR macro at ❶, which is used to make the DOXYGEN variable precious to Autoconf. Making a variable precious causes Autoconf to display it within the configure script's help text as an influential environment variable. The AC_ARG_VAR macro also makes the specified variable an Autoconf substitution variable. At ❷ we come to the heart of this macro—the call to AC_CHECK_PROGS. This macro checks for a doxygen program in the system search path, but it only looks for the program (passed in the second argument) if the variable (passed in the first argument) is empty. If this variable is not empty, AC_CHECK_PROGS assumes that the end user has already specified the proper program in the variable in his environment and it does nothing. In this case, the DOXYGEN variable is populated with *doxygen* if the doxygen program is found in the system search path. In either case, a reference to the DOXYGEN variable is substituted into template files by Autoconf. (Since we just called AC_ARG_VAR on DOXYGEN, this step is redundant but harmless.)

The call to m4_ifval at ❸ brings us to the point of this section. This a conditional macro defined in Autoconf's m4sugar layer; a layer of simple macros designed to make writing higher-level Autoconf macros easier. M4 conditional macros are designed to generate one block of text if a condition is true and another if the condition is false. The purpose of m4_ifval is to generate text based on whether its first argument is empty. If its first argument is not empty, the macro generates the text in its second argument. If its first argument is empty, the macro generates the text in its third argument.

The FLM_PROG_TRY_DOXYGEN macro works with or without an argument. If no arguments are passed, FLM_PROG_TRY_DOXYGEN will print a warning message that the build is continuing without Doxygen support if the doxygen program is not in the system search path. On the other hand, if the quiet option is passed to FLM_PROG_TRY_DOXYGEN, no message will be printed if the doxygen program is not found.

In Listing 10-6, m4_ifval generates no text (the second argument is empty) if the first argument contains text. The first argument is $1, which refers to the contents of the first argument passed to FLM_PROG_TRY_DOXGEN. If no arguments are given to our macro, $1 will be empty, and m4_ifval will generate the text in its third argument shown at ❹. On the other hand, if we pass quiet (or any text, for that matter) to FLM_PROG_TRY_DOXYGEN, $1 will contain quiet, and m4_ifval will generate nothing.

The shell code in the third argument (at ❹) checks to see if the DOXYGEN variable is still empty after the call to AC_CHECK_PROGS. If it is, it calls AC_MSG_WARN to display a configuration warning.

Adding Precision

Autoconf provides a macro called m4_if, a renamed version of the M4 built-in ifelse macro. The m4_if macro is similar in nature to m4sugar's m4_ifval. Listing 10-7 shows how we might use ifelse in place of m4_ifval, if we didn't have m4sugar macros to work with.

```
...
ifelse([$1],,
[if test -z "$DOXYGEN"; then
  AC_MSG_WARN([Doxygen program not found - continuing without Doxygen])
fi])
...
```

Listing 10-7: Using ifelse *instead of* m4_ifval

The macros appear to be identical in function but this appearance is only circumstantial; the parameters are used differently. In this case, if the first argument ($1) is the same as the second argument (the empty string), the contents of the third argument ([if test -z ...]) are generated. Otherwise, the contents of the fourth (nonexistent) argument are generated because omitted arguments are treated as if the empty string had been passed.

FLM_PROG_TRY_DOXYGEN treats any text in its argument as if quiet was passed. In order to facilitate future enhancements to this macro, we should limit the allowed text in this argument to something that makes sense, otherwise users could abuse this parameter and we'd be stuck supporting whatever they pass for the sake of backward compatibility. The m4_if macro can help us out here. This macro is quite powerful because it accepts an unlimited number of arguments. Here are its basic prototypes:

```
m4_if(comment)
m4_if(string-1, string-2, equal[, not-equal])
m4_if(string-1, string-2, equal-1, string-3, string-4, equal-2,
    ...[, not-equal])
```

If only one parameter is passed to m4_if, that parameter is treated as a comment because there's not much that m4_if can do with one argument. If three or four arguments are passed, the description I gave for ifelse in Listing 10-7 is also accurate for m4_if. However, if five or more arguments are passed, the fourth and fifth become the comparison strings for a second *else-if* clause. The last argument in an arbitrarily long set of triples is generated if the last two comparison strings are different.

We can use m4_if to ensure that quiet is the only acceptable option in the list of options accepted by FLM_PROG_TRY_DOXYGEN. Listing 10-8 shows one possible implementation.

```
...
m4_if([$1],,
[if test -z "$DOXYGEN"; then
  AC_MSG_WARN([doxygen not found - continuing without Doxygen support])
fi], [$1], [quiet],, [m4_fatal([Invalid option in FLM_PROG_TRY_DOXYGEN])])
...
```

Listing 10-8: Restricting the argument options allowed by FLM_PROG_TRY_DOXYGEN

In this case we want a message to be printed if doxygen is missing in all cases except when the quiet option is specified as the first argument passed into our macro. In Listing 10-8 I've given FLM_PROG_TRY_DOXYGEN the ability to detect cases when something other than quiet or the empty string is passed in this parameter, and to do something specific in response. Listing 10-9 shows the resulting pseudocode generated by the expansion of FLM_PROG_TRY_DOXYGEN.

```
if $1 == '' then
    Generate WARNING if no doxygen program is found
else if $1 == 'quiet' then
    Don't generate any messages
else
    Generate a fatal "bad parameter" error at autoconf (autoreconf) time
end
```

Listing 10-9: Pseudocode for Listing 10-8's use of the m4_if macro

Let's examine exactly what's going on in Listing 10-8. If arguments one ([$1]) and two ([]) are the same, a warning message is generated when doxygen is not found. If arguments four ([$1]) and five ([quiet]) are the same, nothing is generated or a fatal error (via m4_fatal) is generated by Autoconf when it's executed against the calling *configure.ac* file. It's very simple, once you see how it works, *and* once you get the bugs worked out—which brings us nicely to our next topic.

Diagnosing Problems

One of the most significant stumbling blocks that people run into at this point is not so much a lack of understanding of how these macros work but a lack of attention to detail. There are several places where things can go wrong when writing even a simple macro like this. For example, you might have any of the following problems:

- Space between a macro name and the opening parenthesis
- Unbalanced brackets or parentheses
- The wrong number of parameters
- A misspelled macro name
- Incorrectly quoted arguments to a macro
- A missing comma in a macro's parameter list

M4 is rather unforgiving of such mistakes. Worse, its error messages can be even more cryptic than those of make.[7] If you get strange errors and you think your macro should be working, your best diagnostic method is to scan the definition very carefully looking for the above conditions. These mistakes are easy to make, and in the end most problems come down to some combination of them.

Another very useful debugging tool is the m4_traceon and m4_traceoff macro pair. The macro signatures are:

```
m4_traceon([name, ...])
m4_traceoff([name, ...])
```

All arguments are optional. When given, the arguments should be a comma-separated list of macro names you'd like M4 to print to the output stream as these names are encountered in the input stream. If you omit the arguments, M4 will print the name of every macro it expands.

---

7. The reason for such cryptic messages in both make and M4 is that it's very difficult for these programs to determine the proper context for an error, if the parsing context is drastically different with and without the error. In make, for example, a missing tab character on a command is problematic simply because commands are only commands by virtue of the tab character. Without it, the line looks to make like some other type of construct—perhaps a rule or a macro definition. The same is true of M4. When a comma is missing, for instance, M4 has so little context to go on that it appears as if two intended parameters are simply one parameter. M4 doesn't even complain—it simply processes the errant call as if there was one less parameter than intended (but it has no way of knowing the caller's intention).

A typical trace session in M4 looks something like this:

```
$ m4
define(`abc', `def')dnl
define(`def', `ghi')dnl
traceon()dnl
abc
❶ m4trace: -1- abc
m4trace: -1- def
ghi
traceoff()dnl
❷ m4trace: -1- traceoff
<ctrl-d>$
```

The number between dashes in the output lines at ❶ and ❷ indicates the nesting level which is usually 1. The value of the trace facility is that you can easily see when the traced macros are expanded within the context of the output text generated. The M4 tracing facility can also be enabled from the command line with the -t or --trace options:

```
$ m4 --trace=abc
```

Or more appropriately for this discussion:

```
$ autoconf --trace=FLM_PROG_TRY_DOXYGEN
```

For more information on the use of the M4 trace options, refer to Chapter 7 (specifically, Section 7.2) of the *GNU M4 Manual*.

NOTE *The Autotools rely heavily on tracing for more than just debugging. Various of the Autotools and their supporting utilities use traces on* configure.ac *to gather information used in other stages of the configuration process. For more information on tracing within Autoconf, refer to Section 3.4 of the* GNU Autoconf Manual, *entitled "Using* autoconf *to Create* configure."

Summary

Using M4 is deceptively complex. On the surface it appears simple, but as you get deeper into it, you find ways of using it that almost defy comprehension. While the complexities do exist, they're not insurmountable. As you become truly proficient with M4, you'll find that your way of thinking about certain problems changes. It's worth gaining some M4 proficiency for that reason alone. It's like adding a new tool to your software engineering toolbox.

Because the very foundation of Autoconf is M4, becoming proficient with M4 will give you more insight into Autoconf than you might think. The more about M4 you know, the more about Autoconf you'll understand at a glance.

11

A CATALOG OF TIPS AND REUSABLE SOLUTIONS FOR CREATING GREAT PROJECTS

*Experience is a hard teacher because
she gives the test first, the lesson afterwards.*
—Vernon Sanders Law[1]

This chapter began as a catalog of reusable solutions—canned macros, if you will. But as I finished the chapters preceding this one, it became clear to me that I needed to broaden my definition of a *canned solution.* Instead of just cataloging interesting macros, this chapter lists several unrelated-but important tips for creating great projects. Some of these are related to the GNU Autotools, but others are merely good programming practice with respect to open source and free software projects.

---

1. Nathan, David H. (2000). *The McFarland Baseball Quotations Dictionary.* McFarland & Company.

Item 1: Keeping Private Details out of Public Interfaces

At times, I've come across poorly designed library interfaces where a project's *config.h* file is required by the project's public header files. This presents a problem when more than one such library is required by a consumer. Which *config.h* file should be included? Both have the same name, and chances are that both provide similar or identically named definitions.

When you carefully consider the purpose of *config.h*, you see that it makes little sense to expose it in a library's public interface (by including it in any of the library's public header files), because its purpose is to provide platform-specific definitions to a particular build of the library. On the other hand, the public interface of a portable library is, by definition, platform-independent.

Interface design is a fairly general topic in computer science. This item focuses a bit more specifically on how to avoid including *config.h* in your public interfaces.

When designing a library for consumption by other projects, you're responsible for not polluting your consumers' symbol spaces with useless garbage from your header files. I once worked on a project that consumed a library interface from another team. This team provided both a Windows and a Unix version of their library, with the header file being portable between the two platforms. Unfortunately, they didn't understand the definition of a clean interface. At some point in their public header files, they had a bit of code that looked like Listing 11-1.

```
#ifdef _WIN32
# include <windows.h>
#else
typedef void * HANDLE;
#endif
```

Listing 11-1: A poorly designed public header file that exposes platform-specific header files

Ouch! Did they really need to include *windows.h* just for the definition of HANDLE? No, and they probably should have used a different name for the handle object in their public interface because HANDLE is too generic and could easily conflict with a dozen other library interfaces. Something like XYZ_HANDLE or something more specific to the XYZ library would have been a better choice.

To properly design a library, first design the public interface to expose as little of the library's internals as is reasonable. Now, you'll have to determine the definition of *reasonable*, but it will probably involve a compromise between abstraction and performance.

When designing an API, start with the functionality you wish to expose from your library; design functions that will maximize ease of use. If you find yourself trying to decide between a simpler implementation and a simpler user experience, always err on the side of ease of use for your consumers. They'll thank you by actually using your library. Of course, if the interface is already defined by a software standard, then much of your work is done for you. Often this is not the case, and you will have to make these decisions.

Next, try to abstract away internal details. Unfortunately, the C language doesn't make it easy to do this because you often need to pass structure references in public APIs containing internal details of your implementation that consumers don't need to see. (C++ is just as bad in this area: C++ classes define public interfaces and private implementation details in the same class definition.)

Solutions in C

In C, a common solution for this problem is to define a public alias for a private structure in terms of a generic (void) pointer. Many developers don't care for this approach because it reduces type safety in the interface, but the loss of type safety is significantly offset by the increase in interface abstraction, as shown in Listings 11-2 and 11-3.

```
#include <abc_pub.h>

#if HAVE_CONFIG_H
# include <config.h>
#endif

typedef struct
{
    /* private details */
} abc_impl;

int abc_func(abc * p)
{
    abc_impl * ip = (abc_impl *)p;
    /* use 'p' through 'ip' */
}
```

Listing 11-2: An example of a private C-language source file

```
typedef void abc;
int abc_func(abc * p);
```

Listing 11-3: abc_pub.h: A public header file describing a public interface (API)

Notice how the abstraction conveniently alleviates the need to include a bunch of really private definitions in the library's public interface.

Solutions in C++

In C++, hiding implementation details with interface abstraction can be done in a few different ways, which include using virtual interfaces and the *PIMPL (Private IMPLementation)* pattern.

The PIMPL Pattern

In the PIMPL pattern, implementation details are hidden behind a pointer to a private implementation class stored as private data within the public interface class, as shown in Listings 11-4 and 11-5.

```
#include <abc_pub.h>

#if HAVE_CONFIG_H
# include <config.h>
#endif

class abc_impl
{
    /* private details */
};

int abc::func(void)
{
    /* use 'pimpl' pointer */
}
```

Listing 11-4: A private C++-language source file showing the proper use of the PIMPL pattern

```
❶ class abc_impl;
   class abc {
❷   abc_impl * pimpl;
   public:
     int func(void);
   };
```

Listing 11-5: abc_pub.h: The public header file exposes few private details via the PIMPL pattern.

The C++ language allows the use of a *forward declaration* (like the one at ❶) for any types used only through references or pointers (as at ❷) but never actually dereferenced in the public interface. Thus, the definition of the implementation class need not be exposed in the public interface, because the compiler will happily compile the public interface header file without the definition of the private implementation class.

The performance trade-off here generally involves the dynamic allocation of an instance of the private implementation class, and then accessing class data indirectly through this pointer, rather than directly in the public structure. Notice how all internal details are now conveniently hidden, and thus not required by the public interface.

C++ Virtual Interfaces

Another approach when using C++ is to define a public *interface* class, whose methods are declared *pure virtual*, with the interface implemented internally by the library. To access an object of this class, consumers call a public *factory* function, which returns a pointer to the implementation class in terms of the interface definition. Listings 11-6 and 11-7 illustrate the concept of C++ virtual interfaces.

```
#include <abc_pub.h>

#if HAVE_CONFIG_H
# include <config.h>
#endif

class abc_impl : public abc {
    /* implementation of virtual methods */
};
```

Listing 11-6: A private C++-language source file implementing a pure virtual interface

```
#define xyz_interface class

xyz_interface abc {
public:
    virtual int func(void) = 0;
};
```

❶ abc * abc_instantiate(/* abc_impl ctor params */);

Listing 11-7: abc_pub.h: A public C++-language header file, providing only the interface definition

Here I use the C++ preprocessor to define a new keyword, xyz_interface. By definition, xyz_interface is synonymous with class, so the terms may be used interchangeably. The idea here is that an interface doesn't expose any implementation details to the consumer. The public *factory* function abc_instantiate at ❶ returns a pointer to a new object of type abc_impl, except in terms of abc. Thus, nothing internal need be shown to the caller in the public header file.

It may seem like the virtual interface class method is more efficient than the PIMPL method, but the fact is that most compilers implement virtual function calls as tables of function pointers referred to by a hidden *vptr* address within the implementation class. As a result, you still end up calling all of your public methods indirectly through a pointer. The technique you choose to use to help you hide your implementation details is more a matter of personal preference than performance.

When I design a library, I first design a minimal, but complete, functional interface with as much of my internal implementation abstracted away as is reasonable. I try to use only standard library basic types, if possible, in my function prototypes, and then include only the C or C++ standard header files required by the use of those types and definitions. This technique is the fastest way I've found to create a highly portable and maintainable interface.

If you still can't see the value in the advice offered by this item, then let me give you one more scenario to ponder. Consider what happens when a Linux distro packager decides to create a *devel* package for your library—that is, a package containing static libraries and header files, designed to be installed into the */usr/lib* and */usr/include* directories on a target system. Every header file required by your library must be installed into the */usr/include* directory. If your library's public interface requires the inclusion of your *config.h* file, then by extension, your *config.h* file must be installed into the */usr/include* directory. Now consider what happens when multiple such libraries need to be installed. Which copy of *config.h* will win? Only one *config.h* file can exist in */usr/include*.

I've seen message threads on the Autotools mailing lists defending the need to publish *config.h* in a public interface and providing techniques for naming *config.h* in a package-specific manner. These techniques often involve some form of post-processing of this file to rename its macros so they don't conflict with *config.h* definitions installed by other packages. While this can be done, and while there are a few good reasons for doing so (usually involving a widely used legacy code base that can't be modified without breaking a lot of existing code), these situations should be considered the exception, not the rule, because a well-designed project should not need to expose platform- and project-specific definitions in its public interface.

If your project simply can't live without *config.h* in its public interface, explore the nuances of the `AC_CONFIG_HEADERS` macro. Like all of the instantiating macros, this macro accepts a list of input files. The `autoheader` utility only writes the first input file in the list, so you can hand-create a second input file that contains definitions that you feel must be included in your public interface. Remember to name your public input file so as to reduce conflict with other packages' public interfaces.

NOTE *Also, explore the `AX_PREFIX_CONFIG_H` macro, found in the Autoconf Macro Archive (see "Item 8: Using the ac-archive Project" on page 298), which will add a custom prefix to all items found in* config.h.

Item 2: Implementing Recursive Extension Targets

An *extension target* is a make target that you write to accomplish some build goal that Automake doesn't automatically support. A *recursive extension target* is one that traverses your project directory structure, visiting every *Makefile.am* file in your Autotools build system and giving each one the opportunity to do some work when the extension target is made.

When you add a new top-level target to your build system, you have to either tie it into an existing Automake target, or add your own make code to the desired target that traverses the subdirectory structure provided by Automake in your build system.

The SUBDIRS variable is used to recursively traverse all subdirectories of the current directory, passing requested build commands into the makefiles in these directories. This works great for targets that must be built based on configuration options, because after configuration, the SUBDIRS variable contains only those directories destined to be built.

However, if you need to execute your new recursive target in all subdirectories, regardless of any conditional configuration that might exclude a subdirectory specified in SUBDIRS, use the DIST_SUBDIRS variable instead.

There are various ways to traverse the build hierarchy, including some really simple one-liners provided by GNU make–specific syntax. But the most portable way is to use the technique that Automake itself uses, as shown in Listing 11-8.

```
my-recursive-target:
❶        $(preorder_commands)
         for dir in $(SUBDIRS); do \
           (cd $$dir && $(MAKE) $(AM_MAKEFLAGS) $@) || exit 1; \
         done
❷        $(postorder_commands)

.PHONY: my-recursive-target
```

Listing 11-8: A makefile with a recursive target—WARNING: no support for "." in SUBDIRS

At some point in the hierarchy, you'll need to do something useful besides calling down to lower levels. The preorder_commands macro at ❶ can be used to do things that must be done before recursing into lower-level directories. The postorder_commands macro at ❷ can likewise be used to do additional things once you return from the lower-level directories. Simply define either or both of these macros in any makefiles that need to do some pre-order or post-order processing for my-recursive-target.

For example, if you want to build some generated documentation, you might have a special target called doxygen. Even if you happen to be okay with building your documentation in the top-level directory, there may be times when you need to distribute the generation of your documentation to various directories within your project hierarchy. You might use code similar to that shown in Listing 11-9 in each *Makefile.am* file in your project.

```
# uncomment if doxyfile exists in this directory
❶ # postorder_commands = $(DOXYGEN) $(DOXYFLAGS) doxyfile

doxygen:
         $(preorder_commands)
❷        for dir in $(SUBDIRS); do \
❸          (cd $$dir && $(MAKE) $(AM_MAKEFLAGS) $@) || exit 1; \
         done
         $(postorder_commands)

.PHONY: doxygen
```

Listing 11-9: Implementing post order commands for a doxygen directory

For directories where *doxyfile* doesn't exist, you can comment out (or better yet, simply omit) the postorder_commands macro definition at ❶. In this case, the doxygen target will be harmlessly propagated to the next lower level in the build tree by the three lines of shell code at ❷.

The exit statement at the end of ❸ ensures that the build terminates when a lower-level makefile fails on the recursive target, propagating the shell error code (1) back up to each parent makefile until the top-level shell is reached. This is important; without it, the build may continue after a failure until a different error is encountered.

NOTE *I chose not to use the somewhat less portable -C make command-line option to change directories before running the sub-make operation.*

If you choose to implement a completely recursive global target in this manner, then you must include Listing 11-9 in every *Makefile.am* file in your project, even if that makefile has nothing to do with the generation of documentation. If you don't, then make will fail on that makefile because no doxygen target exists within that makefile. The commands may do nothing, but the target must exist.

If you want to do something simpler, such as pass a target down to a single subdirectory beneath the top-level directory (such as a *doc* directory just below the top), life becomes easier. Just implement the code shown in Listings 11-10 and 11-11.

```
doxygen:
❶          cd doc && $(MAKE) $(AM_MAKEFLAGS) $@

.PHONY: doxygen
```

Listing 11-10: A top-level makefile that propagates a target to a single subdirectory

```
doxygen:
            $(DOXYGEN) $(DOXYFLAGS) doxyfile

.PHONY: doxygen
```

Listing 11-11: doc/Makefile.am: The code to handle the new target

The shell statement at ❶ in the top-level makefile in Listing 11-10 simply passes the target (doxygen) down to the desired directory (doc).

NOTE *The variables DOXYGEN and DOXYFLAGS are assumed to exist by virtue of some macro or shell code executed within the configure script.*

Automake recursive targets are more sophisticated in that they also support make's -k command-line option to continue building after errors. Additionally, Automake's recursive target implementation supports the use of the dot (.) in the SUBDIRS variable, which represents the current directory. You may also support these features, but if you do, your boilerplate recursive make shell code will be messier. For the sake of completeness, Listing 11-12 shows an implementation that supports these features. Compare this listing to Listing 11-8. The bolded shell code shows the differences between these listings.

```
my-recursive-target:
        $(preorder_commands)
        @failcom='exit 1'; \
        for f in x $$MAKEFLAGS; do \
          case $$f in \
            *=* | --[!k]*);; \
❶          *k*) failcom='fail=yes';; \
          esac; \
        done; \
        for dir in $(SUBDIRS); do \
❷         if test "$$dir" != .; then \
            (cd $$dir && $(MAKE) $(AM_MAKEFLAGS) $@) || eval $$failcom; \
          fi; \
        done
        $(postorder_commands)

.PHONY: my-recursive-target
```

Listing 11-12: Adding make -k and a check for the current directory

At ❶ the case statement checks for a -k option in the MAKEFLAGS environment variable and, on finding it, sets the failcom shell variable to some innocuous shell code. If it's not found, then failcom is left at its default value, exit 1, which is then inserted where an exit should occur on error. The if statement within the for loop at ❷ simply skips the recursive call for the dot entry in SUBDIRS. As with the previous examples, for the current directory, the functionality of the recursive target is found entirely within the $(preorder_commands) and $(postorder_commands) macro expansions.

I've tried to show you in this item that you can do as much or as little as you like with your own recursive targets. Most of the implementation is simply shell code in the command.

Item 3: Using a Repository Revision Number in a Package Version

Version control is an important part of every project. Not only does it protect intellectual property, but it also allows the developer to back up and start again after a long series of mistakes. One advantage of version control systems like Subversion is that the system assigns a unique revision number to every change to a project's repository. This means that any distribution of the project's source code can be logically tied to a particular repository revision number. This item presents a technique you can use to automatically insert a repository revision number into your package's Autoconf version string.

Arguments to the Autoconf AC_INIT macro must be static text. That is, they can't be shell variables, and Autoconf will flag attempts to use shell variables in these arguments as errors. This is all well and good until you want to calculate any portion of your package's version number during the configuration process.

I once tried to use a shell variable in AC_INIT's VERSION argument so that I could substitute my Subversion revision number into the VERSION argument when configure was executed. I spent a couple of days trying to figure out how to trick Autoconf into letting me use a shell variable as a *revision* field in my package's version number. Eventually, I discovered the trick shown in Listing 11-13, which I implemented in my *configure.ac* file and in my top-level *Makefile.am* file.

```
SVNREV=`( svnversion $srcdir | sed 's/:.*//' ) 2>/dev/null`
if { ! ( svnversion ) >/dev/null 2>&1 || test "$SVNREV" = "exported"; } ;
❸    then SVNREV=`cat $srcdir/SVNREV`
     else echo $SVNREV>$srcdir/SVNREV
fi
AC_SUBST(SVNREV)
```

Listing 11-13: configure.ac: *Implementing a dynamic revision number as part of the package version*

Here, the shell variable SVNREV is set at ❶ to the output of the svnversion command, as executed on the project top-level directory. The output is piped through sed to remove all text following an embedded colon character. This gives us a raw Subversion revision number—that is, *if* the code is executed in a true Subversion work area, which isn't always the case.

When a user executes this configure script from a distribution tarball, Subversion may not even be installed on his workstation. Even if it is, the top-level project directory comes from the tarball, not a Subversion repository. To handle these situations, the line at ❷ checks to see if Subversion is not installed or if the output from the first line was the word *exported*, the result of executing the svnversion utility on a non-work-area directory.

If either of these cases is true, the SVNREV variable is populated at ❸ from the contents of a file called SVNREV. The project should be configured to ship the *SVNREV* file with a distribution tarball containing the configuration code in Listing 11-13. This must be done because if the svnversion generates a true Subversion repository revision number, that value is immediately written to the *SVNREV* file by the else clause of this if statement at ❹.

Finally, the call to AC_SUBST at ❺ substitutes the SVNREV variable into template files, including the project makefiles.

In the top-level *Makefile.am* file, I ensure that the *SVNREV* file becomes part of the distribution tarball by adding it to the EXTRA_DIST list. Thus, when a distribution tarball is created and published by the maintainer, it contains an *SVNREV* file with the source tree revision number used to generate the tarball from this source code. The value in the *SVNREV* file is also used when a tarball is generated from the source code in this tarball (via make dist). This is accurate because the original tarball was actually generated from this particular revision of the Subversion repository.

Generally, it's not particularly important that a project's distribution tarball be able to generate a proper distribution tarball, but an Automake-generated tarball can do so without this modification, so it should also be able to do so *with* it. Listing 11-14 shows the relevant changes to the top-level *Makefile.am* file in bold.

```
EXTRA_DIST = SVNREV
distdir = $(PACKAGE)-$(VERSION).$(SVNREV)
```

Listing 11-14: Makefile.am: A top-level makefile configured for SVN revision numbers

In Listing 11-14, the distdir variable controls the name of the distribution directory and the tarball filename generated by Automake. Setting this variable in the top-level *Makefile.am* file affects the generation of the distribution tarball, because that *Makefile.am* file is where this functionality is located in the final generated *Makefile*.

NOTE *Note the similarity of the SVNREV filename and the SVNREV make variable [$(SVNREV)] in Listing 11-14. Although they appear to be the same, the text added to the EXTRA_DIST line refers to the SVNREV file in the top-level project directory, while the text added to the distdir variable refers to a make variable.*

For most purposes, setting distdir in the top-level *Makefile.am* file should be sufficient. However, if you need distdir to be formatted correctly in another *Makefile.am* file in your project, just set it in that file as well.

The technique presented in this item does not automatically reconfigure the project to generate a new *SVNREV* file when you commit new changes (and so change the Subversion revision used in your build). I could have added this functionality with a few well-placed make rules, but that would have forced the build to check for commits with each new build.[2]

Item 4: Ensuring Your Distribution Packages Are Clean

Have you ever downloaded and unpacked an open source package, and tried to run **configure && make** only to have it fail half way through one of these steps? As you dug into the problem, perhaps you discovered missing files in the tarball. How sad to have this happen in an Autotools project, when the Autotools make it so easy to ensure that this simply doesn't happen.

To ensure that your distribution tarballs are always clean and complete, run the distcheck target on a newly created tarball. Don't be satisfied with what you *believe* about your package. Allow Automake to run the distribution unit tests. I call these tests *unit tests* because they provide the same testing functionality for a distribution package that regular unit tests provide for your source code.

---

2. My work habits are such that I tend to regenerate a build tree from scratch before releasing a new distribution package, so this issue doesn't really affect me that much.

You'd never make a code change and ship a package without running your unit tests, would you? (If so, then you can safely skip this section.) Likewise, don't ship your tarballs without running the build system unit tests—run **make distcheck** on your project *before* posting your new tarballs. If the distcheck target fails, find out why and fix it. The payoff is worth the effort.

Item 5: Hacking Autoconf Macros

Occasionally you need a macro that Autoconf doesn't quite provide. That's when it pays to know how to copy and modify existing Autoconf macros.[3]

For example, here's a solution to a common Autoconf mailing list issue. A user wants to use AC_CHECK_LIB to capture a desired library in the LIBS variable. The catch is that this library exports functions with C++, rather than C linkage. AC_CHECK_LIB is not very accommodating when it comes to C++, primarily because AC_CHECK_LIB makes certain assumptions about symbols exported with C linkage that just don't apply to C++ symbols.

For example, the widely known (and standardized) rules of C linkage state that an exported C-linkage symbol (also known as the cdecl calling convention on Intel systems) is case sensitive and decorated with a leading underscore,[4] whereas a symbol exported with C++ linkage is *mangled* using nonstandard, vendor-defined rules. The decorations are based on the signature of the function—specifically, the number and types of parameters, and the classes and/or namespaces to which the function belongs. But the exact scheme is not defined by the C++ standard.

Now, stop and consider under what circumstances you're likely to have symbols exported from a library using C++ linkage. There are two ways to export C++ symbols from a library. The first is to (either purposely or accidentally) export *global* functions without using the extern "C" linkage specification on your function prototypes. The second is to export entire classes— including public and protected methods and class data.

If you've accidentally forgotten to use extern "C" on your global functions, well then, stop it. If you're doing it on purpose, then I wonder why? The only reason I can think of is that you want to export more than one function of the same name. This seems a rather trivial reason to keep your C developers from being able to use your library.

If you're exporting classes, now that's another story. In this case, you're catering specifically to C++ users, which presents a real issue with AC_CHECK_LIB.

Autoconf provides a framework around the definition of AC_CHECK_LIB that allows for differences between C and C++. If you use the AC_LANG([C++]) macro before you call AC_CHECK_LIB, you'll generate a version of the test program that's specific to C++. But don't get your hopes up; the current implementation of the C++ version is simply a copy of the C version. I expect that a generic C++ implementation would be difficult at best to design.

---

3. This technique is also an excellent way to learn your way around Autoconf-provided macros.
4. The cdecl keyword or attribute does not decorate the symbol with a leading underscore on some systems.

But all is not lost. While a *generic* implementation would be difficult, as the project maintainer you can easily write a project-specific version of the test code using AC_CHECK_LIB's test code.

First we need to find the definition of the AC_CHECK_LIB macro. A grep of the Autoconf macro directory (usually */usr/(local/)share/autoconf/autoconf*) should quickly locate the definition of AC_CHECK_LIB in the file called *libs.m4*. Because most macro definitions start with a comment header containing a hash mark and then the name of the macro and a single space, the following should work.

```
$ cd /usr/share/autoconf/autoconf
$ grep "^# AC_CHECK_LIB" *.m4
libs.m4:# AC_CHECK_LIB(LIBRARY, FUNCTION,
$
```

The definition of AC_CHECK_LIB is shown in Listing 11-15.[5]

```
# AC_CHECK_LIB(LIBRARY, FUNCTION,
#              [ACTION-IF-FOUND], [ACTION-IF-NOT-FOUND],
#              [OTHER-LIBRARIES])
...
# freedom.
AC_DEFUN([AC_CHECK_LIB],
[m4_ifval([$3], , [AH_CHECK_LIB([$1])])dnl
AS_LITERAL_IF([$1], [AS_VAR_PUSHDEF([ac_Lib], [ac_cv_lib_$1_$2])],
    [AS_VAR_PUSHDEF([ac_Lib], [ac_cv_lib_$1''_$2])])dnl
AC_CACHE_CHECK([for $2 in -l$1], [ac_Lib],
[ac_check_lib_save_LIBS=$LIBS
LIBS="-l$1 $5 $LIBS"
❶ AC_LINK_IFELSE([AC_LANG_CALL([], [$2])],
    [AS_VAR_SET([ac_Lib], [yes])],
    [AS_VAR_SET([ac_Lib], [no])])
LIBS=$ac_check_lib_save_LIBS])
AS_VAR_IF([ac_Lib], [yes],
    [m4_default([$3], [AC_DEFINE_UNQUOTED(AS_TR_CPP(HAVE_LIB$1))
    LIBS="-l$1 $LIBS"
])],
    [$4])dnl
AS_VAR_POPDEF([ac_Lib])dnl
])# AC_CHECK_LIB
```

Listing 11-15: The definition of AC_CHECK_LIB, as found in libs.m4

This apparent quagmire is easily sorted out with a little analysis. The macro appears to accept up to five arguments (as shown in the comment header), the first two of which are required. The bolded portion is the macro definition—the part we'll copy into our *configure.ac* file and modify to work with our C++ exports.

---

5. This version of AC_CHECK_LIB is from Autoconf version 2.63. Portions of the macro were rewritten in version 2.64, but this version is a bit easier to understand and analyze.

Recall from Chapter 10 that the placeholders for M4 macro definition parameters are similar to those of shell scripts: a dollar sign followed by a number. The first parameter is represented by $1, the second by $2, and so on. We need to determine which parameters are important to us and which ones to discard. We know that most calls to AC_CHECK_LIB pass only the first two arguments. The third and fourth parameters are optional and exist only so that you can change the macro's default behavior depending on whether it locates the desired function in the specified library. The fifth parameter allows you to provide a list of additional linker command-line arguments (usually additional library and library directory references) that are required to properly link the desired library.

Say we have a C++ library that exports a class's public data and methods. Our library is named *fancy*, our class is Fancy, and the method we're interested in is called execute—specifically the execute method that accepts two integer arguments. Thus, its signature would be

---

```
Fancy::execute(int, int)
```

When exported with C linkage, such a function would be presented to the linker merely as _execute (or simply as execute, without the leading underscore, on some platforms), but when exported with C++ linkage, all bets are off because of vendor-specific name-mangling.

The only way to get the linker to find this symbol is to declare it in compiled source code with exactly this signature, but we don't supply enough information to AC_CHECK_LIB to properly declare the function signature in the test code. Here's the declaration required to tell the compiler how to properly mangle this method's name:

```
class Fancy { public: void execute(int,int); };
```

Assuming that we're looking for a function with C linkage called execute, the AC_CHECK_LIB macro generates a small test program like the one shown in Listing 11-16. I've bolded our function name, so you can easily see where the macro inserts it into the generated test code.

```
/* confdefs.h.   */
#define PACKAGE_NAME ""
#define PACKAGE_TARNAME ""
#define PACKAGE_VERSION ""
#define PACKAGE_STRING ""
#define PACKAGE_BUGREPORT ""
/* end confdefs.h.   */

/* Override any GCC internal prototype to avoid an error.
   Use char because int might match the return type of a GCC
   builtin and then its argument prototype would still apply.   */
#ifdef __cplusplus
extern "C"
#endif
```

```
char execute();
int
main ()
{
return execute();
    ;
    return 0;
}
```

Listing 11-16: An Autoconf-generated check for the global C-language execute function

Except for these two uses of the specified function name, the entire test program is identical for every call to AC_CHECK_LIB. This macro creates a common prototype for all functions, so that all functions are treated the same way. Clearly, however, not all functions accept no parameters and return a character, as defined in this code. AC_CHECK_LIB effectively lies to the compiler about the true nature of the function. The test only cares whether the test program can successfully be linked; it will never attempt to execute it (an operation that would fail spectacularly in most cases).

For C++ symbols, we need to generate a different test program; one that makes no assumptions about the signature of our exported symbol.

Looking back at ❶ in Listing 11-15, it appears as if the AC_LANG_CALL macro has something to do with the generation of the test code in Listing 11-16 because the output of AC_LANG_CALL is generated directly into the first argument of a call to AC_LINK_IFELSE; it's first argument is source code to be tested with the linker. As it turns out, this macro too is a higher-level wrapper around another macro, the AC_LANG_PROGRAM macro. Listing 11-17 shows the definitions of both macros. I've bolded the macro names for the sake of clarity.

```
# AC_LANG_CALL(C)(PROLOGUE, FUNCTION)
# ----------------------------------
# Avoid conflicting decl of main.
m4_define([AC_LANG_CALL(C)],
❶ [AC_LANG_PROGRAM([$1
m4_if([$2], [main], ,
[/* Override any GCC internal prototype to avoid an error.
   Use char because int might match the return type of a GCC
   builtin and then its argument prototype would still apply.  */
#ifdef __cplusplus
extern "C"
#endif
❷ char $2 ();])], [return $2 ();])])

# AC_LANG_PROGRAM(C)([PROLOGUE], [BODY])
# -------------------------------------
m4_define([AC_LANG_PROGRAM(C)],
❸ [$1
m4_ifdef([_AC_LANG_PROGRAM_C_F77_HOOKS], [_AC_LANG_PROGRAM_C_F77_HOOKS])[]dnl
m4_ifdef([_AC_LANG_PROGRAM_C_FC_HOOKS], [_AC_LANG_PROGRAM_C_FC_HOOKS])[]dnl
int
```

```
main ()
{
dnl Do *not* indent the following line: there may be CPP directives.
dnl Don't move the `;' right after for the same reason.
❹ $2
  ;
  return 0;
}])
```

Listing 11-17: The definitions of AC_LANG_CALL and AC_LANG_PROGRAM

At ❶, AC_LANG_CALL generates a call to AC_LANG_PROGRAM, passing the the PROLOGUE argument in the first parameter. At ❸, this prologue (in the form of $1) is immediately sent to the output stream. If the second argument passed to AC_LANG_CALL (FUNCTION) is not main, an extern "C" function prototype is generated for the function. At ❷, the text return $2 (); is passed as the BODY argument to AC_LANG_PROGRAM, which uses this text at ❹ to generate a call to the function. (Remember that this code will only be linked, never executed.)

For C++, we need to be able to define more of the test program so that it makes no assumptions about the prototype of our exported symbol, and AC_LANG_CALL is too specific to C, so we'll use the lower-level macro, AC_LANG_ PROGRAM, instead. Listing 11-18 shows how we might rework AC_CHECK_LIB to handle the function Fancy::execute(int, int) from a library called *fancy*. I've bolded the places where I've modified the original macro definition of Listing 11-15 on page 283.

```
AC_PREREQ(2.59)
AC_INIT(test, 1.0)

AC_LANG(C++)

# --- A modified version of AC_CHECK_LIB
m4_ifval([], , [AH_CHECK_LIB([fancy])])dnl
❶ AS_VAR_PUSHDEF([ac_Lib], [ac_cv_lib_fancy_execute])dnl
❷ AC_CACHE_CHECK([whether -lfancy exports Fancy::execute(int,int)], [ac_Lib],
   [ac_check_lib_save_LIBS=$LIBS
LIBS="-lfancy $LIBS"
❸ AC_LINK_IFELSE([AC_LANG_PROGRAM(
   [[class Fancy {
      public: void execute(int i, int j);
   };]],
   [[ MyClass test;
     test.execute(1, 1);]])],
     [AS_VAR_SET([ac_Lib], [yes])],
     [AS_VAR_SET([ac_Lib], [no])])
LIBS=$ac_check_lib_save_LIBS])
AS_VAR_IF([ac_Lib], [yes],
   [AC_DEFINE_UNQUOTED(AS_TR_CPP(HAVE_LIBFANCY))
   LIBS="-lfancy $LIBS"
],
[])dnl
AS_VAR_POPDEF([ac_Lib])dnl
```

```
# --- End of modified version of AC_CHECK_LIB
```

AC_OUTPUT

Listing 11-18: Hacking a modified version of AC_CHECK_LIB *into* configure.ac

In Listing 11-18 I've replaced the parameter placeholders with library and function names at ❶ and ❷ and added the prologue and body of the program to be generated by AC_LANG_PROGRAM at ❸. I've also removed some extraneous text that had specifically to do with the optional parameters of AC_CHECK_LIB that I don't care about in my version.

This code is much longer and more difficult to understand than a simple call to AC_CHECK_LIB, so it just begs to be turned into a macro. I'll leave that to you as an exercise. Having read Chapter 10, you should be able to do this without too much difficulty.

Providing Library-Specific Autoconf Macros

This item is about hacking Autoconf macros when you need special features not provided by the standard macros, but the example I used was specifically about looking for a particular function in a library. This is a special case of a more general issue: finding libraries that provide desired functionality.

If you're a library developer, consider providing downloadable Autoconf macros that test for the existence of your libraries, and perhaps version-specific functionality within them. By doing so, you make it easier for your users to ensure that their users have proper access to your libraries.

Such macros don't have to be general purpose in nature, because they're tailored to a specific library. Library-specific macros are much easier to write and can be more thorough in testing for the functionality of the library.

Item 6: Cross-Compiling

Cross-compilation occurs when the *build system* (the system on which the binaries are built) and the *host system* (the system on which those binaries are meant to be executed) are not of the same types. For example, we're cross-compiling when we build Motorola 68000 binaries for an embedded system on a typical Intel x86 platform such as GNU/Linux, or when we build Sparc binaries on a DEC Alpha system. A far more common scenario is using your Linux system to build software designed to run on an embedded microprocessor.

The situation becomes even more complex if the software you're building, such as a compiler or linker, can generate software. In this case, the *target system* represents the system for which your compiler or linker will ultimately generate code. When such a build system involves three different architectures, it's often referred to as a *Canadian cross.*[6] In this case, a compiler or linker is built on architecture A to run on architecture B and generate code for architecture C. Another type of three-system build, called a *cross-to-native* build,

---

6. The name comes from the fact that during early discussions of cross-compilation issues on the Internet, Canada had three political parties.

involves building an architecture-A compiler *on* architecture A to run on architecture B. In this case, three architectures are involved, but the host and target architectures are the same. Once you master the concepts of dual-system cross-compilation, moving on to using a three-system cross-compile mode is fairly simple.

Autoconf generates configuration scripts that attempt to guess the build system type, and then assume that the host system type is the same. Unless told otherwise with command-line options, `configure` assumes that non-cross compilation mode is in effect. When executed without command-line options that specify the build or host system types, an Autoconf-generated configuration script can usually accurately determine system type and characteristics.

NOTE   *Section 14, "Manual Configuration," of the* GNU Autoconf Manual *discusses how to put Autoconf into cross-compilation mode. Unfortunately, the information that you'll need in order to write proper* configure.ac *files for cross-compilation is spread throughout that manual in bits and pieces. Each macro with nuances specific to cross-compilation has a paragraph describing the effects of cross-compilation mode on that macro. Search the manual for "cross-comp" to find all the references.*

System types are defined in the *GNU Autoconf Manual* in terms of a three-part canonical naming scheme involving CPU, vendor, and operating system, in the form `cpu-vendor-os`. But the `os` portion can itself be a pair containing a kernel and system type (`kernel-system`). If you know a canonical name for a system, you can specify it in each of three parameters to `configure`, as follows:

```
--build=build-type
--host=host-type
--target=target-type
```

These `configure` command-line options, with correct canonical system type names, allow you to define the build, host, and target system types. (Defining the host system type to be the same as your build system type is redundant, because this is the default case for `configure`.)

One of the most challenging (and least documented) aspects of using these options is determining a proper canonical system name to use in these command-line options. Nowhere in the *GNU Autoconf Manual* will you find a statement that tells you how to contrive a proper canonical name because canonical names are not unique for each system type. For instance, in most valid cross-compilation configurations, the `vendor` portion of the canonical name is simply ignored, and can thus be set to anything.

When you use the `AC_CANONICAL_SYSTEM` macro early in your *configure.ac* file, you'll find two new Autoconf helper scripts added to your project directory (by `automake --add-missing`, which is also executed by `autoreconf --install`); specifically, `config.guess` and `config.sub`. The job of `config.guess` is to determine, through heuristics, the canonical system name for your user's system—the build system. You can execute this program yourself to determine an appropriate canonical name for your own build system. For instance, from a copy of the *jupiter-libtool-ch6* directory (found in this book's downloadable archive[7]) on my 64-bit Intel GNU/Linux system, I get the following output from config.guess:

```
$ autoreconf -i
...
$ ./config.guess
x86_64-unknown-linux-gnu
$
```

As you can see here, config.guess requires no command-line options, although there are a few available. (Use the --help option to see them.) Its job is to guess your system type, mostly based on the output of the uname utility. This guess is used as a default system type that can be overridden by a user on the configure command line. When cross-compiling, you can use this value in your --build command-line option.[8]

The task of the config.sub program is to accept an input string as a sort of alias for a system type that you're looking for, and convert it to a proper Autoconf canonical name. But what is a valid alias? For a few clues, search for "Decode aliases" within config.sub. You'll likely find a comment above a bit of code whose job it is to decode aliases for certain CPU-COMPANY combinations. Here are a few examples executed from my 64-bit Linux machine:

```
$ ./config.sub i386
i386-pc-none
$ ./config.sub i386-linux
i386-pc-linux-gnu
$ ./config.sub m68k
m68k-unknown-none
$ ./config.sub m68k-sun
m68k-sun-sunos4.1.1
$ ./config.sub alpha
alpha-unknown-none
$ ./config.sub alpha-dec
alpha-dec-ultrix4.2
$ ./config.sub sparc
sparc-sun-sunos4.1.1
$ ./config.sub sparc-sun
sparc-sun-sunos4.1.1
$ ./config.sub mips
mips-unknown-elf
$
```

As you can see, a lone CPU name is usually not quite enough information for config.sub to properly determine a useful canonical name for a desired host system.

---

7. The archive is available from the No Starch Press website at *http://nostarch.com/autotools.htm/*.

8. For normal two-system cross-compilation mode you shouldn't have to specify the build system type, only the host system type. However, for historical and backward-compatibility reasons, always use the --build option when you use --host. Specify the build system type as your actual build system type (such as i686-pc-linux-gnu, on an Intel x86 GNU/Linux system). This requirement will be relaxed in a future version of Autoconf.

Notice too that there are a few generic keywords that can sometimes provide enough information for cross-compilation, without actually providing true vendor or operating system names. For instance, unknown can be substituted for the vendor name in general, and none is occasionally appropriate for the operating system name. Clearly elf is a valid system name as well, and can be enough in some circumstances for configure to determine which tool chain to use. However, by simply appending a proper vendor name to the CPU, config.sub can take a pretty good stab at coming up with the most likely operating system for that pair, and generate a useful canonical system type name.

Ultimately, the best way to determine a proper canonical system type name is to examine config.sub for something close to what you think you should be using for a CPU and a vendor name, and then simply ask it. While this may seem like a shot in the dark, chances are good that if you've gotten to the point of writing a build system for a program that should be cross-compiled, you're probably already very familiar with the names of your host CPU, vendor, and operating system.

When cross-compiling, you'll most likely use tools other than the ones you normally use on your system, or at the very least, additional command-line options on your normal tools. Such tools are usually installed in sets as packages. Another clue to a proper host system canonical name is the prefix of these tools' names. There's nothing magic in the way Autoconf handles cross-compilation. The host system canonical name is used directly to locate the proper tools by name in the system path. Thus, the host system canonical name you use will have to match the prefix on your tools.

Now let's examine a common scenario: building 32-bit code on a 64-bit machine of the same CPU architecture. Technically, this is a form of cross-compilation and it's often a much simpler scenario than cross-compiling code for an entirely different machine architecture. Many GNU/Linux systems support both 32- and 64-bit execution. On these systems, you can often use your build system's toolchain to perform this task with special command-line options. For example, to build C source code for a 32-bit Intel system on a 64-bit Intel system, you would simply use the following configure command line.[9] I've bolded the lines related to cross-compilation:

```
$ ./configure CPPFLAGS=-m32 LDFLAGS=-m32
checking for a BSD-compatible install... /usr/bin/install -c
checking whether build environment is sane... yes
checking for a thread-safe mkdir -p... /bin/mkdir -p
checking for gawk... gawk
checking whether make sets $(MAKE)... yes
❶ checking build system type... x86_64-unknown-linux-gnu
❷ checking host system type... x86_64-unknown-linux-gnu
```

9. Why not use CFLAGS? Using CPPFLAGS (C-PreProcessor FLAGS) has two positive effects: It properly renders C-preprocessor tests that rely on bit size, and it allows C++ compilers (which would normally honor CXXFLAGS over CFLAGS) to correctly define the proper bit size as well. Another popular option is to specify CC="gcc -m32", thereby changing the compiler type to that of a 32-bit compiler. I've added -m32 to both CPPFLAGS and LDFLAGS so the linker will also be notified of the architecture change. If you add -m32 to the CC variable, you don't need to do this because the linker is called via the compiler.

```
       checking for style of include used by make... GNU
       checking for gcc... gcc
       checking for C compiler default output file name... a.out
       checking whether the C compiler works... yes
❸ checking whether we are cross compiling... no
       checking for suffix of executables...
       checking for suffix of object files... o
       ...
```

Notice at ❸ that, as far as configure is concerned, we are not cross-compiling because we haven't given configure any command-line options instructing it to use a different toolchain than it would normally use. As you can see at ❶ and ❷, both the host and build system types are what you'd expect for a 64-bit GNU/Linux system. Additionally, because my system is a dual-mode system, it can execute test programs compiled with these flags. They'll run on the 64-bit CPU in 32-bit mode just fine.

To be even more certain of a proper build on Linux systems, you can also use the linux32 utility to change the personality of your 64-bit system to that of a 32-bit system, like this:

```
$ linux32 ./configure CPPFLAGS=-m32 LDFLAGS=-m32
...
```

We use linux32 here because some subscripts executed by configure may inspect uname -m to determine the build machine's architecture. The linux32 utility ensures that these scripts properly see a 32-bit Linux system.

To get this sort of cross-compile to work on a Linux dual-mode system, you usually need to install one or more 32-bit development packages such as *gcc-32bit*, *glibc-32bit*, and *glibc-devel-32bit*. If your project uses other system-level services, such as a graphical desktop, you will need the 32-bit versions of these libraries, as well.

Now let's do it the more conventional (dare I say, *canonical?*) way. Rather than add -m32 to the CPPFLAGS and LDFLAGS variables, we'll set the build and host system types manually on the configure command line and see what happens. Again I've bolded the output lines related to cross-compilation:

```
$ ./configure --build=x86_64-pc-linux-gnu --host=i686-pc-linux-gnu
       checking for a BSD-compatible install... /usr/bin/install -c
       checking whether build environment is sane... yes
       checking for a thread-safe mkdir -p... /bin/mkdir -p
       checking for gawk... gawk
       checking whether make sets $(MAKE)... yes
❶ checking for i686-pc-linux-gnu-strip... no
       checking for strip... strip
❷ configure: WARNING: using cross tools not prefixed with host triplet
       checking build system type... x86_64-pc-linux-gnu
       checking host system type... i686-pc-linux-gnu
       checking for style of include used by make... GNU
❸ checking for i686-pc-linux-gnu-gcc... no
       checking for gcc... gcc
       checking for C compiler default output file name... a.out
```

```
checking whether the C compiler works... yes
checking whether we are cross compiling... yes
checking for suffix of executables...
checking for suffix of object files... o
...
```

Several key lines in this example indicate that, as far as configure is concerned, we're cross-compiling. The cross-compilation build environment is x86_64-pc-linux-gnu, while the host is i686-pc-linux-gnu.

But notice the highlighted WARNING text at ❷: My system doesn't have a toolchain that's dedicated to building 32-bit Intel binaries. Such a toolchain includes all of the same tools required to build the 64-bit versions of my products, but these are prefixed with the canonical system name of the host system. If you don't have a properly prefixed toolchain installed and available in the system path, configure will default to using the build system tools—those without a prefix. This can work fine if your build system's tools can cross-compile to the host system with proper command-line options, and if you've also specified those options in CPPFLAGS and LDFLAGS.

Normally, you'd have to install a toolchain designed to build the correct type of binaries. In this example, a version of such tools could easily be provided by creating soft links and simple shell scripts that pass additional required flags. According to the configure script output at ❶ and ❸, I need to provide i686-pc-linux-gnu- prefixed versions of strip and gcc.

Generally, such foreign toolchains are installed into an auxiliary directory, which means you'd have to add that directory to your system PATH variable in order to allow configure to find them. For this example, I'll just create them in *~/bin*. Once again I've bolded the output text related to cross-compilation:

```
$ ln -s strip ~/bin/i686-pc-linux-gnu-strip
$ echo '#!/bin/sh
> gcc -m32 "$@"' > ~/bin/i686-pc-linux-gnu-gcc
$ chmod 755 ~/bin/i686-pc-linux-gnu-gcc
$ ./configure --build=x86_64-pc-linux-gnu --host=i686-pc-linux-gnu
checking for a BSD-compatible install... /usr/bin/install -c
checking whether build environment is sane... yes
checking for a thread-safe mkdir -p... /bin/mkdir -p
checking for gawk... gawk
checking whether make sets $(MAKE)... yes
checking for i686-pc-linux-gnu-strip... i686-pc-linux-gnu-strip
checking build system type... x86_64-pc-linux-gnu
checking host system type... i686-pc-linux-gnu
checking for style of include used by make... GNU
checking for i686-pc-linux-gnu-gcc... i686-pc-linux-gnu-gcc
checking for C compiler default output file name... a.out
checking whether the C compiler works... yes
checking whether we are cross compiling... yes
checking for suffix of executables...
checking for suffix of object files... o
checking whether we are using the GNU C compiler... yes
checking whether i686-pc-linux-gnu-gcc accepts -g... yes
...
```

```
$ make
...
```
❶ `libtool: compile:  i686-pc-linux-gnu-gcc -DHAVE_CONFIG_H -I. -I.. -g -O2 -MT print.lo -MD -MP -MF .deps/print.Tpo -c print.c  -fPIC -DPIC -o`
```
...
$
```

This time, `configure` was able to find the proper tools. Notice that the compiler command at ❶ no longer contains the -m32 flag. It's there, but it's hidden inside the i686-pc-linux-gnu-gcc script.

Cross-compilation is not for the average end user. As open source software developers, we use packages like the Autotools to ensure that our end users don't have to be experts in software development in order to build and install our packages. But cross-compilation requires a certain level of system configuration that is beyond the scope of what the Autotools generally expect of end users. Additionally, cross-compilation is used most often within specialized fields, such as toolchain or embedded systems development. End users in these areas usually are experts in software development.

There are a few places where cross-compilation can, and possibly should, be made available to the average end user. However, I strongly encourage you to be explicit and detailed in the instructions you provide your users in your *README* and *INSTALL* documents.

Item 7: Emulating Autoconf Text Replacement Techniques

Say your project builds a daemon that is configured at startup with values in a configuration text file. How does the daemon know where to find this file on start up? One way is to simply assume it's located in */etc*, but a well-written program will allow the user to configure this location when building the software. The system configuration directory has a variable location whose value can be specified on the `configure`, `make all`, or `make install` command lines, as shown in the following examples:

```
$ ./configure sysconfdir=/etc
...
$ make all sysconfdir=/usr/mypkg/etc
...
$ sudo make install sysconfdir=/usr/local/mypkg/etc
...
```

All of these examples take advantage of command-line functionality provided by Autotools build systems, so they must all be carefully taken into account when creating project and project build source files. Let's look at some examples that will explain how to do this.

Now, some conditions simply can't work. For instance, you can't pass a system configuration directory path into C source code from within the makefile when you build your program, and then expect it to run correctly if you change where the configuration files are installed on the `make install` command line. Most end users won't pass anything on the command line, but you should still ensure that they can set prefix directories from the configure and make command lines.

This item is focused on placing command-line prefix variable override information into the proper locations in your code and installed data files as late as possible in the build process.

Autoconf replaces text in AC_SUBST variables with the values of those variables as defined in configure at configuration time, but it doesn't replace the text with raw values. In an Autotools project, if you execute configure with a specific datadir, you get the following:

```
$ ./configure datadir=/usr/share
...
$ cat Makefile
...
❶ datadir = /usr/share
...
$
```

You can see at ❶ that the value of the shell variable datadir in configure is substituted exactly according to the command-line instructions in the make variable datadir in *Makefile*. What's not obvious here is that the default value of datadir, both in the configure script and in the makefile after substitution, is relative to other variables within the build system. By not overriding datadir on the configure command line, we see that the default value in the makefile contains unexpanded shell variable references:

```
$ ./configure
...
$ cat Makefile
...
datadir = ${datarootdir}
datarootdir = ${prefix}/share
...
prefix = /usr/local
...
$
```

In Chapter 2, we saw that we could pass command-line options to the preprocessor that would allow us to consume these sorts of path values within our source code. Listing 11-19 demonstrates this by passing a C-preprocessor definition in the CPPFLAGS variable for a hypothetical program called myprog.[10]

---

10. The escaped double quotes in this example are passed as part of the definition to the preprocessor, and ultimately into the source code. The unescaped double quotes are stripped off by the shell as it passes the option on the compiler command line. The unescaped double quotes allow the value of the definition to contain spaces, which are not protected by the escaped double quotes because the shell doesn't recognize them as quotes.

```
myprog_CPPFLAGS = -DSYSCONFDIR="\"@sysconfdir@\""
```

Listing 11-19: Pushing prefix variables into C source code in Makefile.am or Makefile.in

A C source file might then contain the code shown in Listing 11-20.

```
...
#ifndef SYSCONFDIR
# define SYSCONFDIR "/etc"
#endif
...
const char * sysconfdir = SYSCONFDIR;
...
```

Listing 11-20: Using the preprocessor-defined variables in C source code

Automake does nothing special with the line in Listing 11-19 between *Makefile.am* and *Makefile.in*, but the configure script converts the *Makefile.in* line into the *Makefile* line shown in Listing 11-21.

```
myprog_CPPFLAGS = -DSYSCONFDIR="\"${prefix}/etc\""
```

Listing 11-21: The resulting Makefile line after configure *substitutes* @sysconfdir@

When make passes this option on the compiler command line, the shell dereferences the variables to produce the following output command line (shown only in part here):

```
libtool: compile: gcc ... -DSYSCONFDIR=\"/usr/local/etc\" ...
```

There are a couple of problems with this approach. First, between configure and make, you lose the resolution of the sysconfdir variable because configure substitutes @sysconfdir@ for ${prefix}/etc, rather than ${sysconfdir}. The problem is that you can no longer set the value of sysconfdir on the make command line. To solve this problem, use the ${sysconfdir} make variable directly in your CPPFLAGS variable, as shown in Listing 11-22, rather than the Autoconf @sysconfdir@ substitution variable.

```
myprog_CPPFLAGS = -DSYSCONFDIR="\"${sysconfdir}\""
```

Listing 11-22: Using the make variable in CPPFLAGS *instead of the Autoconf substitution variable*

You can use this approach to specify a value for sysconfdir on both the configure and make command lines. Setting the variable on the configure command line defines a default value in *Makefile.in* (and subsequently in the generated *Makefile*), which can then be overridden on the make command line.

The problem with using different values on the `make all` and `make install` command lines is a bit more subtle. Consider what happens if you do the following:

```
$ make sysconfdir=/usr/local/myprog/etc
...
$ sudo make install sysconfdir=/etc
...
$
```

Here, you're basically lying to the compiler when you tell it that your configuration file will be installed in */usr/local/myprog/etc* during the build. The compiler will happily generate the code in Listing 11-20 so that it refers to this path and the second command line will then install your configuration file into */etc*, and your program will contain a hardcoded path to the wrong location. Unfortunately, there's little that you can do to correct this because you've allowed your users to define these variables anywhere.

NOTE *There are cases where different installation paths are given to the build and install processes on purpose. Recall the discussion of* DESTDIR *in "Getting Your Project into a Linux Distro" on page 48, wherein RPM packages are built and installed in a staging directory so that built products can be packaged in an RPM to be installed into the correct location later.*

Regardless of the potential pitfalls, being able to specify installation locations on the `make` command line is a powerful technique, but one that only works in makefiles because it relies heavily on `shell` variable substitution within compiler command lines.

What if you want to replace a value in an installed data file that isn't processed by the shell on a `make` command line? You could convert your data file into an Autoconf template, and then simply reference the Autoconf substitution variable within that file.

In fact, we did just that in the *doxyfile.in* templates that we created for the FLAIM project. However, this only worked in Doxygen input files because the class of variables used in those templates is always defined with complete absolute or relative paths by `configure`. That is, the values of `@srcdir@` and `@top_srcdir@` contain no additional shell variables. These variables are not installation directory (prefix) variables, which, with the exception of `prefix` itself, are always defined relative to other prefix variables.

You can, however, *emulate* the Autoconf substitution variable process within a makefile, allowing substitution variables to be used in installed data files. Listing 11-23 shows a template in which you might wish to replace variables with path information normally found in the standard prefix variables during a build.

```
# Configuration file for myprog
logdir = @localstatedir@/log
...
```

Listing 11-23: A sample configuration file template for myprog; *to be installed in* $(sysconfdir)

This template is for a program configuration file which might normally be installed in the system configuration directory. We want the location of the program's log file, specified in this configuration file, to be determined at install time by the value of @localstatedir@. Unfortunately, configure would replace this variable with a string containing at least ${prefix}, which is not useful in a program configuration file. Listing 11-24 shows a *Makefile.am* file with additional make script to generate *myprog.cfg* by performing substitution on variables in *myprog.cfg.in*.

```
  EXTRA_DIST = myprog.cfg.in
❶ sysconf_DATA = myprog.cfg

❷ edit = sed -e 's|@localstatedir[@]|$(localstatedir)|g'
❸ myprog.cfg: myprog.cfg.in Makefile
          $(edit) $(srcdir)/$@.in > $@

  CLEANFILES = myprog.cfg
```

Listing 11-24: Substituting make variables into data files using sed in a makefile

In this *Makefile.am* file, I've defined a custom make target at ❸ to build the *myprog.cfg* data file. I've also defined a make variable called edit at ❷, which resolves to a partial sed command that replaces all instances of @localstatedir@ in the template file [$(srcdir)/*myprog.cfg.in*] with the value of the $(localstatedir) variable. In the command where this variable is used, sed's output is redirected to the output file (*myprog.cfg*).

The only nonobvious code in this example is the use of the square brackets around the trailing at sign (@) in the sed expression which represent regular expression syntax indicating that any of the enclosed characters should be matched. Because there is only one enclosed character, this would seem to be a pointless complication, but the purpose of these brackets is to keep configure from replacing @localstatedir@ in the edit variable when it performs Autoconf variable substitution on this makefile. We want make to use this variable, not configure.

I assign *myprog.cfg* to the sysconf_DATA variable at ❶ to tie execution of this new rule into the framework provided by Automake. Automake will install this file into the system configuration directory after building it if necessary.

The files in DATA primaries are added as dependencies to the all target via the internal all-am target. If *myprog.cfg* doesn't exist, make will look for a rule to build it. Since I have such a rule, make will simply execute that rule when I build the all target.

I've added the template file name *myprog.cfg.in* to the EXTRA_DIST variable at the top of Listing 11-24 because neither Autoconf nor Automake are aware of this file. In addition, I've added the generated file *myprog.cfg* to the CLEAN-FILES variable at the bottom of the listing because, as far as Automake is concerned, *myprog.cfg* is a distributed data file which should not be automatically deleted by make clean.

NOTE   *This example demonstrates a good reason for Automake to not automatically distribute files listed in DATA primaries. Sometimes such files are built in this manner. If built data files were automatically distributed, the distcheck target would fail because* myprog.cfg *was not available for distribution before building.*

In this example, I've tied the building of *myprog.cfg* into the install process by adding it to the sysconf_DATA variable, and then placed a dependency between *mydata.cfg.in* and *mydata.cfg*[11] to ensure that the installed file is built when make all is executed. You could also tie into a standard or custom build or installation target using appropriate -hook or custom targets.

Item 8: Using the ac-archive Project

In "Item 5: Hacking Autoconf Macros" on page 282, I demonstrated a technique for hacking Autoconf macros to provide functionality that's close to, but not exactly the same as, that of the original macro. When you need a macro that Autoconf doesn't provide, you can either write it yourself or look for one that someone else has written. This item is about the second option, and a perfect place to begin your search is the Autoconf Macro Archive project.

As of this writing, the Autoconf Macro Archive is hosted by the *GNU Savannah* project at *http://savannah.nongnu.org/projects/autoconf-archive/*. The current ac-archive project is the result of a merger between two older projects, one by Guido Draheim (at *http://ac-archive.sourceforge.net/*) and the other by Peter Simon (at *http://auto-archive.cryp.to*). There is some long history and not a few flame wars on email lists between these two projects. Ultimately, each project incorporated most of the contents of the other, but Peter Simon's is the one that was migrated into the *Savannah* repository, and the new home page is found at *http://www.nongnu.org/autoconf-archive/*.[12]

The value in the archive is that private macros become public and public macros are incrementally improved by many users.

---

11. Note the dependency on *Makefile* as well. If *Makefile* changes, the sed expression or command line may have changed, in which case, *myprog.cfg* should be regenerated. As of this writing, make has no inherent functionality to tie particular commands within the makefile to a given target, so if the makefile changes in anyway, we must assume that it affects *myprog.cfg*.

12. It appears as if Guido has given up because the last updates to his SourceForge project were made in August of 2007.

As of this writing, the macro archive contains over 500 macros not distributed by Autoconf, including the ACX_PTHREAD macro discussed in "Doing Threads the Right Way" on page 210. The latest release of the archive can be downloaded as a tarball from the project home page or checked out from the project website. The site indexes macros by category, author, and open source license, allowing you to choose macros based on specific criteria. You can also search for a macro by name or by entering any text that might be found in the macro's header comments.

If you find yourself in need of a macro that Autoconf doesn't appear to provide, check out the Autoconf Macro Archive.

Item 9: Using pkg-config with Autotools

For many years, developers have struggled with library dependency issues on Unix systems. Many software packages have been inadvertently released without required libraries because Unix systems don't generally require all dependent libraries to be available when linking a library. Additionally, automated build systems have difficulty recognizing and ensuring the existence of secondary library dependencies. Several solutions to this problem have arisen over the years, and the *pkg-config* project is one of the more successful ones.

The pkg-config program looks in well-known and configurable locations in your file system for metadata files describing associated libraries. When you execute pkg-config with the name of a pkg-config–enabled library, the program outputs a list of C-preprocessor and linker flags necessary to use that library. Here are some examples of existing pkg-config–enabled packages installed on my system:

```
$ pkg-config --list-all
blkid                        blkid - Block device id library
gstreamer-tag-0.10           GStreamer Tag Library - Tag base classes
gsf-sharp                    Gsf - Gsf
xf86rushproto                XF86RushProto - XF86Rush extension headers
mozilla-gtkmozembed          mozilla-gtkembedmoz - Mozilla Embedding Widget
fontsproto                   FontsProto - Fonts extension headers
libebackend-1.2              libebackend - Utility library for Evolution
com_err                      com_err - Common error description library
...
$ pkg-config --cflags --libs libebackend-1.2
-I/usr/include/evolution-data-server-2.24 -I/usr/include/glib-2.0 \
-I/usr/lib64/glib-2.0/include  -lebackend-1.2 -lglib-2.0
$
```

In many ways, pkg-config provides a subset of functionality already provided by Libtool but pkg-config provides some additional value. In this item, I'll show you how to use pkg-config with the Autotools.

There are two aspects of using pkg-config with the Autotools. The first involves the generation and installation of pkg-config metadata files for your own projects. The second, the use of pkg-config extension macros in your projects' *configure.ac* files as a way to locate other libraries and configure your projects to use them.

Providing pkg-config Files for Your Library Projects

A pkg-config metadata file consists of a short text file containing what are effectively variable definitions and metadata fields. The variable definitions look and act like simple make variables. The metadata fields are name/value pairs with a colon separating the name and value.

Generating a pkg-config metadata file is as simple as using Autoconf substitution variables in a template version of the file, and then adding the file to the AC_CONFIG_FILES macro in *configure.ac*. Listing 11-25 shows the pkg-config metadata file template for the xflaim project discussed in Chapters 8 and 9.

```
prefix=@prefix@
exec_prefix=@exec_prefix@
libdir=@libdir@
includedir=@includedir@

Name: XFLAIM
URL: http://forge.novell.com/modules/xfmod/project/?flaim
Description: An embeddable cross-platform XML database engine
Version: @PACKAGE_VERSION@
Requires: libflaimtk >= 1.0
Libs: -L${libdir} -lxflaim -lpthread -lrt -lstdc++ -ldl -lncurses
Cflags: -I${includedir}
```

Listing 11-25: xflaim/libxflaim.pc.in: *A pkg-config metadata template for xflaim*

I'm using standard Autoconf prefix substitution variables to set the *lib* and *include* directory paths in pkg-config variables which are then used in the metadata fields at the bottom of the file. The use of variables is optional, but good practice. There is, however, a subtle caveat to the use of such variables. Recall that the Autoconf substitution variable @includedir@ expands not to */usr/local/include*, but rather to ${prefix}/*include*, so we need to be sure to define all of the required variables. In this case, both prefix and exec_prefix must also be defined, even though I'm not using either of these explicitly in the text. If they're not defined, the ultimate value will contain the variable reference ${prefix}/*include*, rather than the properly expanded text */usr/local/include*.

I'm also using the @PACKAGE_VERSION@ substitution variable to carry the package version string over from *configure.ac*. Don't forget to add the output file name to the AC_CONFIG_FILES macro so that the *.pc* file will be generated by configure.

You can place this template anywhere in your project, but a location central to the library to which it belongs seems reasonable. I created separate pkg-config metadata files for each library in the FLAIM project. Each of the four projects creates a single library, so I put my pkg-config templates at the root of each library project directory structure.

Now let's look at installation. Metadata files should be installed in the ${libdir}/*pkgconfig* directory. A simple way to get them installed is to add the code shown in Listing 11-26 into your *Makefile.am* file.

```
...
pkgconfigdir = $(libdir)/pkgconfig
pkgconfig_DATA = libxflaim.pc
...
```

Listing 11-26: xflaim/Makefile.am: Adding installation script for pkg-config metadata files

This is standard Automake fare for defining a new installation location with a dir variable, and then using the associated prefix on the DATA primary. The template file will be distributed automatically in this case, because it's referenced in the AC_CONFIG_FILES macro.

Using pkg-config Files in configure.ac

Using pkg-config packages is even simpler than generating and installing metadata files. The pkg-config package provides a macro file called *pkg.m4* which is installed in */usr/(local/)share/aclocal.* This macro file contains three Autoconf extension macros, PKG_PROG_PKG_CONFIG, PKG_CHECK_EXISTS, and PKG_CHECK_MODULES. Their prototypes are:

```
PKG_PROG_PKG_CONFIG([MIN-VERSION])
PKG_CHECK_EXISTS(MODULES, [ACTION-IF-FOUND], [ACTION-IF-NOT-FOUND])
PKG_CHECK_MODULES(VARIABLE-PREFIX, MODULES, [ACTION-IF-FOUND],
    [ACTION-IF-NOT-FOUND])
```

The last two of these macros ensure that the first one is called via the Autoconf prerequisite framework. Use PKG_CHECK_EXISTS to set package-specific variations of the CFLAGS and LDFLAGS variables for the specific versions of the packages you're interested in. Use PKG_CHECK_MODULE to ensure that desired modules are available, but without specific versions. If either of these macros is called conditionally in your *configure.ac* file, you should also explicitly call PKG_PROG_PKG_CONFIG to ensure that the pkg-config program is available to your toolchain, in case the other pkg-config macros are not called.

NOTE   *You could use the Autoconf AS_IF macro in place of a shell if statement to formulate conditional calls to these macros. Using AS_IF will ensure that prerequisite calls (such as PKG_PROG_PKG_CONFIG) are properly expanded outside the condition.*

Package-specific CFLAGS and LDFLAGS variables for a library called *abc*, for example, are defined as ABC_CFLAGS and ABC_LDFLAGS, if the variable-prefix argument passed to PKG_CHECK_MODULES is ABC. The pkg-config macros call AC_SUBST on these package-specific variables, which makes them available as make variables within your *Makefile.am* files. You can add them to library- or program-specific CPPFLAGS and LDFLAGS Automake variables, as shown in Listing 11-27.

```
PROGRAMS = myprog
myprog_CPPFLAGS = $(ABC_CFLAGS)
myprog_LDFLAGS = $(ABC_LDFLAGS)
...
```

Listing 11-27: Using the results of the pkg-config macros in a Makefile.am file

NOTE   *You can read more about the proper use of pkg-config at* http://pkg-config
.freedesktop.org/. *In addition, Dan Nicholson has written a concise and easy to
follow tutorial on using pkg-config at* http://people.freedesktop.org/~dbn/
pkg-config-guide.html/.

Item 10: Using Incremental Installation Techniques

Some people have requested that make install be made smart enough to install
only files that are not already installed, or that are newer than installed versions of the same files.

This feature is available by default to users by passing the -C command-
line option to install-sh. It can be enabled directly by end users by using the
following syntax on the make command line during execution of make install:

```
$ make install "INSTALL=/path/to/install-sh -C"
```

If you think your users will benefit from this option, consider adding
some information about its proper use to the *INSTALL* file that ships with
your distribution. Don't you just love features you don't have to implement?

Item 11: Using Generated Source Code

Automake requires that all source files used within a project be statically
defined within the project's *Makefile.am* files, but sometimes the contents of
source files need to be generated at build time.

There are two ways to deal with generated sources (more specifically,
generated header files) in your projects. The first involves the use of an
Automake-provided crutch for developers not interested in the finer points
of make. The second involves writing proper dependency rules to allow make to
understand the relationships between your source files and your products.
I'll cover the crutch first, and then we'll get into the details of proper dependency management in *Makefile.am* files.

Using the BUILT_SOURCES Variable

When you have a header file that's generated as part of your build process,
you can tell Automake to generate rules that will always create this file first,
before attempting to build your products. To do this, add the header file to
the Automake BUILT_SOURCES variable, as shown in Listing 11-28.

```
bin_PROGRAMS = program
program_SOURCES = program.c program.h
nodist_program_SOURCES = generated.h
BUILT_SOURCES = generated.h
CLEANFILES = generated.h
generated.h: Makefile
        echo "#define generated 1" > $@
```

Listing 11-28: Using BUILT_SOURCES to deal with generated source files

The nodist_program_SOURCES variable ensures that Automake will not generate rules that try to distribute this file; we want it to be built when the end user runs make, not shipped in the distribution package.

Without a user-provided clue, Automake-generated makefiles have no way of knowing that the rule for *generated.h* should be executed before *program.c* is compiled. I call BUILT_SOURCES a "crutch" because it simply forces the rules used to generate the listed files to execute first, and only when the user makes the all or check targets. The rules created using BUILT_SOURCES aren't even executed if you attempt to make the program target directly. With that said, let's look at what's going on under the covers.

Dependency Management

There are two distinct classes of source files in a C or C++ project: those explicitly defined as dependencies within your makefile, and those referenced only indirectly through, for instance, preprocessor inclusion.

You can hardcode all of these dependencies directly into your makefiles. For instance, if *program.c* includes *program.h*, and if *program.h* includes *console.h* and *print.h*, then *program.o* actually depends on all of these files, not just *program.c*. And yet, a normal hand-coded makefile explicitly defines only the relationships between the *.c* files and the program. For a truly accurate build, make needs to be told about all of these relationships using a rule like the one shown in Listing 11-29.

```
program: program.o
        $(CC) $(CFLAGS) $(LDFLAGS) -o $@ program.o

❶ program.o: program.c program.h console.h print.h
        $(CC) -c $(CPPFLAGS) $(CFLAGS) -o $@ program.c
```

Listing 11-29: A rule describing the complete relationship between an object file and its source files

The relationship between *program.o* and *program.c* is often defined by an *implicit* rule, so the rule at ❶ in Listing 11-29 is often broken into two separate rules, as shown in Listing 11-30.

```
    program: program.o
            $(CC) $(CFLAGS) $(LDFLAGS) -o $@ program.o

❶ %.o: %.c
            $(CC) -c $(CPPFLAGS) $(CFLAGS) -o $@ $<

❷ program.o: program.h console.h print.h
```

Listing 11-30: An implicit rule for C source files, defined as a GNU make pattern rule

In Listing 11-30, the GNU make-specific *pattern rule* at ❶ tells make that the associated command can generate a file ending in *.o* from a file of the same base name ending in *.c*. Thus, whenever make needs to find a rule to generate a file ending in *.o* that's listed as a dependency in one of your rules, it searches for a *.c* file with the same base name. If it finds one, it applies this rule to rebuild the *.o* file from the corresponding *.c* file if the timestamp on the *.c* file is newer than that of the existing *.o* file, or if the *.o* file is missing.

There is a documented set of implicit pattern rules built into make so you don't generally have to write such rules. Still, you must somehow tell make about the indirect[13] dependencies between the *.o* file and any included *.h* files. These dependencies cannot simply be implied with a built-in rule because there are no implicit relationships between these files that are based on file naming conventions, such as the relationship between *.c* and *.o* files. The relationships are manually coded into the source and header files as inclusions.

As I mentioned in Chapter 2, writing such rules is tedious and error prone, because during development (and even maintenance, to a lesser degree) the myriad relationships between source and header files can change all the time, and the rules must be updated carefully with each change to keep the build accurate. The C preprocessor is much better suited to automatically writing and maintaining these rules for you.

A Two-Pass System

There are two ways to use the preprocessor to manage dependencies. The first is to create a two-pass system, wherein the first pass just builds the dependencies, and the second compiles the source code, based on those dependencies. This is done by defining rules that use certain preprocessor commands to generate make dependency rules, as shown in Listing 11-31.[14]

---

13. I use the term *indirect* here to mean that the *.o* file depends upon the *.h* file *through* the *.c* file. That is, the *.o* file is built from the *.h* file by virtue of the fact that it's included by the *.c* file. Technically, the *.o* file's dependency on the *.h* file is just as direct as that of the *.c* file, because when the compiler picks up where the preprocessor leaves off, there are no *.h* files—only a single file comprised of the *.c* file and all included header files—a *translation unit*, in the vernacular.

14. Microsoft has apparently never felt the need to support the make utility to the same degree that Unix compiler vendors have, relying heavily upon their IDEs to create properly defined dependency graphs for project builds. Thus, while the preprocessor option used here is generally portable among Unix compilers, Microsoft compilers simply have no support for this sort of feature.

```
program: program.o
        $(CC) $(CFLAGS) $(LDFLAGS) -o $@ program.o

%.o: %.c
        $(CC) $(CPPFLAGS) -c $(CFLAGS) -o $@ $<

❶ %.d: %.c
        $(CC) -M $(CPPFLAGS) $< >$@

❷ sinclude program.d
```

Listing 11-31: Building automatic dependencies directly

In Listing 11-31, the pattern rule at ❶ specifies the same sort of relationship between *.d* and *.c* files as the one shown at ❶ in Listing 11-30 does for *.o* and *.c* files. The sinclude statement here at ❷ tells make to include another makefile, and GNU make is smart enough, not only to ensure that all makefiles are included before the primary dependency graph is analyzed, but also to look for rules to build them.[15] Running make on this makefile produces the following output:

```
$ make
cc -M  program.c >program.d
cc  -c  -o program.o program.c
cc  -o program program.o
$
$ cat program.d
program.o: program.c /usr/include/stdio.h /usr/include/features.h \
  /usr/include/sys/cdefs.h /usr/include/bits/wordsize.h \
    ... a lot of additional system headers omitted here ...
  /usr/include/bits/pthreadtypes.h /usr/include/alloca.h program.h \
  console.h print.h
$
$ touch console.h && make
cc  -c  -o program.o program.c
cc  -o program program.o
$
```

As you can see here, the rule to generate *program.d* is executed first, as make attempts to include that file. The file contains a dependency rule similar[16] to the one we wrote at ❷ in Listing 11-30. (The reference to *program.c* is missing in our hand-coded rule's dependency list because it's redundant, though harmless.) You can also see that touching one of these included files now properly causes the *program.c* source file to be rebuilt.

---

15. Only GNU make is smart enough to silently include dependency files with sinclude. Other brands of make provide only include, which will fail if any of the included makefiles are missing. GNU make is also the only version smart enough to re-execute itself when it notices the build system has been updated.

16. The GNU toolset supports several non-portable extensions to the classic -M option. For example, the -MM option has the wonderful effect of not bothering to add system header files to generated dependency lists. So, the long list of system headers omitted in the example above need not be present at all if portability is not a concern. The -MD and -MMD options used in the examples are not portable either.

The problems with the mechanism outlined in Listing 11-31 include the fact that the entire source tree must be traversed twice: once to check for and possibly generate the dependency files, and then again to compile any modified source files.

Another problem is that if one header includes another, and the second header is modified, the object file will be updated but not the dependency file included by make. The next time the second level header is modified, neither the object nor the dependency file will be updated. Deleted header files also cause problems: the build system doesn't recognize that the deleted file was purposely removed so it complains that files referenced in the existing dependencies are missing.

Doing It in One Pass

A more efficient way to handle automatic dependencies is to generate the dependency files as a side effect of compilation. Listing 11-32 shows how this can be done by using the non-portable GNU extension compiler option shown in bold.

```
program: program.o
        $(CC) $(CFLAGS) $(LDFLAGS) -o $@ program.o

%.o: %.c
❶       $(CC) -MMD $(CPPFLAGS) -c $(CFLAGS) -o $@ $<

❷ sinclude program.d
```

Listing 11-32: Generating dependencies as a side effect of compilation

Here, I've removed the second pattern rule (originally shown at ❶ in Listing 11-31) and added a -MMD option to the compiler command line at ❶ in Listing 11-32. This option tells the compiler (preprocessor) to generate a *.d* file of the same base name as the *.c* file that it's currently compiling. When make is executed on a clean work area, the sinclude statement at ❷ silently fails to include the missing *program.d* file, but it doesn't matter because all of the object files will be built the first time anyway. During subsequent incremental builds, the previously built *program.d* is included, and its dependency rules take effect during those builds.

Built Sources Done Right

The one-pass method described above is roughly the one that Automake uses to manage automatic dependencies, when possible. The problems with this approach are most often manifested when working with generated sources, including both *.c* files and *.h* files. For instance, let's expand the example shown in Listing 11-32 a bit to contain a generated header file called *generated.h*, included by *program.h*. Listing 11-33 shows a first attempt at this modification. Additions to Listing 11-32 are bolded in this listing.

```
program: program.o
        $(CC) $(CFLAGS) $(LDFLAGS) -o $@ program.o

%.o: %.c
        $(CC) -MMD $(CPPFLAGS) -c $(CFLAGS) -o $@ $<

generated.h: Makefile
        echo "#define generated" >$@

sinclude program.d
```

Listing 11-33: A makefile that works with a generated header file dependency

In this case, when we execute make, we find that the lack of an initial dependency file works against us:

```
$ make
cc -MMD  -c  -o program.o program.c
In file included from program.c:4:
program.h:3:23: error: generated.h: No such file or directory
make: *** [program.o] Error 1
$
```

Because there is no initial secondary dependency information, make doesn't know it needs to run the commands for the *generated.h* rule yet, because *generated.h* only depends on *Makefile*, which hasn't changed. To fix this problem in a *Makefile.am* file, we could list *generated.h* in the BUILT_SOURCES variable, as we did in Listing 11-28 on page 303. This would add *generated.h* as the first dependency of the all and check targets, thereby forcing them to be built first in the likely event the user happens to enter make, make all, or make check.[17]

The proper way to handle this problem is very simple, and it works every time in both makefiles and *Makefile.am* files: write a dependency rule between *program.o* and *generated.h*, as shown in the updated makefile in Listing 11-34. The bolded line contains the additional rule.

```
program: program.o
        $(CC) $(CFLAGS) $(LDFLAGS) -o $@ program.o

%.o: %.c
        $(CC) -MMD $(CPPFLAGS) -c $(CFLAGS) -o $@ $<

program.o: generated.h

generated.h: Makefile
        echo "#define generated" >$@

sinclude program.d
```

Listing 11-34: Adding a hardcoded dependency rule for a generated header file

---

17. Note that you can't rely on dependency order for build order with parallel make (make -j).

The new rule tells make about the relationship between *program.o* and *generated.h*:

```
$. make
echo "#define generated" >generated.h
cc -MMD  -c  -o program.o program.c
cc  -o program program.o
$
$ make
make: 'program' is up to date.
$
❶ $ touch generated.h && make
cc -MMD  -c  -o program.o program.c
cc  -o program program.o
$
❷ $ touch Makefile && make
echo "#define generated" >generated.h
cc -MMD  -c  -o program.o program.c
cc  -o program program.o
$
```

Here, touching *generated.h* (at ❶) causes program to be updated. Touching *Makefile* (at ❷) causes *generated.h* to be re-created first.

To implement the dependency rule shown in Listing 11-34 in an Automake *Makefile.am* file, you'd use the bolded rule shown in Listing 11-35.

```
bin_PROGRAMS = program
program_SOURCES = program.c program.h
nodist_program_SOURCES = generated.h
program.$(OBJEXT): generated.h
CLEANFILES = generated.h
generated.h: Makefile
        echo "#define generated 1" > $@
```

Listing 11-35: Replacing BUILT_SOURCES with a proper dependency rule

This is exactly the same code shown previously in Listing 11-28 on page 303, except that we've replaced the BUILT_SOURCES variable with a proper dependency rule. The advantage of this method is that it always works as it should; *generated.h* will always be built exactly when it needs to be, regardless of the target specified by the user.[18]

If you had tried to generate a C source file rather than a header file, you'd find that you didn't even need the additional dependency rule because *.o* files implicitly depend on their *.c* files. However, you must still list your generated *.c* file in the nodist_program_SOURCES variable to keep Automake from trying to distribute it.

---

18. This technique fails when you try to use program-specific Automake flags. For example, if you use program_CFLAGS, Automake generates a different set of rules for building the objects associated with program and munges the object name to contain the program name. By doing so, these special objects won't be confused with ones generated for other products from the same sources, but your hand-coded dependency rules won't line up with the object file names generated by the compiler. For more information, see the documentation for the AC_PROG_CC_C_O macro in the *GNU Autoconf Manual.*

NOTE *When you define your own rule, you suppress any rules that Automake may generate for that product. In the case of a specific object file, this is not likely to be a problem, but keep this Automake idiosyncracy in mind when defining rules.*

As you can see, all you really need to properly manage generated sources is a correctly written set of dependency rules, and appropriate nodist_*_SOURCES variables.

Item 12: Disabling Undesirable Targets

Sometimes the Autotools do too much for you. Here's an example from the Automake mailing list:

> I use automake in one of my projects along with texinfo. That project has documentation full of images. As you probably know, 'make pdf' makes a PDF document from JPGs and PNGs, whereas 'make dvi' requires EPSs. However, EPS images are insanely large (in this case like 15 times larger than JPGs).
>
> The problem is that running 'make distcheck' results in error since the EPS images that should be there aren't there and 'make distcheck' tries to run 'make dvi' everywhere. I would like to run 'make pdf' instead, or at least to disable building DVI. Is there any way to accomplish that?

First a little background information: The Automake TEXINFOS primary makes several documentation targets available to the end user, including info, dvi, ps, pdf, and html. It also provides several installation targets, including install-info, install-dvi, install-ps, install-pdf, and install-html. Of these targets, only info is automatically built with make or make all, and only install-info is executed with make install.[19]

However, it appears that the distcheck target also builds at least the dvi target, as well. The problem outlined above is that the poster doesn't provide the encapsulated postscript (EPS) graphics files required to build the DVI documentation, so the distcheck target fails because it can't build documentation that he doesn't want to support anyway.

To fix this issue, simply provide your own version of the target that does nothing, as shown in Listing 11-36.

```
...
info_TEXINFOS = zardoz.texi
❶ dvi:  # do nothing for make dvi
```

Listing 11-36: Disabling the dvi target in a Makefile.am *that specifies TEXINFOS primaries*

With the one line addition at ❶, make distcheck is back in business. Now, when it builds the dvi target, it succeeds because it does nothing.

---

19. The *.info* files generated by the info target are automatically distributed, so your users don't have to have texinfo installed.

Other Automake primaries provide multiple additional targets as well. If you only wish to support a subset of these targets, you can effectively disable the undesired targets by providing one of your own. If you'd like to be a bit more vocal about the disabling override, simply include an echo statement as a command that tells the user that your package doesn't provide DVI documentation, but be careful not to execute anything that might fail in this override, or your user will be right back in the same boat.

Item 13: Watch Those Tab Characters!

Having made the transition to Automake, you're not using raw makefiles anymore, so why should you still care about TAB characters? Remember that *Makefile.am* files are simply stylized makefiles. Ultimately, every line in a *Makefile.am* file will be either consumed directly by Automake and then transformed into true make syntax, or copied directly into the final makefile. This means that TAB characters matter within *Makefile.am* files.

Consider this example from the Automake mailing list:

```
lib_LTLIBRARIES = libfoo.la
libfoo_la_SOURCES = foo.cpp
if WANT_BAR
❶        libfoo_la_SOURCES += a.cpp
else
❷        libfoo_la_SOURCES += b.cpp
endif

AM_CPPFLAGS = -I${top_srcdir}/include
libfoo_la_LDFLAGS = -version-info 0:0:0
```

I have been reading both autoconf and automake manuals and as far as I can see the above should work. However the files (a.cpp or b.cpp) [are] always added at the bottom of the generated Makefile and are therefore not used in the compilation. No matter what I try I cannot get even the above code to generate a correct makefile but obviously I am doing something wrong.

The answer, provided by another poster, was simple and accurate:

Remove the indentation.

The trouble here is that the two lines within the Automake conditional at ❶ and ❷ are indented with TAB characters.

You may recall from "Automake Configuration Features" on page 206, where I discussed the implementation of Automake conditionals, that text within conditionals is prefixed with an Autoconf substitution variable that is ultimately transformed into either an empty string or a hash mark. The implication here is that these lines are essentially either left as is or commented out within the final makefile. The commented lines really don't concern us, but you can clearly see that if the uncommented lines in the makefile begin with the TAB character, Automake will treat them as commands, rather than as definitions, and sort them accordingly in the final makefile. When make processes the generated makefile, it will attempt to interpret these lines as orphan commands.

Had the original poster used spaces to indent the conditional statements, he'd have had no problem.

The moral of the story: Watch those TAB characters!

Item 14: Packaging Choices

The ultimate goal of a package maintainer is to make it easy for the end user. System-level packages never have this problem because they don't rely on anything that's not part of the core operating system. But higher-level packages often rely on multiple subpackages, some of which are more pervasive than others.

For example, consider the Subversion project. If you download the latest source archive from the Subversion project website, you'll find that it comes in two flavors. The first contains only the Subversion source code, but if you unpack and build this project you'll find that you'll need to download and install the Apache runtime and runtime utility (*apr* and *apr-utils*) packages, the *zlib-devel* package, and the *sqlite-devel* package. At this point, you can build subversion, but to enable secure access to repositories via https, you'll also need *neon* or *serf* and *openssl*.

The Subversion project maintainers felt that community adoption of Subversion was important enough to go the extra mile, so to speak. To help you out in your quest to build a functional Subversion package, they've provided a second package called *subversion-deps*, which contains a source-level distribution of some of Subversion's more important requirements.[20] Simply unpack the *subversion-deps* source package in the same directory where you unpacked your *subversion* source package. The root directory in the *subversion-deps* package contains only subdirectories; one for each of these source-level dependencies.

You can choose to add source packages to your projects' build systems in the same manner. Of course, the process is much simpler if you're using Automake. You need only call AC_CONFIG_SUBDIRS for subdirectories containing add-on projects in your build tree. AC_CONFIG_SUBDIRS quietly ignores missing subproject directories. I showed you an example of this process in Chapter 8 where I built the FLAIM toolkit as a subproject if it existed as a subdirectory within any of the higher-level FLAIM project directories.

Which packages should you ship with your package? The key lies in determining which packages your consumers are least likely to be able to find on their own.

---

20. You'll still have to download and install the openssl-devel package for your GNU/Linux distribution, or else download, build and install a source-level distribution of openSSL in order to build https support into your Subversion client. The reason for this is that the tricky nature of various countries' import and export laws surrounding openSSL make it rather difficult for anyone but the project maintainers to distribute openSSL.

Wrapping Up

I hope you find these solutions—indeed, this book—useful to you on your quest to create a really great user experience with your open source projects. I began this book with the statement that people often start out hating the Autotools because they don't understand the purpose of the Autotools. By now, you should have a fairly well developed sense of this purpose. If you were disinclined to use the Autotools before, then I hope I've given you reason to reconsider.

Recall the famously misquoted line from Albert Einstein, "Everything should be made as simple as possible, but no simpler."[21] Not all things can be made so simple that anyone can master them with little training. This is especially true when it comes to processes that are designed to make life simpler for others. The Autotools offer the ability for experts—programmers and software engineers—to make open source software more accessible to end users. Let's face it—this process is less than trivial, but the Autotools attempts to make it as simple as possible.

---

21. See *http://en.wikiquote.org/wiki/Talk:Albert_Einstein*. What Einstein actually said was, "The supreme goal of all theory is to make the irreducible basic elements as simple and as few as possible without having to surrender the adequate representation of a single datum of experience."

INDEX

Symbols & Numerals

*_LIBADD variables, 155

@ (at sign)
    as leading control character, 36
    preventing make from printing
        code to stdout, 44
    for substitution variable, 90

@<:@ and @:>@ (quadrigraphs), 117

` (backtick), as default M4 quote
        character, 252

: (colon), for rules, 27

$ (dollar sign), escaping, 24

$$ (dollar sign doubled), for
        variable references, 43

$@ variable, 29

$# variable, 255

$%, to refer to archive member, 29

$0 shell script parameter, 77

" (double quotes), escaped, 294*n*

= (equal sign), in makefile, 24

(hash mark)
    for M4 comments, 252
    for makefile comments, 22

?= (query-assign operator), 54

' (single quote), as default M4
        quote character, 252

[] (square brackets)
    for AC_CHECK_TYPES macro
        parameter, 114
    for macro parameters, 60
    for optional parameters, 76*n*

64-bit file addressing, 209

64-bit machine, building 32-bit code
        on, 290–292

A

ABI (application binary
        interface), 172

aborted process, from missing
        shared libraries, 149

absolute addresses
    CPUs and, 168
    to function calls, 164–165

ac-archive project, 298–299

AC_ARG_ENABLE macro, 108,
        109–111, 211
    formatting help strings with, 112

AC_ARG_VAR macro, 220, 265

AC_ARG_WITH macro, 108–109

AC_CANONICAL_HOST macro,
        reliance on, 234

AC_CANONICAL_SYSTEM macro, 234,
        245, 288

AC_CHECK_HEADERS macro, 85, 103,
        184, 189
    GNU Autoconf Manual
        definition, 102

AC_CHECK_LIB macro, 211, 282,
        283, 284
    parameters, 284

AC_CHECK_PROG macro, 94
    first attempt, 96
    GNU Autoconf Manual, 95

AC_CHECK_PROGS macro, 265

AC_CHECK_TYPES macro, 114

AC_CONFIG_COMMANDS macro, 79, 80, 81

AC_CONFIG_FILES macro, 65, 67, 80,
    139, 156
    adding pkg-config file, 300
    conditional reference for *xflaim/
        docs/doxygen/doxyfile*, 246
    references in *configure.ac*, 154
    specifying mutiple tags, 81

AC_CONFIG_HEADER macro, 78–79

AC_CONFIG_HEADERS macro, 78–79,
    83–84, 85

AC_CONFIG_MACRO_DIR macro, 201–202

AC_CONFIG_SRCDIR macro, 77–78

AC_CONFIG_SUBDIRS macro, 200, 221

AC_DEFINE macro, 91, 212
    conditional use, 212

AC_DEFINE_UNQUOTED macro, 91

AC_DEFUN macro, 260, 262

acinclude.m4 file, 10

AC_INCLUDES_DEFAULT macro, 114–115

AC_INIT macro, 76–77

AC_LANG macro, 206

AC_LANG_CALL macro, 285–286

AC_LANG_PROGRAM macro, 285

aclocal utility, 10–11, 201
    data flow diagram, 11
    macro fle locations for, 203

ACLOCAL_AMFLAGS variable, 203

aclocal.m4 file, 259

AC_MSG_CHECKING macro, 106–107

AC_MSG_ERROR macro, 106, 107

AC_MSG_FAILURE macro, 106, 107

AC_MSG_NOTICE macro, 106, 107

AC_MSG_RESULT macro, 106–107

AC_MSG_WARN macro, 106, 107

AC_OUTPUT macro, 116

AC_PREREQ macro, 76

AC_PROG_CC macro, 91, 92

AC_PROG_INSTALL macro, 74, 93–94

AC_PROG_RANLIB macro, 139, 156

AC_REQUIRE macro, 260

AC_SEARCH_LIBS macro, 59, 99–100,
    184, 189
    GNU Autoconf Manual
        definition, 100

AC_SUBST macro, 90

AC_SYS_LARGEFILE macro, 209

action-if-not-given argument, for
    configure.ac script, 109

ACX_PTHREAD macro, 99, 210–211

age value, in library interface
    version number, 178

AIX archive (*.a*) file, 174

all, 31

all-local target, 242

alternatives scripts, 52*n*

AM_COND_IF macro, 207

AM_CONDITIONAL macro, 206, 221, 245
    substitution variables for, 207

AM_CPPFLAGS option variable, 138, 225

AM_INIT_AUTOMAKE macro, 121
    foreign keyword, 206
    silent-rules option, 143

AM_JAVACFLAGS variable, 232

AM_LDFLAGS option variable, 138

AM_MAINTAINER_MODE macro, 141–142

AM_MAKEFLAGS, passing
    expansion of, 203

AM_PROG_CC_C_O macro, 139, 140

a.out scheme, for library
    management, 172*n*

API design, 272

Apple platforms, 3

application binary interface
    (ABI), 172

ar utility, 169

archives, 136
    $% to refer to member, 29

arguments
    commas as placeholders, 90
    macros with, 60, 255–256
    whitespace around, 255–256

AS_HELP_STRING macro, 112

AS_IF macro, vs. shell if-then
    statement, 211–212

asynchronous processing, 108
    enabling or disabling by default,
        109–111

at sign (@)
    as leading control character, 36
    preventing make from printing
        code to stdout, 44
    for substitution variable, 90

AUTHORS file
    creating, 121
    for FLAIM project, 200
Autoconf, 1, 6–9, 57–88
    vs. Automake, 125
    common problem, 95–98
    configuration scripts, 58–59
    data flow diagram, 8
    determining version installed, 16
    emulating text replacement
        techniques, 293–298
    executing, 61–62
    file generation framework, 78
    files containing variables, 246
    grep of macro directory, 283
    hacking macros, 282–287
    library-specific macros, 287
    and M4 macro language,
        259–269
    message display to user, 106–107
    native support for programming
        languages, 5
    substitutions and definitions,
        90–91
    supporting options features and
        packages, 107–112
    testing for, 59
Autoconf Macro Archive, 210, 233,
    234, 260, 298
    to help build Java applications,
        230*n*
autoconf shell script, 7, 9
autoconfiscating project, 65
autoconf.m4 file, 259
autogen.sh script, 73–75
    executing, 75
autoheader utility, 7, 9
    data flow diagram, 8
    include file template generation
        by, 84–87
autom4te utility, 8, 259
autom4te.cache directory, 61
Automake, 1, 9–11
    --add-missing option, 73, 74, 201
    vs. Autoconf, 125
    build system support for make
        targets, 124
    configuration features, 206–209

--copy, 74
    data flow diagram, 13
    determining version installed, 16
    development history, 119–120
    enabling in *configure.ac*, 121–124
    foreign option, 201
    -hook target, 214–215
    -local target, 214–215
    recursive targets, 276–279
    support for unit testing, 133–134
    text files required, 200–201
    -Wall option, 201
    -Werror option, 201
automatic dependencies, 306–309
    tracking, 124–125
automatic variables, 29
autoreconf program, 7, 61, 74, 85
    ACLOCAL_AMFLAGS for execution, 203
    with -i option, 122–123
    warning messages, 234
autoscan program, 7
    configure.ac file created with,
        71–76
    generating starting point for ftk
        project, 204
autoscan.log file, 72
Autotools. *See also* Autoconf;
    Automake; Libtool
    building Java sources with,
        230–239
    design goals, 5
    installing most up-to-date, 16–18
    Java support, 230–232
    noise from build systems based
        on, 142–144
    purpose, 1
    versions, ix–x
autoupdate utility, 7
awk utility, 55, 67

B

backslash, for command wrap, 25
backtick (`` ` ``), as default M4 quote
    character, 252
binding variables, 26–27
bindir variable, 47–48
bootstrap.sh script, 73

Bourne shell, for Autoconf, 58
Bourne-shell scripts, 2
    referencing variable, 24
-brtl flag, for AIX linker, 174*n*
bug-report argument, for AC_INIT
        macro, 77
build directory, cleaning files in,
        226–227
build environment, of end user, 58
$build environment variable, 234
build process, 28*n*
    hooking Doxygen into, 245–247
    installation path for, 296
    Libtool in, 150–151
build system
    analysis, 126–133
    hooking directories into,
        155–156
    vs. host system, 287
    problems from copying, 71
    reconfiguring and building,
        161–164
    user expectations for, 20
BUILT_SOURCES variable, 302–303
    replacing with dependency
        rule, 308
byte stream, 67

C

C#
    building sources, 239–243
    macros, 233
    manual installation of sources,
        242–243
    unit testing in, 242
C++ programming language, 4
    building JNI sources, 236–237
    classes, 273
    exporting symbols from
        library, 282
    public interface solution,
        273–276
    virtual interfaces, 274–276
.*c* files, compiling into .*o* files, 30
C preprocessor
    comparing M4 to, 60
    macro definition, 91

C programming language, 4
    checking for compiler, 91–93
    function prototypes, 158
    passing structure references, 273
    public interface solution, 273
c89 program, 31*n*
c99 program, 31*n*
C99 standard, 113
    macros for determining
        standardized type
        instances, 113
Canadian cross, 287
canonical names, for system types,
        288–290
cc, 30–31
CC variable, 53
@CC@ variable, 92
CFGDIR C-preprocessor variable, 51
CFLAGS variable, 53
@CFLAGS@ variable, 92
ChangeLog file
    creating, 121
    for FLAIM project, 200
changequote macro, 254
check-news option, for
        AM_INIT_AUTOMAKE, 121
check prefix, 128
check programs, 218
check target, 37, 133
check_DATA variable, 225
check_SCRIPTS PLV, 134
chmod command, 39
.*class* files, 231
    location for, 239
CLASSPATH_ENV variable, 232
clean, 31
clean-local target, 243
CLEANFILES variable, 134, 226,
        239, 298
cleaning files
    in build directory, 226–227
    in distribution package, 281–282
CMake package, 2
Cocoa user interface, 3
COFF (Common Object File
        Format) system, 147*n*
colon (:), for rules, 27

commands
  backslash for wrapping, 25
  in makefile, 23–24
commands argument, in instantiating
      macros, 81
comments, in makefile, 22
commercial software, development,
      244n
common make rules, 27
Common Object File Format
      (COFF) system, 147n
compile process, data flow
      diagram, 27
compile script, 140
compile-time expression, 113
compilers, 28
  checking for, 91–93
  configuring options, 243–245
  -Ipath options, 87
  switching, and setting command-
      line options, 53
compiling, and dependency files
      generation, 306
conditional compilation, 104–106,
      187–188
conditional option, -fPIC as, 168
conditionals
  for Automake, vs. make, 213
  in M4, 264–268
config.guess script, 234, 289
config.h header file, 13, 79, 86, 272
  C preprocessor locating, 87
  config.status to generate, 84
  in /usr/include directory, 276
config.h.in file, 7, 9
config.log file, 14, 62
config.status script, 14, 62–63, 67, 82
  AC_OUTPUT macro to generate, 116
  executing, 63–64
  help for command-line options,
      79–80
  Makefile dependence on, 64
config.sub script, 234, 289
configuration. See also Autoconf
  Libtool and, 162
configuration scripts, 5
  Autoconf generation of, 6
configure: error: cannot find
      install-sh ... error, 74

configure script, 9, 13, 54–55, 82
  data flow diagram, 14
  --disable-shared option, 193–194
  --enable-static option, 168
  user ability to override, 94
configure.ac file, 7, 64–67, 68
  action-if-not-given argument
      for, 109
  activities in, 78
  adding checks for dl library and
      header file, 184
  AM_SILENT_RULES macro in, 143
  Autoconf intialization macros,
      76–78
  and autoreconf, 61
  autoscan to create, 71–76
  documenting substitution
      variable values, 246
  enabling Automake in, 121–124
  for FLAIM toolkit, 205–212
  for ftk, 208–209
  pkg-config files in, 301–302
  placement for subprojects,
      199–200
  shortest, 59
  for top-level flaim directory,
      199, 200
  for xflaim project, 218–221
configure.in file, 57–88
@configure_input@ substitution
      variable, 65
configure.scan file, 71, 72
control characters, leading for make
      command, 35–36
convenience libraries, 128, 168
  reducing complexity with,
      134–138
copy-xml-files.stamp file, 225–226
COPYING files
  default, 123
  for FLAIM project, 200
CPPFLAGS variable, 53
  vs. CFLAGS, 290n
@CPPFLAGS@ variable, 92
CPUs, absolute addressing and, 168
crashing, from program loading at
      wrong address, 165

cross-compiling, 287–293
cross-platform networking software,
    data formatting, 112
cross-to-native build, 287–288
CSI_LIBADD variable, 236
cstest.exe, 242
cstest_script script, 242
current target, reference to, 29
current value, in library interface
    version number, 178
CXX variable, 53
CXXFLAGS variable, 53, 210
Cygwin environment, 2

D

data flow diagram
    for aclocal utility, 11
    for Autoconf, 8
    for autoheader utility, 8
    for Automake, 13
    for compile and link
        processes, 27
    for configure shell script, 14
    for Libtool, 13
    for make program, 16
DATA primary, 131, 247
    files as dependencies, 298
database-management library. *See*
    FLAIM (FLexible
    Adaptable Information
    Management)
datadir variable, pkg version, 128
debug variable, and conditional
    (AS_IF) use of
    AC_DEFINE, 212
_DEBUG_END_ string, 96
debugging
    config.log file for, 14
    macros, 60
_DEBUG_START_ string, 96
default distribution package type,
    changing, 121
default name, for tarballs, 34
default quote characters, for M4, 252
define macro, 253
@DEFS@ substitution variable, 87, 103

Demaille, Akim, 120
depcomp wrapper script, 125
dependencies
    automatic, 306–309
    managing, 303–306
    preprocessor to manage,
        304–306
dependency chains, 24
dependency files
    generating as compile side
        effect, 306
    renaming, 164
dependency libraries, in *libxflaim.la*
    file, 225
dependency list, 29
dependency rules, 29–30
    adding hardcoded to header
        file, 307–308
    automatic tracking, 124–125
dereferencing shell variable, 24
DESTDIR variable, 49–50, 52
destination directory structure, 133
/dev/null
    redirecting output to, 163
    redirecting stdout to, 143
df utility (Linux), 148
directed graph, 24
directive (dot-rule), 33
directories
    adding source to distribution
        package, 140
    adding to SUBDIRS variable, 138
    destination structure, 133
    include, 153–156
    root-level, 44
    structure for projects, creating,
        20–22
disable-fast-install option, for
    LT_INIT macro, 157
disable-shared option, for LT_INIT
    macro, 157
disable-static option, for LT_INIT
    macro, 157–158
dist-hook target, 214–215
dist modifier, for PSVs and
    PLVs, 132

dist-* options, for AM_INIT_AUTOMAKE, 121

dist target, 33, 34, 208

distcheck target, 36, 75, 281
    make to test install and uninstall targets, 42–44
    modifying commands, 67

distdir rule, forgetting to update, 36

$(distdir) target, 75

distdir variable, 34

distribution package
    automatically testing, 36–37
    changing default type, 121
    cleaning, 281–282
    contents, 140
    timestamps on source files, 141

DIST_SUBDIRS variable, 276

dkopen function, return type, 191

dl interface functions, 188
    switching to *ltdl* in source code, 190–191

dl POSIX interface, 151

dlclose function, 151

DLL Hell, 175

DLLs. *See* Dynamic Link Libraries (DLLs)

dlopen function, 150, 151, 188
    checking for, 184

-dlopen option, for *ltdl* library, 189

dlopen option, for LT_INIT macro, 157

dlsym function, 150, 151

dnl macro, 254

doc_DATA variable, 213, 247

docs directory, 245

documentation. *See also* Doxygen
    distributing generation of, 277
    for macros, 263–264
    targets, 309
    Texinfo for, 131

dollar sign doubled ($$), for variable references, 43

dollar sign ($), escaping, 24

dot-rule (directive), 33

double compile feature, 163–164

double quotes ("), escaped, 294*n*

doxyfile.in file, 246

Doxygen
    hooking into build process, 245–247
    tarball, 247
    variables in templates, 296

doxygen program, 213

Draheim, Guido, 298

DRY principle, 158

dual-mode build approach, 103

Duret-Lutz, Alexandre, 120

.dvi documentation files, generating rules to build, 131

Dynamic Link Libraries (DLLs), 147
    versioning, 175

dynamic linking
    automatic at runtime, 148–149
    at load time, 147–148
    manual at runtime, 149–150

dynamic loader, source file that checks functionality, 86

E

echo statement
    after AC_OUTPUT for user information about build, 116
    vs. Autoconf macros for message display, 107
    leading @ sign on, 36

Eclipse, 146

ELF (Executable and Linking Format) system, 147*n*

--enable-static option, for configure command, 168

end-user's system, vs. maintainer's system, 5

environment variables, 24
    Autoconf macros to create, 108
    for multithreading, 210
    setting in local environment, 54

equal sign (=), in makefile, 24

Erlang, 4

error messages
    from M4, 268
    for missing TAB characters, 23

escaped double quotes, 294*n*

escaping dollar sign ($), 24

exec_prefix variable, 47

executable

    absolute addressing in, 165

    building, 9

    custom installation location, 238

    entry point for, 177

    hardcoding runtime directories into, 51

    interface between shared libraries and, 146

    on Unix systems, support for embedded runtime library search path, 174

Executable and Linking Format (ELF) system, 147n

@EXEEXT@ variable, 92

export keyword, 40

export-level versioning, 172

export statements, 67

exporting C++ symbols from library, 282

extension target, recursive, 276–279

external reference table, 147

external versioning, 172

EXTRA prefix, 128

EXTRA_DIST variable, 140, 203, 213

F

factory functions, 274, 275

files, setting mode, 39

filesystem hierarchy standard (FHS), 44–45

filesystem rights, 38

Fink, 3

FLAIM (FLexible Adaptable Information Management)

    adding macro subdirectory, 201–202

    analysis of legacy system, 197–199

    basics, 196

    directory tree, 198

    getting started, 199–204

    reasons for project conversion, 196–197

    subprojects, 197–198, 204–218

    top level *Makefile.am* file, 202–204

FLAIM toolkit, 196

    configure.ac file, 205–212

    Makefile.am file, 212–215

    Makefile.am file for *src* and *utils* directories, 215–217

flaimsql project, 197–198

FLM_FTK_SEARCH macro, 221

FLM_PROG_TRY_* macro, 220

FLM_PROG_TRY_CSVM macro, 242

FLM_PROG_TRY_DOXYGEN macro, 206, 233, 265, 266

FLM_PROG_TRY_JNI macro, 238

FORCE rule, 35

foreign keyword, in AM_INIT_AUTOMAKE, 206

formatting help strings, 112

Fortran, 4

Fortran 77, 4

forward declaration, in C++, 274

-fPIC option, for compiling code, 163

free-floating external references, 148

Free Software Foundation (FSF), 20

frozen macro file, 259

ftk project, autoscan to generate starting point, 204

FTKINC variable, 221

FTK_INCLUDE variable, 221

FTKLIB variable, 221

FTK_LTLIB variable, 221

functions

    absolute addresses to calls, 164–165

    vs. macros, 60

G

gcc, 26n

gcj compiler, 4, 230

global processes, makefile and, 33

GNU Autoconf Manual, 78, 264

    naming convention for macros, 264

    on quadigraphs, 117

    system types defined, 288

GNU Automake Manual, 11
    on `AC_PREREQ`, 76
GNU build system, variables
        referenced by, 52
GNU Coding Standards, 119, 121
    on installation targets, 243
    on targets and variables, 45
GNU compiler
    for Java (gcj), 4, 230
    options to generate make
        dependency rule, 124
GNU distribution source archives,
        installing Autotools
        from, 17
GNU Libtool Manual, 151
    and interface versions, 180
    on packaging *ltdl* library with
        project, 189
    symbol-naming convention
        for maintaining
        uniqueness, 192
GNU M4 Manual, 252
GNU Make Manual, 30, 32
GNU projects, files required by
        GCS for, 121
GNU Savannah project, 298
GPL, text in *COPYING* file, 123
grep utility, 37
    for Autoconf macro
        directory, 283
    testing output string, 37
greptest.sh shell script, 185
gzip utility, 3

H

handle, for loaded library, 150
hash mark (#)
    for M4 comments, 252
    for makefile comments, 22
`HAVE_CONFIG_H` macro, 87, 103
`HAVE_DOXYGEN` conditional name, 207
`HAVE_PTHREAD_H` macro, 103, 111
header file template, from
        autoheader, 7
header files
    adding hardcoded dependency
        rule to, 307–308
    checks for, 98–107

config.status to generate, 83
    generating rules to create first,
        302–303
    location, 87
    location in source file, 159
    for plug-in interface, 183
header for macros, documentation
        in, 263–264
`HEADERS` primary, 131, 154
heap manager, preloading, 148
help
    for config.status script
        command-line options,
        79–80
    formatting strings, 112
Hewlett Packard, Unix library-level
        versioning, 175
-hook target, for Automake, 214–215
$host environment variable, 234
host system
    vs. build system, 287
    canonical names, 290
.*html* documentation files
    generating, 247
    generating rules to build, 131

I

IBM AIX library versioning,
        173–174
if statement, 44
if-then statement, vs. AS_IF macro,
        211–212
ifdef keyword, 213
ifeq keyword, 213
ifnames program, 8
ifndef keyword, 213
ifneq keyword, 213
image directory, building, 34
implicit rules, 30–31, 303–304
include directives, 87
include directories, 153–156
include file, autoheader to generate
        template, 84–87
include guard, 86, 159
include statement, for .*m4* macro
        files, 202
includedir variable, 154
    pkg version, 128

indirect dependencies, 304
infinite recursion by macro, 257
.info files, 131
    generating rules to build, 131
`info_TEXINFOS` product list
        variable, 131
`init-cmds` argument, in instantiating
        macros, 81
initialization macros, in *configure.ac*
        file, 76–78
input text
    M4 procedure for processing
        stream, 257
    macro to discard, 254
`install-data-hook` target, 247
INSTALL files
    default, 123
    for FLAIM project, 200
`install` target, 39, 52
`install` utility (Unix), 74
`@INSTALL@` variable, 93
installation location prefixes,
        127–128
installing
    Autotools, 16–18
    choices, 40–41
    Libtool, 152
    path for, 296
    prefixes not associated with,
        128–129
    products, 38–44
    from tarball, 5
    testing, 42–44
`@INSTALL_PROGRAM@` variable, 93
`@INSTALL_SCRIPT@` variable, 93
instantiating macros, 78–87
integer types in C, 112
interface abstraction, hiding
        implementation details
        with, 273–276
interface versioning, library
        versioning as, 177–180
interfaces
    design, 272
    between executable and shared
        libraries, 146
    public, 160, 272–276
internal name of library, 176

internal versioning, 172
internationalization, 58*n*
`intN_t` type, 113

J

.jar files, 230
    make rule for building, 238
Java, 4, 52*n*
    building sources with Autotools,
        230–239
    defining list of source files in
        variable, 231
    wrapper classes, 237–239
Java Native Interface (JNI)
    C++ sources, 236–237
    header files, 232
`JAVA` primary, 130, 230
    caveat about using, 239
Java Virtual Machine (JVM), 230
`JAVAC` variable, 232
`JAVACFLAGS` variable, 232
`javah` utility, 232, 238
`JAVAROOT` directory, 235
`JAVAROOT` variable, 232, 238
JNI. *See* Java Native Interface (JNI)
`JNI_LIBADD` variable, 236
Jupiter project, 32, 37
    adding libraries, 137
    adding location variables to,
        47–48
    adding multithreading, 99
    adding shared libraries, 152–170
    changes to use *ltdl* library, 189
    `CPPFLAGS` statement, 160
    fixing PIC problem, 167–170
    modules directory, 185
    multiple threads or serialized
        execution, 104
    plug-in interface to modify
        output, 181
    remote build, 70
    single-threaded version, 107
    temp directory, 125
    for users without *pthreads*
        library, 103
`jupiter_LDADD` statement, 160
JVM (Java Virtual Machine), 230

K

Kernighan, Brian, 58

L

.la file extension, 160
large files, 209
lazy binding, 148
lazy entry, 149
LDADD variable, 225
ldconfig utility, 173
LDFLAGS variable, 53
LD_PRELOAD environment variable, 148
leading whitespace, around
    arguments, 256
*_LIBADD variables, 155
libdir variable, pkg version, 128
libdl.so file, 151
libexecdir variable, pkg version, 128
libjupcommon.a static library, 153
libltdl, 181–194
    necessary infrastructure,
        181–183
LIBPATH (AIX), 174
libraries. *See also* shared libraries
    adding to program linker
        command line, 137
    Autoconf macros specific to, 287
    building, 138–140
    checks for, 98–107
    design, 272
    exporting C++ symbols from, 282
    internal name of, 176
    patch level of, 173
    providing pkg-config files for,
        300–301
    referencing those external to
        project, 155
    renaming with Libtool -release
        flag, 180–181
    static, 139. *See also* static libraries
    testing for required, 211
LIBRARIES primary, 130
library interface functions, names
    for, 159–160
library management interface, 151
library versioning, 59, 171
    IBM AIX, 173–174

as interface versioning, 177–180
Libtool scheme for, 176–181
*library_*LIBADD POV, 137
@LIBS@ substitution variable, 100, 101
libs.m4 file, 283
Libtool, 1, 11–12, 145–170
    abstracting build process,
        150–151
    abstraction at runtime, 151–152
    -avoid-version option, 186
    customizing with LT_INIT macro
        options, 157–161
    data flow diagram, 13
    determining version installed, 16
    indicating earliest version for
        project processing, 156
    installing, 152
    library versioning scheme,
        176–181
    new files for project, 161
    preloading multiple modules,
        192–193
    reasons to use, 201
    -version-info option, 177, 181
libtool script, 12
    --mode-link option, 164
    --mode=compile option, 163
libtoolize shell script, 12
libxflaim.la file, dependency
    libraries, 225
link process, data flow diagram, 27
linker
    compiler to call, 28
    name entry, for library
        install, 173
    and object files, 136
    symbols table maintenance, 147
Linux
    getting project into distribution,
        48–50
    library versioning, 172–173
    proper build on, 291
load time, dynamic linking at,
    147–148
loader domain, 174
loader, version information for, 177

loading program, crash from loading at wrong address, 165

-local target, for Automake, 214–215

location variables, 47–48

ltdl library, 12, 151, 181
    converting to, 188–192
    -dlopen option, 189
    initializing, 191
    Jupiter project changes to use, 189
    shipping source code with package, 190

lt_dlopen function, 152
    return type, 191

LTDL_SET_PRELOADED_SYMBOLS macro, 189, 191

lt_dlsym function, 152, 192

LT_INIT macro, 156, 184, 201
    options, 157–161

LTLIBRARIES primary, 130, 151, 153, 155, 168

*ltlibrary*_LIBADD POV, 137

ltmain.sh script, 150, 151, 161
    location, 201

LT_OUTPUT macro, 151n

LT_PREREQ macro, 156

M

M4 macro language, 58
    and Autoconf, 259–260
    comparing to C preprocessor, 60
    conditionals, 264–268
    data as text, 77n
    documenting macros, 263–264
    macro calls, 59
    macro definition, 253–254
    macros with arguments, 255–256
    placeholders for parameters, 284
    problem diagnosis, 268–269
    procedure to process input text stream, 257
    quoting rules, 258–259
    recursive nature of, 256–259
    suggested body closing style, 264
    text processing, 252–256

text replacement, 260–263
whitespace around arguments, 256
writing Autoconf macros, 260–268

M4 macro processor, 251

.m4f extension, 259

m4_if macro, 266–268

m4_ifval macro, 265–266

m4_include statement, 10

m4sugar, 259

m4_traceoff macro, 268–269

m4_traceon macro, 268–269

Mac OS X, 3

MacKenzie, David, 6, 119

MacPorts, 3

macros, 60–61
    and Autoconf, 58
    hacking, 282–287
    instantiating, 78–87
    library-specific Autoconf, 287

main function, new plug-in module from, 187

maintainer-defined command-line options, 212

maintainer mode, 141–142

maintainer's system, vs. end-user's system, 5

major version number, 173

make all, 296
    prefix override for, 51

make check, 218

make clean, 226

make dist, 140

make install, 296
    incremental techniques, 302
    prefix override for, 51

make program, 126
    vs. Automake conditionals, 213
    data flow diagram, 16
    designing new target, 32
    executing commands in separate shells, 25
    information display by, 142
    leading control characters, 35–36
    output, 162–163
    running, 15

make rule, for building *.jar* file, 238
make targets, Automake support for, 124
make variables, defining on command line, 41
makefile
  basics, 22–32
  commands and rules, 23–24
  general layout, 23
  generating. *See* Automake
  resources for authors, 32
  variable definitions, 24–25
  writing, 9
makefile templates, generating, 10
Makefile.am file, 10, 125–126
  adding -dlopen option to LDADD, 191
  adding SUBDIRS variable, 155–156, 185
  AM_CPPFLAGS option variable, 138
  AM_LDFLAGS option variable, 138
  conditional actions, 207
  for *cs* directory, 239
  dist and nodist modifiers, 132
  enabling silent rules, 143
  EXTRA_DIST list, 280–281
  for FLAIM project *src* directory, 235–236
  for FLAIM project top level, 202–204
  for FLAIM toolkit, 212–215
  for *ftk/src*, 215–217
  for *ftk/util*, 217–218
  for *include* directory, 154
  includedir variable or pkginclude prefix in, 154
  Java installation directory defined in, 231
  for *libjup*, 155
  modifying to use shared library, 160
  nobase modifier, 133
  study of, 215
  substituting make variables into data files using sed, 297
  TAB characters in, 310–311
  top level, 126
  for *xflaim/src*, 222–223
  for *xflaim/src/java*, 236–237
  for *xflaim/src/java/wrapper*, 237–239
makefile.in file
  Automake generation of, 123
  updating, 75–76
Makefile.in template, 13
  from empty *Makefile.am* file, 126
MAKEFLAGS environment variable, 279
makeinfo utility, 131
man pages, 131
man_MANS product list variable, 131
manN_MANS product list variable, 131
MANS primary, 131
messages
  multiline, 107*n*
  printing, 106–107
Meyering, Jim, 120
MinGW approach, 2
minor version number, 173
MSYS environment, 2
multiline messages, 107*n*
multiple commands, executing by same shell, 25
multiple targets, 31–32
multithreading, 210
  adding to project, 99
  vs. single thread, 101
mutexes, 108

N

name token
  replacing with macro definition, 253
  word parsed as, 258
names
  of Automake-generated tarballs, 76
  for library interface functions, 159–160
  in M4, 252
  of projects, 21
NEWS file
  creating, 121
  for FLAIM project, 200

NeXTSTEP/OpenStep, 3
Nicholson, Dan, 302
nobase modifier, for PSVs and
       PLVs, 133
nodist_program_SOURCES variable, 303
noinst prefix, 128, 136, 168
noinst_HEADERS PLV, 136n
noise, from Autotools-based build
       systems, 142–144
non-pic option, for LT_INIT
       macro, 158
nonstandard targets, 247–249
notrans modifier, for PSVs and
       PLVs, 133
Novell eDirectory, 196
Novell GroupWise server, 196

O

.o (object) files
    compiling .c files into, 30
    linkers and, 136
Objective C, 4
objects, precompiled, 29
@OBJEXT@ variable, 92
obs directory, 248
open source software projects,
       platforms for, 20
openSUSE Build Service, 248
optimization for fast install,
       disabling, 157
OUT[:INLIST] construct, 79
output files, templates for, 63

P

package build system, generating,
       5–6
@PACKAGE_BUGREPORT@ substitution
       variable, 77
@PACKAGE_NAME@ substitution
       variable, 77
packages
    building, 13–15
    choices, 311
    configuring, 54–55
    installing multiple versions, 52n

repository revision number use
       in version, 279–281
    uninstalling, 41–42
@PACKAGE_STRING@ substitution
       variable, 77
@PACKAGE_TARNAME@ variable, 77, 248
@PACKAGE_URL@ substitution
       variable, 77
@PACKAGE_VERSION@ variable, 77,
       248, 300
packaging systems, 49
parallel-tests option, for
       AM_INIT_AUTOMAKE, 122
patch level, of library, 173
pattern rules, 304
per-product flags, wrapper scripts
       around compiler for, 139
Perl interpreter, for Autoconf, 58
.PHONY rule, adding -local and -hook
       targets to, 214
phony targets, 31, 226
    make execution of commands
       associated with, 33
pic-only option, for LT_INIT
       macro, 158
PIC. See position-independent
       code (PIC)
picket fences, 96
PIMPL (Private IMPLementaton)
       pattern, 273–274
pkg-config program, 299–302
    providing files for library
       projects, 300–301
pkg installation location
       variables, 128
PKG_CHECK_EXISTS macro, 301
PKG_CHECK_MODULES macro, 301
pkginclude prefix, 154
pkg.m4 file, 301
PKG_PROG_PKG_CONFIG macro, 301
plug-in interface, 146
    adding, 183–184
    to modify Jupiter project
       output, 181
plug-in modules, scope of data
       references for, 186
PLV. See product list variables (PLV)

pointer, to call public methods, 275
portability
    of build systems with non-
        mainstream languages, 4
    of shell code, 6
position-independent code (PIC),
        164–166
    default behavior for creating, 158
    fixing problem in Jupiter,
        167–170
    and shared libraries, 166
POSIX/FHS runtime
        environment, 2
POSIX shared-library API, 151
POSIX standard, 29n
    threads (*pthreads*) library, 98–99
postorder_commands macro, 277
POVs (product option variables),
        136–138
precious variables, 206, 220, 265
precompiled objects, 29
prefix variable, 41
    build vs. installation overrides,
        50–52
prefix variables, 44
    ability to change, 48
    default values, 46–47
$(prefix), vs. @prefix@, 67
prefixes
    installation location, 127–128
    not associated with installation,
        128–129
preorder_commands macro, 277
preprocessor
    comparing M4 to C, 60
    conditional construct, 159
    definitions from autoheader, 85
preprocessor variables, 90
primaries, 129–131
print statement
    after AC_OUTPUT for user
        information about
        build, 116
    vs. Autoconf macros for message
        display, 107
printing
    code to stdout, preventing, 44
    messages, 106–107

print_routine function, adding
        salutation, 181–182
Private IMPLementaton (PIMPL)
        pattern, 273–274
product list variables (PLV),
        127–131
    modifier-list portions of
        templates, 132–133
product option variables (POVs),
        136–138
product source variables (PSVs), 132
    modifier-list portions of
        templates, 132–133
product versions, vs. shared-library
        versioning, 177
*product*_CFLAGS POV, 137
*product*_CPPFLAGS POV, 137
*product*_LDFLAGS POV, 137
products
    installing, 38–44
    preventing install during specific
        build, 128
prog-to-check-for parameter, in
        AC_CHECK_PROG macro, 97
program, checking for existence, 94
*program*_LDADD POV, 137
programming language. *See also*
        specific language names
    choosing, 4
programs, checking for
        existence, 220
PROGRAMS primary, 130
programs.m4 macro file, 95
projects. *See also* build system
    autoconfiscating, 65
    directory structure creation,
        20–22
    getting into Linux distribution,
        48–50
    organization techniques, 19
    structure, 21–22
.ps documentation files, generating
        rules to build, 131
PSVs. *See* product source
        variables (PSVs)
PTHREAD_CC variable, 210
PTHREAD_CFLAGS environment
        variable, 210

pthread_create function, finding
library containing, 100
PTHREAD_CXX variable, 210
PTHREAD_CXXFLAGS environment
variable, 210
PTHREAD_LIBS environment
variable, 210
pthreads (threads) library, 98–99, 170
output if missing, 105
proper use, 210–211
public interface
call through, 160
contents, 272–276
pure virtual methods, 274–275
PYTHON primary, 130

Q

quadrigraphs, 117
query-assign operator (?=), 54
quiet builds, 142
quote characters in M4
default, 252
using, 262–263

R

ranlib utility, 139*n*
readme-alpha option, for
AM_INIT_AUTOMAKE, 122
README file
creating, 121
for FLAIM project, 200
real target, for make, 9
recursive build system, 21
recursive extension target, 276–279
recursive targets, 204
Red Hat Package Manager
(RPM), 49
package files, building, 248–249
redirecting stdout, to */dev/null*, 143
redundancy, eliminating, 29
references, to external libraries, 155
regeneration rules, 65
reject parameter, in AC_CHECK_PROG
macro, 97–98
relative addresses, 166
-release flag, of Libtool, 180–181

remote build, adding functionality
to makefile, 68
replacing text, emulating Autoconf
techniques, 293–298
repository revision number, using
in package version,
279–281
revision value, in library interface
version number, 178
Ritchie, Dennis, 58
rm command, 120
leading control character for, 35
root-level directories, 44
root-level rights
for installing products, 38–39
for uninstall, 42
root permissions, for installing into
system directory
hierarchy, 52
RPM. *See* Red Hat Package
Manager (RPM)
rpmbuild utility, 249
rpmcheck target, 249
rpms target, 203
rules, 27–32
dependency, 29–30
forcing to run, 34–35
implicit, 30–31
in makefile, 23–24
runtime
automatic dynamic linking at,
148–149
manual dynamic linking at,
149–150
runtime directories, hardcoding
into executable, 51

S

SCons package, 2
scope of data references, for plug-in
modules, 186
SCRIPTS primary, 130
security risks, from free-floating
symbols, 148
sed command, 55, 67
substituting make variables into
data files, 297

separator characters, for commands, 25

serialized execution, vs. multithreading, 104

shared libraries, 11, 102, 145. *See also* Libtool

  aborted process from missing, 149

  adding to Jupiter, 152–170

  benefits, 146, 153

  default behavior for creating, 157

  header file, 158

  how they work, 146–150

  and *include* directories, 154

  initial contents of source file, 158

  modifying *Makefile.am* to use, 160

  and PIC objects, 166

  versioning, vs. product version, 177

  warning about linking against static library, 164

shared-library interface, 171

shared-library table, 147

shared object name (soname), of library, 173

shared option, for LT_INIT macro, 157

shell code

  make passing variable reference to, 43

  portability, 6

shell variable

  creating substitution variable from, 90

  dereferencing, 24

shim libraries, 2

side-by-side cache (SxS), 175

.SILENT directive, 36

silent rules, 142–144

  for AM_INIT_AUTOMAKE, 122

Simon, Peter, 298

sinclude statement, 305

single quote ('), as default M4 quote character, 252

.sl file extension, 175

Solaris, library versioning, 172–173

soname (shared object name), of library, 173

source code

  classes in C or C++ project, 303

  compiling, 164

  shipping *ltdl* library with package, 190

  using generated, 302–309

source directory

  adding to distribution package, 140

  building outside, 15

source distribution archive. *See also* tarballs

  creating, 32–36

source files

  timestamps on, 141

  in variable definition, 28

SourceForge.net, 196

SOURCES variable, library name in, 168

spec file, 49, 248

square brackets ([])

  for AC_CHECK_TYPES macro parameter, 114

  for macro parameters, 60

  for optional parameters, 76*n*

$(srcdir) prefix, prepending on files, 232

@srcdir@ substitution variable, 68, 296

srcrpm target, 203

stack overflow, from infinite recursion by macro, 257

staged installations, *GNU Coding Standards* on, 49

stamp files, 226*n*, 232, 238, 247

stamp targets, 225–226

standard targets, 46

standard variables, 46–47

static libraries, 139, 161

  default behavior for creating, 157–158

  generating PIC objects in, 167

  header file, 158

  Libtool generation of, 168

  warning about linking shared library against, 164

static option, for LT_INIT macro, 157–158

stderr, 144
    redirecting, 75, 163
stdout
    preventing make from printing
        code to, 44
    redirecting, 75, 163
    redirecting to */dev/null*, 143
stream editor, 67
strings for help, formatting, 112
structure definitions, checking for,
        112–115
SUBDIRS variable, 203
    adding directory to, 138
    adding to *Makefile.am* file, 185
    conditional definition of
        contents, 223
    for make, 126–127
    recursively traversing
        subdirectories with, 276
substitution variables
    AC_PROG_CC macro definition of, 92
    for AM_CONDITIONAL macro, 207
    creating from shell variable, 90
    defining, 207
    documenting values in
        configure.ac file, 246
    macro to specify, 265
Subversion, 279–280, 311
subversion-deps source package, 311
suffix rules, 30
Sun Microsystem, external library
        versioning by, 172
SVNREV file, 280
SxS (side-by-side cache), 175
symbol-level versioning, 172
symbols table, linker maintenance
        of, 147
sysconfdir variable, 51, 295
system directory hierarchy, root
        permissions for installing
        into, 52
system-specific versioning, 172–176

T

TAB character, 25*n*, 310–311
    in makefile, 23
    missing, in make, 268*n*

tags, OUT[:INLIST] construct as, 79
tar utility, 3
tarballs
    checking for completeness, 281
    creating, 32–36
    as dependency of rpms target, 249
    names for, 34, 76
    process for building and
        installing software from, 5
$target environment variable, 234
target system, for cross-compiling,
        287, 288
targets
    disabling undesirable, 309–310
    multiple, 31–32
    nonstandard, 247–249
    phony, 31, 33, 226
    reference to current, 29
    in rules, 27
templates
    conditionally processing, 208
    config.status to generate
        makefiles from, 64–67
    generating files from, 62, 67–68
    for output files, 63
test files, cleaning, 227
testing
    for Autoconf, 59
    distribution, automatically,
        36–37
    install and uninstall, 42–44
    for required libraries, 211
    unit, 37–38
TEXINFOS primary, 131, 309–310
text files, generating from *.in* file, 67
text processing
    emulating Autoconf text
        replacement techniques,
        293–298
    with M4, 252–256
threads (*pthreads*) library, 98–99
    output if missing, 105
    proper use, 210–211
threads, single vs. multithreading,
        101

timestamps, on distribution source files, 141

tokens in M4, 252

@top_srcdir@ variable, 296

touch command, 121, 206

trailing whitespace, aroung arguments, 256

troff markup, 131

Tromey, Tom, 119

type checks, in Autoconf, 114

type definitions, checking for, 112–115

U

uint*N*_t type, 113

uname command, 234

uninstall rule, package manager and, 49

uninstalling
package, 41–42
testing, 42–44

unit testing, 37–38, 281
Automake support for, 133–134
in C#, 242
XML files for, 225

Unix systems
compilers, 28
executable support for embedded runtime library search path, 174
Hewlett Packard, library-level versioning, 175

user-defined macros, adding to Autoconf project, 10

user variables, 52–54, 92, 138
defining, 40

/usr/bin directory, file ownership, 39

/usr directory, 44

/usr/include directory, *config.h* file in, 276

/usr/local directory, 45
for Libtool default install, 152

utility scripts, 141

V

valgrind package, 148

variables. *See also* substitution variables
$$ (dollar sign doubled) for referencing, 43
automatic, 29
binding, 26–27
location, 47–48
in makefile, 24–25
standard, 46–47
user, 40, 52–54

verbose mode, for autoreconf, 61

version argument, for AC_INIT macro, 77

-version-info flag, of Libtool, 181

version of library, 171

version option, for AM_INIT_AUTOMAKE, 122

VERSION variables, 77

versioning, 217
Dynamic Link Libraries (DLLs), 175
library, 171
repository revision number use in, 279–281
system-specific, 172–176

virtual search path (VPATH), 68–70

W

warnings
for autoscan utility, 72
response to, 164

-warnings=category option, for AM_INIT_AUTOMAKE, 122

-W*category* option, for AM_INIT_AUTOMAKE, 122

which command, 16–17

whitespace characters, in M4, 252–253

Wikipedia, on position-independent code, 166*n*

Wildenhues, Ralf, 120

Windows operating system loader, symbole resolution, 147

Windows runtime environment, 2
wrapper scripts, for per-product
flags, 139

X

X Windows, 3
xfcs_sources variable, 242
xflaim library, 230
xflaim subproject, 197–198
    build system design, 218–227
    configure.ac file, 218–221
    ftk search code from, 261
    java directory structure, 234–235
    Java wrapper classes, 235
    Makefile.am file for *src* directory,
        222–223, 235–236
    pkg-config metadata template
        for, 300
    util directory, 223–227
XML files, for unit tests, 225

The Electronic Frontier Foundation (EFF) is the leading organization defending civil liberties in the digital world. We defend free speech on the Internet, fight illegal surveillance, promote the rights of innovators to develop new digital technologies, and work to ensure that the rights and freedoms we enjoy are enhanced — rather than eroded — as our use of technology grows.

PRIVACY EFF has sued telecom giant AT&T for giving the NSA unfettered access to the private communications of millions of their customers. eff.org/nsa

FREE SPEECH EFF's Coders' Rights Project is defending the rights of programmers and security researchers to publish their findings without fear of legal challenges. eff.org/freespeech

INNOVATION EFF's Patent Busting Project challenges overbroad patents that threaten technological innovation. eff.org/patent

FAIR USE EFF is fighting prohibitive standards that would take away your right to receive and use over-the-air television broadcasts any way you choose. eff.org/IP/fairuse

TRANSPARENCY EFF has developed the Switzerland Network Testing Tool to give individuals the tools to test for covert traffic filtering. eff.org/transparency

INTERNATIONAL EFF is working to ensure that international treaties do not restrict our free speech, privacy or digital consumer rights. eff.org/global

EFF.ORG
ELECTRONIC FRONTIER FOUNDATION
Protecting Rights and Promoting Freedom on the Electronic Frontier

EFF is a member-supported organization. Join Now! www.eff.org/support

THE ART OF ASSEMBLY LANGUAGE, 2ND EDITION

by RANDALL HYDE

Widely respected by hackers of all kinds, *The Art of Assembly Language* teaches programmers how to understand assembly language and how to use it to write powerful, efficient code. Using the proven High Level Assembler (HLA) as its primary teaching tool, *The Art of Assembly Language* leverages your knowledge of high-level programming languages to make it easier for you to quickly grasp basic assembly concepts. Among the most comprehensive references to assembly language ever published, *The Art of Assembly Language, 2nd Edition* has been thoroughly updated to reflect recent changes to the HLA language. All code from the book is portable to the Windows, Linux, Mac OS X, and FreeBSD operating systems.

MARCH 2010, 760 PP., $59.95
ISBN 978-1-59327-207-4

THE IDA PRO BOOK

The Unofficial Guide to the World's Most Popular Disassembler

by CHRIS EAGLE

Hailed by the creator of IDA Pro as the "long-awaited" and "information-packed" guide to IDA, *The IDA Pro Book* covers everything from the very first steps with IDA to advanced automation techniques. You'll learn how to identify known library routines and how to extend IDA to support new processors and filetypes, making disassembly possible for new or obscure architectures. The book also covers the popular plug-ins that make writing IDA scripts easier.

AUGUST 2008, 640 PP., $59.95
ISBN 978-1-59327-178-7

THE ART OF DEBUGGING WITH GDB, DDD, AND ECLIPSE

by NORMAN MATLOFF *and* PETER JAY SALZMAN

The Art of Debugging with GDB, DDD, and Eclipse illustrates the use of three of the most popular debugging tools on Linux/Unix platforms: GDB, DDD, and Eclipse. In addition to offering specific advice for debugging with each tool, authors Norm Matloff and Pete Salzman cover general strategies for improving the process of finding and fixing code errors, including how to inspect variables and data structures, understand segmentation faults and core dumps, and figure out why your program crashes or throws exceptions. You'll also learn how to use features like catchpoints, convenience variables, and artificial arrays and become familiar with ways to avoid common debugging pitfalls.

SEPTEMBER 2008, 280 PP., $39.95
ISBN 978-1-59327-174-9

HACKING, 2ND EDITION

The Art of Exploitation

by JON ERICKSON

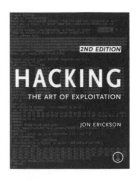

While many security books merely show how to run existing exploits, *Hacking: The Art of Exploitation* was the first book to explain how exploits actually work—and how readers can develop and implement their own. In this all new second edition, author Jon Erickson uses practical examples to illustrate the fundamentals of serious hacking. You'll learn about key concepts underlying common exploits, such as programming errors, assembly language, networking, shellcode, cryptography, and more. And the bundled Linux LiveCD provides an easy-to-use, hands-on learning environment. This edition has been extensively updated and expanded, including a new introduction to the complex, low-level workings of computers.

FEBRUARY 2008, 488 PP. W/CD, $49.95
ISBN 978-1-59327-144-2

GRAY HAT PYTHON

Python Programming for Hackers and Reverse Engineers

by JUSTIN SEITZ

Gray Hat Python explains how to complete various hacking tasks with Python, which is fast becoming the programming language of choice for hackers, reverse engineers, and software testers. Author Justin Seitz explains the concepts behind hacking tools like debuggers, Trojans, fuzzers, and emulators. He then goes on to explain how to harness existing Python-based security tools and build new ones when the pre-built ones just won't cut it. The book teaches readers how to automate tedious reversing and security tasks, sniff secure traffic out of an encrypted web browser session, use PyDBG, Immunity Debugger, Sulley, IDAPython, PyEMU, and more.

APRIL 2009, 216 PP., $39.95
ISBN 978-1-59327-192-3

PHONE:
800.420.7240 OR
415.863.9900
MONDAY THROUGH FRIDAY,
9 A.M. TO 5 P.M. (PST)

FAX:
415.863.9950
24 HOURS A DAY,
7 DAYS A WEEK

EMAIL:
SALES@NOSTARCH.COM

WEB:
WWW.NOSTARCH.COM

MAIL:
NO STARCH PRESS
38 RINGOLD STREET
SAN FRANCISCO, CA 94103
USA

UPDATES

Visit *http://www.nostarch.com/autotools.htm* for updates, errata, and other information.

Autotools is set in New Baskerville, TheSansMono Condensed, Futura, and Dogma.

The book was printed and bound at Malloy Incorporated in Ann Arbor, Michigan. The paper is 60# Spring Forge, which is certified by the Sustainable Forestry Initiative. The book uses a RepKover binding, which allows it to lie flat when open.